W9-BNH-371

Public Religion and Urban Transformation

Faith in the City

EDITED BY

Lowell W. Livezey

BENEDICTINE UNIVERSITY LIBRARY
IN THE KINDLON HALL OF LEARNING
5700 COLLEGE ROAD
LISLE, IL 60532-0900

New York University Press

NEW YORK AND LONDON

200
.977311
P976

NEW YORK UNIVERSITY PRESS
New York and London

© 2000 by New York University
All rights reserved

Library of Congress Cataloging-in-Publication Data
Public religion and urban transformation : faith in the city / edited by
Lowell W. Livezey.
p. cm. — (Religion, race, and ethnicity)
Includes bibliographical references and index.
ISBN 0-8147-5157-1 (alk. paper) —
ISBN 0-8147-5158-X (pbk. : alk. paper)
1. Chicago (Ill.)—Religion.   I. Livezey, Lowell. II. Series.
BL2527.C48 P83 2000
200'.9773'11—dc21   99-050622

New York University Press books are printed on acid-free paper,
and their binding materials are chosen for strength and durability.

Manufactured in the United States of America

10 9 8 7 6 5 4 3 2 1

Contents

    Edge-City Technoburb   187
    Paul D. Numrich

PART III: Religion and the New Metropolitan Context

9   Catholic Spirituality in a New Urban Church   213
    Elfriede Wedam

10 Recent Immigrant Religions and the Restructuring
    of Metropolitan Chicago   239
    Paul D. Numrich

11 Catholic Planning for a Multicultural Metropolis,
    1982–1996   269
    Peter R. D'Agostino

PART IV: Epilogue

    Epilogue: Building Religious Communities at the
    Turn of the Century   295
    R. Stephen Warner

    *Appendix: Religious Organizations Studied and Names
       of Principal Contact Persons*   *309*
    Bibliography   *319*
    Contributors   *343*
    Index   *345*

Illustrations

Maps

Photographs

Tables

Preface and Acknowledgments

The Religion in Urban America Program at the University of Illinois at Chicago has been from the beginning a collective, collegial undertaking. The authors of this book were all members of the staff during the program's first three years, 1992–1995, when we conducted most of the field research, and each author studied the congregations, organizations, and neighborhoods he or she writes about here. Several researchers participated at each site, however, because we wanted to observe our subjects "through each other's eyes," aware that we had different capacities for perception and distortion. We tried, wherever possible, to include a relative insider (for example, a Muslim observing a mosque) and an outsider (a Euro-American Catholic observing a black Protestant church). In forming the group to work at each site, we also considered the academic discipline, language skills, gender, age, and temperament of each researcher. As a result, we all have used field research conducted by other authors.

We also wish to acknowledge the contributions of research associates and assistants who are not authors of this volume but whose field research provided data and whose ideas enriched the discourse that we have drawn on for our chapters. Research associates included Julie Kaufman, Lois Gehr Livezey, Anthony Mansueto, Larry G. Murphy, William Peterman, Uma Sharma, and Ariel Zamarripa. Research assistants included Susana Angélica Bañuelos, Danit Ben Ari, Joy Bostic, Shalanda Dexter, Karen Ephraim, Jennifer Feenstra, Jeannie Lukacek, Damien McAnany, Evelyn Parker, April Payton, Reece Pendleton, Mari Philipsborn, Iraida Rodriguez, Sabri Samirah, and Authens Smith. In addition, the whole project depended heavily on the intelligent and cheerful support of undergraduate office assistants including Alex Gervacio (who made the computers work for us), Stephanie Prazak (who managed the bibliographic database and much more), Jennifer Chang, Monique Malek, Tricia Mazzone, Cynthia Suarez, and Julianna Whiteman.

Nearly everyone in the Religion in Urban America Program contributed to the research for multiple chapters and to the rich discourse
that has been sustained over several years by the research team. Accord-
ingly, as chapter authors, we acknowledge our deep sense of gratitude to
one another and to the rest of the team. With rare exceptions, we do not
identify each member of the team who contributed to a particular chapter, in order to avoid repetition and to emphasize the overriding importance of every person's contribution to the whole.

Academic colleagues and religious and civic leaders have been generous
with advice. To launch the advisory process, we convened a meeting in
October 1992 with Michael Conzen, Theo Feliciano, Sr. Mary Hennessey,
Philip Nyden, Wardell Payne, George W. Pickering, Calvin Pressley, Yolanda
Rios Rangel, Rabbi Herman Schaalman, Eldin Villafañe, R. Stephen Warner,
and Julian Wolpert. Many of these, and others including Msgr. John Egan;
Robert Franklin; Rev. Joseph Hacala, S.J.; Nancy Ammerman; and Carl
Dudley, advised us intermittently throughout the project. R. Stephen
Warner thoroughly reviewed our work and counseled with us insightfully
at a midpoint retreat.

We also benefited greatly from comments on papers we presented between 1993 and 1997 at meetings of the American Academy of Religion, the
Association for the Sociology of Religion, the Religious Research Association, the Social Ethics Seminar, and the Chicago Area Group for the Study
of Religious Communities. Discussants at these meetings included (in
chronological order) Msgr. Philip J. Murnion, Mark Chavez, Rima Schultz,
Alan B. Anderson, Rhys H. Williams, Helen Rose Ebaugh, Preston N.
Williams, Anthony Orum, Dennis McCann, Donald E. Miller, and Nancy L.
Eiesland. Their public comments and continued dialogue with us have contributed substantially to this book.

Undoubtedly, the most generous and resourceful contributors to the
research underlying these chapters are the congregations and other organizations, their members and leaders, their clergy and laity, who talked
with us and allowed us to observe and participate in their religious activities. These people and organizations are the sources of our primary data,
and we are most grateful for their considerable time and effort. Moreover,
we recognize that they included us in some of their most intimate moments and entrusted us with information about themselves that could
easily be misused. To protect their privacy and the confidentiality of our
conversations with them, in the chapters that follow we use pseudonyms
(except for clergy and chief executives of organizations, whose identity is

evident from the organization itself). We know full well, however, that their trust will have been justified only by the accuracy of our description and by our insightful, appreciative use of the information they so generously shared.

We attempted to make the field research as interactive as possible, inviting our subjects to review and correct our work in progress. We are grateful for the responses of clergy and lay leaders (listed in the appendix) to interim reports and preliminary analyses of their organizations. When the field research was nearly complete in 1995, we held a conference, "Religion and Community in a Restructuring Metropolis," with workshops designed to provide for dialogue among the people of the neighborhoods and religious organizations we had studied, scholars and religious leaders, and ourselves. We wish to acknowledge all who attended, and particularly the community people and academics who spoke formally at that conference: Edwin David Aponte; Assad Basool; Warren Copeland; Larry Greenfield; Eileen Heineman; Rev. Juan J. Huitrado, M.C.C.J.; Joseph Levin; Dominic Pacyga; George W. Pickering; Ellen Skerrett; Rev. Michael J. Slattery, O.S.A.; Robert H. Stockman; and Rev. Eugene Winkler. We are also grateful to Professors Jay P. Dolan, Diana Eck, Albert Hunter, Peter J. Paris, and R. Stephen Warner for their concluding comments.

The dialogue continued during 1996 and 1997 at five "Neighborhood Forums on Religion in Chicago." Speakers and participants in these forums discussed our research with one another and with us, making a unique contribution to the thinking presented in the chapters that follow. We wish to thank Jay Caponigro, Rev. Jeffery Haynes, and Victoria Verala for participation in the "Chicago's Southwest Side" forum; Sr. Dominga Zapata, S.H., Rev. Julio Loza, and Raul Raymundo for participation in the "Pilsen's Challenge to Its Churches" forum; Rabbi Philip Lefkowitz, Robert W. Matanky, Rabbi Michael M. Remson, and Rabbi Herman Schaalman for participation in the "Jewish North Side" forum; Rev. Erwin Lutzer, Rev. Eugene Winkler, and Rev. Robert McLaughlin for participation in the "Church at the Heart of the City" forum; and Kale Williams, Imam Ahmed Rufai, Rabbi Henry Balzer, and Cathy Vates for participation in the Rogers Park forum, which was cosponsored with Loyola University.

Maps produced by UIC cartographer Raymond Brod for our 1996 research report, *Religious Organizations and Structural Change in Metropolitan Chicago,* served as a point of departure for the maps provided here. It was, however, Professor Mark Bouman and cartographer Brian Twardosz, who accepted the challenge of creating maps that would undergird the arguments and amplify the themes that appear in the text. We are also grateful to the clergy, staff, and laypeople of the congregrations who provided a wide selection of photographs.

Both of our institutional sponsors, the University of Illinois at Chicago and the Lilly Endowment, have fostered the collegial character of the Religion in Urban America Program. The University of Illinois at Chicago is an excellent venue, not only because we fit the research agenda of an urban land-grant university but particularly because we have the good fortune to be situated in the Office of Social Science Research (OSSR). OSSR's director, Professor John Gardiner, is an exemplary colleague who deftly provided the optimal mix of breathing room, intellectual challenge, and support, while ensuring the proper administration of our grants and a congenial work environment. Iris Tillman, the secretary/administrator, and a series of research coordinators have cheerfully and efficiently provided logistical support. We have also benefited from interacting with other projects based at OSSR, including R. Stephen Warner's New Ethnic and Immigrant Congregations Project, Dick Simpson's research on Chicago city government, Marcia Farr's field studies of literacy among Mexican immigrants, and the Historical Encyclopedia of Chicago Women Project.

We are deeply grateful for three generous grants from the Lilly Endowment and a supplemental grant from the Lilly-funded Louisville Institute that made our work possible. But the sense of partnership with Lilly goes well beyond our funding. The initial idea for this program derived from discussions around Lilly's long-standing commitment to urban ministry and to grounding urban ministry in the best possible analysis of its urban and ecclesiastical contexts. The decision to pursue a research agenda much broader, and thus more expensive, than urban ministry alone—investigating the work of all the major religions and a wide range of religious activities—resulted from extensive discussions with Craig Dykstra, Lilly's vice president for religion, and program directors James Hudnut-Beumler, Jacqui Burton, and James P. Wind. They all, as well as a later program director, Edward Queen III, and Louisville Institute director James W. Lewis, have continued to be insightful commentators and critics. In addition, Lilly and the Louisville Institute have convened consultations with related research projects in other cities, including the Religion and Civic Order Project at University of Southern California, the Religion and Urban Culture Project at Indiana University–Purdue University at Indianapolis, and the Center for Social and Religious Research at Hartford Seminary. Thus they have fostered at the national level the collegiality we have tried to practice locally.

As editor of this volume, and as director of the program, I am deeply grateful to the other authors of this book and am even more indebted than they to our colleagues in the Religion and Urban America Program and to the many scholars and practitioners who have assisted us. I pay special tribute to three persons for their exceptional collaboration and support. William A. Simpson has followed our work closely, consistently, and thoughtfully from its conception, and his highly original thinking was ever evident in his critique of our work. Elfriede Wedam effectively combined the roles of research associate and program coordinator, rising naturally to become my partner in the leadership and serving as associate director. I shall be eternally grateful for her willingness to share overall responsibility for the program and for her intelligence, mature judgment, and grace. Finally, among the many blessings of being Lois Gehr Livezey's husband are her loyalty and her wise counsel. Both have been abundant, not only in her choosing to devote her sabbatical to participation as a theologian in the research team but in her discerning after-hours discussion of the intellectual and organizational concerns of the program. Bill, Elfriede, and Lois exemplify the larger pattern of collegiality and commitment to the whole that we were so fortunate to have in the Religion in Urban America Program, and for which I am grateful to the entire team.

Lowell W. Livezey, Director
Religion in Urban America Program

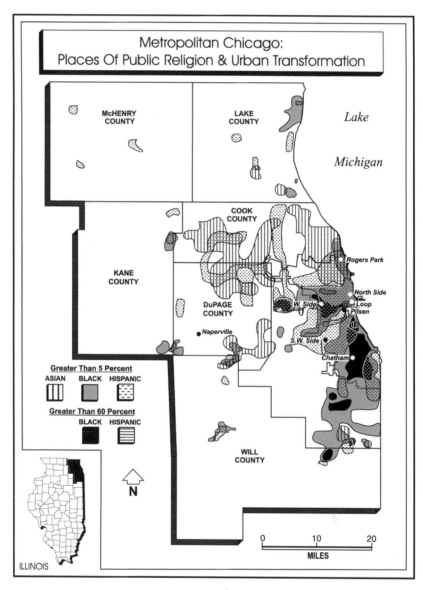

Metropolitan Chicago:
Places Of Public Religion & Urban Transformation

McHENRY COUNTY

LAKE COUNTY

Lake

Michigan

COOK COUNTY

Rogers Park

KANE COUNTY

North Side

DuPAGE COUNTY

W. Side · Loop · Pilsen

• Naperville

S.W. Side

Chatham

Greater Than 5 Percent

ASIAN   BLACK   HISPANIC

Greater Than 60 Percent

BLACK   HISPANIC

WILL COUNTY

N

ILLINOIS

0   10   20

MILES

The places named on this map locate the congregations discussed in chapters 2 through 9, while chapters 10 and 11 encompass much of the region. The population distribution shows that racial and ethnic diversity are important considerations for these congregations. Map by Brian Twardosz, BMT Printing and Cartographic Specialists.

Chapter 1

The New Context of Urban Religion

Lowell W. Livezey

"Viva Mexico!" calls the youthful nun, standing in full habit at the front of the large Gothic Catholic church. "Viva Mexico! Viva Mexico!" respond a thousand voices from the crowded pews and aisles. The evening is in early December 1993, and like thousands of others in this large Midwestern American city, these Mexican families have gathered in Catholic churches to serenade La Virgen de Guadalupe, the Mother of Jesus who appeared to the peasant Juan Diego and thus to the indigenous poor of Mexico.

Thousands of red roses adorn the Virgin in a brightly lit shrine that is easily seen from anywhere in the nave. People of all ages kneel in prayer and present her with more roses, which they have purchased from young boys outside the church. The worshipers then move to the already crowded pews and join in singing love songs to the Virgin and in shouting patriotic slogans.

Only a few blocks away and a month later, a committee gathers in a Protestant church located between the city's wealthiest neighborhood and a public housing project, home to the "ghetto underclass." The committee represents the churches of the wealthy neighborhood. Laypeople and clergy, mostly white Protestants, are listening to one of their members explain the intricacies of a city policy that will gradually dismantle the adjacent public housing project, which has become notorious for its level of violence and gang warfare. What concerns the committee is the fate of the families now living in the project. The committee members have expertise and "good connections," but they don't fully agree about what to do; so they authorize some research and decide to meet again soon.

Every Sunday morning, about twenty-five African American children gather in a multipurpose room at another of the city's public housing projects. Sports equipment has been moved to the corners, and a few adults from the nearby Baptist church are putting up posters with Bible verses and pictures of black biblical characters. The adults begin singing children's choruses; the children join in. One of the church's many ministers, an African American woman, then asks for quiet and, ignoring the continuing low-level chatter, offers a passionate prayer, greets the children effusively, and directs them to adjacent rooms according to their age.

The prosperous black Baptist church also conducts Sunday school in its well-appointed educational plant, but, the ministers say, the children from the housing projects will not come to Sunday school at the church (only two blocks away). So the church takes the Sunday school to the projects.

On a Saturday morning in spring 1994, in a neighborhood sometimes called the bastion of the black middle class but now threatened by the loss of nearby employers, the Christian Men's Fellowship is cooking breakfast. Eggs and sausage, biscuits and gravy, and grits. The breakfast is for the Save Our Sons program—boys mostly from the neighborhood but not from the families of the church. The men have long been involved in the church with their wives and children, nieces, nephews, and cousins. But recently they have been hearing a new message about what it means to be a Christian man. As people of African heritage, they have been told from the pulpit, men must be fathers to all the boys of the neighborhood. The church is family to all the children and young people. So even if these men and their families have moved to other parts of the city and suburbs (following the jobs), they return to mentor the new generation of neighborhood kids. After breakfast, the boys and men will study the Bible together, recite African proverbs (in Swahili or Zulu), and go on an outing to a forest preserve or a theme park.

That same Saturday morning, in still another part of the city, the Khutbah Committee of a large mosque is meeting. The mosque, a converted theater that accommodates fifteen hundred for prayers, is alive with the voices of more than three hundred children attending Islamic school and the smell of curries being prepared for a wedding feast. The committee meets in the corner of a large room that also serves as a thoroughfare among other activities. The dozen members are all men and relatively young. Except for one African American, they are immigrants—mainly from Jordan, India, and Pakistan. There is also an Egyptian and a Nigerian. The committee chairman, Muhammad Said, is the Egyptian. His fluency in Arabic is an important qualification for the committee, which selects an Arabic-speaking *khatib* to give the *khutba* (sermon) at the *jum'ah* prayer each Friday. In this mosque, a measure of theological, political, and ethnic diversity is maintained by rotating the honor of speaking each week. This in turn gives the committee a great deal of prestige. At this meeting, the man who had been designated the *khatib* for the next Friday was called to Palestine on business for his engineering firm, and a substitute was needed. Some members objected to the fact that all the candidates were Indo-Pakistani, which, they said, had been the nationality of all the recent *khatibs*.

It is Tuesday, a few minutes after 7 A.M., and as on most weekday mornings, the rabbi is reading psalms to several other men seated in chairs on one side of the modern synagogue. Each man wears the *kippah* (skullcap), the *tallith* (prayer shawl), and the *tefillin* (the small leather box containing bits of Torah scroll that is lashed to the forehead by strips of leather). They have gathered for morning prayers, but the order of service cannot begin until a *minyan* (a minimum of ten men) is present. Two more men arrive, carefully remove the *tallith* and *tefillin* from their pouch, and put them on. Then another enters, and after a few minutes—and several more psalms interspersed with greetings—the tenth.

Most of the men know the place in the prayer book and turn to it comfortably as the rabbi indicates the page. They chant the prayers, psalms, and scriptures with ease and confidence acquired over decades of repetition. But they do not chant completely in unison, for each voices a cantillation learned in his country of origin—Turkey, Morocco, Spain, Israel, Armenia. After prayers, the men's breakfast includes baked eggs as well as lox and bagels.

Middle-class blacks appropriating African folk culture on the South Side, Indo-Pakistani immigrants planning their mosque's prayer service on the Northwest Side, Moroccan cantillations in a North Side synagogue . . . these are only glimpses of what the authors of this book have seen and heard since beginning research with the Religion in Urban America Program in 1992.[1] But they also point beyond specific people and congregations in this particular city to the larger reality of religion interacting with changing urban environments.

Studying Urban Religion in the Late Twentieth Century

Since World War II, change in American cities has been so fundamental as to be termed "urban restructuring." During the same period, organized religion has been undergoing a widespread, pervasive change that is now commonly called, following the title of Robert Wuthnow's important book, the restructuring of American religion.[2] Both structural changes are further linked to the social transformation of the 1960s and 1970s, which extended the presumption of individual autonomy and the moral legitimacy of personal choice at the expense of traditional collective authorities, including religion.

By studying more than seventy-five congregations in eight quite different neighborhoods of Chicago, Illinois, we have witnessed a complex interaction among religion, urban structure, and social change during this extraordinary episode in the history of urban America. Congregations are adapting to profound changes in context, but our interest goes beyond their strategies of survival and adaptation to consider how and to what extent they may reflect, resist, or influence the change itself.

In the 1920s, Chicago became the research site for the early members of the Chicago School of urban sociology,[3] and it has been fertile ground for urban and religious scholars ever since. In making research in this city the basis for this book, we do not claim that Chicago is typical of American cities. It is larger and more diverse than most, and unlike cities that have come of age more recently, it was structured decisively by the requirements of the industrial economy of the late nineteenth century. But it does represent many of the dimensions of late-twentieth-century urban life with which religious organizations are learning to interact. The congregations and neighborhoods we studied include people who are wealthy, middle-class, working poor, and urban underclass. They include white, black, Hispanic, Asian, African, and Middle Eastern people. They include recent immigrants and descendants of the immigrants of many generations ago. They include adherents to most of the world's religions. And they include congregations that have been organized—some recently and some generations ago—to meet the religious needs and give expression to the religious beliefs and practices of these diverse populations. Despite its differences from other cities, Chicago exemplifies the three processes of urban restructuring, religious restructuring, and social transformation with which religious organizations must interact if they are to participate effectively in urban life today.

Urban Restructuring and the Erosion of Neighborhood Ties

As an industrial city, Chicago has undergone a pattern of city-building—the phases of entrepreneurship, growth, consolidation, and decline—that is quite common in the United States, much like the building of Milwaukee, Detroit, Cleveland, and other cities that grew with the shift from a predominantly agrarian to predominantly industrial American economy.[4] And Chicago's attempt to become a successful postindustrial city, to make a transition comparable to those of Minneapolis–St. Paul and Pittsburgh, is well underway. But Chicago also exemplifies many of the challenges associated with postindustrial growth—economic polarization, spatial dislocations, and the lack of public authority at the metropolitan level to match the metropolitan reach of the economy.[5]

The congregations discussed in this book are coping with these challenges. In chapter 3, Matthew Price explores the efforts of "Gold Coast" churches to deal with problems of the notorious Cabrini Green public housing projects nearby, which were addressed at the meeting on public housing described earlier. These churches must negotiate the economic polarization between their Gold Coast neighborhood, whose people prosper with jobs in the technical and financial sectors, and Cabrini Green, whose residents do not qualify for the new jobs and are increasingly marginalized economically and victimized by violence. Similarly, the black middle-class churches discussed in David Daniels's chapter 7 recall our earlier account of male leadership responding to a situation brought on by the exodus of heavy industry, which until recently had undergirded the neighborhood's prosperity and cohesion. Many of these churches' members now live in the suburbs, where employment is more readily available. But as Daniels shows, their return to their churches not only to worship but to care for the at-risk youth is fostered by theological innovation that transcends class boundaries.

Similarly, the Baptist Sunday school we visited is in the Henry Horner public housing project on Chicago's West Side, home of what William Julius Wilson[6] has termed the "ghetto underclass," a population whose skills matched the requirements of manufacturing jobs of the previous era but do not meet the technical qualifications of the present. In chapter 4, Lowell Livezey and Isaac Laudarji explore how churches are responding to the resulting social isolation. In contrast, the Mexican Americans of Pilsen whom we saw serenading the Virgin of Guadalupe are mostly "working poor" immigrants and transmigrants, who fill the poorly paid manufacturing and service jobs that have remained in the city. In chapter 2, Janise Hurtig examines the role of churches in the "ethnicization" of these working-poor newcomers.

Other congregations throughout the city are made up of people who are financially successful but always on the move—commuting to work, taking the kids across the city to school, driving to shopping malls. The "edge-city" congregations reviewed in Paul Numrich's chapter 8 perhaps best illustrate this reality, but the recent Muslim, Hindu, and Sikh immigrants (see Numrich's chapter 10) too are highly mobile and widely distributed. Thus the local ties of the more prosperous congregations of all faiths are weakened by the centrifugal forces of people on constant reassignment and the speed of capital allocation. These cause members to spend little time in their own neighborhoods and to have few occasions to work with neighbors on problems and projects of common concern.

How did the city's deindustrialization and restructuring come about? Chicago's charter was granted in 1833, but as built space, most of Chicago dates from the Fire of 1871. Over the 125 years since the fire, most of the city's neighborhoods have been rebuilt at least twice, and some high-rises are the third buildings erected on certain sites. Before World War II, the entire design and layout of buildings, railroads, ports, streets, and highways were uniformly directed toward the expansion and consolidation of an industrial city. But since the war the city of Chicago, and more recently, industrial suburbs near the city, has suffered the loss of the manufacturing industries on which its economy primarily was based and around which the physical layout was organized. From 1947 to 1980, Chicago's employment in manufacturing dropped by more than 50 percent and in "TUC" (transportation, utilities, and communication) by 25 percent. Even with employment expansion in the government, service, and "FIRE" (finance, insurance, and real estate) sectors, the city of Chicago suffered a net loss of 189,000 jobs. In contrast, suburban employment increased dramatically (over 300 percent) during the same period. Yet despite this increase, employment in manufacturing and TUC in the Chicago Standard Metropolitan Statistical Area (SMSA) as a whole suffered a net decrease of 62,000 jobs.[7] By the 1990s, metropolitan Chicago had fundamentally changed both where and how it made its living.

Rapid and disruptive change is not new to the urban landscape. The changes that had taken place in Chicago neighborhoods and in the city as a whole since the late nineteenth century were of great interest to the founders of the Chicago School of urban sociology in the 1920s.[8] Indeed, the Chicago School was influential precisely because it provided an explanation for the dynamics of urban change associated with industrial growth.

But in the last decades of the twentieth century, Chicago and other large industrial cities were to undergo a different kind of change. A new metropolitan structure was emerging, one that was highly decentralized and multipolar, with edge cities[9] and other concentrations of employment and commerce distributed throughout the metropolitan area.[10] Moreover, although Chicago's central business area continued to prosper and grow as a focal point for employment, it had been transformed from the control center for Chicago-area enterprise into a niche in a global matrix of capital and information flows. Thus business decisions affecting the lives of Chicagoans were made not only in Chicago but in the major financial centers around the world. In turn, Chicago's economic power, represented in its thriving downtown and in its edge cities, increasingly was exercised over a global labor force and a worldwide network of productive enterprises. The city's labor force was competing in a growing global market, made possible by easier migrations of workers and technologically supported flows of capital. And major corporations now needed not brawny laborers, living near factories, ports, and railroads, but rather a highly educated workforce, which could afford to live in safe, pleasant residential areas with good schools and cultural amenities. These structural changes have complicated religious social ministries that once focused on issues of justice in an industrial economy.

The Changing Voices of Religion

Chicago's religious organizations grew up as part of the social and institutional structure characteristic of an American industrial city, representing what Daniel Bluestone calls "a parallel moral power."[11] The city's first settlers built churches and synagogues along with shops and houses near the Chicago River and its confluence with Lake Michigan. Some of these congregations, such as Old Saint Patrick's Roman Catholic Church (chapter 9) and First United Methodist Church, Chicago Temple (chapter 3), remain strong spiritual forces in the central city. But beginning before the Fire of 1871 and continuing through the 1920s, with the expansion and consolidation of the industrial infrastructure along waterways and railroads, many churches and synagogues moved from the central commercial district to the densely populated residential neighborhoods that were integral to that infrastructure. Bluestone argues that this represented a partial dissociation of religion from the commercial and public affairs of the city and a primary association of religion with morality and femininity, with the social and nurturing functions of community life.

Many of these congregations formed part of the growing denominationalism that was to be a hallmark of disestablished American religion. From 1916 to 1939, Archbishop George Mundelein led the Roman Catholic Archdiocese of Chicago to prominence as an exemplar of the "American Church," which evolved as a distinctive religious presence in a country in which Protestantism was culturally dominant but not officially established. Under his leadership, the archdiocese exercised effective institutional authority over territorially defined parishes that, in turn, established Catholic cultural hegemony in neighborhoods throughout much of Chicago, including Pilsen (chapter 2) and the Southwest Side (chapter 5). As in other American industrial cities, labor unions built supportive relationships with Catholics and their parishes. After the Second World War, the Chicago Archdiocese provided essential support for Saul Alinsky's innovative organizing in the Back of the Yards neighborhood, which launched the strategy of church-based organizing that has since been implemented in urban neighborhoods throughout the United States.

Although Chicago was home to as many Protestants as Catholics, most Protestant churches were smaller than Catholic parishes, and they were divided among so many denominations and sects that they could not hope to speak in a single public voice, as the Catholic Church could. The Protestant denominations, as H. Richard Niebuhr[12] argued, reflected not only doctrinal and organizational alternatives but the ethnic, racial, and class divisions of American society. Nevertheless, the Protestants of Chicago organized their numerous congregations in an Episcopal diocese, a presbytery, Methodist districts and a conference, synods of the various Lutheran churches, and various associations of congregations. These structures provided internal discipline, vehicles for social mission, and the capacity to speak publicly in the affairs of a burgeoning industrial city. Although fewer in number and membership, Jewish organizations served the same function.

Like Protestant churches in other major cities, soon after 1900, Chicago's churches crossed denominational lines to form clergy associations at the neighborhood level as well as citywide organizations. The Church Federation of Greater Chicago was founded in 1907 and continued until the late 1980s.[13] While it never united all Protestant churches, it was sufficiently strong to be recognized as an authoritative Protestant voice, a presence parallel to the Catholic Archdiocese of Chicago and the Chicago Board of Rabbis. Black churches, including those of black Protestant denominations, operated more autonomously, but many joined in issue-specific coalitions, especially when the civil rights movement came north in the 1960s.

Just as Chicago's ecumenical and denominational organizations were reaching the peak of their strength in the 1950s, however, they were also beginning to reflect the national process now known as religious restructuring.[14] While the people of the United States remain among the most likely in the world to believe in God, pray, and go to church, their religious institutions are being fragmented and realigned. The national and regional institutions of the mainline Protestant churches—the Church Federation of Greater Chicago and its member denominations, for example—have been disbanded or seriously weakened as local congregations have withheld support and questioned their authority and as individuals have directed support more to religious special-purpose organizations than to their own denominations and ecumenical agencies. This means not only that the mainline Protestant churches' economic base is attenuated but that increasingly each denomination cannot speak on public issues in a single, unified voice. Such has been the fate of the very institutions that most actively sought to have an impact on government and other public institutions and policies, that were the main expressions of what was generally considered "the public church."[15]

The Roman Catholic and Evangelical churches' concern with public policy has increased, however, and the "New Christian Right" has become a force to be reckoned with in electoral politics.[16] While the public prominence of the Chicago Archdiocese is hardly new, its visibility as a force in public life is accented by the retreat and fragmentation of Protestantism. Yet even these elements of increased strength in public religion appear to be only loosely related to the denominational structures that evolved before the Second World War.

The public role of religion was never limited to denominational and ecumenical bodies, of course, and restructuring has enhanced the relative stature of congregations and parishes. Their public importance is particularly impressive when one takes their cultural activity into account. This book highlights the publicly significant cultural work of congregations by examining the symbolic images and language, narrative stories, and social identities that they generate.

Since the 1960s, the rapid immigration from South and East Asia, the Middle East, Africa, and Latin America has altered the shape and character of religion in Chicago and in other large American cities, as Paul Numrich shows in chapter 10.[17] By most accounts, metropolitan Chicago is now home to at least three hundred thousand Muslims, seventy-five thousand Hindus, seventy-five thousand Buddhists, and smaller numbers of Sikhs, Jains, and Zoroastrians. All but a few thousand of these have arrived or were born here since 1960, but they have already formed well over a hundred thriving worship centers. Moreover, for the first time in U.S. history Christians have been arriving in large numbers from countries in which Christianity is not the majority religion or the religious basis of the predominant culture. Thus, for example, Methodists and Syrian Orthodox from India and Presbyterians from Korea add significantly to Chicago's cultural and religious diversity. Although these immigrants have largely been ignored in the literature, several scholars[18] have recently demonstrated their nationwide distribution and impact on American religious and cultural pluralism. Chapters 2, 5, 6, 8, and 10 in this book include studies of congregations that the recent wave of immigrants has created, and explore the new dimensions of pluralism that have resulted.

Social Transformation and the Refocus of Moral Culture

In Chicago as elsewhere, both urban and religious restructuring have been intimately linked to what some critics have called the "social revolution" of the 1960s and 1970s. The rejection of traditional values and extrication from traditional authorities during these decades are most often interpreted as a triumph of individual freedom and choice at the expense of community. Drawing on Philip Rieff's "triumph of the therapeutic," Christopher Lasch's "culture of narcissism," Robert Bellah's "expressive individualism," and Phillip Hammond's rise of "personal autonomy," scholars of culture John R. Hall and Mary Jo Neitz describe—and for the most part, decry—a fundamental shift in moral culture, from one in which authority lies with collectivities and their traditions to one that recognizes the authority of individual choice.[19] This thesis concerning the "loss of community" and the resulting amoral character of American society suggests one dimension—an ambiguous one, to be sure—of what has been happening in Chicago. Chicago is known as a "city of neighbor-hoods,"[20] and it is widely believed, not without reason, that these neigh-borhoods have had a moral character. While they never have been as ho-mogeneous, stable, and cohesive as Chicago mythology would have it, there is little reason to doubt that in many neighborhoods a moral cul-ture was shaped by overlapping interactions among people who were brought together by jobs, shopping, schooling, worship, and various ser-vices that were located relatively close together. Among immigrants, a common language and culture reinforced these material incentives to fol-low a shared path. For Catholics, the parish structure not only required them to attend church in their areas of residence but also established the sacredness of those particular spaces and thus of the relationships and cultural norms within them. Among industrial workers, the solidarity that the labor unions fostered reinforced the solidarity of workers and working-class families in their neighborhoods, which were typically not far from their places of employment.

These moral cultures, nostalgically recalled by Alan Ehrenhalt in *The Lost City*,[21] were inevitably eroded by urban restructuring, which caused people to spend less time, meet fewer of their needs, and achieve fewer of their aspirations near home. Moreover, these "natural communities" and their moral cultures were, in fact, morally ambiguous, as became increas-ingly apparent during the civil rights era, when many of them proved to be "defended neighborhoods."[22] Several chapters in this book—most poignantly chapter 5, on the Southwest Side parishes—offer lenses on congregations struggling with problems of boundaries and change as they attempt to preserve or reconstruct the moral cultures considered es-sential to social life.

But the old moral cultures and forms of social control have been chal-lenged not only by economic and demographic change but by religion it-self. In the Catholic Church, the Second Vatican Council's *Declaration on Religious Freedom* offered increased recognition of freedom of con-science. As Elfriede Wedam (chapter 9) and Peter D'Agostino (chapter 11) argue, the implementation of Vatican II in the Chicago Archdiocese has also afforded Catholics greater flexibility in associating with parishes and schools and has enhanced their authority and responsibility for the shape and direction of parish life. Mainline Protestant churches, perhaps more historically rooted in American individualism than other religious groups, train pastoral counselors in methods and settings that share many of the assumptions and principles of the therapeutic culture.[23] The mainline Protestants, along with Reform Jews, led the way in advocating removal of legal restrictions on divorce, and more recently, many have urged the same for abortion and the practice of a homosexual lifestyle, making all these increasingly a matter of individual choice and less subject to social control.

Yet the rise in personal autonomy has not been the only thrust of the social transformation. While many traditional sources of collective authority (such as neighborhoods, parishes, and unions) have been weakened, and others (churches) have chosen to support a greater degree of personal choice, there has been a simultaneous increase in the recognition of new collectivities and their moral claims. The events of the 1960s were fostered by social movements that both depended on and articulated group solidarities. The civil rights movement had as its goal increasing the individual rights of black people, but the movement presumed solidarities both among blacks and between blacks and whites that had not yet been articulated. These presumptions remain evident, newly reformulated, in the activities and cultures of the neighborhoods and congregations discussed in this book. Even though the feminist movement sought to advance the individual rights of women, sometimes at the expense of their communal ties, it also has both identified and fostered an "ethic of care"[24] in which individuals see themselves constituted by and embedded in their relationships, not as autonomous selves. And the two major 1990s community-organizing initiatives in Chicago, led by the Gamaliel Foundation and the Industrial Areas Foundation, suggest that the thrust of social change is not all in the direction of individualism and personal autonomy. In contrast to the personal growth and self-awareness movements, the prevailing idioms of these efforts are "relational power" and collective action for the "common good."

During the 1960s and 1970s, America underwent a profound discontinuity in its moral culture, and this is evident in the congregations discussed in this book. But if a new moral paradigm is emerging, it is doing so by fits and starts. Old authorities may be in disrepute and moral communities in disarray, but many individuals still repair to existing communities or attempt to build new ones in order to find their moral bearings. Some of these communities are congregations, whereas others compete with congregations for the hearts and minds of urban people.

Chicago: The Known City

Chicago has proved itself many times to be a rich resource and a fertile setting for both urban and religious research.[25] As Richard Sennett has argued, the early Chicago School sociologists distinguished themselves from their German teachers in part by examining and analyzing the gritty details of Chicago's neighborhoods and by studying its subpopulations and neighborhood organizations. By assembling these scholars' writings in *Classic Essays on the Culture of Cities,* Sennett shows that Georg Simmel (with whom Robert Park had studied at Heidelberg), Max Weber, and Oswald Spengler sought to contrast the distinctive city culture with that of farm and village and thus concerned themselves with what was common to cities, rather than with the variety and differentiation within them. In contrast, Park and his colleagues sought to discern the urban culture in its own "ecology," in the ways in which it was internally divided and operative. As Sennett puts it, Park believed that a city's "functional, tangible character would ultimately reveal the cultural and ethical possibilities for life within it."[26]

It was in Chicago, during the decades of its growth and consolidation as a great industrial city, that this central notion was developed and the city's specific physical and social realities, including religious life and organizations, were examined. Early Chicago School studies were conducted in some of the same neighborhoods that are the subjects of this book. The meeting concerning the demolition of public housing described at the beginning of this chapter took place in the LaSalle Street Church, which is located in what Chicago School sociologist Harvey Warren Zorbaugh[27] called the "area of furnished rooms," which separated what was then Little Sicily (now occupied by the Cabrini Green public housing project) from the wealthy residential area to the east, known from that day to this as the Gold Coast (see chapter 3). Nels Anderson's *The Hobo,* one of the earliest sociological studies of homeless men, achieves its insight into the homelessness of the time not only by charting the relationships (or lack of relationships) between the homeless and other people but by monitoring their interaction with their physical surroundings. Anderson spent his research time in the areas he called "Hobohemia," certain blocks on the fringes of Chicago's business district, including some in Old Saint Patrick's Parish, which is discussed in chapter 9. Louis Wirth's *The Ghetto,* a study of Chicago's Near West Side, a port of entry for Jews from Eastern Europe beginning in the late nineteenth century, showed how the attempt to understand the people of a neighborhood points beyond the neighborhood to "the natural history of an institution and the psychology of a people."[28] Since the 1920s, the people of Wirth's ghetto have migrated within Chicago, first westward to Lawndale, then north to West Rogers Park, where they comprise one of what Livezey (chapter 6) calls the "religiously based, ethnoracial enclaves" that characterize the community.

Chicago School methods were also used to study churches. Shortly after Graham Taylor arrived in Chicago in 1892 to teach at Chicago Theological Seminary, he established the Chicago Commons Association on the Near West Side as a laboratory for his students.[29] Preparation for Christian ministry required field studies, using direct observation and social survey. Samuel Kincheloe, a successor to Taylor, was particularly concerned to understand the inability of Chicago's Protestant neighborhood churches to cope with the influx of non-Protestant and nonwhite populations. Kincheloe's "The Behavior Sequence of a Dying Church,"[30] was based on data from declining congregations, including the West Side's Douglas Park Christian Church, which Kincheloe, as a young pastor, had been unable to keep alive when large numbers of Catholic immigrants replaced the Protestants of its neighborhood. Kincheloe's work anticipated the challenges to congregations from immigration and neighborhood change that this book explores. Kincheloe's research, however, reflecting the ecological approach of his Chicago School mentors, is preoccupied with the ability—or inability—of a church to adapt when the conditions that have sustained it change. His essays give little attention to the spiritual and social missions of the churches or to whether or not the churches create congregational cultures and goals distinct from the secular momentum of urban life.

After the Great Depression and World War II, research in and about Chicago continued to demonstrate and develop the use of field methods for understanding both urban and religious culture and organizations. Some of the landmark sociological studies in Chicago that undergird present research, including that presented here, are St. Clair Drake and Horace Cayton's *Black Metropolis*, Morris Janowitz's *The Community Press in an Urban Setting*, Gerald Suttles's *The Social Order of the Slum*, and Albert Hunter's *Symbolic Communities*.

Studies in social ethics, history, and politics have also demonstrated the value of direct, local observation for discerning human agency and for appraising strategies of transformation. For example, *The Edge of the*

Ghetto[31] examines the dynamics of race in Chicago's Southwest Side, providing a window on the encounter, repeated throughout the United States, of "white ethnic" communities with the assertion of African Americans' civil rights. Similarly, a detailed study of Chicago's civil rights organizations in the mid-1960s, *Confronting the Color Line*,[32] and various books on the dimension of race in Chicago politics during the campaigns and incumbency of Chicago's only elected African American mayor, Harold Washington,[33] anticipate that the problematic of race continues to pervade all aspects of life in metropolitan Chicago.

Finally, Chicago-based research is not particularly rich in studies that take the metropolitan area as a system or a unit of study. The present volume makes a modest move in that direction by attempting to show how each neighborhood is linked to a metropolitan system, and how change at the metropolitan level affects the neighborhood and its congregations. One antecedent is to be found in *Sacred Sands*, J. Ronald Engel's[34] study of voluntary associations' fight to save the Indiana Dunes and the Lake Michigan shore in the state of Indiana, southeast of Chicago. Engel shows how the movement to save the Dunes was built largely by Chicago-based organizations and movements that recognized the inextricable link between Chicago and the Dunes.

The writings discussed above focus on organizations' agency more than on their adaptive capacities. This is not to say that all the organizations studied actually made a difference; indeed, the main conclusion of *Confronting the Color Line* is that after years of civil rights struggle, the color line was left intact. But these accounts show how organizations may simultaneously adapt to change and participate in shaping outcomes. And they further illustrate how research in and about Chicago can illuminate issues of wider interest and can help explain the dynamics of large cities coping with structural change.

Since the early 1970s, "congregational studies" has emerged as an interdisciplinary field of research, signaled by the publication in 1986 of the *Handbook for Congregational Studies*, succeeded by *Studying Congregations* in 1998.[35] The Chicago-based Church and Community Ministry Project,[36] which seeks to understand the factors that sustain church activities intended to transform their communities, contributed greatly to the concepts presented in these books and to the development of this nascent field. The field has also been shaped by studies of the ecologies of congregations-in-community and of congregational adaptation to neighborhood change, most recently exemplified in Nancy Ammerman's

Congregation and Community,[37] and by studies of congregational cultures, perhaps still best represented by James Hopewell's *Congregation.*[38] Although the field as a whole is concerned mainly with Protestantism, John T. McGreevy's *Parish Boundaries*[39] examines the complex church-and-neighborhood interaction on the race issue in the Catholic parishes in Chicago and other American industrial cities. And in *Gatherings in Diaspora,* scholars convened by R. Stephen Warner present ethnographic case studies of eleven "new ethnic and immigrant" congregations.[40]

The Evolution of Method

The Religion in Urban America Program continued this history of religious and community research in Chicago with particular attention to the responses of religious organizations to postwar urban and religious restructuring and social transformation. We proceeded inductively in order to avoid privileging social services and community action, the urban ministries that were prominent when cities made their living mainly by manufacturing and shipping and when Will Herberg's *Protestant-Catholic-Jew*[41] described the extent of religious pluralism. We made ethnographic case studies of congregations the core of the investigation in order to look at urban religion as much as possible "from the native's point of view," recognizing, as Clifford Geertz[42] did, that this could only be approximated. We believe the ethnographic method helped us to be equally attentive to self-initiated mission and adaptive strategies and to analyze a full range of public actions, including cultural production as well as social service and community organizing. We selected organizations as case studies without regard to the nature or extent of their engagement in such activities but with the objective that, collectively, they would reflect the social, economic, demographic, and religious diversity of metropolitan Chicago.

Because we wanted to examine congregations in relation to their geographic and social contexts, we first selected neighborhoods that, taken together, would represent the city's range of social, economic, demographic, and religious characteristics. We then inventoried congregations and other religious organizations in each neighborhood and selected from five to eight of them for investigation as case studies. These selections mainly reflected the religious diversity of the neighborhoods, but we also sought to ensure that the selections for the study as a whole would represent the religious diversity of the metropolitan area. We selected a higher proportion of organizations representing Islam, Hinduism, Buddhism, and other religions that had not been much discussed in the literature of American religion.

Thus the Religion in Urban America Program's investigative method both continues and complements the ecological model of community research that has been developed and practiced in Chicago for nearly a century. It is the Chicago empirical method in a new phase. This book presents a ground-level view of the results.

Congregations and Urban Transformation

In the chapters that follow, we offer narratives of what we saw and heard as we studied Chicago-area religious organizations in their local settings. The essays in part 2 explore the interaction between religious congregations and the neighborhoods and social settings in which they are located. The social functions of neighborhoods are changing and often declining. Consequently, many congregations are reorganizing themselves to depend less on their immediate neighborhoods, to relate to their geographic surroundings in new ways, and to emphasize more symbolic and communicative frames of reference.

The essays in part 3, therefore, are concerned with some of the ways in which religious organizations constitute themselves and serve constituencies beyond the neighborhood. Many of these, exemplified by Old Saint Patrick's Church in chapter 9, are "niche congregations" that are surviving neighborhood change and reconstituting themselves as viable, possibly growing congregations by devising programs and communal styles that appeal to specialized constituencies. Others, such as the recently established Buddhist, Hindu, Sikh, and Muslim worship centers discussed in chapter 10, have deliberately chosen their locations to accommodate participants who are dispersed throughout the metropolitan area.

Finally, despite the erosion of denominational power, these structures still have the institutional responsibility for the entire city or metropolitan area. Peter R. D'Agostino's analysis in chapter 11 of Chicago's largest denominational structure, the Roman Catholic Archdiocese, complements the ethnographic examination of parishes presented in chapters 2, 4, 5, 6, 7, and 9, enabling the reader to see the interaction between the neighborhood and the metropolitan levels of religious organization. This is particularly important at a time of adjustment to a postindustrial economy, and D'Agostino's chapter focuses specifically on the archdiocesan response to urban restructuring under the episcopacy of the late Joseph Cardinal Bernardin, who died in 1996, shortly after our field research was completed.

The narratives of all ten chapters reveal congregations and other religious institutions responding, often creatively, to the opportunities and pressures of urban change. The congregations demonstrate a combination of internal and external concerns, delivering what organizational theorists call "member benefits" as well as "public benefits." Most of the congregations principally serve their own members, with service to the wider community and advocacy for public causes relegated to small committees and discretionary portions of annual budgets. The chapters presented in this book suggest that while social action is a significant form of religious engagement, one that makes an appreciable contribution to human welfare in the city, it is not the central dynamic of urban religion.

This finding suggests a considerable expansion, if not an outright shift in focus, for the question of the urban contribution of religious organizations. At least since the Progressive Era and the Social Gospel movement, both scholarly and ministerial interest in religion's contribution has focused on benefits to poor, marginalized, and subordinated populations, whether through the salvation of souls, the delivery of social services, or the reform of the public order. In short, religious agency has been considered important in the city mainly insofar as it directly and measurably benefited, in Elam Davies's memorable expression, "the least, the last, the lost, and the lonely."[43] In the late 1990s, this long-standing expectation of religion has been expressed as part of the trend toward the privatization of services briefly considered the proper responsibility of government.

The studies presented in this book confirm that congregations of all the major faiths are collectively engaged in good deeds to benefit the "disadvantaged other," continuing the long-standing tradition known in Christianity as social ministry. But they also conclude that programs of social service and social action account for but a fraction of the religious contribution to the quality of urban life. To understand that contribution fully, it is necessary to examine the cultural life of religious organizations and to recognize that cultural production and community formation are not necessarily inward-looking and private but are often effective forms of public action. R. Stephen Warner addresses this point in the epilogue.

The religious organizations of metropolitan Chicago are shaped by their members' experience of living in extremely kinetic conditions, in which the communities and cultures of their past appear to be defunct, inaccessible, or irrelevant. This is most obvious among recent immigrants, especially those from non-European countries that were never fully dominated by European culture, the English language, and Christianity. But it is also true for American citizens whose ties to a local community have been severed by their own relocation, or by the replacement of their former neighbors by new neighbors of different language or culture or experience, or by the daily pressures preventing their interaction and cooperation with persons whose residences are nearby. And it may also be true for some who, even though geographically settled and organizationally connected, are unable or unwilling to assent to the moral authority or share in the common culture of the institutions and groups to which they belong. In short, the institutions of urban religion are made up of people whose frames of reference have been shaken by some combination of structural and cultural change.

In response, these churches, temples, synagogues, and mosques produce the cultural material that enables their members and adherents to locate themselves with respect to the places and time in which they currently live, to identify with others, to find their moral bearings, and to achieve some measure of efficacy with respect to their own needs and aspirations. Mainly through worship, education, and social activities, these congregations appropriate symbols and generate new ones, claim and revise traditions, defend and bridge social boundaries, articulate and invent meanings and values by which to make sense of changing circumstances.

This much is not new but rather a recognized role of religion in society and an expression of the fact that, as Geertz[44] has argued, religion is— whatever else it may also be—a cultural system. The importance lies in both the process and the content of that cultural production, which are complex subjects. The process of producing religious cultural material, as Robert Wuthnow explains in *Producing the Sacred*,[45] is very similar to that of creating music, art, and entertainment. The production of new cultural material always begins with what already exists. Just as even the most original painting reflects the pigments, tools, and media that the present technology and economy supply, so the sermons, music, and liturgies of every congregation are conditioned by the particular people, artifacts, technologies, theologies, and beliefs available to it. These raw materials of cultural production are different for every congregation, and the congregations discussed in this book were selected precisely to reflect as much variety as possible. Although they are located in a single metropolitan region, the differences of neighborhood, race and ethnicity, economic resources, age, and religious heritage mean that the starting point is unique to each congregation.

Yet, as we have observed the expressions and practices of urban religion, it has been possible to discern patterns and to identify some of the ways in which the cultural activities of these congregations are important to life in the city. Culture is inherently public, so cultural production by religious organizations is one kind of religious public action. Cultural production has many dimensions, but we have been particularly impressed with the ways in which it is concerned with theology, morality, and community.

First, since congregations are specifically religious, their cultural innovation is in part theological. Their central symbols are about their god or gods, and the meanings they share and the authority they exercise almost always include some claims about their relationship with the Divine. Thus, while the chapters that follow are not explicitly theological, they examine congregations that are engaged in theological discourse, and they show how that discourse has public and political as well as private and spiritual implications. For example, the incorporation of black popular culture into the worship life of a middle-class black church evokes an understanding of the God of the entire African diaspora, and this in turn provides a basis for bridging the boundary between the black middle class and the poor. Similarly, the mandatory inclusion of multiple ethnic groups in the governing structure of a mosque not only symbolizes the theological principle of the inclusiveness of the Muslim *ummah*, or "nation," but also institutionalizes procedures to ensure that diverse cultural traditions interact and evolve. The result is that Indians, Pakistanis, Palestinians, Egyptians, and African Americans, among others, find common interests and purposes that go far beyond the conduct of the mosque.

Second, most of the congregations discussed here are engaged in cultural activities that have a prominent moral dimension. This does not mean that they or the authors writing about them view culture itself as inherently good. While many of these congregations exhibit the aesthetic refinement and intellectual achievement associated with "high culture," this is incidental to the fact that they all generate systems of meaning and value that are embodied and expressed in symbols. Cultural symbols mark both the good and the bad, the better and the worse, the acceptable and the unacceptable—whether the subject is art, food, government, or personal or group behavior. And since religion is a cultural system, our focus on religious congregations enables us to ask how and to what extent congregations may be fostering collective norms and patterns of social accountability.

The picture that emerges from the essays taken together is one of multiple religious communities in which people share a concern for speaking and acting in ways they consider proper. Virtually every subject that has a "right-and-wrong" dimension came up sooner or later in the congregations we studied. But we were particularly impressed with how frequently congregations or groups within them were concerned with questions of race or ethnicity, sometimes without even articulating the relevant choices in racial or ethnic terms. Whether or not to conduct a worship service in an additional language, whether to add or change a picture or icon, how hard to try to evangelize a neighborhood or to recruit new members from a wider region—choices such as these entail racial values and choices. And the decision of whether to articulate the racial dimension or to leave it latent beneath the surface is itself a moral choice, one that the congregations discussed in this book often made and sometimes articulated. Thus, although only a small percentage of these congregations engaged in political action on race "issues," the problem of race in our society and in their own religious groups was frequently central to their cultural work.

Finally, while different congregations and groups foster different and sometimes conflicting values, their social accountability and the authority they attribute to their respective traditions contrast markedly with the individual moral autonomy sustained by the secular culture. For all their differences, congregations are collectives—associations, groups, communities. In general, the religious communities discussed in this book tend to preserve traditional values by reinterpreting them in new contexts, rather than to reject and replace them. Thus the cultural activities of religious congregations tend more toward preserving and reclaiming traditional collective goods (neighborhoods, families) than toward promoting either new collective goods (economic equality) or individual rights and freedoms. This runs counter to the individualism and moral autonomy that were central to the social revolution of the 1970s and that many alarmed critics, such as Bellah and Hammond, claim have become the dominant features of the common culture. This line of argument is more implicit than explicit in following chapters, but the reader will find rich and multifaceted evidence to support it.

NOTES

The entire Religion in Urban America Program team contributed greatly to the knowledge and perspective reflected in this introductory chapter. I am also particularly grateful to William A. Simpson for his discerning critiques and creative suggestions.

1. The authors are all members of the Religion in Urban America Program at the University of Illinois at Chicago and conducted field research—along with our colleagues in the program—in the congregations and neighborhoods we discuss in our chapters.

2. Wuthnow, *Restructuring of American Religion.*

3. See Park, "City as a Social Laboratory."

4. Orum, *City-Building in America.*

5. Soja, *Postmodern Geographies;* Orum, *City-Building in America.*

6. Wilson, *Truly Disadvantaged.*

7. Haider, "Chicagoland 2005."

8. Park and Burgess, *The City;* Wirth, "Urbanism as a Way of Life"; Hunter, *Symbolic Communities* and "The Gold Coast and the Slum Revisited."

9. Garreau, *Edge City.*

10. Soot et al., *Analysis of Employment Hubs.*

11. Bluestone, *Constructing Chicago,* 62ff.

12. Niebuhr, *Social Sources of Denominationalism.*

13. Richesin, "Eighty Years of Ministry 1907–1987."

14. Wuthnow, *Restructuring of American Religion.*

15. Marty, *Public Church.*

16. Casanova, *Public Religions in the Modern World,* esp. 135–166.

17. Also see Numrich, "Recent Immigrant Religions."

18. Williams, *Religions of Immigrants;* Warner and Wittner, eds., *Gatherings in Diaspora;* Haddad, ed., *Muslims of America;* Eck, ed., *World Religions in Boston.*

19. Hall and Neitz, *Culture,* 20–43. Their sources include Rieff, *Triumph of the Therapeutic;* Lasch, *Culture of Narcissism;* Bellah et al., *Habits of the Heart;* and Hammond, *Religion and Personal Autonomy.*

20. Pacyga and Skerrett, *Chicago.*

21. Ehrenhalt, *Lost City.*

22. Suttles, *Social Construction of Communities,* 21–43.

23. Browning, *Fundamental Practical Theology,* 245–46.

24. Gilligan, *In a Different Voice,* esp. 62–63.

25. The title for this section comes from Richard Wright's introduction to Drake and Cayton, *Black Metropolis,* xviii.

26. Sennett, ed., *Classic Essays,* 13.

27. Zorbaugh, *Gold Coast and the Slum.*

28. Wirth, *The Ghetto,* xi.

29. Stockwell, "Graham Taylor—Urban Pioneer."

30. Kincheloe, "Behavior Sequence of a Dying Church."

31. Fish et al., *Edge of the Ghetto.*

32. Anderson and Pickering, *Confronting the Color Line.*

33. See Grimshaw, *Bitter Fruit;* Green and Holli, eds., *Restoration 1989;* Travis, *"Harold" the People's Mayor.*

34. Engel, *Sacred Sands.*

35. Carroll, Dudley, and McKinney, eds., *Handbook for Congregational Studies;* Ammerman et al., eds., *Studying Congregations.* Also see Hopewell, *Congregation;* Dudley, Caroll, and Wind, eds., *Carriers of Faith;* Wind and Lewis, eds., *American Congregations,* vols. 1 and 2; Ammerman, *Congregation and Community.*

36. Dudley and Johnson, "Congregational Self-Images."

37. Ammerman, *Congregation and Community.*

38. Hopewell, *Congregation.*

39. McGreevy, *Parish Boundaries.*

40. Warner and Wittner, eds., *Gatherings in Diaspora.*

41. Herberg, *Protestant-Catholic-Jew.*

42. Geertz, *Local Knowledge,* chap. 3.

43. Scroggs, "Making a Difference," 507.

44. Geertz, *Interpretation of Cultures,* chap. 4.

45. Wuthnow, *Producing the Sacred,* chap. 1.

Part II

Religion in a City of Neighborhoods

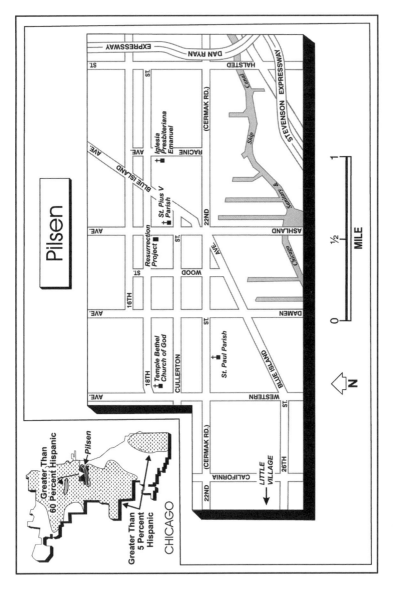

Map 2. Pilsen, a major port of entry for Mexicans, is a symbolic center of the Hispanic population of metropolitan Chicago. Map by Brian Twardosz, BMT Printing and Cartographic Specialists.

Chapter 2

Hispanic Immigrant Churches and the Construction of Ethnicity

Janise D. Hurtig

Every Sunday morning Rosario and her family walk four blocks to Saint Pius V, their neighborhood parish. Saint Pius is a Roman Catholic church located in the heart of Pilsen—a poor, inner-city neighborhood that over the past forty years has come to form part of Chicago's densest and most populous Mexican American district, as well as a principal port of entry for Mexican immigrants to the Chicago area. As Rosario walks up the steps of the unimposing red-brick building, she joins hundreds of her fellow parishioners—most of whom also live nearby—to attend one of three Spanish-language masses held each Sunday; two more masses are held in English. Over the course of the day, more than twenty-five hundred people attend mass at Saint Pius, and often there is standing room only in the wood-beamed sanctuary that seats around six hundred. Most of those attending, like Rosario, are Mexican immigrants; and many of them, like Rosario, speak little or no English.

While Rosario walks to Saint Pius, Lucia drives into Pilsen, with her Salvadoran husband and their two young children, from a lower-middle-class, predominantly Hispanic[1] neighborhood several miles away, to attend services at Emmanuel Presbyterian Church. Located only blocks away from Saint Pius, Emmanuel Presbyterian is an evangelically oriented, burgeoning congregation whose two hundred Sunday worshipers consistently overflow the rather modest sanctuary. As at Saint Pius, the Sunday service is attended largely by young families—parents accompanied by their children and, at times, the grandparents. The worshipers at Emmanuel, however, tend to be slightly better off economically than Saint Pius's parishioners; and while the Presbyterian congregation is entirely Hispanic, it is nationally quite diverse.

Although many of the adults and their children are bilingual, Sunday services at Emmanuel are held in Spanish.

We[2] met Rosario and Lucia in the winter of 1994, in the course of conducting comparative research on religious organizations in Pilsen. Our objectives were, first, to learn what Pilsen's religious organizations considered to be the pressing issues for their members and communities and, second, to analyze and compare how individual organizations addressed those issues, spiritually and programmatically. We gathered information in part through the observation of religious rituals, programs, and other activities and in part through interviews with clergy, laity, and community leaders. Rosario and Lucia were among the lay leaders we interviewed at their churches.

This chapter draws on the growing research in congregational studies that looks at urban churches not as institutional mirrors of the larger secular society, nor as havens from the profane urban world, but rather as "subcultures," distinguishable from but interacting with the larger urban environment of which they are part. Each church subculture is guided by a particular logic or worldview that integrates the spiritual, social, educational, and community life of the church. It also projects certain values, identities, and social orientations that members often turn to for guidance and inspiration in their daily lives.[3]

The worldviews of immigrant churches are informed in part by their model or vision of "ethnicization"—the process by which immigrants become ethnics. Thus the orientation an immigrant church offers its members also implies a path for their incorporation into an ethnic community. Located in a Mexican American neighborhood and serving predominantly Hispanic constituencies, Pilsen's churches play an active role in the constitution and spiritual legitimation of Mexican American and Hispanic ethnicities.

By "ethnicity" I am referring to a culturally constructed category that stands for a collective identity emergent in the interaction between immigrant groups and the mainstream society. Historically, ethnicity has been represented in the popular and academic imaginations as a transcendent cultural form, thought to abide in such traits as descent, cultural heritage, and national origin and to be expressed and reproduced through shared language, customs, and traditions. Discussions of the nature of ethnicity—implicitly figured in terms of the experiences of (white) European immigrants—have been inseparable from debates regarding the likelihood and civic value of immigrant incorporation (assimilationism) on the one hand and the persistence of separate "ethnic minorities" (cultural pluralism) on the other.[4] Even the current celebration of multiculturalism and ethnic diversity, while embracing pluralism wholeheartedly, has encouraged a new wave of ethnic essentialism among scholars, cultural critics, and social activists.

In a provocative article contesting essentialist notions of ethnicity, Kathleen Conzen and her colleagues suggest instead that ethnicity be thought of as "a process of construction or invention which incorporates, adapts, and amplifies preexisting communal solidarities, cultural attributes, and historical memories."[5] Their constructivist approach to ethnicity is compelling, first, because it historicizes ethnicity as an ongoing and contested process and, second, because it emphasizes the active participation of immigrants themselves in the construction and transformation of ethnic identities and ethnic group boundaries. Ethnicity, they argue, does not inhere in immigrants; rather, it emerges through *"relationships* among specific immigrant groups and between them and the dominant ethnoculture."[6] By implication, immigrant churches would not simply offer up a preconstituted ethnic identity to their members. Rather, the invention or construction of ethnicity occurs at the intersections of the church, its members, the larger religious institutions to which it is tied, and the wider secular society with which it interacts. In the context of the urban neighborhood of Pilsen, this perspective encourages us to consider the significance and impact of each church's model of ethnicization in terms of such factors as the racialization of Hispanic ethnicity by the dominant (Anglo) society[7] and the location of Pilsen and many of its residents within a transnational, migratory circuit.

The Religious Landscape of a Transnational Neighborhood

Pilsen is a small but densely populated neighborhood bounded on the north and west by railroad tracks, on the east and south by the South Branch of the Chicago River. The boundaries signal the neighborhood's historical role as port of entry and residence for poor, laboring Eastern European immigrants, who found jobs on the rail and shipping lines and in the lumberyards, factories, and processing plants that had surrounded the area since the mid-1800s.[8]

By the turn of the century, Pilsen—named for a small town in Bohemia—had become a "tenement district": it suffered the highest concentration of poor immigrant families, the most congested and unsanitary housing, and the most militant labor force in the city.[9] Pilsen's immigrant population was also solidly Catholic, and the neighborhood was organized around national parishes—Czech, Slovak, Polish, Croatian—often built by the parishioners and run by "native" priests. For the early residents of Pilsen parish, community, faith, and national identity were of a piece.[10] It was as parish communities that Pilseners waged battles over language, ethnic discrimination, employment, housing, and education, in their efforts to assimilate into the urban U.S. mainstream while maintaining symbolic and material ties to their homelands. They also contended with the Archdiocese of Chicago for their native languages, religious practices, and clerical representation. Similar battles, both secular and spiritual, continue to be fought today by Pilsen's Mexican residents.[11]

Pilsen's population began to change from Eastern European to Mexican in the 1950s, when the coincidence of U.S. postwar prosperity and Mexican economic crisis stimulated a dramatic increase in Mexican immigration. At the same time, patterns of national and transnational migration began to shift as Mexican migrants increasingly relocated from rural agricultural to urban industrial areas on both sides of the border, under the pressures of a changing global labor market. By 1980, over 80 percent of the Mexican workforce in the United States was located in urban areas, and Chicago's Mexican population was growing dramatically: from 106,000 in 1970, to 206,000 in 1980, and to 348,000 by 1990—figures that do not take into account the tens of thousands of undocumented Mexican immigrants. The rapid influx of Hispanics into Pilsen was magnified in the 1960s by two major urban renewal projects to the north and east that displaced substantial numbers of Hispanics. At the same time, acculturated "white ethnic" residents moved to urban and suburban neighborhoods where they could buy houses and move up the socioeconomic ladder. By the 1970s, Pilsen had become a solidly Hispanic and primarily Mexican district; by the 1990s, many of the industries providing accessible, low-skill employment for immigrants had relocated elsewhere or closed.

Present-day Pilsen is a thoroughly Mexican neighborhood. The 1990 U.S. Census statistics, which tell us that over 81 percent of its nearly fifty thousand residents identify themselves as Mexican (with another 12 percent identifying themselves as Latin Americans of other national backgrounds), give us little feel for the myriad ways in which Mexican cultural and social life permeates the neighborhood. Its main streets are lined with restaurants, grocery stores, and bakeries that sell primarily Mexican food and dry goods. The sweet smell of corn tortillas wafts across every street corner. Bookstores sell Spanish-language books, magazines, and newspapers, and most street conversation and store signs are in Spanish. Mexican popular music pours out into the streets from music stores, apartment buildings, and car windows. In the spring and summer months, *paleteros* selling ice cream and *eloteros* selling corn on the cob and tropical fruit ambulate up and down the streets ringing their bells. Seven of Pilsen's nine Catholic parishes offer one or more Sunday masses in Spanish, and many church interiors include shrines to the Virgin of Guadalupe, the patron saint of Mexico and symbol of Mexican popular religious culture.

But Pilsen is not a town in Mexico. Its immigrant residents work for U.S. companies and deposit money into U.S. banks; their children attend either public or parochial schools; and the neighborhood parishes are under the jurisdiction of the Archdiocese of Chicago, which is part of the U.S. Roman Catholic Church. Pilseners face struggles common to poor, inner-city communities the United States: under- and unemployment, inadequate housing and school facilities, high rates of crime and violence, pervasive gang and drug involvement, and low levels of academic achievement among youth. These problems are exacerbated by the material and ideological barriers created by language differences, and by the gender and generational conflicts created by tensions between the cultural values and social relations of the societies of origin and of settlement.

In both the struggles Pilsen's Mexican residents face and the tendency to address those problems through their religious organizations, Pilsen's current inhabitants resemble their European predecessors. Several interrelated factors, however, distinguish the Mexican experience from that of earlier Eastern European immigrants: the neocolonial relationship of Mexico to the United States; the institutionalized, racialized discrimination against Mexican immigrants;[12] the precariousness of many immigrants' civil status, exacerbated by the current wave of anti-immigration legislation targeting Mexicans; and the circular, transnational dimension of their migration experience.

While many of Pilsen's churches address the first three of these issues spiritually and programmatically, transmigration is not on the religious agenda. And yet, Mexican migration into Chicago has become increasingly transnational in its orientation and cultural consequences. Certainly, the intention of eventual return to the homeland is not new to the immigrant experience; nor is the creation of formal and informal structures for maintaining circular flows of communication, money, and other material and cultural goods between the United States and the homelands. (Indeed, immigrant churches have often facilitated such circuits.) What distinguishes contemporary transnational communities is the rapidity, frequency, and relative ease with which family members come and go between various points of residence, so that *migration itself* becomes formative of the cultural and social life of such communities.

As ethnographers of transnational communities have suggested, transmigratory practices do not simply produce two distinct local or national cultures; rather, they create a distinct, transmigratory cultural system that sustains multiple and often conflicting social and cultural identities,[13] as well as "a powerful ideology of return migration."[14] This dream—which for many is linked to the very impetus to migrate to the United States in the first place—circulates as a force organizing many families' daily lives and thus pours out into the larger community of Pilsen as well. Moreover, transmigration supports a cultural logic in which returns to the homeland are among the strategies immigrants adopt in adjusting to life in the host society. Thus we can understand the common practice among Mexican American families in Pilsen of sending teenage children back to Mexico, for summers or during the school year, to "keep them out of trouble"—where trouble refers to gang involvement, drug use, or premarital sexual activity.[15] Notably, while most of the religious organizations we studied devoted considerable energy and programming to the needs of neighborhood youth, none of them considered sending youth back to Mexico as a strategy for avoiding gang involvement or drug use.

In their extensive study of Mexican migration, Douglas Massey and his colleagues found that while few Mexican immigrants come to the United States with the intention of staying, many find themselves slowly abandoning the dream of return to their homeland as they become increasingly caught up in and committed to life in the United States. And yet, established immigrants do not separate from but rather support other network members' transmigratory patterns.[16] In other words, transmigration is not a stage in a continuum from mobility to settlement; rather, the two migratory tendencies are intimately interconnected. Thus neighborhoods like Pilsen are not simply the point of entry to a unidirectional pathway that leads immigrants up and out of the poor inner city and into the suburban mainstream. Rather, they are incorporated economically, socially, and culturally into a larger, spatially dispersed, transmigrant culture. As Roger Rouse puts it, "In the United States as well as in Mexico, the *place* of the putative community—whether regional or national—is becoming little more than the *site* in which transnationally organized circuits of capital, labor, and communications intersect with one another and with local ways of life."[17] By extension, parishes like Saint Pius are themselves enmeshed in this transnational migratory flow. Emmanuel Presbyterian, a church with a substantial outsider membership and fewer recent immigrant members than Saint Pius, has a less direct relationship to the transnational social reality that permeates Pilsen. Nonetheless, it too engages with that reality: not only does it evangelize within and serve the local community, but many of its members maintain familial ties to the neighborhood.

Within the context of Pilsen's emergent transmigratory culture, the Catholic parishes, schools, health facilities, and community centers have maintained their centrality as a religious presence and defender of the people. Certainly, Pilsen has produced an impressive array of secular, community-based organizations that operate in the service and defense of Pilsen's Hispanic immigrants; some of these are descendents of community organizations that once served Pilsen's Eastern European residents. But the Catholic community of Pilsen has continued to play a central role in advocating for its immigrant residents. At the same time, it is engaged with its Protestant competitors in a battle over souls that dates back to the founding of Protestant-based settlement houses at the turn of the century.

Over the past thirty-five years, the neighborhood parishes have consolidated their efforts through the structure of the Pilsen Catholic Cluster—an association of parishes active for social justice. The Cluster describes itself as "a clearing house to share information and ideas and to assist on joint action among the parishes and other invited groups."[18] Cluster parishes work together on liturgy and sacramental programs, social-justice issues affecting the neighborhood and the wider Hispanic Catholic community, evangelization, educational issues, and youth programs.

One religious event that enacts and illustrates the integration of faith, popular culture, and social action characteristic of the Pilsen Cluster is its annual dramatization of the Via Crucis (Stations of the Cross), held on Good Friday of Saints' Week. In Mexico and across Latin America, Saints' Week is one of the most important moments in the annual ritual cycle, and the Via Crucis is a public performance vividly enacted with all the dramatis personae in full regalia. The Cluster's decision to enact the Stations of the Cross in the street exemplifies the incorporation and symbolic transformation of "native traditions": parishioners and clergy alike recognized that a street celebration not only would draw on a familiar Mexican religious practice but would also "represent Christ's passion publicly in relation to Pilsen people's everyday lives" and reaffirm "the immigrant community's identity as . . . a people on the move."[19]

The Pilsen Via Crucis has become renowned throughout the city as a powerful expression of Mexican popular religion and community solidarity. Thousands of people—Hispanics and Anglos alike—come from around the city to walk slowly and somberly behind the cross-bearing figure of Jesus from station to station. As Jesus carries the cross down the streets of Pilsen, accompanied by Mary, Joseph, Mary Magdalene, the disciples, and Roman soldiers, the procession stops at each of the twelve stations, located in front of parishes and at sites of social and political significance to the community. Among the stations of the cross included in the 1994 Via Crucis that I attended was the Rudy Luzano Public Library, a site of bittersweet significance. Named for a martyred community activist, the modern, well-equipped library is a source of tremendous community pride. The procession also stopped at the site of a drive-by gang shooting and, later, at the newly opened Guadalupano Family Center, located in a former Saint Vitus Parish building. This passionate, public display of popular religion consolidates the community around symbols of local struggle, which are made sacred as they become integral to Mexican American ethnicity.

Fig. 2-1. Jesus bearing his cross in the 1998 Via Crucis in Chicago's Pilsen neighborhood. Photo courtesy of Saint Pius V Roman Catholic Church.

Fig. 2-2. Father Charles Dahm, pastor of Saint Pius V Roman Catholic Church in Pilsen, memorializing a neighborhood killing as part of the 1998 Via Crucis. Photo courtesy of Saint Pius V Roman Catholic Church.

In the 1960s and 1970s the Pilsen Catholic Cluster also provided the structure and inspiration for the creation of a church-based neighborhood community organization and a development corporation, two separate entities that merged in 1994 to form the Resurrection Project. The Resurrection Project runs a neighborhood cleanup program, low-cost housing development and rental programs, and the Guadalupano Family Center. While the Resurrection Project is not directly accountable to the Cluster, its mission—"to shape the future of our community and the quality of its life by building relationships, organizing people with common goals and values and putting those values into practice through education, leadership training, and action"[20]—clearly echoes the Cluster's liberationist spirit. Its programs, directed against the twin threats of urban blight and Anglo gentrification, are aimed at empowering residents by increasing their pride in, control over, and ownership of the community. It is interesting that the unidirectional vision of immigrant incorporation implicit in Resurrection Project's efforts to empower Mexican immigrants by facilitating settlement is entirely in keeping with the long-standing policy of the Catholic leadership to promote home ownership as a strategy for building and sustaining the parish community.[21]

The Catholic presence in Pilsen extends beyond the parishes, schools, and church-based community organizations. Many secular community organizations and agencies also cooperate with the Pilsen parishes, in part because of the sizable population base the parishes represent and can mobilize. Cooperation is also fostered by the politically progressive orientation of the parishes and Cluster and by the recognition that the local parishes are advocates for the Mexican community. This is often expressed through their appeals to the middle-class, Anglo Archdiocese of Chicago, which much of the Hispanic Catholic community perceives as having only a token interest in its large but poor Hispanic constituency and as unwilling to promote Hispanic leadership.

As the Cluster struggles to gain both recognition and autonomy from the archdiocese while uniting with the regional Hispanic Catholic community, it finds itself contending with a growing, though relatively small, Protestant presence. In the mid-1990s there were three mainline Protestant congregations in Pilsen and fifteen small and often transitory evangelical, fundamentalist, or Pentecostal "storefront" churches, many of which have a significant outsider membership. Of these non-Catholic churches, only Saint Matthew Lutheran Church and the multiethnic Church of God are actively engaged in social-justice issues in the community. Ana Maria Díaz-Stevens and Anthony Stevens-Arroyo attribute the pastoralism of Pentecostal and evangelical churches to their millennial vision, which "often precludes concerns for social and political change."[22] While these organizations may implicitly construct Hispanicity through the homogeneity of their membership, they do not explicitly link spirituality and religious identity with ethnic identity.

Nonetheless, Catholic parishes and Protestant congregations are equally invested in recruiting souls into the faith, establishing a commitment to their religious community, and cultivating lay leadership among their members—all efforts that encourage a unidirectional model of ethnicization that prefigures their immigrant constituencies as moving along a path toward eventual, permanent settlement in the Chicago area.

Saint Pius Parish: An Immigrant Parish
Committed to Social Justice

Rosario had been living in Chicago for close to six months when she first walked up the steps of Saint Pius Parish. She, her husband, and their two young daughters had come to Pilsen from a small hamlet in the central state of Michoacán, Mexico. It was February, and the brutal Chicago winter matched the harsh urban landscape and the rough sounds of English that accosted Rosario's uncomprehending ears.

Just before leaving her native village, Rosario's pastor had counseled her: "Where the tree is, there the branches and the root should also be. The wife should follow the man. Wherever you may be, look for the pastor and your religion." His simple message made it profoundly clear that the continuity of and commitment to family and religious life were not only morally imperative but part of the natural order of things. Implicit in his counsel was the assumption of a certain universality to Catholicism—that it knows no cultural boundaries and transcends the materiality of national frontiers. Historically, this theological premise has existed in tension with the equally fundamental parochialism of that same religion, one that emphasizes the geographic and cultural situatedness of each parish and its parishioners.[23]

Perhaps the presumption of and commitment to a universal religious culture gave Rosario the courage to first walk into the parish sanctuary and attend mass when, six months after her arrival, her pastor's words resonated through her growing sense of isolation and estrangement. And in a sense he had been right: something spiritually and personally reassuring was indeed to be found in the mere act of attending Mass. And certainly, the comfort the act produced was enhanced by hearing the Mass conducted in Spanish. As Rosario told us the story of her entry and gradual immersion into parish life, she made it clear, however, that the inviting familiarity she encountered in many of the parish's ritual practices and religious symbols was due to their being specifically *Mexican,* not "universally" Catholic: the nine-day celebration (*novena*) dedicated to the Virgin of Guadalupe, the patron saint of Mexico, whose altar shines with particular brilliance inside the sanctuary; the dramatic Via Crucis procession; the Quinceañera program, which prepares young women turning fifteen for their important rite of passage; the Christmas *posadas,* house visits that symbolize the arrival of the infant Jesus.

This is not to say that Saint Pius offers its immigrant parishioners a replica of Mexican Catholic religious culture, although we heard several parishioners describe parish life as "like being in Mexico." To begin with, the very act of incorporating these familiar symbols and practices into the religious life of an urban U.S. immigrant parish imbues them with a distinct spiritual and cultural significance. Relocated, resacralized, and relegitimated as "native traditions," these components of religious life take on new meaning as ethnic symbols, effectively linking local cultural practices to a common *national* heritage. This use of ethnic symbols contributes to the nationalization of ethnicity, a process of social and symbolic relocation in which immigrants from different communities and cultural groups within Mexico are assimilated into the ethnic category "Mexican Americans."[24]

Historically, the process of transforming religious practices associated with the country of origin into cultural traditions that stand for and preserve a nostalgic identification with the homeland has been a fundamental dimension of immigrant-church subcultures in this country.[25] At a progressive, liberationist parish such as Saint Pius, however, these elements of Mexican religious life become more than performative symbols of Mexican American identity; they are also deployed as vehicles of community formation and empowerment. As one of the parish's religious staff commented, "We seek to empower our parishioners *through* their traditions" (my emphasis).

One way in which Saint Pius empowers its parishioners is to offer them positions as leaders of the groups organizing religious rituals and programs. Several lay leaders described at length the modifications they had made or planned to make in a particular religious festival or program, often in order to better capture the spirit and qualities of the festival as it was practiced in Mexico. Olivia, never an active parish member in Mexico, had been a volunteer in the Devotional Group to Our Lady of Guadalupe (the Guadalupano Group) for ten years when she assumed the position of coordinator, dedicating herself more to the group "in order to do more things, and do them differently." As she explained, she had found the activities at Saint Pius "poor, lacking" in comparison to the festivities for the Virgin of Guadalupe back in Mexico. Both the pastor and the Guadalupano Group have supported her in her efforts to embellish and enrich the group's activities and the festival. The support Olivia has received in taking a creative and determinative role indicates the parish's commitment to empowering and promoting leadership among its parishioners. Moreover, by encouraging lay participation in the renewal and transformation of these rituals,[26] Saint Pius also supports its immigrant parishioners in the construction of their emerging ethnic identities—even though for some parishioners it may also contribute to the construction of a national Mexican identity.

While signs of Mexican popular religious expression are ubiquitous at Saint Pius, most practices and programs at the parish combine familiar elements from Mexico with features that are quite new to its immigrant parishioners. But the newness is not necessarily disorienting. Indeed, it is precisely this juxtaposition of the familiar with the strange that imbues those native traditions with a spiritual significance that guides immigrant parishioners toward new, specifically ethnic identities and dispositions. Saint Pius enacts its incarnational theology by focusing spirituality on so-cial-justice issues that affect the parish community, as well as the neigh-borhood of Pilsen more generally. Thus, as Saint Pius offers parishioners a social location, spiritual mission, and ideological orientation, it also le-gitimizes an ethnic identity that is based in their local struggles as immi-grants and in their experiences of oppression as a racialized minority.

This ethnically infused localism—the very aspect of immigrant parish culture that exists in tension with its claims to transcendence—is a par-ticularly important dimension of how Saint Pius offers guidance and ori-entation to its immigrant parishioners. It tells them who they were, who they are, who they should become, and how to do so. In other words, Saint Pius "invents" ethnicity in the process of fulfilling its mission to serve an immigrant community, by engaging its parishioners in struggles for social justice. However, Saint Pius's model of ethnicization and its concomitant social/civic orientation may not be identical to parishioners' experiences and orientations as transnational migrants who maintain fa-milial, social, and economic commitments to two communities, in and between two distinct cultural contexts.

Saint Pius was first established as an Irish parish in 1874. It had become pre-dominantly Polish by the 1920s and served a primarily Polish congregation until the 1950s. During the 1960s, the Spanish-speaking membership of the parish was on the rise at the same time that the parish's and neighborhood's Eastern European residents were moving out along the suburban corridor. In 1972 a shrine in honor of the Virgin of Guadalupe was installed, further testimony to the growing presence of Mexican Americans within the parish. By the end of the 1960s, Spanish masses had been integrated into the regu-lar parish schedule, as was true at other increasingly Hispanic parishes such as Saint Vitus and Saint Procopius. Their current prevalence belies the long and fierce struggle for Spanish-language masses, a local initiative that uni-fied the Spanish-speaking Catholic newcomers of Pilsen in opposition to the Anglo Catholic establishment.[27]

The use of Spanish not only in masses but as the predominant language of parish life has a complex cultural significance in a transnational neighborhood like Pilsen, where recent immigrants share the block with established immigrants or second-generation Mexican Americans, many of whose children, bilingual and bicultural, are ambivalent about their "mother tongue." The presumption of a shared language in Mexico here becomes a vehicle both of continuity with the homeland and of community formation in the host society.[28] At the same time, the church as a sacred institution imbues the Spanish language (and, by extension, Hispanic cultures) with a legitimacy that is continually under assault by the dominant Anglophone society. Nonetheless, several clergy members we spoke with referred to the problems parishes have reaching out to "English-speaking" youth, which suggests that the construction of a monolingual Mexican ethnicity may not be as meaningful to Pilsen's youth as to their parents.

Parishioners at Saint Pius frequently commented that their pastor speaks Spanish "as if he were one of us," using language to symbolize the pastor's commitment to, and perhaps his ability to stand for, the parish as an ethnic community. While the pastor's language is comfortingly familiar, the ritual form and liturgical content of the masses express the parish's distinct subculture. The pastor's homilies have a consistently liberatory orientation, emphasizing social justice and community empowerment. Various aspects of the masses symbolize an egalitarian, participatory theology: the priest speaking from a podium located close to the pews, the inclusion of parishioners in the service, the occasional clapping from congregants—all features that are quite different from the masses Rosario attended at her village chapel in Mexico.

The masses also offer a clear symbolism of the parish's model of ethnicization. The liberationist liturgy draws frequent analogies between the spiritual and historical role of Jesus, Mexicans as an oppressed third-world people in struggle, and Mexican immigrants as an oppressed minority in the United States. These associations have commonly been drawn through allusion to the Zapatista movement in the Mexican state of Chiapas, a reference that encourages parishioners to generalize their associations beyond their ongoing ties to specific home communities (which for most are not located in Chiapas) to the struggles of the Mexican peasantry more generally. The liturgy also links parishioners both to a national Mexican immigrant community, for example, through references to repressive immigration legislation in California (specifically Proposition 187), and to a local Hispanic community, by calling for opposition to such legislation in Illinois.

The church's pastor, Father Charles Dahm, a Dominican priest, is one of the most important Catholic leaders in Pilsen and a leading figure on the Catholic Left in Chicago. Since coming to the parish, he has continued to stimulate its growth while taking it in a direction more progressive than that of his predecessors. In "Religious Rituals and Class Formation," a study of ritual life and class struggle at the now-defunct Saint Vitus Parish, Robert Stark identifies the orientation of the Pilsen parishes according to a three-part typology of participation in social and political life: service, patronage, or protest. He characterizes Saint Pius in the early 1970s as being oriented toward patronage, due to its close affiliation with Mayor Richard J. Daley. Under its subsequent pastor it became more service oriented, and Fr. Dahm has continued this trend while incorporating a strong social-action dimension. If Saint Pius is not a "protest" type of parish, this may be a sign more of the politically conservative times than of the political position of the parish leadership.

In an interview, Fr. Dahm characterized his theology as "incarnational and nondualistic," the focus being on God as incarnated in the world—a vision and orientation that appear to be enthusiastically respected and shared by the parish staff. While Fr. Dahm cautioned against any facile characterization of the parish's orientation as one of "liberation theology," a liberationist spirit does undergird Saint Pius's primary identity, mission, and purpose: to integrate spirituality with social justice in a way that empowers the congregation and "builds community," as Fr. Dahm put it.

Despite Fr. Dahm's reluctance to reduce the theological orientation of Saint Pius to an Americanized liberation theology, we heard parish staff make frequent reference to the Latin American theological movement, which seemed to stand as a symbol for the "this-worldly," human rights focus of the parish's spiritual discourses and practices. This association is enhanced by the significant effort Saint Pius devotes to the development of activist-oriented block groups, commonly known in the Hispanic Catholic world as CEBs, *comunidades eclesiales de base* (base Christian communities). Despite the association in the United States of CEBs with Latin American Catholicism, few of Saint Pius's parishioners were familiar with liberation theology or its application through CEBs before their arrival at the Pilsen parish. The centrality of CEBs to the lifework of Saint Pius was clearly conveyed by the associate pastor, who described CEBs as the model of the parish. He also characterized CEBs as "Latin American," in order to signal a contrast between the suburban (and, implicitly, non-Hispanic) block groups, which focus on scripture study, and the CEBs organized by the Hispanic churches, which are geared—like their Latin American counterparts—toward social action.

The CEB program enacts the parish's model for immigrant incorporation, organizing liberationist spiritual training around local struggles in a way that locates the participants simultaneously within a neighborhood community and an ethnic community. The organizational centrality of CEBs, coupled with the discourse of liberation theology, associates local social-justice struggles with religiously inspired grassroots liberation struggles in Latin America. By implication, it legitimizes a specifically Latin American radical Catholicism as the principal source of inspiration and guidance for the parish. The emphasis on liberation theology links Saint Pius symbolically to both the radical Catholic community in Latin America and the U.S. Hispanic Catholic community. Notably, the Hispanic Catholic community has actively and vocally embraced CEBs, with their this-worldly spirituality, as a propitious structural and symbolic framework for organizing Hispanic Catholics as an oppressed minority within the United States.[29]

Thus, while only a tenth of Saint Pius's parishioners are actively involved in CEBs, the CEBs' visibility and organizational centrality have several important effects: they focus parishioners spiritually, socially, and politically on local struggles; they legitimate those struggles theologically; they generalize and abstract ties to the homeland as ties to Latin America; and they contribute to the construction of a Catholic Hispanic ethnicity, by linking Saint Pius's CEBs to a wider, regional Hispanic CEB organization. While Fr. Dahm and several clergy acknowledged that the individual block groups were moving slowly through the stages from "seeing" to "social action," they had no doubts that the CEBs were effective in promoting communication, developing trust, and thus building community among parishioners. The staff also shared the perception that the CEBs functioned *to replace* the familial and fictive kin networks from which some parishioners apparently became dissociated in their migration to Chicago. And indeed, many parishioners establish local ties of godparenthood through participation in CEBs. For those parishioners, however, who maintain their connections with transnational networks of family, fictive kin (*compadrazgo*), and friends, one wonders whether the CEBs replace or supplement preexisting social networks, commitments, and identities.

An important moment in the ritual cycle at Saint Pius, and a vivid display of the construction and sacralization of ethnicity, is the nine-day festival (*novena*) honoring the Virgin of Guadalupe. This elaborate festival, celebrated in early December, is organized annually by the Devotional Group to Our Lady of Guadalupe, who is the patron saint of Mexico. The Virgin of Guadalupe is a symbol of Mexican nationalism who asserts a specifically Mexican, mestizo[30] culture, identity, and popular religious expression. As an apparition that came to the native "Indian" Juan Diego during the time of the Spanish Conquest, the Virgin of Guadalupe serves as a potent reminder that the origins of the Mexican people lie in the brutal history of conquest and colonization. Guadalupe is thus a religious icon laden with political, ethnic, and racial symbolism.

Members of the Devotional Group participate in the monthly Mass for the Virgin of Guadalupe, taking down the Virgin's banner and carrying it around the sanctuary in a small procession for the Virgin. On those Sundays they also sell candles and food after Mass. The money the Guadalupano Group raises funds the elaborate nine-day festival for the Virgin, traditionally celebrated with a feast and a mariachi band. Through the festival the parish establishes symbolic, social, and material ties to Mexico. For instance, they commission an elaborate altar; the one we saw was prepared by a man who was on a return trip to Mexico at the time of our study. Most years the group also brings a Mexican priest to preach during the *novena*. But the Devotional Group is particularly proud of the contribution it makes to its U.S. parish through its fund-raising efforts. Olivia, the group's coordinator, boasted to us that the previous year they had donated a new air conditioner to the parish.

In a homily at a *novena* mass for the Virgin of Guadalupe, Fr. Dahm drew on the politicized symbolism associated with Guadalupe to give meaning and direction to the lives and experiences of his parishioners: "Just as Jesus Christ came to include the oppressed, the marginalized, the foreigners, and the excluded, so did his mother come to do the same thing in the sixteenth century . . . and just as Juan Diego, inspired by the apparition of the Virgin, went out to work among the poor, the victims of the conquest, so were they to follow the teachings of Jesus Christ and organize against the oppressions of modern-day conquest, such as NAFTA [the North American Free Trade Agreement]. Just as the Spanish treated indigenous people like animals, so do Mexicans in the U.S. think little of themselves, because of the oppression that prevails in our land." Then the pastor made reference to California's Proposition 187 and described recent incidents of racist violence against Mexican migrants.

Moving back and forth between an emphasis on poverty and on culture (ethnicity), weaving himself in and out of the discourse by alternating the pronouns *you* and *we,* the pastor effectively linked and legitimized class and ethnic identities, integrating class struggle with the battle for cultural recognition and ethnic equality. His analogic narrative effectively transposed Guadalupe, a symbol of Mexican national identity, into a symbol of Mexican American ethnic identity.

As we can see, when Saint Pius integrates spirituality, community-focused struggles for justice, and ethnicity, it offers its parishioners two distinct but not mutually exclusive ethnic identities: as Mexican Americans and as Hispanic Americans. Each of these is associated with functional and meaningful collectivities into which the parish facilitates its parishioners' entry. Importantly, the assimilation of a Hispanic and/or Mexican American identity becomes linked to a disposition toward *locally* based problems and struggles, although the possibilities of community-building and empowerment would seem to imply identification and collective engagement as ethnic *Americans*. In thinking beyond the parish subculture to its impact on parishioners, however, we should bear in mind that the mononational identities and localized orientations these activities assume and encourage may be in tension with the many local identities, affiliations, and commitments parishioners take on as participants in transnational migratory circuits.

Emmanuel Presbyterian Church: A Hispanic Christian Family in Faith

Emmanuel Presbyterian Church is an evangelically oriented, self-identified Hispanic church, unusual theologically for a Presbyterian congregation, and unusual among Pilsen's Protestant churches in that it has a burgeoning membership, with much of its growth due to successful evangelization within Pilsen.

The proximity of Emmanuel and Saint Pius belies a theologically and politically adversarial relationship, while their dramatically contrasting architectures convey distinct relationships to the neighborhood. The accessibility of Saint Pius's rather modest and unimposing architecture is matched by its policy of leaving its doors open "twenty-four hours a day" in order to be a home, shelter, and sanctuary to the community. Emmanuel's modern building and tall metal fence, by contrast, set it apart while implicitly indexing the dangerous nature of the neighborhood. Approached from the street by a metal gate, long sidewalk, and well-groomed lawn, the church conveys an inviting residential comfort while connoting a social class status that is strikingly distinct from the immediate neighborhood. The sanctuary, built in 1965, has a complex and free-flowing design, intended by the architect to convey "both a welcoming and protective shelter"[31]—qualities expressive of the distinction between Emmanuel's relationship to its congregation and to the neighborhood. Thus, where Saint Pius emphasizes its continuity with the larger community of Pilsen, Emmanuel constructs itself as a community of faith by serving and reaching out to Pilsen's residents while distancing itself from the geographic neighborhood.

Emmanuel's pastor, the Reverend Rolando Cuellar, a Peruvian with a Pentecostal background, is a warm, intelligent, and rather charismatic man in his mid- to late forties. Rev. Cuellar first came to Emmanuel in 1983, while a student at McCormick Theological Seminary in Chicago. At the time there were only thirty people worshiping at the church. Soon after, when the congregation's student pastor, (it had no regular pastor) graduated and went to Dallas, Rev. Cuellar was invited to serve as Emmanuel's student pastor, and later as its full-time pastor. The decisive role of the congregation with regard to its leadership signals its democratic, nonhierarchical organizational structure, a hallmark of U.S. Presbyterianism and Anglo Protestant religious culture—a quality that contrasts with the decidedly hierarchical Catholic Church and the patriarchal nature of Latin American societies.

Rev. Cuellar has revitalized the congregation: he brought the church out of debt, and under his leadership membership has grown steadily, primarily through a vigorous evangelization campaign waged in the neighborhood of Pilsen. In 1994, Emmanuel had a growing congregation of 120 members, with close to two hundred people overall attending the Sunday worship service, overflowing the sanctuary. In fact, the congregation had built up its membership to such an extent that they were actively looking for a larger building—one that would house not only an expanding congregation but also a variety of programs their current location could not contain. This effort constituted one of Emmanuel's principal ministries, known as "Pro Templo."

Although the pastor and lay leaders involved in the ministry preferred to relocate within Pilsen, they eventually chose to move to a nearby suburb, one with a substantial and growing Hispanic population who tend to be more affluent and settled than Pilsen's residents. The decision, however, appeared to have been made for financial rather than demographic reasons; in relocating, Emmanuel opted to occupy a space within an "American" Presbyterian church, as described by the pastor. In conversations about the

Fig. 2-3. Youth group of Iglesia Presbiteriana Emanuel of Pilsen, performing while on a visit to a church in suburban Wheeling, Illinois. Photo courtesy of Iglesia Presbiteriana Emanuel.

move before and after it took place, Rev. Cuellar focused on control and administration of the space but did not mention the ethnic composition of the host congregation. Nonetheless, the congregation still evangelizes in Pilsen and offers social programs to the community, and Rev. Cuellar continues to preach at the Pilsen sanctuary.

That ethnicity did not play an explicit role in the congregation's decision about location attests to its vision or worldview. As Rev. Cuellar put it, "The main focus of the church is first to proclaim the message of Christ and provide peace and hope for the people." Thus, unlike Saint Pius, Emmanuel does not link its status as an immigrant congregation explicitly to its theology or mission. Nor does it directly implicate its model of ethnicization in its statement of mission. Nonetheless, through its ritual life, social programs, ministries, and missions, Emmanuel enacts and expresses a particular Hispanic ethnicity that is intimately related to the model of ethnicization the church presumes for its actual and potential congregants. By projecting certain values, identities, and social orientations for its members, Emmanuel incorporates them into a larger Hispanic Christian "family in Christ," offering them both an ethnic community and identity within the U.S. mainstream.

Emmanuel's faithful represent a diversity of national backgrounds, including Mexicans, Central Americans, Puerto Ricans, and South Americans. The diversity of Emmanuel's congregation is a quality that Rev. Cuellar pointed out to us with apparent pride during our initial interview. This emphasis on national diversity contributes to the construction of *Hispanic* ethnicity as a collective identification that homogenizes and abstracts the varied social and political experiences of those it incorporates.[32] In distinction to nationally referential ethnic constructions such as "Mexicano" or "Mexican American," the construction of a Hispanic ethnicity focuses collective identification away from the country of origin (and thus away from nationally specific native traditions) and toward an abstract community created in the host country. As we will see, where Saint Pius constructs Hispanicity in part through a spiritual and political association with Latin America, Emmanuel constructs a thoroughly U.S. Hispanic ethnicity.

Nonetheless, the majority of Emmanuel's congregants are first-generation immigrants from Mexico. And while a significant number of Emmanuel's Mexican members commute to attend Emmanuel, many of them once lived in Pilsen and have familial ties to the neighborhood. Take Lucia, for instance. She was born and raised in Pilsen by immigrant Mexican parents who came from a town not far from Rosario's native village in Michoacán. Lucia and her Salvadoran husband moved out of Pilsen to a "better neighborhood" in 1992, one year after they'd joined Emmanuel. Nonetheless, Lucia still feels ties to Pilsen and its residents. Even though she is native to this country, Lucia explained, she feels she has a lot in common with "the Mexican community." "Sometimes I'm in the middle. I understand the position of older people who have lived here a long time, but I also understand the younger ones." She likes being in this position: "*Agarro dos mundos*" ("I take hold of two worlds,") she said. Lucia's comments convey her identification with Pilsen and with the Mexican community more generally, as well as a bicultural sensibility expressed by the notion of "taking hold of two worlds."

In a sense, Lucia's position differs from her church's disposition toward Pilsen and toward the immigrant Mexican community more generally. As a Hispanic Christian congregation, Emmanuel has an ambivalent relationship with Pilsen's Mexican residents. On the one hand, it differentiates the church from those Pilseners who, as Catholics, are "Others"; on the other hand it identifies itself with them, both as "potential

Christians" and as Hispanics. Unlike a national parish like Saint Pius, which asserts the *Mexican-ness* of its parishioners ritually and discursively, Emmanuel Presbyterian downplays its members' national identities and negates native traditions, constructing instead a Hispanic Christian identity for its congregants. Emmanuel constructs this ethnicity through both negation and affirmation. It negates a nationally based ethnicity, linking conversion (to Protestant Christianity) to a rupture with former religious beliefs and nationally specific cultural affiliations. Where Saint Pius embraces its members' native traditions, Emmanuel eschews them, precisely because of the intimate interconnection between Mexican popular culture and Catholicism. More than one lay leader at Emmanuel made the point that "they [Mexican Catholics] don't distinguish between religion and tradition." Particularly striking is the relationship congregants drew between the process of ethnicization and that of religious conversion. Not only were both figured as processes of rupture and rediscovery, but they also were causally linked. Lucia made this relationship explicit in our conversation. She said that "being here [in the United States], with time people begin to realize the connection between Hispanic culture and Catholicism. . . . With time they go through a rediscovery of what are the legitimate traditions."

At the same time, the congregational subculture of Emmanuel affirms and reinforces its congregants' Hispanicity through myriad aspects of its ritual, educational, and organizational life. To begin with, despite a substantial bilingual presence, Emmanuel conducts all its services in Spanish. As Chicana poet Gloria Anzaldúa puts it, "Language is twin-skin to identity";[33] and a congregation's choice of language is a forceful and formative symbol of its worldview. In the case of Emmanuel, it attests not only to its identification as a Hispanic congregation but also to its evangelizing orientation toward recent immigrants.

Nonetheless, as Lucia signaled in her identification of a *generational* distinction between the positions of the older and younger immigrant populations, Emmanuel faces the challenge of reconciling the differences between more settled and more recent immigrants, on the one hand, and between immigrant parents and their second-generation, bilingual, and bicultural children. In our conversations with Rev. Cuellar and lay leaders, this challenge was often expressed in terms of language. In fact, discussion of increased incorporation of English into worship services and religious education carried a certain urgency. The pastor explained that the services held by young people were bilingual because the youth preferred to speak English—although he added that "they are open because we also have young people who recently came from Mexico; they also speak in Spanish at home." While this ready embracing of English might suggest a more assimilationist perspective at Emmanuel than we encountered at Saint Pius, the difference may also reflect responses to distinct constituencies: where Saint Pius serves a constantly replenished population of recent immigrants and transmigrants, Emmanuel's membership ranges from recent immigrants to second-generation and settled first-generation immigrants who use English in their daily lives.

Many other features of Emmanuel's congregational life attest to the centrality of Hispanic ethnicity. For instance, the congregation belongs to the Hispanic Council within the Presbyterian Church, a body composed of lay and pastoral representatives who discuss the specific needs of the Hispanic community. Emmanuel devotes attention to those needs programmatically through worship services it holds on issues of discrimination and immigration. Emmanuel also participates in worship services with other Hispanic Christian churches in the metropolitan area. Finally, while Emmanuel does not emphasize explicit ties to Latin America through religious symbology and iconography, it does carry on formal interchanges with Latin American preachers. The relationship between ethnicity and spirituality at Emmanuel, however, is carefully bounded. The church's festival calendar, for instance, is distinctly not Latin American but rather (Anglo) American. In addition to the religious holidays of Christmas and Easter, the congregation celebrates Thanksgiving, Mother's Day, and New Year's Day—three thoroughly U.S. American *secular* holidays that are imbued with familial significance. Thus Emmanuel's ritual calendar expresses the congregation's model of ethnicization: the incorporation of mainstream, Anglo American traditions as integral to the construction of a Hispanic American lifestyle.

For several lay leaders we spoke with, it was not the tenets of Presbyterianism per se that attracted them to Emmanuel but rather a union of spiritual and interpersonal qualities that they had found lacking in their specific parish or in Catholicism more generally. Lucia told us that she preferred Emmanuel's more fundamentalist approach to scripture and the greater emphasis on reading and studying the Bible in its entirety. Lucia admitted to an early wariness as she described her initial response to the lively religious services, which had seemed loud and raucous compared to the more sober and restrained Catholic masses to which she was accustomed. But now, Lucia admitted timidly, she even likes the drumming, the rock music, and the pastor's bold preaching style—ritual practices that certainly produce an intense spirit of communality.

But the qualities Lucia most emphasized were interpersonal: communication among congregants and between pastor and the congregation, a spirit of caring and warmth that she had found absent at the more anonymous parish, and a sense not only of belonging but of being needed. "Here everyone has a role, a function," she commented. Notably, Lucia and other congregants we spoke with drew on the image of *family* to convey this combined sense of belonging and intimacy. This is not incidental. A leaflet passed out before Sunday services offers the following invitation to newcomers: "If you do not have a church, make Emmanuel your family in faith" (*si no tiene una iglesia, haga de la Iglesia Emanuel su familia en la fe*). And indeed Emmanuel, whose membership is made up primarily of families, forms a congregation that is essentially a network of families. Moreover, congregants seem to have a primary identity as members of that church; the church's identity as Presbyterian seems to be relatively unimportant and is certainly secondary to its identity as a Hispanic Christian evangelical church.

Indeed, family is the central theme running through the liturgy, program discourse, and ministry at Emmanuel. Church social events and celebrations tend to be organized around the family. The appeal of secular festivals such as Mother's Day and Thanksgiving can be understood in part in terms of their familial orientation. The church also assists its needy members on an individual or family basis (offering economic assistance, clothing, employment, counseling), rather than through participation in grassroots struggles that would locate church members within an oppressed community of Hispanics and/or "the poor."

Family issues and problems are the focus for many church ministries, including the women's club, the ministry for couples, the youth club, and the children's club. Of these ministries, the most extensive are the youth group and the children's club. The Club de Niños en Acción (Club for Children in Action) is a weekend program offering Bible study, educational and recreational activities, and a meal for children under thirteen years of age. As one club volunteer explained, the children's club was promoted with the needs of the community in mind, "to serve the community where the church resides." Of the sixty enrolled children, most are from the community. The program director noted that, while some parents have joined the church because of the quality of the program, its purpose is not to evangelize but rather to teach the children to "grow with a love of God, with positive goals, not thinking about things like gangs."

The youth group is essentially a continuation of the children's club, with a strong leadership-development component. The group meets weekly to talk, support one another, and plan a range of activities, including a youth worship service, field trips, Presbyterian Church youth retreats, and "spiritual campaigns" such as the annual "street festival," a worship service held each summer and intended to reach out to youth in the community. Several youth see their group as an alternative to gangs because it provides the kind of peer support and sense of family that youth who join gangs are looking for. In our conversations, youth emphasized the supportive sense of family, as well as social and spiritual growth, that group participation gives them.

While Emmanuel constitutes itself symbolically as a "family in Christ," structurally it is made up of a close-knit network of mostly nuclear families, many of whom seem to find their primary identification with the church. While several people we spoke to rejected Mexican culture out of hand as being inextricably bound to Catholicism, they commented that the primacy given to family was a positive quality found in "Hispanic culture" more generally. One lay leader associated the ability to discern between the positive values within Hispanic culture and the negative ones—such as *machismo*—with the process of spiritual rediscovery. In this sense, Emmanuel contributes to the construction of a Hispanic Christian ethnicity based on familial roles and identities that fit squarely within the U.S. mainstream.

As we can see, Emmanuel offers its members a location within an ethnically defined spiritual community that is wholly derived from shared religious practices (be they devotional or social), rather than from a shared neighborhood or shared struggles as oppressed immigrants, as is the case for Saint Pius's parishioners. However, Pilsen is hardly irrelevant to the construction of ethnicity at Emmanuel. To the extent that congregants work together to help a poor Hispanic neighborhood, their engagement with the geographic community—through the children's club, ministry to the local jail, distribution of food and clothing—further unites the congregation in common cause or mission. Yet these outreach efforts, as they are called, maintain the neighborhood at a distance, as the object of good works and evangelization. Moreover, Emmanuel's pluralistic, evangelical subculture is thoroughly at odds with the transnational subculture of Pilsen. Where Saint Pius's vision of ethnicization may unintentionally and indirectly support a transnational orientation by encouraging symbolic, political, and material ties to Mexico, Emmanuel constructs a Hispanic American ethnicity for its congregation on the basis of spiritual severance from those ties.

What does this comparison of two immigrant churches that are radically different—theologically, ideologically, politically, and culturally—suggest about their roles in the construction of ethnicity? To begin with, it highlights the distinct subcultures that can emerge at the intersection of a church's vision of ethnicity and its theological and political positions. Moreover, because the churches themselves constitute distinct subcultures, they also contribute to the construction of distinct ethnicities, despite the fact that both churches evangelize and serve Mexican immigrants and that both are tied into wider Hispanic religious networks. And while both churches assume and espouse positions of ethnic pluralism, their pluralistic visions and related models of ethnicity are ideologically quite distinct, as evidenced by the dramatically different strategies they adopt to guide and assist their members in making the social, civic, and psychic transition from immigrants to ethnics.

However, when examined in relation to the transmigratory circuit that incorporates Pilsen and its residents into its socioeconomic and cultural flows, a striking commonality emerges through the two churches' differences, namely, their *unidirectional* vision of immigration and ethnicization: both churches expect that settlement and incorporation into the host society entail a process of becoming an ethnic *American;* both churches are intent on helping their members make that transition; and both churches prefigure their members' struggles on that basis. Conversely, neither church actively supports the transmigratory lifestyle or culture of their members or the neighborhood, although either church may do so indirectly and unintentionally. It will be the task of further research to discern the ways in which these spiritually imbued visions of ethnicization are taken up by Pilsen's residents as they fashion their various collectivities and identities.

NOTES

1. Though it is often criticized as an assimilationist label, I use the term *Hispanic* rather than *Latino* because of its predominance in the spoken and written discourses of both churches. See Moore, "'Hispanic/Latino'"; Padilla, *Latino Ethnic Consciousness.*

2. Research for this chapter was conducted by Susana Angélica Bañuelos and myself.

3. Wind and Lewis, *American Congregations*, vol. 2, 6–7.

4. Omi and Winant, *Racial Formation*, 15.

5. Conzen et al., "Invention of Ethnicity," 4–5.

6. Ibid., 8.

7. Sánchez, *Becoming Mexican American*, 6–7.

8. Adelman, *Pilsen and the West Side*, 4–5; Stark, "Religious Ritual and Class Formation," 27.

9. Stark, "Religious Ritual and Class Formation," 27–31.

10. Liptak, *Immigrants and Their Church*, 117–118; Castelli and Gremillion, *Emerging Parish*, 15.

11. See D'Agostino, chapter 11 in this book.

12. Díaz-Stevens and Stevens-Arroyo, *Recognizing the Latino Resurgence*.

13. Rouse, "Questions of Identity"; Schiller, Basch, and Blanc, "From Immigrant to Transmigrant"; Oboler, *Ethnic Labels, Latino Lives*, 88; Rouse, "Mexican Migration." For the Chicago case, see Farr, "Language, Culture, and Literacy."

14. Massey et al., *Return to Aztlan*, 6.

15. From interviews with congregants and parishioners, and data from Marcia Farr's research on transmigrant family networks based in Pilsen (personal communication with Farr, Evanston, IL, May 16, 1999). See also Orellana and Thorne, "Year-Round Schools," 464.

16. Orellana and Thorne, "Year-Round Schools," 285–314.

17. Rouse, "Mexican Migration," 16.

18. From Pilsen Catholic Cluster, "Our Vision," Chicago May 1993.

19. Stark, "Religious Ritual and Class Formation," 210–211.

20. Pilsen Resurrection Development Corporation (PRDC), "Mission Statement," Chicago 1994. (The PRDC was merged into the Resurrection Project the same year.)

21. McGreevy, *Parish Boundaries*, 27.

22. Díaz-Stevens and Stevens-Arroyo, *Recognizing the Latino Resurgence*, 205–206.

23. Gilkey, "Christian Congregation"; Castelli and Gremillion, *Emerging Parish*.

24. See Conzen et al., "Invention of Ethnicity," 22–23.

25. Liptak, *Immigrants and Their Church*.

26. See Bass, "Congregations and the Bearing of Traditions," 170.

27. Stark, "Religious Ritual and Class Formation," 170–172.

28. See Hunter, *Symbolic Communities*, 67.

29. Sandoval, *On the Move*.

30. *Mestizo/a* refers to the racial mixture of indigenous and Spanish. Recognition of and pride in mestizo ancestry and culture has been an important dimension in the development of contemporary Mexican national identity.

31. Adelman, *Pilsen and the West Side*, 58.

32. Oboler, *Ethnic Labels, Latino Lives*, 3.

33. Anzaldúa, *Borderlands/ La Frontera*, 74.

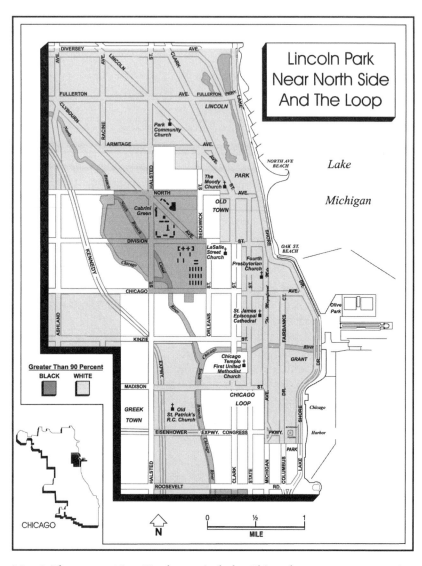

Map 3. The greater Near North area includes Chicago's greatest concentration of wealth and power only a few blocks from the "ghetto poverty" of Cabrini Green public housing. Map by Brain Twardosz, BMT Printing and Cartographic Specialists.

Chapter 3

Place, Race, and History
The Social Mission of Downtown Churches

Matthew J. Price

The prestigious downtown churches of the Loop and greater Near North Side have a unique place in the religious landscape of Chicago. They serve their immediate neighborhoods, and their congregations reflect the increasingly affluent and predominantly white population of the area. They also serve the larger metropolitan area, drawing on a religious constituency with an unprecedented willingness to travel in search of the church that serves their needs. In this they share certain characteristics with suburban megachurches outside Chicago, such as Willow Creek Community Church in suburban Barrington. But the central location of the downtown churches means that they address the city as a whole in a way that other churches do not: they are, symbolically and sometimes literally, the city's cathedrals.[1]

Like the prestigious "signature" buildings of architects that define the skyline of downtown, these churches are signature religious buildings at the heart of the city. For example, First United Methodist Church, Chicago Temple, the city's oldest congregation, is situated right across from City Hall. The building, according to church literature, "combines the grace of the French gothic with the practicality of an American sky-scraper." With its Sky Chapel, spire, and twelve foot-high cross at its peak, the 568-foot structure is considered to be the world's tallest church building, "a beacon to the city." Like the European cathedrals that inspired its architecture, the Methodist temple, along with the other downtown churches, attempts by its physical presence to ordain with religious meaning the sense that the city as a whole has of itself.

Many of the churches studied in this chapter came of age at the beginning of the twentieth century with the rise of the corporation and its downtown headquarters. The civic-minded philanthropy of their members sought to create the epicenter of a "great city" that would present to the world the city's power and prestige and that of its professional-managerial class as one and the same. But philanthropists and advocates of the Social Gospel also attempted to fashion the image of the city as a single, corporate entity by reaching across the boundaries of class, race, and nationality through highly visible acts of compassion and social redemption. It is this combination of centrality, concentration of power and prestige, and acts of compassion articulating a responsibility for the city as a whole that still defines these churches of the downtown Loop and Near North Side.[2]

While many downtown churches in other cities have struggled, Chicago possesses a remarkable set of vibrant and strong center-city churches that not only show no signs of decline but are confident about their future growth and prospects. If, as Lyle E. Schaller claims with regard to downtown churches, "only a fraction are large, strong, vital, future-minded, and exciting congregations that today are able to attract new generations of church goers," then it seems that Chicago has a disproportionate number of such cases.[3] Nevertheless, the success of these churches is dependent on an unpredictable balance of the contradictory forces of center-city revitalization and urban decay. The churches need the former to maintain their affluent congregations and influential place within the city, but the latter also is a key part of their historic sense of mission and purpose. The churches are in control of neither force, and while from the mid-1960s through the late 1980s it looked as if the downtown churches might be overwhelmed by the forces of urban decay, in the late 1990s it was, ironically, the force of downtown revitalization that promised to transform the mission fields of these churches, removing the adjacent neighborhoods as objects of philanthropy.

Because the large downtown churches are predominantly affluent and white and the adjacent neighborhoods are predominantly poor and black, the issue of race is ever present in the churches, although rarely in the simple form of a dialectical opposition of two groups. A combination of sometimes contradictory desires and forces has created a complex racial dynamic. First, the churches' outreach theology is based on the possibility of societal redemption through a social transformation brought about by the ameliorative impact of church programs on the individual lives of the poor and, for some churches, by the advocacy of public policies that will help the poor in collective terms. Yet after thirty years of operation, the urban ministry programs begun in the late 1960s and early 1970s seem no nearer to achieving their goal of ending poverty. The seeming intractability of the problems of the urban poor has led to the construction of larger programs and the creation of a large pool of volunteers who have little or no relationship with the churches. Such programs have also led to the recruitment of full-time program staff, some of whom seem to have concluded that the problems of these areas might indeed be unsolvable. Second, the outreach theology of these prestige churches charges them to maintain their place as centers of civic leadership while also being servant churches to poor minority communities. In fulfilling this vision of a servant church, the churches have given autonomy to the programs and their administrators, some of whom see the wider white society in which the churches operate as having interests that are fundamentally opposed to the poor black communities the programs serve.

Thus powerful, mainly white churches are connected to their proximate poor black communities by a host of large outreach programs, but the connection is not a direct one. Standing between them are the army of volunteers from outside the church as well as the program staff, whose ideas about the programs can be radically different from those presented to the congregation from the pulpit. The mediating role of the volunteers allows the churches symbolically to construct their large programs as redemptive, transformative, and racially integrative while signifying the continued importance of the church in the city. But because most members of the congregation do not see the programs in action over a sustained period, they neither experience the doubts of the full-time workers nor discover the guiding philosophies of some of the programs.

The complex racial dynamic that characterizes these churches is a product of their history, one they share with many other predominantly white downtown churches in America. It has molded their sense of place and space, their role in civic leadership, and their vision of their mission to the poor and downtrodden, all of which have been, and are still, shaped by wider forces of urban restructuring.

An Overview of the Area and Its Congregations

Chicago's combined Loop and greater Near North area includes the Loop and the Near North Side, as well as the community area of Lincoln Park and the southern census tracts of Lakeview (See Map 3). Because of gentrification, this area constitutes an almost unbroken block of business employment and residential affluence running from Roosevelt Road in the south, along the lakefront in the east, to Belmont Avenue in the north, with a western boundary that varies from Wells Street at its southern end to Ashland Avenue at its northern end. Alongside this sphere of affluence lies Cabrini Green, a public housing development occupying twenty blocks in the western third of the Near North community area. While Cabrini Green is racially and economically segregated from the Loop and the greater Near North, the outreach efforts of the downtown churches are a significant point of connection. These areas—the Loop, the greater Near North, Cabrini Green, and the Near West Side—taken together make up a functionally integrated system for the churches, sustaining their sense of place and purpose. The Loop sustains a large professional-managerial class, many of whom reside in the greater Near North area, providing a demographic base for the churches.[4] Cabrini Green and the Near West Side, in turn, are the mission fields for these churches, allowing them to sustain their claims to stand symbolically for the city as a whole.

In the Loop and Near North area, the Religion in Urban America Program conducted a comprehensive survey of all religious institutions listed in phone books and directories. We then selected six churches as sites for in-depth case studies and carried out interviews or observations at eight more.

In the mid-1990's—the time of our study—Fourth Presbyterian was a church of more than three thousand members, situated along Michigan Avenue's "Magnificent Mile." The church describes itself as "a light in the city," attempting urban ministry through large-scale programs for the residents of the Cabrini Green public housing development, with whom it sees itself as sharing the neighborhood.

Old Saint Patrick's Church (the focus of chapter 9), with a membership of fifteen hundred, sees itself as a "crossroads" where people from all over the city can meet in an atmosphere that exudes warm hospitality and a strong sense of Christian service. Its Community Outreach Group has five hundred members and sponsors seven ongoing sites and a half dozen periodic activities, including two Franciscan homeless shelters, an athletic program for Hispanic youth, and adult literacy programs at one Catholic and two non-Catholic locations.

The 950-member First United Methodist Church, Chicago Temple, has led a coalition of churches in a successful campaign for the construction of a single-occupancy hotel in the southern part of the downtown to ease the problems of homelessness.

LaSalle Street Church stands as a "bridging church" between the affluent Gold Coast and the public housing development of Cabrini Green. While the church has only 350 members, it was been the driving force in the creation of two affordable housing complexes near the church and has founded two high-profile ministries on the North Side, the Cabrini Legal Aid Clinic and the Community Youth Creative Learning Experience.

Moody Church, built in honor of the Chicago evangelist Dwight L. Moody, is the largest evangelical church in central Chicago, with more than fifteen hundred members. Although in the 1960s it considered a move out to the suburbs, as the area around the church was deteriorating, the church has benefited from adjacent gentrification and is once again solidly established in the city.

The Episcopal Cathedral of Saint James, seat of the Episcopal Diocese, lies just off Michigan Avenue's Magnificent Mile. This congregation of five hundred members saw its halcyon days during the Progressive Era, when it was a leader in social reform movements. It now operates a food pantry and a homeless shelter for men, contributes money and volunteers to a women's homeless shelter, and has an AIDS outreach ministry. At Saint James, a simple black cross, about eight feet high, stands in the cathedral plaza, where it was dedicated at Easter 1994. On it the cathedral inscribed the names of all the children who were murdered in Chicago in the previous year. Shoppers from Michigan Avenue frequently pause for a few moments by the cross. The cross and the outreach activities listed above show how the downtown churches challenge people to reach across the barriers of race and class as the churches seek the welfare of the city as a whole.

We also made on-site observations or conducted face-to-face interviews at Holy Name Cathedral, the center of the Chicago Catholic Archdiocese; Park Community Church, a member of the Willow Creek Association; Saint Paul's Lutheran Church; Saint Joseph's Catholic Church and School; Saint Luke's Church of God in Christ; and Saint Matthew's United Methodist Church, the last two of which are African American churches with strong outreach programs to Cabrini Green. In addition, we conducted interviews with organizations based in the Cabrini Green area that are involved in outreach projects.

An Evolving Racial Dynamic: Power, Responsibility, and Community

The downtown churches have historically been the places of worship for the powerful and influential citizens who lived on Chicago's Gold Coast. In *The Gold Coast and the Slum,* Harvey Zorbaugh saw the Gold Coast as "the only element in the city's life that sees the city as a whole, dreams dreams for it as a whole."[5] For Zorbaugh, these were the people who had built the city, whose "imaginations play with its future."[6] Unlike the residents of Little Sicily, now Cabrini Green, or the lodgers in "world of furnished rooms," whom Zorbaugh saw as "merely part of the landscape," "the Gold Coast has, as no other group, a sense of its . . . responsibility for the future of the city."[7]

The discourse of the destiny of the city and the responsibility of its leading citizens was heavily tinged with religious imagery. The Chicago Fire of 1871 was pictured as a divinely sent time of trial, which had ushered in a period of reform that would lead to Chicago achieving the destiny God had planned for it.[8] In 1893, British journalist William T. Stead posed the provocative question: "If Christ came to Chicago what would he wish me to do?"[9] The formation of the Chicago Civic Federation, which included such notables as Marshall Field, Cyrus McCormick, Albion Small, Jane Addams, and the pastor of Moody Church, was a direct response to Stead's revelations of poverty and squalor in Chicago's poorest neighborhoods.[10] His call to action was grounded in the growing turn-of-the-century interest in the social dimension of Christianity. This was also reflected in the ethos of Fourth Presbyterian Church, which Marilee Munger Scroggs sees as seeking to "provide for the welfare not only of church members but of whole cities."[11]

The 1890s saw the start of the tutoring programs at Fourth Presbyterian, with Cyrus McCormick Jr., among others, spending Saturday evenings tutoring immigrant men.[12] These programs expanded during the Progressive Era, and in 1913, *The Continent,* a Chicago religious journal, commented, "The great mission of Fourth Church will be to grapple with the conditions by which it is surrounded."[13] The underlying assumption in all such efforts was that wealthy native Protestants would remain in control of the destiny of the city. The great city that would be formed by the stewardship of Chicago's leading citizens would benefit all, regardless of race or ethnicity. But these visions of the city as a manifestation of God's Kingdom were not pluralistic; rather, they had within them an implicit Protestant triumphalism and an unquestioned leadership by the "enlightened," who were white, native, and Protestant.

While the downtown churches exhibit strong patterns of continuity with the Progressive Era, the 1960s brought about significant modifications to the churches' missions and their theological underpinnings. The demographic shift on the city's Near North and Near West Side, from a population that was predominantly made up of working-class white ethnics to one of poor unemployed African Americans, meant that the outreach efforts of the downtown churches now involved the crossing of racial as well as class boundaries. While the sense of insecurity that came with this change was new to many once-powerful churches, it also allowed them to articulate a mission that was more urgent and attractive to a younger generation of Christians, raised in the Civil Rights era. These churches also realized that meeting the needs of this population would require a much greater effort on their part.[14]

A 1967 report prepared under the direction of Pastor George Sweeting for the board of Moody Church, which had just a few years earlier considered leaving the city altogether, called for much greater involvement in Cabrini Green:

> We would strongly recommend that Moody Church make plans to minister to the nearly 20,000 Negroes . . . who live within the shadow of the church. . . . It seems inconceivable to us that a church that sends $1,000,000.00 a year to evangelize people of another color miles across the sea can ignore them on their back porch.[15]

It was also during the 1960s, under the pastorship of Elam Davies, that many of Fourth Presbyterian's current outreach programs were started, and it was during the early 1970s, under the Reverend Bill Leslie's leadership, that LaSalle's main ministries were initiated—Community Youth Creative Learning Experience, or CYCLE; the Cabrini Green Legal Aid Clinic; the Near North Counseling Center (now the Center for Life Skills); Young Life at LaSalle; and the ministry to seniors, including a senior housing development. The five ministries formed during the first fifteen years of Bill Leslie's pastorate account for all but one of the current outreach ministries of LaSalle.[16]

The 1960s brought the agenda of the Civil Rights movement, with its calls for racial inclusion, equality, and greater opportunity.[17] Churches were not simply to reach down with assistance to those in the adjacent communities but to make their congregations racially and economically inclusive, placing the task of racial integration in the forefront of the churches' social agenda. The churches were also asked to respect the integrity of those who lived in poor communities and to include those communities as neighbors and equals in the task of community renewal. Writers on urban ministry continue to stress the importance of this partnership approach, with programs envisioned as a means of creating a single community rather than a world of servers and clients, an ideal to which the churches in Chicago's downtown still adhere.[18]

In the late 1960s the rise of the community-organizing movement among the Protestant mainline churches, operating under the conviction that a maximum degree of autonomy should be given to community-based organizations, brought with it a cadre of program leaders who saw the existing church as an encumbrance to the progress of the communities they were serving.[19] Activist-scholar John McKnight warned against church people who had been "misled by the modern secular vision." He asked:

> Have they substituted the vision of service for the only thing that will make people whole—community? Are they service peddlers or community builders? Peddling services is unchristian—even if you're hellbent on helping people. Peddling services instead of building communities is the one way you can be sure not to help.[20]

Churches were asked to question their established practices, with the voices of the poor, now empowered by community organizing, acting as "a sorely needed check on the self-centeredness and sin which Christians should know infect all their most well meaning and charitable actions."[21]

In the late 1960s and the 1970s encounters between the activists, who saw themselves on the front lines of the fight for social justice, and the established church membership proved to be contentious and difficult. Those encounters rarely occur today, having been replaced by what theologian Langdon Gilkey has described as a "conspiracy of silence" about these contentious issues; and as we shall see, those working with church programs in poor communities may still have very different views from those espoused by their congregations.[22] The wall of separation between the thoughts and feelings of the congregations, on the one hand, and the attitudes of both those who run the programs and those who benefit from them, on the other, has been reinforced by the professionalization of urban ministry, with full-time staff assuming the major responsibilities, an intellectual subculture of urban ministry with its own institutes

and centers, and the bureaucratization that has come with the need to so-
licit steady sources of funds from beyond the church in order to maintain
the programs.[23]

This separation has meant that the issues and problems that each new
mission theology raises have remained largely unresolved and have rarely
surfaced at the congregational level. Instead, each stage of mission theology has overlain the previous one without the churches having to face the
potentially contradictory nature of these commitments. These complexi-
ties define the organizational cultures of many downtown churches. A
historic sense of responsibility for the city as a whole, based in a Progressive Era sense of civic leadership, is now combined with a Civil Rights era
orientation, predicated on equality, service, and inclusiveness, directed
toward the predominantly poor African American residents of adjacent
communities. The churches also try to follow some of the precepts of the
community-organizing model by giving the maximum level of autonomy
to the organizations they sponsor within the community, which leads to a
separation from the congregation.

The bounded nature of Cabrini Green as a mission field made it possible for us to gain some sense of the overall level of outreach to this area.
The churches that we studied are immensely effective practitioners of social ministry, and it is because of the "success" of their projects, as understood from the standpoint of urban ministry studies, that the findings of
our research in the Cabrini Green area point to some striking anom-
alies.[24] Our views of the Cabrini area came from interviews with the
salaried program officers, some of whom are white and some of whom
are African American. Through these interviews we noted three other
main actors: the residents of Cabrini Green, the church congregations,
and the program volunteers.

Cabrini Green: Place and Programs

The Cabrini Green public housing development lies in the western half of
the Near North community area, two blocks from LaSalle Street Church
and six to eight blocks from Fourth Presbyterian Church, Moody
Church, and the Episcopal Cathedral of Saint James. In 1992 the development had 6,935 official residents, but church workers in the area believe
this radically undercounts the number of adult men.[25] In many ways
Cabrini Green is similar to other housing developments and deep-

poverty areas in the city. Of its heads of household, 57 percent rely on Aid for Dependent Children as their primary source of income, only slightly lower than the percentage for the Robert Taylor Homes (59 percent). By certain other measures Cabrini Green compares quite favorably with other public housing developments. Despite its notoriety, in 1991 Cabrini's violent-crime rate was only eleventh highest of the nineteen major developments, at fifty-two violent crimes per one thousand persons.[26] Nevertheless, social conditions at Cabrini Green make it a different universe for those who attend the churches of the Loop and Near North Side, for whom Cabrini is defined by the enormity of its social problems.

The social-outreach effort at Cabrini Green is striking by its sheer scale. For example, we estimated that there were, at the time of our research, about fifteen hundred[27] tutors in the tutoring programs. Organizations running tutoring or mentoring programs include Fourth Presbyterian Church, LaSalle Street Church's CYCLE ministry, the Montgomery Ward Cabrini Connections program, Saint Chrysostom's Episcopal Church, Saint Luke's Church of God in Christ, Saint Joseph's Parochial School, Holy Family Lutheran Church, the Moody Bible Institute's Big Brother and Big Sister programs, Saint Matthew's United Methodist Church, and the Lower North Center.[28] In addition to the tutoring programs, we have counted at least forty agencies and organizations that work in the Cabrini area. These include Holy Name Cathedral, which has an established history of outreach missions to Cabrini Green; the imaginative Cabrini Greens, where Cabrini children grow designer vegetables for high-class North Side restaurants; and the summer filmmaking program.[29] This investment of resources in Cabrini Green is in stark contrast to the resources devoted to other deep-poverty areas in the city. For example, the South Side neighborhood of Englewood had a 1990 population five times the size of that in the Cabrini area, with, according to the U.S. Census, 11,911 school-age children, as opposed to Cabrini's 2,500. Yet, according to a comprehensive 1994 survey of Chicago tutoring/mentoring programs, Englewood had only two such programs, serving just 140 students.[30]

Despite the impressive scope of all the churches' outreach programs to Cabrini Green's residents, questions about the combined impact of the many efforts point to the striking absence of social transformation, or even a tangible process of improvement, relative to the major outlay of resources. Although none of these programs addresses the need for well-paying jobs for the residents, nevertheless the scale of the effort put forward by voluntary and government sectors in Cabrini is more than just a "drop in the ocean." What effect have these programs had on Cabrini Green? Unfortunately, the programs we looked at did not compile statistics that would have given an overall measure of success.

Perhaps one indicator of the impact of the programs is that the population of Cabrini Green dropped by two-thirds between 1970 and 1993. As those who have been helped by the educational programs have tended to move out of Cabrini, the population decline may be a sign of the programs' ability to help residents move up and then out of the housing project. Moreover, according to a youth worker in Cabrini, the very presence of so many white middle-class volunteers has had a cooling effect on gang conflict, because the gangs believe that the death of a white volunteer would almost certainly bring the National Guard into Cabrini. Thus these substantial efforts by the churches and other agencies have helped many individuals and given them opportunities that would have otherwise been unavailable, and they may well have made some small contribution to the gang truce and a more peaceful atmosphere in Cabrini.

Nevertheless, Cabrini is not significantly different from other Chicago Housing Authority projects. Hence we have to ask: Why have not fifteen hundred tutors and more than forty programs made more of a difference to the children who remain?

Church versus Community and the Dilemmas of Social Outreach

The tutoring programs of LaSalle Street Church and Fourth Presbyterian Church reflect by their size a sense of the magnitude of Cabrini's social problems. But the vast size of the programs complicates the church's relationship to them. The evolution of the programs illustrates the complications that can arise when attempting to conform to a mission theology whose goal is to answer the needs that develop out of overwhelming social problems, yet at the same time attempt to build community. Both LaSalle and Fourth Presbyterian are well aware of the need to help rather than hinder the creation of a strong community at Cabrini, but attempts to achieve this goal seem to distance the church from its ministries there and complicate the possibility of building a partnership between the congregation and the residents.

Both tutoring programs started small but, in order to meet the needs of the Cabrini community, expanded their pool of volunteers well beyond that of church members. LaSalle's program, Community Youth Creative Learning Experience, or CYCLE, is its oldest ministry, started in the church basement in the early 1960s. By 1994 more than three hundred CYCLE volunteers were giving about two hours each week to the learning center. Most of the volunteers at the time of our interview were young, white, middle-class professionals in marketing and accounting, and 60 percent were women. Yet, while the make-up of the volunteers resembles the LaSalle Street congregation in age, race, class, and sex, only four or five are members. To address more fully the problems of the Cabrini community, CYCLE's activities have expanded from simple tutoring to leadership development among community youth, college scholarship programs, job placement, and a GED (general equivalency diploma) and job-training program for adults. The need for money to support these ambitious programs, a full-time staff, and its own building has made CYCLE look well beyond the church for funds, with 75 percent coming from foundations, 20 percent from the public sector, and only 5 percent from individual contributions.

LaSalle's CYCLE program also adapted to Cabrini's overwhelming social problems by making a conscious decision to be closer to the Cabrini community through the relocation of CYCLE's activities from the church basement to 1441 North Cleveland, more than a mile away from the church and just to the north of the Cabrini itself, in an area that is still predominantly poor and African American. This impulse also came out of a criticism of the Progressive Era model, where social outreach by middle-class white churches was done *to* the community rather than *with* the community. Although the move made CYCLE more a part of the community it serves, it further distanced CYCLE from LaSalle; and while this has been an incredibly successful program, the growth of CYCLE and its relocation have meant that the material contribution of LaSalle members to CYCLE has become, in proportional terms, negligible. This became painfully clear to the congregation when a representative of CYCLE came to the church to talk on Ministry Sunday; it became obvious that she had no idea LaSalle and the program she worked for had ever been connected. In 1998, CYCLE moved back to LaSalle Street. The program is located in the new Cornerstone Center, just opposite the church, with the hope that the church will once again play a large part in its life.

Fourth Presbyterian Church also has struggled with the dilemmas of church versus community. Their program tutors 470 children, one-to-one, three nights per week. In Fourth Presbyterian's program, about 20 percent of the tutors are from the church. Although 90 percent of the children in the tutoring program are from Cabrini Green, the tutoring takes place at the church on Michigan Avenue, a "habitus" that, as James Wellman has pointed out, is much closer to that of the volunteers (who for the most part are professionals working downtown, single, white, and twenty-five to thirty-five years old) than to that of the children.[31]

To address the issue of community-building at Cabrini, Fourth Presbyterian opened the Center for Whole Life in 1993. The church located the center on the ground floor of a Cabrini high-rise that was scheduled for demolition. The center attempts to do three things. First, it is visible presence inside Cabrini Green and thus builds a much more direct relationship between the residents and the church than is possible with the tutoring program. Second, through the center the church can be part of the process of building community and may possibly serve in an advocacy capacity. Third, and most important, the center offers support and resources to young mothers and their children. Yet, while the Center for Whole Life is closer than the church itself to the Cabrini community, most of the program is carried out by paid staff members and a small number of volunteers; unlike the tutoring program, it does not bring many church members into contact with Cabrini residents.

Thus both churches find themselves in a dynamic in which the closeness of a program to the community it serves gives it more legitimacy and greater effectiveness than would be the case if it were seen as being carried out on the terms of the predominantly white and middle-class congregation. But the risk of such distancing is that the congregations themselves may become so uninvolved that the programs are only nominally tied to the churches. This problem of an ever-increasing divide between church congregations and the people who volunteer in their outreach programs is not confined to tutoring. In the case of Cabrini Alive—an organization sponsored by Fourth Prebyterian, LaSalle, and other Near North churches—that rehabilitates Cabrini Green apartments, observations and interviews indicate that, apart from a core of church volunteers, the bulk of the labor power comes from college and seminary students.

Fig. 3-1. Fourth Presbyterian Church and the "Magnificent Mile" in Chicago's Near North Side. Photo courtesy of Fourth Presbyterian Church.

Fig. 3-2. The Center for Whole Life at the Cabrini Green public housing development, Chicago, is a project of Fourth Presbyterian Church. Photo courtesty of Fourth Presbyterian Church.

Processing the Absence of Change

In discussions with those who work for the churches in the Cabrini area we found an underlying awareness of the absence of a social transformation, even a lack of a general sense of progress, at the housing development. Some felt the lack of progress at Cabrini was due to the existence of a deeply ingrained culture of poverty, based more on the dynamics of class than of race, and saw themselves as essentially outside any possibility of change. But others identified with the community in seeing forces in society actively maintaining a system that oppresses the residents of Cabrini Green primarily on the basis of their race. This difference in the explanations of why the programs have not achieved greater success was not a simple division between white and African American program workers, although racial background made it more likely that one would adopt a particular view. African American program workers might well share Cabrini residents' experiences of police harassment, making a causal argument based on white supremacy seem more plausible to

them.[32] Moreover, the middle-class position of African American program workers may, according to Jennifer Hochschild, make it more likely
that they will ascribe responsibility for the problems of Cabrini Green to
whites than would either whites or poor African Americans.[33] Similarly,
whites might be in a difficult position if they were to identify themselves
as part of the problem while having a calling to be part of the solution, although this is not unheard-of.[34] Thus, although we are not inferring
hard-and-fast racial divisions, the different positions that program workers adopt in relation to the absence of success at Cabrini Green are part of
the complex racial dynamic of the outreach missions.

Among those who have adopted the "culture of poverty" argument,
most of whom have worked in Cabrini for many years, the mood might
best be described as weary. Although these workers share a strong sense
of spiritual purpose, founded on a belief that this work fulfills a religious
calling, we found little faith among them that their efforts would transform Cabrini Green itself. Most of these volunteer workers focused on
the possibility of helping a limited number of people. One volunteer, who
has been working in Cabrini Green since the 1970s, saw himself as running the modern equivalent of the Underground Railroad in helping
people to escape from Cabrini. He believed that all the families who
could leave Cabrini had left, and that those who remained were trapped
in overlapping and reinforcing social pathologies. Another experienced
church worker said that she felt the residents of Cabrini had a fatalistic
vision of life and did not see themselves as changing. While these culture-
of-poverty perspectives articulate a strong sense of the intangible nature
of the social problems at Cabrini, none of the program workers ever directly blamed the residents for their plight. Rather, like William Julius
Wilson in *The Truly Disadvantaged,* they saw a pattern caused by structural circumstances beyond the control of individuals. In a more pes-
simistic vein than Wilson, they also saw a pattern of low expectations that
has become ingrained because generations have lived in deep poverty,
isolated from mainstream culture. Thus, although the people we interviewed work for programs and missions that present themselves as redemptive and transformative, their observations are closer to a culture-
of-poverty perspective than that of a social activism and community
transformation model.

Some workers associated with the ministries of the predominantly
white downtown churches were uncertain about the possibility of transforming Cabrini Green through the existing programs. While issues of

family and low church membership among Cabrini residents were raised, the barrier to change was also located within the larger structure of racial domination. On two occasions we were referred to Jawanza Kunjufu's *Countering the Conspiracy to Destroy Black Boys* (1985–86) as giving an explanation of the problems faced by children in Cabrini Green. Kunjufu's book offers suggestions for providing role models to young black boys, and it does so from the premise that there is a genetically driven conspiracy of whites to maintain their racial purity through dominating other races, and in particular by destroying black males. To counter this conspiracy requires a much greater involvement by older black males in the lives of young black males and creation of a curriculum that would take advantage of the learning skills of black males rather than stifling them, as a predominantly female and white teaching force tends to do. In one interview, a church worker said that the predominance of white tutors gave the children of Cabrini the idea that success was based on race and not on merit. Another worker stressed that it was a major concern of the program that there were relatively few black tutors.

The sentiments of some of the program workers who took up the viewpoint of the community as a group facing racial domination in a white society have peculiar dissonances. These programs that are addressed to a presumed white conspiracy are sponsored by white churches; they receive most of their funding from white individuals and corporate foundations; and their volunteer base is mainly white and female. The sentiments expressed by some of the African American workers and the Afrocentric philosophy of Kunjufu's *Countering the Conspiracy* seem to be at variance with the importance placed on unity within diversity in the mission statements of the churches and in the sentiments expressed in a congregational survey we administered at the LaSalle Street Church. In the survey, members stated that they valued the church because it was a place "where people from various backgrounds get together to share in Christ," because of its "diversity," because of "the variety of people at LSC [LaSalle Street Church]—different races, different socio-economic statuses." The pessimism some of the white church workers expressed and the very notion of an intractable culture of poverty also run counter to LaSalle Street Church's stated mission of fostering "Christian renewal and revitalization" in Cabrini Green.

What effect do these differing perceptions of outreach have on the programs that are at the core of these churches' identity and claim to status and influence in the city? Despite the differences between the worldviews of the program workers and the institutional culture of churches as represented by mission and vision statements, the understanding that Loop/Near North churches have of Cabrini Green as a site of redemptive activity has remained. Nevertheless, part of what sustains this image may be the separation of the congregations from the concerns and fears of those who actually work in the field. This separation is sustained by the labor of a majority of volunteers who have little relationship to the churches but who seem to move into and out of the programs through a revolving door, and so gain very little sense of how effective their efforts are in terms of the wider Cabrini community. It is a system that permits a number of mutually contradictory constructions of the interactions between middle-class white churches and a poor African American community. It is a system that aids in the continuation of the historic leadership role of the downtown churches, but it is an inherently unstable system, where a sharp fall in the number of outside volunteers or the boiling over of frustrations and disappointments by some of the full-time workers could lead to the unraveling of the delicate balance between the churches and the community they attempt to serve.

Finally, if hard questions need to be asked about the effectiveness of the programs at Cabrini Green and the subcultures of social outreach that have grown up around them, similar projects in other parts of the city also need to face these issues. On the one hand, our findings suggest that any notion that the churches can "pick up the slack" left by the curtailment of the welfare state is completely delusional; even with a limited mission and relatively substantial resources, the churches have been unable to change Cabrini Green fundamentally. On the other hand, in an era marked by increasingly hardening attitudes toward the poor, it is more important than ever that the churches formulate projects that both work and involve their members, and that there be an honest and realistic dialogue within churches about their programs' effectiveness and underlying philosophies.

New Demographics and Old Missions

Just as economic and demographic changes have challenged the churches and reshaped their mission in the past, so in the late 1990s downtown and its adjacent neighborhoods are changing again, presenting new challenges and opportunities. Although the total combined population of the

Loop and Near North Side has remained almost constant between 1970 and 1990, this seeming stability hides a massive change in the composition of the population. In 1970 roughly one-third (22,722) of the residents of this combined Loop and Near North area lived in the census tracts between Orleans Street and the Chicago River, in the area dominated by the Cabrini Green housing development—an area that was predominantly poor and African American.[35] This is the dark-shaded portion of map 3. In 1990 only one-sixth (11,142) of the population of the Loop and Near North Side lived in these tracts. Our on-site observation since 1992 indicates that even within these several tracts the composition of the population is shifting from one that is poor and predominantly black to one that is prosperous and increasingly white. This strength of the professional-managerial class can also be seen in changes in income levels. Between 1979 and 1989, the median household income of Loop residents rose by 313 percent, that of Lincoln Park residents rose by 126 percent, and that of Near North residents rose by 108 percent. Along with the contiguous neighborhood of Lakeview just to the north of Lincoln Park, these neighborhoods were the only ones in the city that had more than 100 percent increases in their median household incomes.[36]

In general, the churches have been anchor institutions in this transformation, and LaSalle Street Church with its housing program has been successful in its goal of neighborhood revitalization. By the late 1990s the area around the church had been transformed, spurred by LaSalle's Atrium Village development. In the blocks surrounding LaSalle, the percentage of workers who are managers and professionals rose from 4 percent in 1970 to 22 percent in 1990.

In the late 1990s the trend toward an enlarged presence for the professional-managerial class showed no signs of abating and, if anything, accelerated. An examination of city building permits for the greater Near North from 1991 to 1997 shows a net addition of roughly nine thousand new homes in this area, almost all by private developers and many of which consist of townhouses and condominiums.[37] It is impossible to tell if the many renovations and conversions going on in the area are adding to the total population, but they are almost certainly continuing the trend toward a more affluent population. The biggest change in the area, and the one that will transform the entire raison d'être of some of the churches that we studied, is yet to come: the comprehensive redevelopment of the Cabrini Green housing development. The city aims to redevelop the existing site into one of low-rise apartments and townhouses that will be occupied by a mixture of existing Cabrini residents, low-income tenants, and tenants paying a market rent.

The guiding philosophy behind the project is that of William Julius Wilson, as laid out in his book *The Truly Disadvantaged*. To prevent a concentrated population of the nonworking poor and a resulting a culture of poverty, the nonworking poor will be interspersed with those who work, as has been the case in the Chicago Housing Authority's Lake Shore Drive condominiums. The developer who will reshape Cabrini Green has had a number of successes already in Chicago with mixed-income housing projects, but his success has in part been based on a rigorous screening process in which roughly two-thirds of existing tenants have left the redeveloped properties.[38] This process may end up institutionalizing distinctions between the respectable and the unrespectable poor, distinctions that from the 1960s onward the churches have tried hard to shed.

Thus, in the late 1990s, with the neighborhoods around the churches undergoing a radical transformation as old railyards have been converted into more than two hundred townhouse developments for the returning middle classes, the churches have faced two main challenges, one from outside the congregation and one from within. First, if the downtown and its adjacent neighborhoods are strong, the churches have a strong demographic base for their congregations and are able to maintain their prestige place in the wider metropolitan religious world. But if the neighborhoods adjacent to the churches were to gentrify—if there were, to use Harvey Zorbaugh's terminology, only an expanded Gold Coast and no slum—the churches' sense of identity would undoubtedly change. In the late 1990s these churches have been facing the dilemma of whether they should serve what will be, after the redevelopment is complete, a very different Cabrini population working with many who are the working poor but not the desperately poor on public assistance, or whether they should look to other neighborhoods in the city to find, in Elam Davies's words, "the least, the last, the lost and the lonely."[39]

The theological self-imagery that undergirds the churches' outreach missions to the very poor is infused by the language of proximity and extremes, which brings with it both a sense of urgency to the task at hand and a certain charge that would be lacking if missions were further afield or if they were to a population that is not as desperately poor. In *Being Church, Becoming Community*, John Buchanan, pastor of Fourth Presbyterian Church, states:

> The fact is that one mile from Bloomingdales and the Four Seasons is a community living in Third World squalor. Thirteen thousand people live there, mostly women and children, in high-rise apartments where most of the elevators . . . are commandeered by gang members and operated for a fee, where the smell of urine assaults everyone who walks in.[40]

While the missions of these churches and the sense of the churches' historic responsibility to the city as a whole would carry on even if the locale of their efforts were to shift to a more distant neighborhood, the sense of a shared destiny is easier to articulate when there is such a visible image of a shared space. Buchanan again cogently states the theological charge given by the proximity: "Cabrini Green represents the most dramatic contrast to the affluence of the near north side and is therefore God's clearest call to mission for the church."[41] I argue that should the proximate areas of poverty disappear, then part of the churches' identity and sense of purpose would disappear with them, a part of what makes these downtown churches so attractive to the socially conscious residents of the Near North Side. Thus the vitality of the churches depends on a contingent balance of historically volatile and unpredictable forces over which they have limited control.

The second challenge is that, with the decision of many couples with children to stay in the city, the downtown churches are finding themselves having to address new needs among their congregants that are associated with the stresses experienced by working families, something that suburban churches are used to but that has not been a major part of the downtown churches for many years. The challenge will be to meet the needs of the church members and still carry out the well-established traditions of outreach to those beyond the church door. In response to this, some of the churches have developed new mission activities that simultaneously serve the members of their congregations and aid members of the surrounding communities. This model of the church as a place where people of different socioeconomic backgrounds may have common needs fulfilled as they participate in a faith community is finding its way into the life of LaSalle Street Church and Fourth Presbyterian. Both have renovated and expanded their day-care facilities, largely at the request of their own member families, but the onset of welfare reform has provided an opportunity to share these facilities with mothers from Cabrini Green who are entering the workforce. For both the schools and the church day-care centers it is important that the scholarship parents pay some part of the cost, so the parents do not feel they are being treated as charity cases but rather all pay in accordance with their means.

This may indeed be a propitious moment to make the congregation itself a vehicle of social outreach. While the congregation's social make-up and seemingly "inward" concerns were once seen as an obstacle to the church's public mission, a new appreciation of the congregation's role gives it the potential to be more than just a bridge between public and private; indeed, it may become a moral community in and of itself.[42] Although those served by programs such as expanded day-care facilities will not be the poorest of the poor, they will still be a large population of working poor with great needs—needs that are held in common with other members of the church. Through these programs the churches may be able to achieve that as yet unfulfilled aspiration from the 1960s, namely, building an economically and racially diverse congregation.

As the churches expand services to their congregations, examples of how to build an outreach element into these services are already available to them. At Saint Joseph's Parochial School on Orleans Street, Sister Stephanie Schmidt, who runs the school's tutoring program, seems to have found a way to combine building strong institutional ties within the church with an outreach to those who live in Cabrini Green. At Saint Joseph's, a volunteer is assigned to every child. Most of the children are from Cabrini Green, and most of the volunteers live on the Near North Side or in Lincoln Park, few of them congregants at Saint Joseph's Church; this makes the program no different from those found in other area churches. But because the tutoring is centered in the school, Sister Stephanie places the tutor within a network of people that includes the student, the student's parents, the student's homeroom teacher, and Sister Stephanie herself. Moreover, although the volunteers may not be from Saint Joseph's, they are from other local Catholic parishes, and Sister Stephanie feels that she is responsible for the spiritual development of the tutors as well as the students. Thus the tutors and students are part of an organic faith community. A school as an instrument of outreach is a concept also seen at Old Saint Patrick's Church. The school is "church-sponsored" but "not parochial" and is deliberately racially, religiously, and ethnically diverse; 45 percent of the current enrollment is nonwhite. The school financially maintains 30 percent of its enrollment, with over four hundred places for "scholarship children."

Despite the promise of such an approach, this is a pattern of outreach mission that will likely benefit the working poor more than the desperately poor. In this way, the churches may start to institutionalize the same distinctions between different categories of poor people as the new developers at Cabrini Green are employing. Despite the dangers of this, such a change would, I believe, break the current dynamic of separation and subcultures that has built up between the various actors in the world of Cabrini outreach. The churches will able to bring the Cabrini community into their congregational world on the basis of common need, and the process of transforming Cabrini may well become easier if the bulk of the population is the working poor. This is a radical change for the churches. It will mean accepting the limited possibilities of "the least, the last, the lost and the lonely" as a transformative force, while still acknowledging a need to care for this part of the population, and realizing that its other goals of being in community with those of a different race and class may be more realistically realized by reaching out to a working-poor population that have not been prominent in the churches' outreach theologies.

The transformation is taking place in Cabrini Green through the workings of the market system, not through the churches. The question for the churches is: With such a transformation already occurring, what are the churches going to do? If they decide to minister to a reshaped Cabrini Green, with all their doubts about the reshaping process, they may have an opportunity to create the church as a community of diverse people living lives of mutual accountability and interdependence. In fact, because of their centrality and accessibility, it is these old downtown churches, rather than the suburban megachurches situated many miles from even the working poor, who can be on the cutting edge of creating a new type of church, while still carrying on their mission to create a better city for all its residents.

NOTES

1. These churches are similar to the "Old First" churches of Jones and Wilson, *What's Ahead;* and Bakke, *Expanded Mission,* 1–4; to "pillar churches" and "crusader churches" in Dudley and Johnson, "Congregational Self-Images for Social Ministry"; and to "Downtown Baptist" in Roozen, McKinney, and Carroll, *Varieties of Religious Presence.*

2. On the downtown Social Gospel church as the church of the whole city, see Lewis, *Protestant Experience in Gary;* and for its potential as a community of memory, see Wind and Lewis, "Memory, Amnesia, and History," 20–22.

3. See Edington, *Downtown Church,* foreword by Lyle E. Schaller, 12–13.

4. Roughly one-half of the members of churches discussed here reside within the Loop/greater Near North Side area.

5. Zorbaugh, *Gold Coast and Slum*, 274.

6. Ibid., 277.

7. Ibid., 274–275.

8. Smith, *Urban Disorder*, 37–38.

9. Stead, *If Christ Came to Chicago!* 432.

10. Smith, "When Stead Came to Chicago."

11. Scroggs, "Making a Difference," 464.

12. Ibid., 482.

13. Ibid., 484.

14. On the changing environment of downtown churches, see Jones and Wilson, *What's Ahead;* and Bakke, *Expanded Mission.*

15. "Report to the Board of Moody Church," Prepared under the direction of Pastor George Sweeting, Chicago, 1967. Copy provided by Billy Graham Center, Wheaton College Library, Wheaton, Illinois.

16. See Scroggs, "Making a Difference," 500–503; and Hefley, *Church That Takes on Trouble* (1976).

17. On the Civil Rights movement and the church, see Green, "History," 16.

18. Meyers, ed., *Envisioning the New City.*

19. See Faramelli, Rodman, and Scheibner, "Seeking to Hear and Heed," 106–108.

20. Quoted in Van Engen, "Constructing a Theology," 246.

21. From Todd, "Presbyterian Ministry," 165.

22. Gilkey, "Christian Congregation," 107.

23. See the example of Downtown Baptist in Roozen, McKinney, and Carroll, *Varieties of Religious Presence*, chap. 7.

24. Compared with the most exemplary churches cited in Dudley, *Basic Steps,* the downtown Chicago churches better understand and respond to the needs of their neighborhood.

25. From Chicago Housing Authority, *Statistical Profile,* 1991–1992 (Chicago: Chicago Housing Authority, 1993).

26. For crime statistics, see "Without Sweeps," 1 and 9.

27. *Tutor/Mentor Connection* 2 (September 1994), published by Montgomery Ward's Cabrini Connections program, puts the number of children tutored in Cabrini Green at fourteen hundred, but some children are in more than one program, which may account for our estimate of tutors being higher than Cabrini Connections' estimate of students.

28. *Tutor/Mentor Connection* 2 reported fourteen tutoring/mentoring programs in Cabrini Green.

29. See "Growth Is at the Root"; and "Cabrini Youths," 1.

30. See *Tutor/Mentor Connection* 2; and the 1990 U.S. Census.

31. Wellman, "Counter-Example"; also see Livezey, "Fourth Presbyterian Church."

32. See Cose, *Rage of a Privileged Class.*

33. Hochschild, *Facing Up to the American Dream.*

34. For example, Andrew Hacker, who is white, argues in *Two Nations* that inequalities between white and black are based on white supremacy, while William Julius Wilson, the African American author of *Truly Disadvantaged,* argues that class explains more than race.

35. This includes census tracts 804, 805, 806, 807, 808, 818, and 819. The dark-shaded portion of map 3 includes all of these except tract 818.

36. Census data published in *Chicago Sun Times* on June 3, 1992, 23.

37. This figure is a net estimation calculated by subtracting all demolition permits from new construction permits as listed by the City of Chicago. The demolitions include the destruction of a number of the tower blocks at Cabrini Green.

38. See "Developer Building a Dream."

39. Scroggs, "Making a Difference," 500.

40. Buchanan, *Being Church,* 27–28.

41. Ibid.

42. Marty, "Public and Private," 136–38 and 145–46.

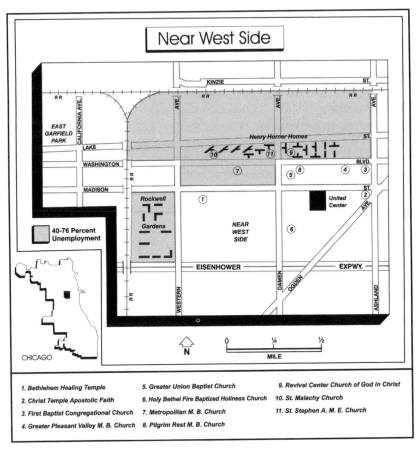

Map 4. The Near West Side, with high concentrations of unemployment and poverty, suffered from the loss of manufacturing jobs in the 1960s and 1970s. Map by Brian Twardosz, BMT Printing and Cartographic Specialists.

Chapter 4

The Churches and the Poor in a "Ghetto Underclass" Neighborhood

Isaac B. Laudarji and Lowell W. Livezey

It is 11:30 A.M., the appointed hour of Sunday worship at the Revival Center Church of God in Christ. Sunday school has just been dismissed by Brother Jerome Seavers, the secretary, after a brief report of the attendance and offering and reminders of upcoming Bible study and prayer meetings. Billy Williams is tapping rhythmically at a small set of drums under the watchful eye of Brother Benjamin, who will take over the drums when the service gets underway. Not far from the entrance, Sister Mary Perkins, the pastor's nurse and head usher, is greeting friends while she reorganizes the bags of food she and the Helping Hands Ministry plan to distribute.

Pastor Benjamin Bowman is still in the kitchen, checking the cornbread and greens that will be shared after service. But he soon exchanges his apron for a perfectly pressed dark suit coat and, with a well-worn Bible in his hand, emerges to mingle with the thirty or forty people gathering in the all-purpose basement. Making his way slowly to the pulpit area, shaking hands, hugging, and talking, he passes the drums, the Hammond B-3 electric organ, and the wooden lectern used for the Sunday school lesson and then half jumps up the three steps to the pulpit and grasps the microphone. "Let's gather round," he says in a raspy voice and a deep Mississippi dialect. "Gather round now, we gon' praise the Lord today."

He begins conversationally, noting that worship will be "right here" rather than in the sanctuary above. He shares information about members and neighborhood people he has seen during the week, about Sister

Josephine and the fact the doctors don't give her much of a chance but, with prayer, God will give her a chance. He mentions matter-of-factly that he "took the kids to Dwight" yesterday—meaning he had taken some of the children to visit their mother in the women's prison in Dwight, Illinois, some eighty miles from Chicago. He begins to pray, prayers of gratitude for the day, for the light, for the church, for health, for healing, for God's power. Gradually, people start repeating, "Thank you Jesus. Praise the Lord." The organist plays softly, then builds as more voices are lifted in thanks and praise. The drummer accents the beat; more people voice their praise; some begin moving about the floor, clapping, singing, and praying, while more worshipers come into the church. The reading from God's Holy Word, the recitation of the Statement of Faith, and selections by the choir of four adults and fourteen children prepare the congregation, now about eighty-five people, for the morning message.

Sister Katrina reads the biblical story of Jehoshaphat, the embattled king of Judah, and the prophets' assurance that however numerous and brutal the enemy tribes may be, the ensuing battle is God's to fight, not the king's, and God will win it. The pastor then spins out the analogy to his people living in the West Side. The tribes are the devil, and the devil's weapons are the "D" weapons of Doubt, Discouragement, and Despair. Just as they worked on Jehoshaphat, they work on each of us. But our God is the same God that delivered Jehoshaphat, and God will deliver us. Therefore we praise God today and every day.

As the sermon builds to its climax, the drums tap quietly, then louder, and the sweet chords of the Hammond B-3 organ complement the pastor's voice. He makes his way to floor level, and his movements evolve into the "holy dance" for which he is locally renowned. By now, half the congregation are standing, moving, singing, shouting, and a few are "slain in the spirit" (briefly fainting and falling, to be lovingly caught by a nearby worshiper). The cadence and tone of the service peak and then quiet again, and people line up for anointing with oil, laying on of hands, and prayers for healing.

At about 2 P.M. the service concludes and the pastor says a benediction, but people continue to move about, now greeting and hugging one another (including visitors), and children play in the open areas. Some are staying for greens and cornbread; a few have arrived only in time for the food. They will all take a the break in the late afternoon, some walking to their apartments in Henry Horner or driving to other neighborhoods. At least half will return for the evening service.

The Revival Center is one of twelve churches located within walking distance of the Chicago Housing Authority high-rise apartments, Henry Horner Homes, in Chicago's Near West Side neighborhood. The Near West Side is one of Chicago's poorest neighborhoods, serving as part of the empirical basis of William Julius Wilson's theory of "ghetto poverty" and the "urban underclass."[1] And, as is evident in Map 4, in the two census tracts that comprise Henry Horner (and surround the Revival Center), the 1990 Census recorded a population that is 100 percent black, with unemployment rates in the two tracts of 40 percent and 66 percent, respectively, and with an astounding 74 percent and 86 percent living in poverty. These rates had increased dramatically since 1980, caused in part by the exodus of employed and employable people as their manufacturing jobs relocated away from the city of Chicago, leaving the unemployed and unemployable even more concentrated and isolated.[2] Alex Kotlowitz brought national attention to Henry Horner in *There Are No Children Here*[3] after ten-year-old resident Lafayette Rivers told him in an interview, "If I grow up, I'd like to be a bus driver." That "if" caught Kotlowitz's attention.

Thus the vicinity of Henry Horner provides an opportunity to explore the interrelationship between churches and very poor people who live in neighborhoods of extreme poverty. For this reason, we and our colleagues in the Religion in Urban America Program surveyed all the churches in the neighborhood and conducted ethnographic studies of four that, taken together, represent the variety of its religious life. Because Henry Horner, more than the West Side in general, is characterized by "extreme" and "concentrated" poverty, we also selected churches that either include Henry Horner residents among their members or serve them through their social ministries.

Across Damen Avenue from the Revival Center is Saint Stephen African Methodist Episcopal (AME) Church, a large, well-maintained stone structure with stained-glass windows and brightly painted red doors. At Saint Stephen, the Sunday-morning worship service starts promptly at 11 A.M., with two hundred or more well-dressed people already seated. The dignified processional, the elegantly robed choir and ministers, and the beautifully appointed sanctuary and finely tuned organ all signify a prosperous congregation. Much of the service is sung, including prayers and responses, giving the service a "high church" feeling. Yet the hymns are traditional Protestant hymns, recalling biblical, often rural, imagery and anticipating a personal salvation.

It is only slightly atypical that on this particular Sunday the procession includes a bishop visiting from Africa, for the congregation is actively dedicated to benevolent activities at home and abroad, and its pastor is a leader in the AME denomination and in the local community. One of the announcements asks members to attend a "claiming and cleansing" ceremony at the property and to come dressed for work. For most, this will be a strictly charitable undertaking, caring for the neighborhood of their church, even though they have long since moved into cleaner, quieter, and safer places of residence.

Continuing west on Washington Boulevard, one sees the security screens and shabby exterior of the small grocery and liquor store, old row houses and "two-flat" buildings in various states of disrepair, and vacant lots. In the third block we arrive at Saint Malachy Roman Catholic Church, the seat of the parish that includes Henry Horner. By midday, Saint Malachy's Sunday mass has concluded, and the only people remaining are members of the parish pastoral council, a lay advisory body. The mass was inspirational to them, celebrated in the small but elegant church, its Greek-revival architecture expressing deep roots in Catholic tradition, while the tradition was made contemporary by percussion and piano performed in a manner suggestive of urban Gospel music. The cantor, like half the congregation, grew up in the church. His rich baritone voice has adapted well to the post–Vatican II hymnody, and he rarely invokes the Gregorian chants for which he was trained. Only a few of the congregation and its leaders have walked to church, but for those who did not, the drive or bus ride was short compared with the commuting time of those attending nearby Saint Stephen. Saint Malachy is their "parish," and they live in the modest West Side row houses and rented apartments (but not in Henry Horner) where they have lived for many years, some for their entire lives.

Like many Catholic parishes, Saint Malachy has an elementary school and a convent, and it is mainly through these that it has been connected to the poorest people of the neighborhood. The school was recently made part of West Side Catholic Education Ministries, which the archdiocese is forming to provide quality Catholic education in poor neighborhoods (see chapter 11). The convent is the Chicago home of Mother Teresa's

Missionaries of Charity, which operates a shelter for abused and homeless women and a soup kitchen that offers hot meals every day.

Retracing our steps, past Saint Stephen and the Revival Center, continuing along the southern boundary of Henry Horner Homes, we pass more churches and the United Center, new home of the Chicago Bulls and Black Hawks, a major example of commercial interests exploiting the opportunities that decades of disinvestment and urban blight have generated. Then, tucked inconspicuously beneath the overpass of the "El" (Chicago's elevated rapid transit), one finds the Greater Pleasant Valley Missionary Baptist Church. Its members are mainly people of modest means, both working poor and welfare recipients, who come not from the immediate neighborhood but from many parts of the city because of their relationship with the minister or to participate in the particular kind of spirituality the church affords.

A block further east, just beyond the last Henry Horner high-rise building, we come to a very large, old church of light sandstone and a bulletin board displaying the words "First Baptist Congregational Church, Rev. Arthur D. Griffin, Pastor." Turning the corner to enter from the main steps, proceeding further up a red-carpeted staircase and through a large walnut-paneled vestibule, we find the thousand-seat sanctuary comfortably full of worshipers. Ten ministers, four of them women, are seated behind the pulpit one level up from the congregation. Above them, at balcony level, the choir director is conducting a classical anthem performed by the fifty-member Celestial Choir and several soloists, arranged for accompaniment by the large pipe organ, a concert grand piano, an electric organ, and an elaborate set of drums. At the conclusion, a ripple of "Amens" can be heard, marking the transition from the solemnity of the anthem to more spontaneous participation in the rest of the service. From the anthem onward the pipe organ is silent, and the urban Gospel sound accents Pastor Griffin's message of personal salvation as the ground of public responsibility. Before the benediction, people are reminded not to miss weekday Bible study, that more volunteers are needed for the weekly soup kitchen, and to please join the "Take Back the Streets" march against drugs that the Interfaith Organizing Project (IOP) is sponsoring the next Saturday. "Even if you don't live in this neighborhood," an assistant minister exclaims, "we worship here, our church is here, our God is here, and we believe the streets can be safe and secure for the community. So working with the IOP is our ministry, and God needs us on the streets next Saturday."

The Black Church and the Urban Poor

The black church has been an anchor of the black community in the United States from the time of slavery, through Reconstruction, Jim Crow, and the migration to the segregated cities of the North, to the present enjoyment of civil rights but simultaneous creation of an enduring ghetto underclass. In their comprehensive analysis *The Black Church in the African American Experience,* C. Eric Lincoln and Lawrence H. Mamiya show that historically "the Black Church has no challenger as the cultural womb of the black community,"[4] and that the churches of the historic black denominations continue to be vital centers of religious, social, economic, and political activity. Resisting the segmenting and differentiating processes of urban society, they argue, the black churches have remained complex, multifunctional institutions that both foster inward spirituality and unite the religious with the economic, political, and cultural dimensions of African American community life. Yet Lincoln and Mamiya voice concerns about the ability of the black churches to sustain this role, in view of growing numbers of "unchurched" blacks and because of institutional limitations their research identified. They also express concern that the black church may be increasingly divided between a middle-class church and a "church of the poor . . . , consisting largely of independent, fundamentalist, and Pentecostal storefront churches."[5]

Others scholars have extended, complemented, and qualified Lincoln and Mamiya's work in ways that inform our analysis of churches in Chicago's West Side. The writings of Cheryl Sanders, David Daniels, and Robert Franklin[6] have revised the apolitical image of Pentecostal churches and established their importance as public actors and agents of resistance to the marginalization and subordination of African Americans. Peter J. Paris and others have elaborated the black churches' role in fostering a racially inclusive and racially just society, despite the exclusion that led to their creation as racially separate institutions.[7] Cheryl Townsend Gilkes, Evelyn Brooks Higgenbotham, and others have probed questions about the status and contributions of women in the church that Lincoln and Mamiya raised but did not fully explore.[8] All these scholars interpret the black church as a culturally powerful institution that transcends the boundaries of class and that integrates religious, economic, political, and social functions to an extent that contrasts markedly with the fragmentation of modern urban life in general. The Religion in Urban America Program's studies of black churches in Chicago, discussed here and in chapter 7, generally support these mainstream perspectives on the role and character of the black church.[9]

But the black church literature, despite its general agreement about the importance of the church for the poor, offers little information about how and to what extent the poor participate in the churches. While Lincoln and Mamiya confirm the "class stratification" of the black church, they recognize that little is known about the participation or nonparticipation of the "dependent poor" (what social science calls the urban underclass) and speculate that the black church may be losing its presumed capacity to bridge the boundaries of class in the inner city.[10] A number of insightful ethnographic studies show how Pentecostal, independent, and storefront churches increase "human capital" in poor urban communities,[11] but these studies provide only general socioeconomic information on the churches' members and nothing about the participation or nonparticipation of area residents. Moreover, a few observers such as Robert Franklin[12] have recently noted the widespread decline in church participation by black men and the growing emphasis on reclaiming black men as a strategy of both church growth and urban mission.

When poor people are conspicuously absent from predominantly middle-class churches near their homes, this may mean not that the poor have opted for a Pentecostal or storefront church but rather that they are absent from church altogether. But it has been widely accepted, at least since the 1987 publication of William Julius Wilson's *The Truly Disadvantaged,* that one of the major causes of the persistence of urban poverty is the extreme *concentration* of the poor in *isolation* from mainstream institutions and societal functions,[13] so it is important to know whether and how churches either reflect or reduce the isolation. Unfortunately, the literature on urban churches tells us more about church programs to benefit the poor than about their interaction with the poor, including the participation of the poor in the churches.

This chapter explores how four black churches interact with people who live near them in conditions of "extreme" and "concentrated" poverty and in "social isolation." The ethnographic case studies we conducted allowed us to explore both this interaction and the differentiation by class and place of residence of members of four quite different black churches. We consider how churches may affect or mitigate the dimensions of isolation that poor people concentrated in residential complexes like Henry Horner Homes may experience. In view of the historic role of the black church, it was to be expected that many churches would offer social services for poor people and advocate public policy for their bene-fit. But if social isolation is an important factor perpetuating poverty, then it is important to see if church ministries involve the poor as partic-ipants as well as recipients. One point to consider is whether or not poor people attend the same churches as middle-class people, and if so, whether or not they engage in the same activities and social networks as those middle-class members. There is anecdotal evidence[14] that small, in-dependent churches, including storefronts, are not necessarily neighbor-hood churches but may be constituted as networks based on factors such as family ties, friendship, history, and religious preference that are much stronger than local geography.

Although any church participation would be a way for poor people to get out of their social isolation, it is particularly important for them to build relationships in their residential neighborhood. Here they are most likely to generate interrelated social networks in which the same people know one another in multiple contexts—for example, as friends, as shop-pers at the same stores, as parents of children at the same school, and as members of the same church. These overlapping relationships enhance an individual's effectiveness more than relationships that are limited to a single function or purpose. In the language of social science, "social capi-tal" (the networks and patterns of activity that people accomplish to-gether) increases "human capital" (the capacities of individuals to be pro-ductive and effective). Moreover, these multiple layers of interrelation-ship seem to be an important ingredient of social capital. For example, James Coleman, a seminal theorist of social capital, found that children did better in school if the children's parents knew one another.[15] Simi-larly, the individual capacities of people in poor neighborhoods are af-fected not only by their individual relationships but by the networks of people in their families, their apartment buildings, and their organiza-tions (if any), including churches. By focusing on churches near Henry Horner, we can examine how the churches may be part of the networks.

The Churches in a Neighborhood of "Extreme Poverty"

Because the Henry Horner Homes had the Near West Side's greatest con-centration of the ghetto poor, we surveyed pastors of the twelve churches located within walking distance of the housing development to deter-mine the extent of Henry Horner residents' involvement in those churches. To our surprise, of the twelve churches, only the Revival Center claimed participation of Henry Horner residents as members or regular attenders, although several spoke of ministries to them, including evangelization and social services. We also conducted informal interviews on the Henry Horner grounds, asking people at random whether and where they and their friends went to church and which church they considered a resource for the community. Confirming what we learned from the pastors, with one exception, they mentioned only the Revival Center as a church they attended, and it was also described as a church one could use (for a funeral, for example) without being a member. Other churches were known for their soup kitchens, food pantries, and free clothing.

We selected the Revival Center Church of God in Christ, Saint Stephen AME, Saint Malachy Roman Catholic, and First Baptist Congregational to ensure that the case studies would include the major recognized forms of public ministry to the inner-city poor[16] and a reasonable sample of the different denominational "families." And because we were treating residence in Henry Horner as a marker of concentrated poverty and social isolation, we included churches that had different ways of connecting with this public housing complex, as well as a distribution of larger and smaller, wealthier and less prosperous churches. Saint Stephen AME Church and First Baptist Congregational Church represent the Baptist and Methodist church families, which are historically the most prominent parts of the black church. While both churches conduct active public ministries, this chapter emphasizes Saint Stephen's social service ministries and First Baptist Congregational's widely recognized leadership role in community organizing. Saint Malachy represents Roman Catholicism, a denomination whose black population is small but increasing. The Revival Center represents the rapidly growing Pentecostal newcomer (in 1907) to the list of historic black denominations.

Most churches located in the poor black neighborhood minister to a wide cross section of the black community, including the poor, and fulfill the inherited image of the vibrant, multifaceted, socially relevant institution that serves as a sorely needed anchor for both the geographic neighborhood and the black community. Yet evidence builds throughout this chapter that, however great their contributions to and on behalf of the poor, most churches—especially those with the resources to provide substantial social ministries—find it very difficult to include the socially isolated poor as participants as well as recipients. It is possible that most of the very poor do not go to church in the neighborhood and may not at-

Fig. 4-1. Revival Center Church of God in Christ and Saint Stephen AME Church, Near West Side, Chicago. Photo by Lowell W. Livezey.

tend any church, anywhere. In addition to interviewing residents and pastors, for several weeks we watched the pedestrian traffic on Sunday mornings and saw virtually no people walking to church from Henry Horner. In any event, our discussions of Saint Stephen and Saint Malachy show how both a commuter and a parish church provided social ministries to benefit the poor, and our discussion of First Baptist Congregational depicts a church that not only provided major social ministries to the poor but mobilized political and economic power to defend and transform the neighborhood. Finally, we discuss the Revival Center as a church whose social ministries were limited to mutual aid but in which persons who were not only poor but otherwise socially isolated were active participants.

Social Ministries, Social Services, and Social Isolation

Little did Saint Stephen AME Church know when it purchased the building that the 1930s depression was around the corner. Nevertheless, the church held onto the building and paid off the debt. It was a neighborhood church, where members lived around the block and looked out for one another. Sixty years later, older members would lament that the church had become primarily a commuter congregation.

Yet, despite its loss of a shared residential neighborhood and the inter-related social networks that fostered, Saint Stephen's members still find at the church a vital community. They hear and recite a common story of salvation, one that is rooted in the Bible but that extends into the present,

Fig. 4-2. Saint Malachy Roman Catholic Church and the former parish school, now part of West Side Catholic Education Ministries. Photo by Lowell W. Livezey.

in which God's saving power is manifest in human agency—including their own. As Pastor Albert Tyson III put it in an interview, they are "not just actors in a play, they are the scriptwriters." This personally empowering self-concept is nurtured through acts of mutual support. A lay ministry of care for shut-ins, a health services program led by volunteer professional nurses, and an economic development committee that matches unemployed members with jobs enable the members to take charge of their own destiny by acting collectively.

The pastor's sermons call for spiritual transformation as a source of political, social, and economic change. Politicians are recognized from the pulpit and occasionally are invited to speak from it. Ministers and church leaders call on these politicians to make good on their promises and be faithful in their stewardship.

Even though fewer than ten of the nearly seven hundred members live near enough to walk to church, Saint Stephen directs much of its social ministry to West Side residents. Its weekly food pantry and clothing closet are intended to meet immediate needs of the local residents and to bridge the social gap between them and church members. The church offers volunteers to shop for needy people, but it seldom gives out money, for fear the recipients may use it for non-essential needs. Residents walk in and out of the church facility when they come to receive material help, just as they would do in a shop. Children in the neighborhood partake of the summer afternoon lunches provided through the church but seldom join in the Sunday school or other church activities oriented to member families.

In contrast, Saint Malachy is a parish church in the Catholic tradition in which, as historian John T. McGreevy puts it, "the individual came to know God, and the community came to be church, within a particular, geographically defined space."[17] If the national pattern held in the Near West Side, we expect that the priests of Saint Malachy were still urging their members to buy homes, invest in the parish school, and put down roots in the neighborhood during the 1970s and 1980s, when Protestants were joining the "black flight" to the suburbs. Not that all the Catholics stayed; but many did, and others would return later to live with younger generations in their family bungalows and "two-flats." Thus the communal, parish values associated with white ethnic Catholics (see chapter 5) led many black Catholics to remain on the West Side.

This was not lost on the 150 families of Saint Malachy parish in the late 1990s. From the name of parish newsletter—*Believers, Neighbors, and Friends*—to requests for voluntary contributions and services, to the concerns addressed in homilies and lifted up in prayers, members and participants were reminded that "to be church" was to celebrate and care for the neighborhood and its people. The evangelization effort, initiated with the help of archdiocesan staff, began with door-to-door visitation on the block where the church building stands and fanned out from there.

Saint Malachy's social ministries also reflect the parish ideal of care for all the souls within its boundaries. Saint Malachy's school, soup kitchen, and women's shelter provide major resources for the residents of Henry Horner and for the homeless who survive on the streets. Yet the social ministries are offered with minimal contact between the recipients and the members and staff of the church.

Ironically, it was precisely to make Catholic education available to the poor, even in parishes that could not afford the costs, that Saint Malachy School was incorporated into the West Side Catholic Education Ministries. But because of its structural independence, the school no longer brings children and their families into direct contact with parishioners. Even so, the prayers, celebrations, and symbols of community life at Saint Malachy symbolically create a sacred space that includes the school, the children, and the neighborhood.

The soup kitchen operated by the Missionaries of Charity, Mother Teresa's order, is the only source of free hot meals available daily in the neighborhood, and they are offered with a minimum of moralizing or religious requirements. Each morning and afternoon, forty-five to fifty men and women (mostly men) form a line at the door of the dining room. In random interviews, only a few told us they attend church, none of them at Saint Malachy; but they knew the neighborhood churches for their feeding programs, their clothing supplies, or their shelters.

Few church members volunteer at the soup kitchen, but they take pride in it, in the shelter for homeless and abused women, and in the fact that the nuns visit the sick and shut-in and work with the children who live in Henry Horner. The mention of these ministries gives immediacy and poignancy to prayers for the poor and suffering that are included in the mass and special rituals. The "we" who have come "this far by faith" includes the food pantry, the Sisters, and the school. In short, although direct interaction between church members and the poor of the neighborhood rarely occurs, the symbolic construction of the parish identity includes not only the collective action of service to the poor but the recognition of the poor—often specifically mentioning Henry Horner residents—among the people who make up Saint Malachy Parish.

Public Ministry on Behalf of the Poor

As First Baptist Congregational Church celebrated its fiftieth anniversary in 1994, it was obvious that its history on the West Side reflected dramatic changes in the neighborhood and in its membership. The onetime community church had become a commuter church; the one-time haven for blacks of all social classes and economic levels now attracted primarily middle-class, well-educated blacks. And by the end of the 1990s, partly as a result of the church's own efforts, incipient gentrification was foreshadowing the likelihood that white folks would move in nearby, implicitly challenging the church to make good on its racially inclusive ideals. If this comes to pass, the church may benefit from its affiliation with the predominantly white American Baptist and United Church of Christ denominations, in addition to the black National Baptist Missionary Convention.

But in the 1990s, the challenge to First Baptist Congregational Church was how to include the poorest residents of the West Side. Finding that virtually no residents of Henry Horner attended the church Sunday school, the church organized a separate Sunday school at Henry Horner. During good weather, the church's ministers preach open-air sermons, and its choirs perform for residents who sit at their windows or stand on the walkways to listen. Evangelization is intentionally directed to Henry Horner.

Like Saint Stephen and Saint Malachy, First Baptist Congregational provides a feeding program, a food pantry, and clothing closet. A tutoring program enlists more than twenty church members. Information about jobs and educational opportunities is displayed on bulletin boards and provided through the church office. The Drug Ministry, led by four ministers who are themselves former drug users and dealers, offers a spiritually grounded approach to recovery and celebrates an extraordinarily low (10 to 20 percent) recidivism rate.

These social ministries are available to all, including Henry Horner residents. The Drug Ministry seems to have a metropolitan clientele reached by a word-of-mouth network of people who have been helped by it. As at Saint Stephen and Saint Malachy, the volunteer service providers do not seem to have continuing social contact with the recipients, and the recipients do not participate in the worshiping community. Yet we were told that First Baptist Congregational members offer their church as a resource to people they personally know to be in need, so to this extent the church is part of a loose social network across boundaries of neighborhood and class.

Yet it is more as a political "player" that First Baptist Congregational ministers to the West Side neighborhood, including the poor of Henry Horner. While recognition from its pulpit, as at Saint Stephen, has long been a prize coveted by politicians, the church's real clout comes from its role in creating and leading the Interfaith Organizing Project (IOP), a Saul Alinsky–style community organization that has had a formative impact on the course of events in the Near West Side from its founding in 1985. "It was right here in this room," Pastor Griffin explained in an interview, extending his arm sacramentally around the cluttered Sunday school classroom, "that Bill Wirtz and Jerry Reinsdorf came to terms with us for the United Center."

The Interfaith Organizing Project was born in 1985 out of the need to bring together "peoples of various faiths and denominations"[18] to work for community interests by linking "our congregations and neighborhoods." The new organization elected Pastor Griffin as its first president and Earnest Gates, a neighborhood resident and business owner, as its vice president. With its incorporation in 1986, IOP was faced with the challenge of mobilizing the community, empowering the people to protect their interests against the Chicago Bears' plan to build a new stadium.

The linking of congregations and neighborhoods as the focus of IOP took place through its two arms—the ministers group, comprised of pastors, which met every Saturday, and the Thursday-night group, consisting mainly of residents and business owners, not limited to church members. Guided by the professional organizers, the pastors networked with one another and mobilized their members (wherever they lived), while the Thursday-night group networked within the Near West Side area. As Thursday-night members told us later,[19] the pastors mobilized people for weekend rallies and demonstrations, but during the week it was the Thursday-night leadership who could make a show of strength from the neighborhood. Despite tensions as to who best represented neighborhood interests, the two branches maintained a close working relationship, defeated the Bears' stadium, and forced the Chicago Bulls to negotiate favorable terms with IOP in the "joint venture" to build the United Center.[20]

The taste of IOP's triumph was still palpable at First Congregational Baptist Church for several years after its successes with the Chicago athletic teams, but IOP's agenda then shifted to the daily struggle against drugs and violence on the streets. The building of housing to replace that sacrificed to the United Center was mainly "spun off" to new, specialized organizations, in which lay neighborhood residents were more prominent than clergy. And some of the clergy (including the influential Pastor Albert Tyson of Saint Stephen) withdrew in conflict over goals, constituency, and leadership styles. It became harder to raise funds for the less-dramatic projects, so staff was reduced.

Yet the IOP remained a central ministry of First Baptist Congregational Church, with the assistant pastor, the Reverend George Daniels, assuming the presidency. This sustained the congregation's identity as a public actor for the neighborhood. While the members for the most part did not know neighborhood residents personally, they knew that the neighborhood was God's concern and that their destiny as a congregation was tied up with it.

Spirit-Filled Ministries, Social Isolation, and Social Capital

The Revival Center follows the practices, disciplines, and traditions of the Church of God in Christ and has the usual components of church structure, such as the Sunday school, Sunday-morning and -evening worship, the Young People Willing Workers (youth group), and the Young Women's Christian Council. People are baptized (by immersion) and may receive Holy Communion as soon as they are saved and confess Christ as Lord and Savior. The church holds funerals and weddings when they are requested, not only for members but for anyone in the community.

The church evangelizes the neighborhood partly by praying with all who come for food, clothing, or help with their children. Elders, missionaries, and other active members also visit their neighbors in Henry Horner, those who used to be their neighbors, and those whose children are in the Sunday school or choir. Even if the recipients of services and evangelization do not come to church, they sustain enough of a relationship that the church knows when something goes wrong and the people know where to come when they are in trouble. If they come, pastor told us, "we're just so happy they've come."

Revivals are important at the Revival Center, but they are not totally distinct from other services. During revivals, church people "tarry for the Holy Ghost" and pray for healing and for spiritual renewal. It is a time to bring inactive members into the church and to reclaim the backsliders. "Everyone who comes through that door—we gon' love them, and God will deliver them."

Like other black "sanctified" churches, the Revival Center draws on the resources of African American Christianity, including rituals of shouting, healing, and holy dancing.[21] It also brings a bit of the rural South into the city, thus preserving for urban people some of what the quintessentially urban scholar Robert M. Franklin calls "the humane culture of agrarian life."[22] This is evident in the relaxed Sunday schedule, with many people staying at church most of the day and sharing a meal, which helps make the church a family-like community. The meal, open even to those who come late and miss the sermon and especially to the children who need a rare hot meal, exemplifies the communal values for which the black church, especially in its Southern roots, is renowned. The pastor's sermons, prayers, and Bible-study illustrations also draw examples from his childhood in the South and communicate the values of practical self-help over commercial or governmental services, of community and mutual care over individual choice, and of respect for nature as God made it over human technology.

The Revival Center shares in what Lincoln and Mamiya have called the "black sacred cosmos,"[23] in which all creation is sacred and is dominated by the God whose "avenging, conquering, liberating" actions in history are mostly recorded in the Old Testament but whose full revelation is in Jesus Christ. The Old Testament epics show that all of life is a great struggle between good and evil, between the power of God and the power of Satan. This cosmic power struggle is still going on in the West Side, where the power of Satan is manifest as violence, drugs, racism, despair, and illness, just as it was manifest as the Egyptian pharaohs' armies and as the tyranny of Babylonian kings.

This means, first, it is God, and not the people themselves, fighting the battles against evil; and second, God is all powerful and He will win. So, at the Revival Center, when people pray for assistance, healing, and deliverance, they mainly praise God for the *fact* that He will deliver them. This does not mean they do nothing themselves to fight off evil; indeed, returning to church or calling the pastor to help with the kids may be a major initiative. But it does mean that the core of what they do is to join in God's fight and to believe in His deliverance. In contrast with Saint Stephen's members' being told that they are not only actors in the play, but they write the script, Revival Center members learn that they are just understudies. But they also learn that the play is a great cosmic epic, and that because God is both the author and the hero, "every thin' gonna be all right!"

The Revival Center's function as an extended family is also deeply rooted in the black church. As Cheryl Townsend Gilkes[24] has shown, the common use of "Brother" and "Sister" as titles of respect and, particularly in the Church of God in Christ, the formal office of "Church Mother" reflect a pattern of social relations in which childrearing, moral education, spiritual formation, and social control have long been shared within the church. Gilkes argues that the family role of the church is especially strong in times of structural pressure on the black family—slavery, urban migration, and now deindustrialization and social isolation.

Pastor Bowman's role as father and grandfather sets the tone. Every service of worship, prayer, and praise begins with the pastor or an elder or missionary talking informally, with concern about people who are absent. His overview always presupposes that concern, and if there is any exhortation, it is about *how* to express that concern. In preparation for a funeral, for example, we observed the pastor recruiting assistance with the "repast" and then giving advice about how to talk with the bereaved—how to be available and loving, but allowing the bereaved to be alone if that is their wish.

But church-as-family was also evident in the routine behavior of adults and children. Children were constantly being trained for good behavior and adult responsibilities. The pastor estimates that about one-third of the fifty or sixty children come with parents, both married and single, and the rest are unrelated to adults in the church. Adults are expected to show the children—especially the two-thirds who come to church without their parents—how to live and to give them pride and self-respect in the process. Preschool and elementary-age children playing around the church learn standard English grammar, ways to resolve conflicts without fighting, how to address adults, and to be quiet when adults are talking. The adults interlace instruction with hugs, pick the children up, give them food, and at least one member makes a ministry of designing and sewing cloths for children who might otherwise be poorly attired. Thus the church is a loving yet disciplined environment for children, and no child is to be excluded for bad behavior. "We just love them into good behavior," Pastor Bowman says. Everyone raises all the children.

Adults also feel the Revival Center's family-like discipline, especially if the forces of evil (drink, drugs, violence, etc.) overtake them. How does the church respond? "God is married to the backslider," the pastor explained, so

> we try to find them and bring them back into church. If people are active in the church they mostly live right. So we go out and find them. The pastor goes, or the active members, elders, missionaries, they go out and say, "Pastor Bowman want to see you." If they come around, if there's a crisis, we always welcome them, never chastise them. We know it's the devil at work; these are not bad people, they were just not able to resist the devil. But God loves them and so do we.

The Revival Center is something like a "parish," which has a ministry to all the people in a given geographic area. Some members also come from further away, but most previously lived in the immediate vicinity and grew up with many of those now remaining in Henry Horner. The image of parish begins with the pastor's sense of his ministry to the people of Henry Horner and the immediate vicinity. He says that in addition to the active membership of about a hundred, there are two hundred to three hundred who occasionally come to church and call him at a points of crisis, and whose children come to church or play there during the week. He and others in the church visit the children's parents—possibly in the hospital or in prison—or the adults' parents in a nursing home.

The church is open for various programs at least five evenings each week, all day Saturday and Sunday, and much of Wednesday, so it offers an open door and a safe haven in a dangerous neighborhood. It is a social center in which friendships are fostered, visitors are welcome, and both visitors and members are helped.

Active members include a few who are paid union-scale wages or are professionals, many working poor, and a few on welfare or disability. Most of the worshipers are poor, but not desperately, chronically poor—we learned, however, about several who had been chronically poor before they joined the church. Celia, a leader of the Helping Hands Ministry, was on welfare until the pastor persuaded her to get her GED; she later became a nurse and now tithes. Alex, who came after being released from prison, has remained employed, drug free, and legal—and employed. One of the elders used to be "the project drunk" before he was saved, joined the church, then got a good job and kept it. We heard several other stories like these, all told to show that if people stay active in the church, they can help one another resist the temptations of the devil and therefore remain reliable workers. The inactive members and the nonmembers who still identify the church as "theirs" are another story—60 or 70 percent are desperately poor, are on welfare and have been for a long time, and may be addicted or in trouble with the law. But they have people reaching out to them, praying for them, trying to find them and connect.

The Revival Center is a good example of the traditional "introverted forms of black Pentecostal social intervention,"[25] with no political activity beyond the occasional circulation of the nominating petition of a Church of God in Christ member seeking public office. The members give generously, but it is a mutual aid organization, not a charitable giving program and much less a broker of government funds or secular philanthropy. It is mutual aid, however, among a group that constantly reaches beyond those who regularly give, to bring in those who constantly need.

Conclusion: A Few Children, Very Few

It was in one of the Henry Horner high-rise buildings that LaJoe Rivers gave Alex Kotlowitz the title of his best-selling book. "But you know, there are no children here," she said. "They've seen too much to be children."[26] Through the eyes of Rivers's sons Lafeyette and Pharoah, Kotlowitz saw, and enabled us to see, the violence, hunger, loneliness, and degradation experienced daily by people of all ages at Henry Horner. Through their eyes we also saw their isolation, not only from the world outside but also from one another—people too fearful to connect.

Yet, for an hour a week in First Baptist Congregational's extension Sunday school, for an hour or two when a nun from Saint Malachy visits, and for much of the week at the Revival Center, a few kids from Henry Horner can be children again. Not that they will forget what they have seen; to the contrary, they will find a way to build a social network that does not remove them from Henry Horner but helps them cope with it. Those who come to the Revival Center might be fortunate enough to find an adult who already knows a parent or grandparent or cousin; or the kids might come *with* their parents. But Kotlowitz's compelling story and most social science accounts of ghetto poverty fail to mention the communities of faith that attempt to bridge the isolation of people living in concentrated poverty.

But the bridging is meager. For individuals like Celia and Alex, the Revival Center is a blessing. But with respect to the social isolation of the neighborhood's ghetto underclass, the church activities reported here suggest an underdeveloped potential, not a major contribution. The feeding programs and clothing closets mitigate the physical impact of acute poverty and will undoubtedly become more important as part of a privatized safety net made necessary by late-1990s changes in welfare policy. But we found little evidence that these charitable activities built social networks, enabling people in concentrated poverty to interact with and participate in a wider world. Similarly, Saint Malachy School provides the children of the Near West Side not only a quality education but a safe space where they can "be children," but the restructuring by which the archdiocese has arranged to maintain the school financially also separates it from the social network of the parish membership.

The participation of Saint Stephen and Saint Malachy and the central leadership of First Baptist Congregational in the Interfaith Organizing Project demonstrated the continuing importance of the black churches as powerful public institutions that can anchor neighborhood redevelopment. But the well-being of Henry Horner residents was less central than justice for owners of the modest homes nearby in IOP's confrontations with the Bears, Bulls, and the City of Chicago. And while IOP's marches against drugs, gangs, crime, and violence have obvious relevance to the Henry Horner Homes and to other poor residents, they are more directed at the deviant residents than toward enlisting the struggling victims of isolation, like Celia and LaJoe.

Our discussion of the Revival Center has shown that a small church with meager financial resources and a modest physical plant can serve as the basis for social networks bridging the boundaries that generally divide urban underclass people from mainstream society. The church has shared food and clothing as a rural family might feed a needy neighbor or stranger by adding a potato and extra water to the soup. Moreover, the pastor and lay leaders never mentioned social isolation and did not talk of providing social services; their concern was to help people find salvation in Christ, that they might be delivered from the power of Satan. Having found salvation, they would become part of a family-like network in which the saved would provide mutual reinforcement in the Christian life; backsliders would be nurtured and reclaimed; and the backsliders' children, spouses, and parents would be prayed for and cared for in their absence.

The practice of this Christian family network was the main evidence of the church interacting with, as opposed to serving, ghetto underclass people. A major difference between Celia and LaJoe Rivers, between ex-convict Alex and LaJoe's imprisoned son, LaShawn, is that Celia and Alex found the Revival Center, and it became their extended family. How much difference does one little church really make? How many other examples of isolation-bridging Christian community might we have missed? Members of First Baptist Congregational Church steer people they know into the Drug Ministry and the Henry Horner Sunday school, and there are undoubtedly other such connective tissues being fostered by churches on the Near West Side. Yet the Revival Center appears to be unique, not only in having Henry Horner residents as active members but also in its intense and interpersonal way of evangelizing in Henry Horner—visiting people in their apartments there and taking the initiative to maintain relationships that would otherwise atrophy. Overall on the Near West Side, we found the number of people who, through the ministries of the churches, were being woven into networks that bridged the social isolation of the poor to be exceedingly small. We hope we have only scratched the surface, and that others will further investigate the social networks of urban churches and the extent to which they bridge the social isolation of urban underclass people.

NOTES

We are particularly grateful to April Payton Bernard for exceptional assistance in field research for this chapter.

1. Wilson, *Truly Disadvantaged.*
2. Data are from the U.S. Census, 1980 and 1990, as reported in Chicago Fact Book Consortium, *Local Community Fact Book Chicago Metropolitan Area 1990.* See also Wilson, ed., *Ghetto Underclass,* 3; Kasarda, "Urban Industrial Transition."
3. Kotlowitz, *There Are No Children Here,* preface.
4. Lincoln and Mamiya, *Black Church,* 8.
5. Ibid., 384.
6. Cf. Sanders, *Saints in Exile;* Daniels, "Cultural Renewal"; and Franklin, "Safest Place on Earth."
7. Paris, *Social Teaching.*
8. Gilkes, "Storm and Light"; Higgenbotham, *Righteous Discontent.*
9. Interpretations of the black church are still contested and debated. Cf. Lincoln, *Black Church since Frazier;* and Lincoln and Mamiya, *Black Church,* on the legacy of Frazier *(Negro Church in America)* and on the "myth of the black church and politics" advanced by several black intellectuals, such as Adolph L. Reed Jr. and Gary Marx.

10. Lincoln and Mamiya, *Black Church*, 138 and 383–385.

11. Kostarelos, *Feeling the Spirit;* Paris, *Black Pentecostalism;* Sanders, *Saints in Exile.* However, Williams, *Community in a Black Pentecostal Church;* and Mukenge, *Black Church in Urban America,* provide socioeconomic profiles of members of churches studied.

12. Franklin, *Another Day's Journey.*

13. Wilson, *Truly Disadvantaged;* Wilson, ed., *Ghetto Underclass;* and Wilson, *When Work Disappears.* See also Copeland, *And the Poor Get Welfare;* and Blank, *It Takes a Nation,* which as a national, not just an inner-city, study of poverty focuses less than Wilson on concentration and social isolation. Anderson, in *Streetwise* and "Code of the Streets," focuses on the self-destructive behavior patterns adopted by those living in extreme and long-term poverty.

14. Kostarelos, *Feeling the Spirit;* and Policy Research Action Group, *Black Churches of West Humboldt Park,* also show that members of small, poor churches located in poor neighborhoods do not necessarily live in those neighborhoods.

15. Coleman, "Families and Schools," "Social Capital," and *Foundations of Social Theory.* There is a growing and increasingly popularized literature on social capital, including, for example, Putnam, "Bowling Alone." Putnam's notion of "generalized reciprocation"—the presumption that assistance rendered will be returned, but not necessarily by the direct recipient—presupposes a social network—hence reinforcing our determination to see if churches can foster such networks among the otherwise socially isolated poor.

16. Franklin, *Another Day's Journey,* 51.

17. McGreevy, *Parish Boundaries,* 4.

18. This historical information is derived from Interfaith Organizing Project, *New "West Side Story,"* and from interviews with current and former board members.

19. Earnest Gates, interview with the authors, April 12, 1995.

20. Agreements reached between the owners of the Chicago Bulls and IOP include the replacement of demolished buildings or payment of full market value of each building plus $30,000; the provision of $600,000 no-interest loan to IOP for the construction of homes for sale in the West Side; the building of a new public library in the West Side by the joint venture; provision of $75,000 to assist in reopening Mile Square Health Center; and the construction of a park in the community.

21. Sanders, *Saints in Exile;* Franklin, "My Soul Says Yes."

22. Franklin, "My Soul Says Yes."

23. Lincoln and Mamiya, *Black Church,* 2–6.

24. Gilkes, "Storm and Light," 186ff.

25. McRoberts, "Understanding the 'New' Black Pentecostal Activism," 48.

26. Kotlowitz, *There Are No Children Here,* preface.

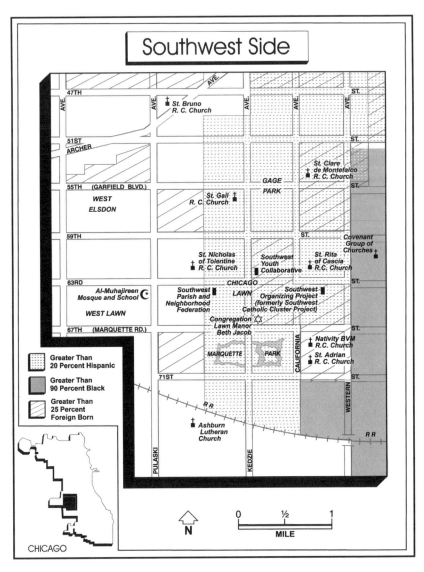

Map 5. The Southwest Side, a classic blue-collar, white-ethnic area, is now receiving Hispanic, Arab, African American, and Polish newcomers. Map by Brian Twardosz, BMT Printing and Cartographic Specialists.

Chapter 5

"God Doesn't Ask What Language I Pray In"
Community and Culture on Chicago's Southwest Side

Elfriede Wedam

The blue-collar neighborhoods in Chicago were long known for the brightest Christmas lights in the area. Some houses had neat designs, others were gaudy. All were expressive and delightful to children's eyes, as reflected in the reactions of my siblings and me. Some blocks looked as though the neighbors had decided together what the year's style or motif would be. On others, it appeared as if there were a competition for the best, or at least the biggest, design. But however it was done, these neighborhoods distinguished themselves with the amount of light that streamed from them. Later, I wondered if the enthusiasm for Christmas decorations had to do with the Catholic propensity for material faith, since these neighborhoods were also predominantly Catholic.

Summers revealed impeccable lawns and trimmed bushes. They were curiously limited, however, in their flower gardens, at least to the eye of the passing motorist. There was just enough color to rescue the panorama from dullness, but far less of the floral vanity that stylish yards emit. There was not much space for the gardens because these small, vigorously maintained bungalows and two- and three-flat apartment buildings rested on narrow lots, arranged in soldierly rows.

The expressive quality of these homes and neighborhoods did not occur by chance. Every locale is defined by culture in the broadest sense, and these neighborhoods reflected the particular class, religious, racial, ethnic, national, and language characteristics of their residents. The outward appearance of the neighborhoods symbolized shared understandings about their meaning. It is neighborhoods like these, in five community areas on the Southwest Side of Chicago, that are the focus of this chapter. Here, residents are reexamining their self-understandings as they confront changing urban realities. I try to unravel some of these shared meanings and self-understandings. I use observations I conducted during the mid-1990s of two Catholic parishes, Saint Nicholas of Tolentine and Saint Bruno, and of a community organization, the Southwest Organizing Project, and I include data from several additional congregations, Protestant, Jewish, and Catholic, as well as other community-based groups.

The neighborhoods are located about five to seven miles southwest of the Loop, Chicago's downtown business district. I argue that these neighborhoods have been strong moral communities, not chiefly because of their high standards of behavior but because the residents act in negotiation with one another for the collective standards to which they hold each other. Historically, these neighborhoods have exemplified the "defended neighborhoods," as Gerald Suttles has described them,[1] that have responded in particular political ways to challenges by groups considered "outsiders." Defended neighborhoods contain a type of social order within which the residents can secure themselves against common apprehensions. This analysis attempts to identify the fundamental causes of those apprehensions, why the neighborhoods take the shape they do, who benefits, who loses, and how the changes in the order (or disorder) in the neighborhoods can be explained.[2] I argue that the kinds of changes that occur are related to the success or failure of new and old residents to negotiate on the basis of a shared sense of a moral order.

Community and Moral Culture in the Southwest Side

The power of community as a concept and a reality is its ability to point to a fundamental human process: the "sense of a primacy of belonging."[3] There is a "presumptive good" to community.[4] Community ties are essential for both healthy individuals and functioning civil society. For example, the strong sense of a collective identity among first-generation immigrant Poles contributed to their community mental health.[5]

The "loss of community" theme gains much of its strength from the acknowledgment that geographic mobility and changes in family life— divorce and blended families—have created certain instabilities in our expectations. Much public discourse and social criticism contrasts idealized tight-knit communities with the extreme individualism that life in modern society permits. In these critiques, moral authority is seen to have been exercised by parents, neighbors, congregations, and even politicians in customary and public ways prior to the privileging of individual rights since the 1960s. The focus on authority limited individual choices, but it also fostered lasting relationships embedded in community ties and legitimated rules that enforced social order. When authority, order, and community were rejected by the baby-boom generation, as Alan Ehrenhalt argues, they were replaced with unlimited choice, personal privacy, and free-market domination. This resulted in a loss of community accountability and an expansion of economic determinism into all areas of our lives.[6] Some of this criticism reveals an "American small town" nostalgia that overlooks the closing of ranks in the face of outsiders, often of another race or class. But it also suggests that community relationships depend on an acknowledgment of interdependence, not merely on the assertion of individual and civil rights.

Studying the culture of community is, in the largest sense, about studying "meaning" and "moral order," argues sociologist Robert Wuthnow.[7] It is studying the relations among individuals and groups in a social system that make organized, collective life possible. Meaning mostly has been analyzed as the property of individuals, but Wuthnow directs sociological inquiry toward meaning revealed in the group life of actors. In the case of the religious dimension of culture, this refers to how individuals relate in the context of their congregations and community organizations. One way to put this, then, is that culture is about how our collective life makes sense to us collectively.

Moral culture includes shared assumptions about the nature of relationships and about the norms and rules that are taught and enforced. For example, a former Southwest Side resident interpreted her neighborhood as a "village" where, when she was growing up, she and other children could roam safely. Her parents were confident that if a neighbor became a "problem," "everyone else felt the same way about it." The adherence to collective standards by members of these Euro-American ethnic neighborhoods was by no means inviolable, but widely understood norms existed by which neighbors could gauge one another's behavior. Yet norms change over time as a result of conflict, created, for example, when community members married into a different religious, ethnic, or racial group.

Interaction among residents who have different social and demographic characteristics and hold different beliefs and values creates a neighborhood community in the urban context. The Southwest Side neighborhoods were never exclusively one ethnic or cultural group,[8] but a significant degree of homogeneity distinguished certain areas—the Lithuanian neighborhood, the Polish corridor, and the like. These neighborhoods are, in the words of *Habits of the Heart*, "communities of memory."[9] They are moral communities in which the residents are connected to one another through norms of authority and stories about "who we are" and "how we do things here." These values and beliefs are taught and practiced in the schools, the neighborhood associations, and the churches.

The negative side of communal ties—the propensity to turn outsiders into enemies—has been discussed by critics of *Habits*.[10] The insider/outsider dilemma is a recalcitrant aspect of American social divisions, because recognizing and constructing others as different permits us to form identities through communal bonds that are lasting, stable, and exclusive. At the same time, tight-knit communities, including the ones of the Southwest Side, have been losing members in large numbers, partially because of economic restructuring in the latter half of the twentieth century but also because they impose restrictions on behavior and create identities that have been increasingly rejected. Participants in the churches and organizations studied here have suggested new approaches to relationships with newcomers. Where racial and ethnic diversity stimulated fears in the past, some residents are initiating discussions that search out human commonalities rather than perpetuate differences between people. Instead of simply seeing the rejection of tightly knit neighborhoods as a "decline in community," we need to examine how the new immigrants to these neighborhoods have interacted and negotiated with the current residents to re-form community cohesion and redraw the boundaries of the insider group.

The urban Catholic churches have had a long history of connecting the family with the local parish in a social and religious ecology that created a particular meaning of neighborhood. Property bought within the parish boundaries sacralized the space of the parish, argues social historian John McGreevy, and created a bond for residents with the neighborhood and with their neighbors not comparable to bonds in predominantly non-Catholic neighborhoods.[11] This interpretation was confirmed in urban historian Thomas Sugrue's account of the deindustrialization of Detroit, when he noted the ways in which neighborhoods developed an identity for their Catholic homeowners despite the fact—or perhaps because of it—that the economic foundations on which these residents made their lives was so precarious.[12] The houses "were close together on small lots. Day-to-day life was structured by countless small interactions among neighbors; little was private. Property maintenance, behavior, and attitudes seldom escaped the close scrutiny of neighbors."[13] When the residents also shared a religious identity, these bonds were reinforced.

Another norm, "to keep up the property," also expresses unity and the ability to accept community standards. In fact, individualistic standards are not well tolerated in tight-knit communities. In the Southwest Side neighborhoods I frequently heard residents unabashedly state that newcomers needed to "follow the rules" and "do the same as I do." While these rules appeared unitary in some respects, they were also reciprocal—"You treat me right and I'll treat you right," explained one resident. These were rules about civic participation and neighborly expectations. Indeed, the enforcement of these rules, another resident explained, was not about power but about "love of the neighborhood." In the words of one Catholic pastor, the meaning of neighborhood for his parishioners emerged from relationships based on and in an "emotional geography." As the ethnic, racial, and religious composition of the members in these neighborhoods has changed, the old residents have negotiated with new residents for a new local meaning based on a different emotional geography.

Two parishes and a community organization illustrate how these new relationships are being formed. The discussions among their members are about two things: first, how to create relationships between newcomers and established members, and second, how these relationships reflect the neighborhoods around the parishes and community groups and, in turn, what effect the new relationships have on those neighborhoods. In the Polish national parish of Saint Bruno, the parishioners are discussing how the Polish language and culture affect their parish. Saint Nicholas of Tolentine is a cosmopolitan parish now experiencing racial change with the steady in-migration of Hispanics and some African Americans. In the Southwest Organizing Project, initially supported by the Archdiocese of Chicago to explore the role of the church in responding to racial and ethnic changes, the members are connecting with an ever-widening array of interfaith neighborhood groups.

The Southwest Side lies several miles southwest of the Loop and includes Gage Park, Chicago Lawn (Marquette Park), West Lawn, West Elsdon (bordering Midway Airport), and Archer Heights on the northwest corner. Marquette Park and Gage Park have a mixed ethnic and racial composition, while the other three areas remain predominantly white and European. Marquette Park shifted from about 83 percent white in 1980 to 47 percent white (a small number of whom are from the Middle East), 27 percent Hispanic, and 26 percent African American in 1990. In Gage Park, the number of Hispanic residents grew from 11 percent in 1980 to almost 40 percent in 1990, and the black population increased from 1 percent to 5 percent. Archer Heights is approximately 90 percent white, with a small increase in Hispanic numbers since 1980. West Lawn and West Elsdon are about 95 percent white. The percentage of home ownership in the neighborhoods, over 70 percent, has changed little from 1960. Among the residents are six major language groups: English, Polish, Slovak, Lithuanian, Arabic, and Spanish.

The expansion of Midway Airport during the 1990s has anchored the economy of the area, which had become precarious when some of the trucking industry and light manufacturing plants left. A rapid transit line linking the airport with the Loop opened in the early 1990s. Its positive economic impact, especially as reflected in increasing real estate value, has become a symbolic and practical vehicle for connecting the neighborhoods to the outside world. Sixty-third Street, the principal east-west corridor and popular shopping district during the mid-century, still has considerable foot traffic despite the competition of nearby malls.

The Southwest Side is home to nineteen major Catholic institutions: eleven parishes, two high schools, two religious-order motherhouses, one abbey, a press headquarters, a hospital, and a home for mentally retarded children. They comprise the Southwest Cluster, designed to promote communication among geographically proximal parishes. Through the cluster, the archdiocese reinforces the spatial relationships on which parishes are based but makes each parish less insular than in the past, less a "kingdom" and more a collaboration. Alongside the Catholic institutions are approximately forty-seven Protestant churches, a Conservative Jewish synagogue, and three Sunni Muslim mosques.

Saint Bruno Parish

Surrounded by tidy brick bungalows in the middle of Archer Heights sits Saint Bruno Catholic Church, its school, and its rectory. The parish was founded in 1923 by a committee of twelve laymen, who gathered support for establishing a Polish national church by circulating petitions in the neighborhood.[14] Ground for the modern church, a cream-colored brick in a simple yet imposing design, was broken in 1955; a second school building and modern rectory were added in 1975. Saint Bruno is one of three churches in the cluster that holds Sunday masses in Polish, and one of forty-two such in the archdiocese. Our Lady of Czestochowa, a popular saint in Poland, is honored with an outdoor shrine, fittingly graced with flowers in the summer and Christmas lights in the winter.

Saint Bruno is both a national and a territorial parish, served by three full-time Polish-speaking priests; one is himself a recent immigrant. About 80 percent of the 1,850 member families live within the parish boundaries. The parish school is just shy of its capacity of three hundred children. The composition of the parish population is about half new immigrants (one-third of whom are undocumented) and half Americans of Eastern European, mostly Polish, descent. Hispanics, about 6 percent of the church's registration, play a minor but growing role in the parish. For the time being Father Joseph Grembla, the pastor, does not use his fluency in Spanish, because these Hispanics are mostly second generation and English-speaking.

Saint Bruno's extensive agenda of social, devotional, and educational activities is offered in Polish and English. The religious education program—Confraternity of Christian Doctrine, or CCD—for public school children, staffed by fifteen to twenty volunteers, serves close to four hundred children in bilingual classes. Many children from outside the parish come for instruction in Polish. The eighty-member, strong-voiced choir sings in both languages and is often a guest choir in other churches. Saint Bruno holds two out of five weekend masses in Polish. The parish elementary school has English-language tutoring for children who need help, although it offers no classes in Polish. The parish bulletin and the parish newspaper, *St. Bruno Beat,* are written in both English and Polish.

The use of both Polish and English has different meanings for different members. American Poles and new immigrant Poles share an ethnicity but not a nationality. This has opened some important opportunities for understanding how culture is both a resource to draw on and a boundary line that is negotiated daily in parish activities.

Language and Community

The annual confirmation ceremony is an important parishwide event for the young teens, their sponsors, and parents, as the young people publicly accept their adult religious responsibilities. Because of its public, ritual importance, the ceremony is held in English. When one of the parish priests included some Polish prayers, the congregation became ill at ease. Afterward, complaints flowed in to the pastor, the parish council members, and even the choir director. One parish council member suggested that no one was prepared to hear Polish, and consequently, people did not know how to respond. The sense of unpreparedness, if this was indeed the case, revealed a deeper ambivalence.

At Saint Bruno, the Polish language is a symbol of the way in which immigrants are both included in the new world and separate from their American neighbors and fellow parishioners. The multiple meanings of language permitted the congregation to make multiple interpretations, opening a debate that included ordinarily muted, negative interpretations of bilingualism. What was the *meaning* of using Polish during an English mass? Was this an attempt surreptitiously to add Polish into a formal liturgy that should represent the parish as a whole? Did the decision communicate a preference for a second language through which the parish will no longer speak as majoritarians? Was this a symbol of further ethnic encroachment, changing the identity of the parish from one that serves Poles to one that is a Polish parish? Does this mean we are no longer Americans?

The pluralist-versus-assimilationist conflict continues over the bilingual religious education classes for children of members who attend public schools. Most of the new Polish immigrant children do not attend Saint Bruno's elementary school. To fulfill the requirement for training in the faith, Polish parents send their children to the CCD program on Saturday mornings. The assimilationists in the parish wish to offer the classes only in English, whereas the pluralists see no advantages to this, only the loss of their heritage.

The conflict between pluralism and assimilation shows how divisive nonracial cultural differences can be. This conflict is about different generations of immigrants of the same national origin whose experiences are set in contrasting cultural contexts. Those contexts permit different interpretations of the meaning of the Polish language in worship and religious education and of its symbolic importance in positioning oneself in American society. Consequently, a common heritage and tradition—elements of a primordial identity—are not sufficient to create community at Saint Bruno. Rather, negotiating the *interpretations* of that heritage

Fig. 5-1. Devotion to Our Lady of Czestochowa at Saint Bruno Roman Catholic Church, Southwest Side, Chicago. Photo courtesy of Saint Bruno Roman Catholic Church.

and tradition is the cultural process through which relationships, and thus community, are formed.

Church and Neighborhood

The Archer Heights Community Organization pays special attention to housing, and it is again no accident that Saint Bruno members are active in it. One evening, the Parish Pastoral Council engaged in heated discussion on the matter of illegal housing conversions by Polish landlords who took in new immigrants. These conversions involved making additional rooms in the basements and attics of single-family houses. One of the parish leaders argued that following the housing regulations was a way of maintaining the neighborhood "as a precious asset" that must be preserved, for the good of the church and for the common good of all residents. "If the neighborhood goes down," this member asserted, "the church will go down too."

The immigrants were less appalled at the suggestion that some of their peers were trying to bend the rules for their own gain than at their perception that critics lacked sympathy for their difficulties of being uprooted and reestablished in a new world. "Immigrants have it hard," one immigrant member explained, "they have much to learn. We sacrifice a lot to try and fit in, yet, if those people [American Poles] don't have any feeling for us, you are set back." Another immigrant stated that the council should discuss such matters as the school and finances, but "they shouldn't worry about immigrants." The council should be aware of what's happening in the community but not "pick on one ethnic group."

This exchange exemplifies how the physical appearance of the neighborhood is a public and political matter, shared among long-term residents, that they scrutinize and evaluate, whereas newer residents simply feel besieged. Older residents claim that poor housing standards result in people leaving the neighborhood, and "we can't afford to lose good parishioners." Newer residents are less likely to focus on the public aspect of what is essentially—in the American definition—a private commodity, one's home. When American Poles emphasize assimilation to American rules and the values that support them, they are focusing on the muted communalist strain in American culture, rather than on the currently more pronounced individualist strain.

The economic dimension of this issue is rooted in the immigrants' continuing ties to their country of origin; for some, their "real parish" is still in Poland. Many Poles, like the Mexican immigrants discussed in chapter 2, have adopted a transnational identity, with connections to their home country continually renewed by travel, communication, and the circulation of money. These exchanges are enriching to the cultures of both the United States and the country of origin. But they are also a social and economic resource drain in each local context, because the tentativeness of commitment precludes a stable and secure involvement. The illegal conversion problem is especially irksome to some parishioners who feel that those who take advantage of American opportunities should share more of the costs. Nevertheless, the new immigrants increase parish rolls, and Fr. Grembla reported a 20 percent increase in giving as a result of a greater appeal to the newcomers. In the end, housing is highly important to long-term residents because it affects their community identity, not just their economic well-being.[15]

The matter of illegal housing conversions raised in the Parish Pastoral Council was withdrawn from discussion when the immigrant Poles on the council successfully argued in a later meeting that this was a civil issue and should not be the subject of church business. Privately, one immigrant Pole recounted to me that a number of new Polish immigrants in the neighborhood are not Catholics, or at least are not registered or practicing Catholics. (This is similar to the migration of black Protestants into heavily Catholic neighborhoods.) These people are harder for the church members to reach. But appealing to a church-state separation reduces the ability of the church to participate in the civic dialogue about what the definition of an American is and where it lies on the continuum from a whole-hearted idealism and patriotism to a crass economic opportunism.

The limitations the parishioners themselves place on the dialogue within the church also weakens its role as a moral community. In response to the push to relegate the housing issue to the civil domain, the council president argued, "Because of our ability to reach out in the Polish language, Saint Bruno Parish is in a unique position to act on this issue. We can communicate, educate, and be an agent of peace to our community. Does this sound like part of our mission as Church?" He suggested further that community issues are issues of justice on which parishioners may eventually be faced with decisions. While community issues continue to push through to become council business, they are perhaps mostly those, like community policing, on which members already agree.

For longtime residents of the Southwest Side, the neighborhood is not just a place to live but a place to which one must contribute. Several members related to me their conviction that a strong neighborhood made a strong church, not the reverse, and that because of the consequences for the church, members have a moral duty to protect the neighborhood. Maintaining control over the neighborhood was not only a response to the structural features of economic insecurity that blue-collar neighborhoods suffered but also an expression of their beliefs in community, family, and God.

Lay Leadership and Parish Planning

Saint Bruno's Parish Pastoral Council—which itself is required by the archdiocese (see chapter 11)—is using parish planning as a tool to form a more integrated parish community. The formation of the council was accompanied by different views about its role and purpose in the parish. Some members wondered, "Why get involved in this? Let the priests do it." Others were gratified that their views were being considered but worried that the council might develop its own agenda, independent of individual parish members.

In response to the statement "The toughest job of the council is to dream dreams and lay out broad visions," a member commented that as a Catholic parishioner, he had never been asked to "dream dreams." In fact, he noted that creativity was not a mark of this working-class parish. But the lay leadership at Saint Bruno is redefining the relationship between parishioners and their parish in order to reconceive their Catholic, parish, and, ultimately, community identity.

Saint Bruno's Parish Pastoral Council conducted a survey of parishioners in both Polish and English to help the council determine the administrative, spiritual, educational, and social priorities of the parish. The planning process stimulated new developments such as *St. Bruno Beat,* the parish newspaper. But it revealed many issues that affect participation and communication between ethnic groups and between generations. While steady leadership in some parish organizations provided continuity and stability, it also sometimes shut out potential leadership from younger people with new ideas. Three of Saint Bruno's council members attended archdiocesan leadership classes that included learning methods of organizing parish groups so as to overcome the tendency to form cliques. A number of parishioners requested that the parish develop a more welcoming atmosphere at church, beginning with expanding the role of the ushers beyond the taking of the collection.

The parish survey confirmed the widely shared opinion that the bilingual choir has made important strides in bridging the language communities at Saint Bruno. Before the current music director was hired, the church had two choirs, one for each language group. Through the combined choir, the members learned "not to be afraid of each other," the music director said.

The survey also confirmed a lack of inclusion of teens in parish activities, especially the liturgies. The council resolved to invite teens to become lectors and take on other lay ministerial roles, and it renewed its commitment to form a teen club that would better connect young people with the parish. Similarly, the council resolved to raise the visibility of young adults through a Parish Commission for Young Adult Ministry that would connect directly with the archdiocesan program.

Through the planning process, the council members saw how parish leadership could change their role from carrying out intraparish activities to exploring ways for the "church to be a model for the world." The pastor noted, however, that the sense of "mission" is not well understood in the parish, for example, with regard to the role of evangelization. The challenge for the council, then, becomes how to extend the envisioning process that began with the council leaders into the decisions and actions of the members.

Not all new immigrants today participate in the parish-building form of community that molded so many earlier generations of newcomers. Many of the recent Polish arrivals both seek out and are steered by well-meaning American and Polish contacts to established churches, founded generations earlier. Poles in Chicago come to churches like Saint Bruno that provide a historical ethnic mission. For immigrating Poles, Saint Bruno is one kind of "proximal host," the concept employed and adapted to religious communities by the authors of *Gatherings in Diaspora* in order to explain the relationship between new immigrants and the receiving country.[16] This relationship refers to the placement of new immigrants into proximity with Americans whom they resemble, often according to a racialized conception of their identity. Because of this particular context, these immigrants cannot shape parishes to their identities as did their predecessors, who created a refuge for themselves as they struggled with the challenges of their new, often hostile—anti-Catholic, anti-immigrant—environment. Today's Polish immigrants are given a template forged by others and shaped by their memories—which may not be recognizable to the new immigrants. Indeed, one of the parish leaders reported that many parish children remember that "grandpa never got any help." Part of the challenge facing the immigrant Poles is negotiating the fit between their newly forming identities and the templates offered by their hosts.

Neither group fully recognizes either its inclusivity or its resistance. Yet, for some members of Saint Bruno, the diversity in the parish offers alternatives not often found in a parish—it is both modern and traditional in outlook, and the dual languages offer the opportunity for expressing oneself with both an American and a European identity, tradition, and culture.

Through parish planning and the empowerment of lay members, the church has rediscovered the importance of a welcoming atmosphere and how the sharing of stories through music and writing creates opportunities to bridge cultural differences. Opening the boundaries of any in-group must include making the out-group understandable, thus "rendering the unknown into a familiar form."[17]

Saint Nicholas of Tolentine Parish

About two miles away from Saint Bruno, in the heart of the Southwest Cluster and straddling the communities of Chicago Lawn (known locally as Marquette Park, after the large and well-used city park nearby) and West Lawn, sits the parish of Saint Nicholas of Tolentine. It was founded as a mission by the Order of Saint Augustine in 1909 but organized and run as a parish by the Archdiocese of Chicago since 1916.[18] The red-brick church in an English Gothic style stands only one-half block from busy Sixty-third Street. The local public high school faces the church property on one side. There are more than twenty-six hundred registered families and almost six hundred children in the parish school, the largest in the Southwest Cluster.

The parish rolls of Saint Nicholas grew steadily during the 1990s as many first- and second-generation Latino families, mostly from Mexico, moved into this part of the city. During the year of our study, about half of the schoolchildren were Hispanic, half were white, and three African American children had recently transferred from a nearby school, which closed the year before our research visits. The church holds six masses on Sunday, one of which is in Spanish, celebrated by the pastor, Father Stanley Rataj, who recently learned Spanish in order to serve the new immigrant population. Saint Nicholas is one of 5 churches in the Southwest Cluster to offer masses in Spanish, and one of 110 in the archdiocese to do so.

Saint Nicholas has long been a large, active parish, demonstrating leadership in Vatican II liturgy and participating in community organizations. *A History of the Parishes of the Archdiocese of Chicago* calls Saint Nicholas a "cosmopolitan" parish because, despite being surrounded by ethnic parishes, it never favored any language group, having families of East European, Hispanic, Irish, and Italian descent. This is not without its special meaning. As an associate pastor phrased it, there are many boundaries to identify and respect.

The parish supports a wide variety of traditional Catholic organizations and activities, such as the Holy Thursday tour of the churches, and some nontraditional ones, such as the Passover seder and the Covenant Group of Churches, which includes several parishes in West Englewood as well as some Protestant churches. The Covenant Group emerged to work for a prayerful racial reconciliation in the aftermath of the 1992 Los Angeles riots, which erupted at the acquittal of white police officers in the beating of Rodney King. The Liturgy Committee is in high gear most of the time, and an archdiocese-mandated parish-planning effort is taking shape. In the mid-1990s, the Society of Our Lady of Guadalupe and a Latino youth group were formed, and several Latinas are members of the parish council. One Hispanic and one white couple were preparing for the deaconate.

Language and Community

Language differences reveal group boundaries within Saint Nicholas, just as they do at Saint Bruno. Saint Nicholas's strategies to address them are different, making room for a new set of members, mostly Latino, who are, in effect, building a parish in shared space. The building process has been both collaborative and segmented. The old and new members do not share a predominant ethnicity, so the parishioners have had to find ways to cross both language and racial differences.

Few priestly vocations among Hispanics means that unlike immigrants before them, the Spanish-speaking groups have few native clergy who can serve their needs. The relative poverty of Hispanics puts the financial burden of Spanish liturgies—for example, language training for priests—on the archdiocese and on the special efforts of religious orders. The previous pastor at Saint Nicholas resisted demands for a Spanish liturgy in the early 1990s, which Fr. Rataj explained later as concerning the issue of "how to do it right." Subsequently, it took over a year of committed efforts by both clergy and lay members to find and train all the liturgical ministers, altar servers, and lectors as well as ensuring a Spanish-speaking priest to say Mass regularly. While not everyone agrees that this played a role in moving the liturgy effort forward, at the time there was heavy proselytizing by Hispanic Protestants in the neighborhood around the church. One lay leader pointed out two Protestant churches nearby in which the membership changed from predominantly white to predominantly Hispanic in only a couple of years.

The Spanish mass had the unintended consequence of furthering group separation when some white members became alienated because "they didn't get a Polish mass" when they had asked for it years before. Hispanics have been able to claim ownership over language in a way that Poles at Saint Nicholas could not. The tension is not over English-speaking versus Spanish-speaking liturgy in the creation of an American as opposed to a foreign identity but over how cultural power is wielded in the parish.

Fig. 5-2. Ballet Folklorico of Mexico performing at a Cinco de Mayo celebration at Saint Nicholas of Tolentine Roman Catholic Church, Southwest Side, Chicago. Photo courtesy of Saint Nicholas of Tolentine Roman Catholic Church.

When asked why a Spanish mass is problematic—for English speakers who want English as well as for Poles who did not get their Polish mass—when there are Lithuanian, Polish, and Slovak masses in churches within a couple of miles, one elderly resident explains, "The Lithuanians built *their* church, the Spanish did not build *our* church." "Our church" signifies what historian Dominic Pacyga calls a kind of "genetic" ownership that is an important dimension of territory in Chicago ethnic parishes.[19] The sense of ownership tied to one's ethnic predecessors, who in most cases are not kin related, is part of a sense of collective identity that has some exclusionary consequences, especially for people of a different race but also for all non-Lithuanians, non-Poles, or whichever ethnic group predominates.

Yet focusing on owning overlooks the dimension of "building." Including new groups who initially are seen as outsiders requires face-to-face negotiating, addressing cultural differences, and responding to the fears these differences generate. Equally important, it is a negotiation around *perceptions* of cultural differences. As members of any social group, we need to make sense of the continuing changes that are part of ordinary life. We use our past experiences to transform new instances into forms sufficiently familiar that we can make some sense of them. If we cannot, we tend to become frightened.[20] These are often-repeated experiences. Sharing religious experiences offers the possibility of making the strange into the familiar.

Members describe one bridging event between Latinos and white parishioners as "magical" in its effect on the participants and its ability to stimulate cross-cultural understanding. A meeting between whites and Latinos was organized shortly after the forming of the Guadalupe Society to give parishioners what was hoped to be a "wide-open opportunity" to express their fears and hopes about the changing membership. Strong statements were made by both whites and Hispanics, but they came almost entirely from English-speaking participants. Despite the presence of translators, the language had been going only from English to Spanish. Finally, a seventy-eight-year-old non-English speaking Latina stood up. Through a translator, she told the story of how she recently came to live with her children in this country, despite her desire to stay in Mexico. She made a plea for a Spanish mass so that she could "talk to God, because I must talk to God." She was unable to learn English at her age and felt cut off from the liturgy by the language barrier. Her account moved many of the participants in the room. One organizer cited that event as crucial for the institution of the Spanish mass.

Yet, for other leaders in the parish, language is a barrier to the search for commonalities that community requires. I frequently heard the story from parishes with new Hispanic immigrants that "if you can't talk to your neighbors, it's a real problem." One parishioner at Saint Nicholas explained that unless you talk to people and find out how they feel, you cannot overcome stereotypes that blockade the identification of common values. She felt the emphasis on culture creates competition between nationalities. In her own Polish family, culture is unifying within the family context. But at the community level, she asserts, commitment must be to extracultural goals, such as to school, to jobs, and to God. This reflects a style of moral integration that parish life as a center for the neighborhood still contains.

Working on a common project often builds unity because it provides opportunities for interaction between groups. Saint Nicholas began this by raising over $11,000 at their first Cinco de Mayo celebration, a national holiday important to Mexicans. It was a fund-raiser for an orphanage in Mexico, where the orphans themselves came to entertain in a professionally executed performance. Many people, including the majority whites who attended, called it a success. It was important in the effort to create commonalities in order to demonstrate that a joint white-Latino event could be financially successful and equitable, with no sliding scale in the price of admission. The two gatekeepers, one Latino, one white, ensured that all paid, whether or not they were poor immigrants. But the amount of money raised was only part of the motivation. It was as important to demonstrate that parish relationships, that is, community, are not free, and that sacrifices for the collective effort are required.

Church and Neighborhood

"Where are you going to run to?"—asked the leader of Saint Nicholas's seniors group as she described the choices some white parishioners made when immigrants of color began moving into the blocks surrounding hers. In the suburbs, houses cost over $100,000, she exclaimed. Who wanted a mortgage at her age? And if you were not able to drive, you would become a prisoner in your own home. And then, there are no sidewalks in the suburbs. And crime? Her nieces told her there was all kinds of crime in their suburbs.

A few blocks away, Saint Nicholas's Parish Council held their second "block meeting" to which they invited all residents, Catholic and non-Catholic. This strategy was used to create a personal connection with residents and was an invitation for them to become acquainted, hear about the parish, and bring up their issues. One Lutheran couple attending urged their neighbors to "stay together and not move out." Rather than asking, "Why not move, if you have the chance?" they asked, "Why do it?" But the latter alternative is seldom suggested to residents who are confronting racial and ethnic population diversity. The former alternative is all too clear.

Another resident commented that although the fear days of the 1970s and 1980s were over, it nevertheless "scares people when some blacks and Hispanics move in and don't keep up the house." The history of this scenario has only reinforced people's interpretations. "It's hard to always know the reasons why people move in this context," mused one of the lay leaders. "It's hard to put my finger on why—are they running from the graffiti, or is it time to move on because they are empty-nesters, or some other reason?"

The block meetings addressed what urban planners call "tipping points." How many individual decisions have to occur before the result appears as an inexorable ecological process? One associate pastor recounted how quickly change occurs. A particular block near the church had a *Saturday Evening Post* quality to it that he would often admire as he took his evening walk. But he got word that a couple of the families were hassled by gang members, and within days, a "forest of for-sale signs" went up. Gangs are a recent visible reality among the Sixty-third street neighborhoods and present a physical and psychological threat. Graffiti is often the first sign. Saint Nicholas's mothers club sponsored a talk by the Eighth Police District gang specialist on how to recognize and respond to gang presence in the neighborhood. The sergeant's talk was so detailed that several people noted out loud that they were more afraid after the meeting than before.

When an area is perceived to be undergoing racial and ethnic change, the visibility of certain otherwise benign and casual characteristics of neighborhood housing is more salient. Houses that are not "kept up" and lawns that are not mowed take on heightened significance with regard to the neighborhood's desirability and future possibility. The nonstandard condition of even one piece of property in the hands of new in-migrants seems a harbinger of change, pointing to inevitable loss of status. Chatting after the mothers club meeting described above, one elderly resident related to me her concerns about a Hispanic family next door who didn't take care of their lawn, while another Hispanic family nearby "is very nice." Despite the approval, her hope regarding the latter was tentative; "you never know when that might change." We can see in her language that she directly links physical upkeep of the house with moral worthiness. A family that cares for its property is also interpreted to be "very nice."

This resident's apprehensions have been formed and tested by the experience of change across the South Side—in South Shore, Pullman, Englewood, and West Englewood. A leader from the synagogue recounted the climate of fear that existed in her neighborhood during the 1960s and 1970s. Many of her neighbors had moved to the Southwest Side from the Southeast not long before and felt the same kind of transition was going to take place again. She knew that "if people didn't fly, property values wouldn't go down," but many people would not believe it and left anyway. Because she and her husband moved to the Southwest Side by choice, she felt they had a different attitude about it. Since they never felt "they had to move" from a previous location, they had not experienced loss or pressure. A pastor from a neighboring parish recalled the feeling of overwhelming inevitability in the process of change in Pullman-Roseland, where he served during the 1960s: "It felt like a tidal wave coming off the lake [Michigan] and eventually will roll over everything in its path."

In the end, people also move for greed, asserted Saint Nicholas's longtime deacon Frank Sullivan. Reasons for leaving the old neighborhood include the desire for a bigger house, a bigger yard, more shopping opportunities. Decisions such as these deliberately counter the American desire for community.[21] Instead, the deacon and his family "made a decision to put down roots, to belong here." The racial and ethnic succession he observed in the Southwest Side reminded him of his growing-up experience in North Lawndale on the West Side, which is an impoverished African American neighborhood today. The neighborhood had been mostly Irish, with some Jewish areas to the south, when suddenly there was an exodus of the Irish, and into the vacuum came the Italians. The deacon remembered the first Italian-Irish wedding announcement at the local church, which proved so disruptive that the couple had to be married at Holy Name Cathedral downtown.

A narrative strategy for crossing boundaries of race, ethnicity, and cultural practices is to ask the question Saint Nicholas's deacon asked: "What's going on with others?" This opens a discussion to the discovery of other people's cultural stories. Saint Nicholas provided the setting for such storytelling, though not all people participated in it. Cultural styles also vary. Some Hispanics' reticence and preference not to intrude can easily be interpreted as resistance and unwillingness to share responsibility.

Creating culture involves the negotiation of many details of daily life at a parish. Constant discussion of issues that might not seem significant to an outsider is a sign of the cultural process at work. In describing the new model of parish they are working to form, the chair of the Parish Pastoral Council at Saint Nicholas told me, "*Doing* is what we're used to." Holding events, raising money, belonging to parish organizations, some social, others pietistic—these have been the stuff of parish life, creating solidarity and marking off the symbolic territory that parishioners identified with. As part of the archdiocesan restructuring effort, Saint Nicholas is being asked to change its focus from more grounded and insular realities—parish-focused and directed by the priests—to the creation of new visions and goals, where laity decide together with the clergy what those might be. Thus the lay members' negotiation with new residents across the language and racial barriers, essential to the formation of community in the Southwest Side, has a new place in a more open parish structure.

The Southwest Organizing Project

The Southwest Organizing Project is a values-oriented community organization that aims to create meaningful cross-racial, cross-ethnic, cross-generational, and cross-religious relationships for the purpose of creating a viable urban community. The Organizing Project was a direct outgrowth of the Southwest Catholic Cluster Project, an arm of the Catholic parishes and the archdiocesan Office of Peace and Justice.

The Southwest Catholic Cluster Project was formed in 1988 when several clergy and lay members of area churches felt that what was missing from various community efforts to address racial tolerance and neighborhood stability was an organization that "would come at the things they were dealing with in the neighborhood from Gospel values." Several pastors and lay leaders who, during the 1970s and 1980s, had been working in their Southwest Side parishes on racial and ethnic community reconciliation had become exhausted by their individual efforts. With new support from the archdiocesan Office of Peace and Justice, the leaders were able to bring most of the parishes in the Southwest Cluster into the effort and develop a collaboration among them.

The first director described the most important issue facing the neighborhood to be a "sense of powerlessness." Racial and ethnic changes were beginning to occur, and residents needed a way to overcome their feelings of isolation and to discuss these issues from a larger geographic perspective. The project developed a coordinated, areawide program to respond to problems raised by real estate interests, transportation questions, and concern over housing values. Much of the original work of the Cluster Project was to address latent problems of perception and stimulate a dialogue among the residents. Several activities, such as an ethnic parade, a banner display on which parishioners expressed their hopes for the neighborhood, and written reflections in pamphlet form about Christian perspectives on neighborhood integration, addressed residents' needs to express their concerns and come to grips with the changing reality.

In 1995, several participants in the Cluster Project decided that a larger, more aggressive agenda was needed. Mobility in the neighborhood was high; concerns about safety, both realistic and exaggerated, were accelerating. At a strategic planning meeting to decide a course of action, a Pentecost prayer was invoked. The members prayed that they might be emboldened so that they could in turn embolden the church to take necessary action on behalf of their community. They determined that an ecumenical, church-based, values-based, community-organizing model was necessary.

A community organizer trained by the Industrial Areas Foundation (IAF)—the creation of activist Saul Alinsky, whose start was in the nearby Back of the Yards neighborhood—Jerome "Jay" Caponigro had grown up in a neighboring parish. As the new director of the project, he moved quickly to restructure the organization independent of the archdiocese, so as to more easily develop an interfaith base. The Organizing Project has been able to bring several Protestant churches and one of the mosques into active participation. The ethnic balance on the steering committee is evenly divided between Euro-American and Latino, lay and clergy, and male and female.

The project's methods of engagement include a new vocabulary, one centered on "power" and "one relationship at a time." The IAF strategy involves building relationships at the public institutional level; in the Southwest Side, this means primarily the faith-based organizations. Through one-on-one meetings with members of each of the congregations, the project is working to build a community identity around public and inclusive relationships where "trust" rather than "loyalty" is fostered. These relationships form the basis of accountability to one another, that is, a relational stance that helps to refocus on the neighborhood and on one's neighbors. Caponigro regards this as essentially a Christian notion, but one that empowers all participants to become civic actors. Political activity can, he asserts, be based on values, and "relational power is one of inclusion, not exclusion."

With a (cultural) predisposition toward loyalty to and preference for one's own parish, it is but a small step toward expressing that exclusivity against outsiders who are visibly different. But the making of "otherness" cannot be simply reduced to its expression as a racial category. The question is how to help people understand the social process of difference and boundary making, and which dimensions of difference and boundary making are more and less strong in each particular context, in order to permit residents to make changes in these long-standing patterns that they have always perceived as natural. The Southwest Organizing Project has given a voice to community residents who are committed to a religiously based understanding of community in a pluralistic society.

Fig. 5-3. A Southwest Organizing Project interracial outing. In the background are a Chicago bungalow and two-flat apartment buildings characteristic of Chicago's blue-collar neighborhoods. Photo courtesty of Southwest Organizing Project.

Conclusion

This chapter has focused on ways in which Southwest Side residents are shaping the moral culture of their parishes to embrace the pluralist realities of urban life. An understanding of moral culture and its relationship to community should be connected to the economic and policy forces that affect residents. This connection has been missing.

For example, it occurred that a white couple wanted to sell their Southwest Side home and were told by an area realtor that "they would have to lower the price because minorities were moving into the area." The realtor further offered, "You had no idea this was going to happen. Ten years ago this was a good neighborhood." Was this 1967? No, it was 1997, and the incident is cited in a lawsuit claiming federal Fair Housing Act violations.[22] To construct new urban community models that cross language, ethnic, and racial boundaries, favorable economic opportunities, effective political control, and a commitment to cultural work must exist simultaneously. A different kind of culture work can then build on

recognizing past mistakes as well as making visible heretofore underap-
preciated and underrecognized strengths.

The experience of the Southwest Side parishes demonstrates the value
of two recently developed concepts in the social sciences—the social and
cultural construction of ethnicity and the formation of race—fresh explanations for the changes in how Americans experience their relationships to others, especially their neighbors. This approach means we no
longer have to think of race and ethnicity as immutable, biological identities. Instead, we can observe how relationships between social groups
change as members come to understand their ethnic or racial heritage as
partial rather than total frameworks for who they are and for what they
make publicly accessible about themselves. It also means that other social
categories—class, power, education, language, and religion—can be examined in order to see the more inclusive influences in the construction
of racial and ethnic identities.

The Southwest Side has received notoriety in the annals of the civil
rights movement. After all, this is where Martin Luther King Jr. was hit
with a brick during an open housing march in 1966. But the Southwest
Side is not a single entity with a single culture, despite the activities that
led to such a public perception. Events of community change involve
processes of symbolic boundary making and remaking that help us ask
questions about what makes up the character of communities and how
the formation and character of boundaries are related to communal
identities in urban areas.[23] People at both parishes studied in this chapter
reported in various ways how they feel closer together in their "own
group" and can understand the urge to keep separate. At the same time,
they acknowledged the need to overcome the primordial urge to remain
with their in-group. To understand the continuing problems of racism in
the United States, we need to find out about the lives of people who experience the movements of integration and/or resegregation in their neighborhoods. As one pastor asserted, these residents are looking for new
urban models, just as did the members of Old Saint Patrick's Church in
the Loop (see chapter 9). They are looking for ways to combine religious
values and commitments with practical issues of neighborhoods.

The full story of change on the Southwest Side from the 1960s to the
1990s has not yet been told and is still unfolding in the twenty-first century. Much is at stake in those neighborhood changes, from housing eq-
uity and economic sustainability to social and cultural misunderstand-
ings about what neighborhood viability means and how to enforce the

moral norms required to achieve it.[24] In particular, a religious and moral understanding of neighborhood has not been sufficiently explored.[25] This is only a brief account, but it shows how the creation of a viable community involves both structural and cultural factors, a fair distribution of political and economic resources, and, especially, the successful negotiation of a moral order between new residents and old.

NOTES

Many thanks for helpful discussions and comments on earlier drafts are due to my Religion in Urban America Program colleagues and to Robert Aponte, Etan Diamond, Robert Lammers, Mary Mapes, Steve Warner, and Rhys Williams.

1. Suttles, *Social Construction of Communities*, 21–43.
2. Squires et al., *Chicago*, 5.
3. Cohen, *Symbolic Construction of Community*, 5.
4. Stout, "Place of Religion," 117.
5. Parot, *Polish Catholics in Chicago*, 225.
6. Ehrenhalt, *Lost City*.
7. Wuthnow, *Meaning and Moral Order*.
8. Pacyga, "Chicago's Ethnic Neighborhoods," 606.
9. Bellah et al., *Habits of the Heart*, 152–153.
10. See Wallwork, "Constructive Freudian Alternative"; and Harding, "Toward a Darkly Radiant Vision."
11. McGreevy, *Parish Boundaries*.
12. Sugrue, *Origins of the Urban Crisis*.
13. Ibid., 213.
14. Koenig, ed., *History of Parishes*, vol. 1, 153–156.
15. Sugrue, *Origins of the Urban Crisis*, 213.
16. Warner and Wittner, eds., *Gatherings in Diaspora*. See esp. McAlister, "Madonna of 115th Street Revisited," 147.
17. Cohen, *Symbolic Construction of Community*, 99.
18. Koenig, ed., *History of Parishes*, vol. 1, 659–662.
19. Dominic Pacyga. Comments at conference, "Religion and Community in a Restructuring Metropolis," University of Illinois at Chicago, June 5, 1995.
20. Cohen, *Symbolic Construction of Community*, 99.
21. Slater, *Pursuit of Loneliness*, 7–28.
22. Lydersen, "Lawsuits," 5.
23. Lamont and Fournier, eds., *Cultivating Differences*.
24. Rieder, *Canarsie*; McGreevy, *Parish Boundaries*.
25. Conzen et al., "Invention of Ethnicity"; McGreevy, *Parish Boundaries*.

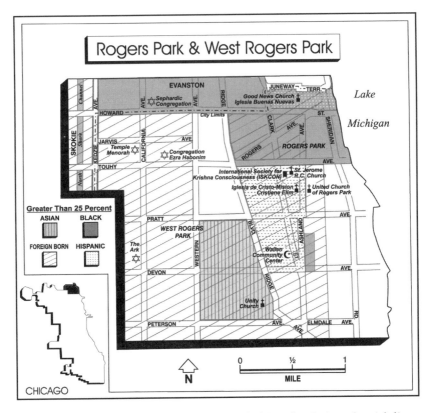

Map 6. The "Rogers Parks" represent much of Chicago's ethnic and racial diversity among their 125,000 people. Map by Brian Twardosz, BMT Printing and Cartographic Specialists.

Chapter 6

Communities and Enclaves
Where Jews, Christians, Hindus, and Muslims Share the Neighborhoods

Lowell W. Livezey

An afternoon walk along Devon Avenue on Chicago's Far North Side gives one a tangible sense of that abstract concept "social diversity." Devon offers a glimpse of the neighborhoods that make up the community areas of Rogers Park and West Ridge (known locally as West Rogers Park), which we discuss here together simply as "Rogers Parks." The area lies between Lake Michigan on the east and the North Shore Channel on the west at the northern boundary of the City of Chicago, about two and a half by two miles in size. Its total 1990 population of 125,000 showed a slight increase from ten years previous, a fact that could be claimed by very few Chicago neighborhoods. The positive population trend was due to a combination of immigration (34 percent of the residents are foreign born) and in-migration from other parts of the city (mostly blacks and Hispanics moving to a better neighborhood). The residents of these neighborhoods represent an extraordinarily wide range of the racial and ethnic groups, social and economic classes, and religious faiths of the Chicago metropolitan area. And because many small shops along Devon are operated by the local residents and cater to them, the street provides a colorful lens on the cultures of the people who live nearby.

Research by the Religion in Urban America Program from 1993 to 1998 provides the basis for my analysis of the religious dimension of local culture during that time. I argue that cultural innovation by religious organizations has encouraged the formation and maintenance of ethnoracial enclaves, which in turn characterize the diversity of Rogers Parks.

The walk eastward from Kedzie Avenue along Devon is a good way to enter the discussion. In the segment between Kedzie and California Avenues, which is officially designated Golda Meir Boulevard, Jewish residents can easily find most of the supplies needed for observance of the *halachah* (Jewish law) as interpreted by Orthodox rabbis. Here one can buy a wide variety of kosher groceries, choosing among alternatives that have been approved by different Jewish authorities determining what is kosher. And if there is any doubt about the requirements of observance, the *beth din* (rabbinic court) is nearby, not far from the *mikvah* (ritual bath) and the Kollel (a major center for adult religious study, which is visible in figure 6-1). Moreover, this part of Devon Avenue goes through an *eruv*, a geographic area constituted under Jewish law as the legal equivalent of the household—with the result that observant Jews can legally carry things on the Sabbath and on the High Holy Days.

Of the many Jewish institutions in Rogers Parks, we studied three in depth. Ezra Habonim is a Conservative congregation, the result of a merger of two German-speaking congregations. Although the older generations of its three hundred members are Germans and Austrians, it seeks to attract younger Jews of any nationality. The Sephardic Congregation is a community of about 250 Sephardic families who have come, either directly or by descent from immigrants earlier in this century, from the various Mediterranean countries in which the Spanish Jews settled. The congregation practices Orthodox observance, so most of its members live close enough to the synagogue to walk to services. Finally, we studied The Ark, a social service agency that follows *halachah* and conducts Shabbat services for staff, persons in their shelter, and many recent Jewish immigrants from Eastern Europe and the former Soviet Union.

The time was when the Jewish dominance of Devon Avenue extended much further east than the corner of California Avenue, but now the brown sign indicating the honorary street name shows the next segment to be Gandhi Marg, and the vegetarian groceries, South Asian spices, and silk saris set the tone. The religious symbolism of the community is not as obvious as on Golda Meir Boulevard, in part because Indian culture involves many different religions—Hinduism, Islam, Sikhism, Jainism, and Christianity. Moreover, the religious practices of Hinduism are not directly tied to neighborhood geography. Despite an Indian population of more than six thousand in Rogers Parks, with more in the immediately adjacent suburbs, there is only one Hindu temple here, organized and staffed by the International Society for Krishna Consciousness (widely known as Hare Krishna). In conducting our case study we learned that, although a few "new age," youthful Americans responded to Hare Krishna recruitment, the leadership and financial support for the temple come from Indian immigrants, mostly from Gujarat and Punjab, and that the temple is organized very much on the model of American congregations. Indian Christians also form American congregations, such as the First Telugu Methodist Church, which is hosted by the United Church of Rogers Park.

Continuing east on Devon, especially in the segment designated Mohammed Ali Jinnah Way, it is not uncommon to see meat markets and groceries with "Halal" signs indicating the availability of religiously approved foods for observant Muslims. Most Indian and Pakistani Muslims in Rogers Parks identify themselves as "Indo-Pakistanis," and they, along with a few Jordanians, Palestinians, Iranians, and Africans, constitute the membership of the five mosques located here. We studied one of these, the Al-Madina Islamic Center, just off Devon Avenue, where two hundred or more Muslim men of many nationalities gather for the jum'ah prayers early every Friday afternoon. But it is the Indo-Pakistanis—some speaking only Urdu, except for enough Arabic to say the prayers—who live in the rental apartments near the mosque, who support it and develop its programs and activities.

About halfway across Rogers Parks, Ridge Avenue marks a local watershed, and the terrain begins to slope gently downward toward Lake Michigan. Now the Mexican *taquerias* and restaurants become prominent and frequent, signaling the presence of Latino immigrants and transmigrants who live and work nearby. Those who participate in religious organizations mostly attend either Catholic parishes that offer the mass in Spanish or Spanish-speaking Protestant churches. We will see how Saint Jerome Roman Catholic Church organizes itself to include the Hispanic, Haitian, and white "American" Catholics living within its parish boundaries, just as in previous generations it struggled to make the Irish, German, Lithuanian, and Polish parishioners feel equally at home and spiritually nourished. We will also look at Misión Cristiana Elim, a Spanish-speaking Pentecostal church whose six hundred members have come from Mexico and Central America. And in the most economically impoverished part of Rogers Parks, "North of Howard," we find another of our case studies, the Good News Church/Iglesia Buenas Nuevas, a two hundred–member congregation of the United Church of Christ, with services in both Spanish and English.

Reaching the end of Devon Avenue, on the shore of Lake Michigan, we find the campus of Loyola, a major Jesuit university, with Saint Ignatius Roman Catholic Church not far away. These and the four other large Catholic parishes remind us that Rogers Parks is historically a "white ethnic" area, and the 1990 U.S. Census figures show that a majority still identify themselves as white.

As we can see, the diversity of Rogers Parks includes religion. By the Religion in Urban America Program's enumeration, in the years 1993–1998, the formally organized religious bodies that met regularly in a designated physical space in Rogers Parks included thirty Jewish congregations, twenty-seven Protestant churches, six mosques, five Roman Catholic parishes and the Croatian Catholic Mission, an Assyrian Catholic church, four Buddhist temples or meditation centers, a Hindu temple, a Sikh *gurdwārā*, and five or more new age meditation and worship centers. Of the Jewish congregations, twenty-one were Orthodox, three Traditional, four Conservative, one Reform, and one Lubavitcher. Of the Protestant churches, five represented mainline denominations, five were immigrant congregations associated with mainline denominations, and the remaining seventeen included Christian Science, Jehovah's Witnesses, and various Pentecostal, Evangelical, and sectarian groups—many with names indicating an ethnic or national identity.

Diversity and Controversy

Diversity is both touted evidence of American inclusiveness and a source of anxiety. At the neighborhood level, diversity often is feared as meaning that "outsiders" have arrived and will soon replace the previous population—which itself, in many cases, had replaced another population one or two generations earlier. In the first half of the twentieth century, the Chicago School of urban sociology developed theories of "invasion and succession"[1] to explain this phenomenon. Since the Second World War, the concept of "racial tipping"[2] has been used to explain and predict the point at which too much diversity will result in "white flight" and thus in the complete turnover of a neighborhood to a racially or ethnically different population. This is what David Daniels means, in chapter 7 of this book, by the "collapse of integration" in Chatham; it is how Pilsen (chapter 2) became a Mexican American neighborhood; and it is what happened in the Englewood neighborhood that so frightened the Southwest Side parishioners discussed in chapter 5. In this "city of neighborhoods,"[3] many all-white neighborhoods changed within a few years to all-black or all-Hispanic neighborhoods. And at any given time, those whose neighborhoods have recently become diverse may ask, "Will we be next?" In this respect, the Rogers Parks neighborhoods are in the same situation as those of the Southwest Side: despite significant differences (Rogers Parks does not lie next to a "color line" and a poverty ghetto), both areas exhibit a diversity that has the chance of being sustainable. In a twenty-two-city study sponsored by the U.S. Department of Housing and Urban Development, Rogers Park and the Southwest Side's Marquette Park were among the fourteen racially diverse neighborhoods selected as case studies with prospects for avoiding the pattern of tipping and white flight.[4] The study concluded that the capacity of a diverse neighborhood to be stable depends fundamentally on its quality of life, and this includes both economic and physical conditions and the values and attitudes fostered by community institutions. A study of Rogers Park conducted at Loyola University in 1993 reached similar conclusions and found that the residents valued the diversity—except that they feared the consequences of increasing poverty.[5]

Yet, for an area that was 99.5 percent white in 1960, the change has been substantial. By 1990 the population had changed from 0 to 14 percent Hispanic, from 0 to 13 percent Asian, from 0 to 15 percent black. Many of the 83,364 whites are foreign born—not only Jews and others coming from the former Soviet Union and Eastern Europe but also Arabs and nonblack Hispanics.[6] So, in light of the experience of other neighborhoods, the possibility of tipping and white flight cannot be easily dismissed.

Diversity is also controversial for more philosophical reasons. While the diversity of a neighborhood may be the consequence of market forces, attitudes toward it may result from beliefs about what it takes to have a good community and a good society. And the diversity of a particular neighborhood may result from the active creation of enclaves and boundaries, the articulation of rationales for separation, and competition for social benefits—what Iris Marion Young calls "the politics of difference."[7] Indeed, many of the religious organizations discussed in this chapter not only locate themselves in ethnoracial enclaves but help to shape them and to give them character.

The term *ethnoracial* is borrowed from David Hollinger's *Postethnic America*[8] in order to bridge the distinction between ethnicity and race, which, as socially constructed categories, are distinguishable but not separable in a fluid context such as Rogers Parks. In the late-twentieth-century American urban context, the metaphor *enclave* draws on its geopolitical roots but connotes a concentration of a subpopulation in an identifiable locale rather than a completely homogeneous population within fixed physical boundaries. While Rogers Parks is diverse, many of the microneighborhoods that make it up are much more ethnoracially concentrated, and that concentration is often fostered and defined by religious groups.

This tendency of diversity to be expressed as group self-identification and difference, often labeled "multiculturalism," is welcomed by many who perceive that the more homogeneous American culture of previous eras imposed itself on minority groups in ways that not only were unjust but that also erased the cultural enrichment of the whole society. From this perspective, some kind of politically self-conscious development of groups defined by separate identities would be necessary to prevent the conformist requirements of "coercive pluralism"—in Lawrence Fuchs's apt phrase[9]—imposed on blacks, Latinos, and immigrants as the price for participation in the wider society.

In opposition to this positive view of multiculturalism, public intellectuals such as Arthur Schlesinger Jr. were warning of "the disuniting of America," and Todd Gitlin could write nostalgically about the "twilight of common dreams,"[10] meaning that even the leftist aspirations were being fragmented by the conflicting claims of ethnic and racial groups. The American ideal of *e pluribus unum* is in danger, they said, because "the many" were identifying too much with their separate groups, rather than with the "one."

Historian David Hollinger, who agrees with the multiculturalist claims that racial and ethnic minorities have been subordinated and muscled into conformity with the norms of the dominant classes, nevertheless worries that the affirmation of separate subcultures actually undermines the social justice it seeks to promote. In *Postethnic America* he argues that the self-identification as separate groups common in the 1990s will ultimately contribute to further marginalization and loss of status of their members. There are many conflicting perspectives on multiculturalism. Minority groups' self-assertion in terms of their group identity will be viewed—positively by some and negatively by others—as fragmenting a presumably common, American culture.

Religious Congregations and Ethnoracial Enclaves

Religious organizations of all faiths produce and reproduce cultural forms that both incorporate and influence the ethnic and racial identities of their people.[11] This process defines and enforces both geographical and symbolic boundaries that distinguish the insider from the outsider, ethnically and racially as well as religiously. At the same time, these religious cultures express values and attitudes about the people, communities, and society beyond their boundaries.

Religiously defined ethnoracial enclaves are as old as the Jewish ghetto and the Catholic national parish, and many Protestant neighborhoods—such as the heavily Lutheran Swedish "Andersonville"[12] in Chicago—have had similar characteristics. But to have such enclaves within an extraordinarily diverse setting such as Rogers Parks, and in an era of highly contested multiculturalism, raises the question of whether and how they contribute to the livability and sustainability of the wider community. Of the nine congregations we examined as religious case studies in the Rogers Parks neighborhoods, seven function either as ethnoracial enclaves or as loose constellations of two or more such enclaves. Moreover, although one congregation, the United Church of Rogers Park, succeeds in its effort to be inclusive and diverse, even it is the host to the First Telugu Methodist Church, which functions as a Telugu-speaking, South Asian enclave. In this chapter we examine the internal dynamics of these enclaves and their relations with their neighborhoods.

The Jewish Community and the Neighborhood

Undoubtedly, the purest example of an ethnoracial enclave in Rogers Parks is the Jewish community. Like all ethnoracial enclaves in Rogers Parks, it shares space with many other ethnoracial and religious groups. But while the geographic space is not homogeneous or exclusive, the Jewish population is highly concentrated, and the cultural infrastructure is very dense. In a 1990 survey, more than twenty-six thousand people in 10,960 households in West Rogers Park identified themselves as Jewish. Included in these households were more than six thousand Jewish children and more than two thousand Jewish teenagers, 97 percent of whom lived with both parents. Levels of synagogue affiliation (56 percent), religious observance, and communal and civic involvement were far higher among West Rogers Park Jewish residents than among the overall Jewish population of metropolitan Chicago.[13] West Rogers Park is also the home of an extraordinary concentration of Jewish religious and cultural organizations, including a growing number of *shuls* (more than twenty-five), day schools, and social service agencies operated by and for Jews according to Jewish law and custom.[14]

The Jewish population's migration within the city is reflected in the founding of Congregation Ezra Habonim, created when Congregation Habonim moved from the South Side to join Congregation Ezra in the early 1970s. The Sephardic Congregation moved from the West Side and built its present synagogue in 1970; The Ark moved to West Rogers Park from the Albany Park neighborhood soon thereafter.

Congregation Ezra Habonim, affiliated with the Conservative branch of American Judaism, is a "Holocaust congregation" founded by refugees from Nazi Germany. As required in Ezra Habonim's bylaws, Kristallnacht, the day in 1938 when synagogues and Jewish-owned businesses were vandalized and destroyed en masse by Nazis and their supporters in Germany and Austria, is memorialized in a very moving service each year.

The intermingling of German identity with the refugee status of members has created a distinct character for this synagogue. These immigrants brought a frugal fiscal style that served them well as they struggled to start a new life in a foreign country without the benefit of public support. They bonded with one another as refugees, and the synagogue became their main social center as well as their place of worship.[15]

By the 1980s the congregation was experiencing fundamental changes, such as the aging of its founding generation; the migration of a large portion of the Jewish population, including some of its members, to the suburbs; the "social revolution" of the 1970s, with its appeal for greater equality and individual rights; and the somewhat countervailing trend within Conservative Judaism toward the reclaiming of deeper roots in Jewish tradition. Since the skills and interests of the younger generation were not the same as those of their forebears, the 1980s was inevitably a time of transition. The question of staying in West Rogers Park remained an underlying issue, but the immediate concerns were how to maintain a viable synagogue home for diverse members—no longer united by the German language and direct experience of the Holocaust—and how to educate their children in Judaism, the meaning and observance of which were being renegotiated.

Responses to these concerns reflect a combination of the immigrant/ refugee experience and the urban situation in which the members live. The congregation had been a "community of memory," whose "constitutive narrative" consisted decisively in retelling the Holocaust experience. As Robert Bellah notes, "A genuine community of memory will . . . tell painful stories of shared suffering that sometimes creates deeper identities than success."[16] Indeed, the Holocaust narrative was constitutive for Ezra Habonim during the very decades, prior to Israel's 1967 Six-Day War, about which Nathan Glazer wrote that he "could see no major impact of the Holocaust . . . on the internal life of American Jews."[17] So, just as the wider Jewish community was beginning to find Holocaust history to be a source of communal identity (the national Holocaust Museum being a concrete result), Ezra Habonim's members who actually experienced the Holocaust began to retire, move to retirement homes, and die. Thus the memory could be sustained only by deliberate measures such as the Kristallnacht services and the content of religious education programs.

During the 1990s, young families with children formed a strong element in the membership of Ezra Habonim. The school, run by a professional staff and a volunteer board, provides a comprehensive education in Jewish life and customs, law and liturgy, theology and ethics, and history and language. Classes begin for prekindergarten children and continue through the high school youth group, which meets with other youth groups from the city and suburbs. In addition to classes, attendance at Shabbat services is mandatory. Both the rabbi and the *hazzan* (cantor) teach regularly in the school in addition to tutoring bar and bat mitzvahs preparing for initiation into religious adulthood. Three youth groups complement and extend the work of the school.

The progressive cultural innovation within Judaism and the wider culture was reflected in the congregation's decision to become "egalitarian," calling women to the Torah and counting them in the *minyan* (the traditional minimum of ten adult males needed for communal prayers)—the first Conservative synagogue in the Chicago area to do so. A decade later, a female *hazzan* was hired. Women can, and some do, wear the *kippah*, the same head covering as men, and they wear the *tallith* (prayer shawl). These changes identified the congregation with the liberal side of the Conservative movement, yet the general trend toward traditional observance in Judaism[18] was present here as well. The congregation hired an Orthodox rabbi, who was a good fit with the services, with most prayers in Hebrew and much interactional and joint praying. The rabbi tolerated, while seeking to correct, the members' limitations in observance of the law and their lack of Jewish "literacy."

The congregation's philanthropy is directed both to members and to nonmember Jews. The first is through a specially constituted fund for persons in need called the Gemiluth Chesed, meaning "acts of loving kindness." The anonymity of this activity is in keeping with the Jewish injunction to conduct charity privately. Second, Ezra Habonim has been active in supporting Russian Jewish immigrants by providing space for English classes, free tuition at the Hebrew school, and free initial memberships to the synagogue. Most of the Russian families, however, drop their participation as soon as the free tuition and memberships run out.

By the mid-1990s, the major concern for Ezra Habonim was to decide about the congregation's location in the heart of the only remaining Jewish neighborhood in Chicago. With most Chicago-area Jews, especially the non-Orthodox, now living in suburbs, the congregation could have increased membership by moving to a suburban location, but it decided to remain on Touhy Avenue. They thought their distinct historical identity would contribute to a viable urban Jewish life, one in which Conservative Jews who value the tough cosmopolitanism and diversity of the city could find a religious community. And the congregation itself would benefit from the dense Jewish infrastructure without giving up the broader diversity of the city. They were proactive, deciding both to strengthen their internal programs, particularly in religious education, and to market their presence to the unaffiliated Jews, especially young people, who live in the Loop, Near North, and Far North Sides of the city. Although the congregation later divided, the part of the congregation that remained in Rogers Parks are the younger families who tend toward increasing religious observance. This strong Conservative congregation, rooted in but transcending the Holocaust identity, is committed to maintaining the current Jewish enclave in an urban rather than suburban setting.

The Sephardic Congregation's members are, by constitution, all Sephardic, though multinational and multilingual by custom and practice. Sephardim[19] are descendants of the Jews of Spain, who developed a distinct subculture as a suppressed minority before the Expulsion in 1492. Elements of that subculture are evident in the Sephardic Congregation, including special rituals and customs, variations in the prayers, the use of the Ladino language (parallel to the Askenazim's use of Yiddish) in conversation and Aramaic (as well as Hebrew) in scripture study, and certain foods (such as baked eggs and Mediterranean delicacies). Because the Sephardim dispersed widely after the Expulsion, they have come to Chicago from many countries—Italy, Greece, Turkey, Iran, Israel, Egypt, Yemen, Morocco, among others. Moreover, since some came to the Western Hemisphere with the early European explorers and colonists, they are now "natives," welcoming the new immigrants from Mediterranean countries. No single group predominates in this synagogue, so the religious services reflect an amalgam of several religious and cultural traditions.

All public activities follow the norms of Sephardic Orthodox practice as interpreted by the rabbi. Services are conducted daily, with the morning prayers (described in the introduction to this book) attended by a few men and the principal Shabbat service on Saturday morning by 150 or more men and women, including the very pious who live in the immediate neighborhood or walk a considerable distance in conformity with *halachah*. The three-hour Shabbat service is conducted entirely in Hebrew except for a short sermon and announcements and involves much participation in prayers and scripture readings. The men ceremoniously remove a Torah scroll from the ark and carry it around the sanctuary for worshipers to touch with their prayer shawls before it is placed on the *bimah* and read. Women, seated behind the *mehitza*, a half-height partition, reach through to touch the Torah scroll with their prayer books.

The education of families has two substantive dimensions: what it means to be Jewish and what it means to be Sephardic. Children's programs are conducted during Shabbat service and on Sundays, teaching Bible stories, Jewish ways of living, and the Hebrew language at an early age. But the main role of the synagogue is to urge families to study together at home so that children learn, through their parents' efforts, what it means to be both Jewish and Sephardic.

The congregation's charitable activities include its Special Fund, based in contributions at daily prayers. The fund is given to persons in need, but only those who have been vetted by Agudas Israel, a recognized organization of the Orthodox Jewish community. The congregation and its rabbi are strong supporters of The Ark (discussed below), which provides a full range of social services in accordance with Orthodox interpretation of Jewish law. Congregational support for the Chicago Jewish Federation/United Jewish Appeal promotes the well-being of the Jewish community in general and, to some extent, the wider public good.

The congregation is deeply involved with the American Sephardic Federation, a secular organization that has been a significant force in the assertion of Sephardic identity in America since World War II. Leaders of the congregation are also leaders of the federation at the regional and national levels. The federation holds meetings and programs at the synagogue, which are promoted by the congregation and function, in effect, as part of the congregation's educational program. One partnership between the two organizations was the "Shabboton," a weekend conference held in December 1993, which incorporated elements of spiritual retreat, ethnic education, and social outing. The prayers, rituals, and educational programs provide a kind of social glue that holds the people together as Jews and as Sephardim, despite tremendous differences among members in language and custom. Thus, this congregation represents both the Sephardic subpopulation within Judaism and religiously observant Jews who identify as Sephardim. It is a vibrant Jewish assembly that contributes to the vitality of the Jewish community, especially in West Rogers Park. But it also creates a distinct cultural niche within the Jewish Community that fosters the development of Sephardic identity and religious practice.

The Ark, occupying the large, beautifully renovated Seymour Persky Center only a few blocks from Ezra Habonim and Sephardic Congregation, offers itself as "the Torah's vehicle for sustaining individuals in time of crisis." It is a professional social service center, but one in which Jewish volunteers can both fulfill the Torah's *mitzvot* (commandments) and do *tzedakah* (charitable deeds). The boundaries and distinctions between the many constituencies and population groups that make up The Ark are intentionally and successfully blurred. It is like the biblical Noah's ark—Noah built the ark (providing both religious leadership and skilled labor), but he also needed it as much as anyone else. While staff are well-qualified professionals and most volunteers are securely situated people, The Ark recognizes that no one is completely secure from a "sea of troubles" and thus fosters an attitude of being in this "ark" together. At The

Ark, many of the people being assisted also serve as volunteers—some of them regularly, year after year—and it is believed that their acts of charity and service may be healing for them as well as for those they assist. Staff and volunteers often serve in the same or overlapping roles, and both interact with clients without obvious signs of status.

Staff, volunteers, and clients all embody the fabric of interrelationships between The Ark and the Jewish neighborhood of West Rogers Park. Clients can be referred for religious counseling to neighborhood rabbis, many of whom interact regularly with The Ark's staff members. The Kollel, the Chicago Rabbinical Council, the Jewish Council for Elderly, the Associated Talmud Torah, and many other Jewish agencies located within easy walking distance serve as a network of organizations, professionals, and volunteers who share responsibility with The Ark for the care and nurture of people in need. Thus, The Ark is one of the pillars of neighborhood life.

The Ark's name also recalls the Ark of the Covenant, and the agency is devoted to enabling Jews to live as observant Jews, individually and collectively, regardless of their means. All food distributed through the food pantry is kosher and is available not only to the hungry but also to those who might otherwise not have kosher food. This makes The Ark's program more expensive and resources harder to obtain than they would otherwise be. But the observance is connected with a holistic support system, including a synagogue on the premises, religious services conducted both at The Ark and at secular and Christian agencies that serve Jewish people, and schedules built around observance of *halachah* by staff, volunteers, and those assisted.

Congregation Ezra Habonim, the Sephardic Congregation, and The Ark all enact both their religious and their ethnic traditions in their collective practices, and they transmit the traditions to their children and to newcomers to the neighborhood. But these are not merely acts of transmittal; they are acts of cultural adaptation and innovation, informed by the experience and practice of current adult members' parents but adapted to the requirements and competing values of their present situations.

The collective activities of these organizations are intensely local, both presupposing and promoting a high concentration of Jewish residents and an intricate infrastructure of Jewish institutions in the central part of West Rogers Park. Insofar as the three organizations look beyond

Fig. 6-1. The Ark and the Chicago Community Kollel, an adult study center, are essential to the Jewish infrastructure of West Rogers Park, Chicago. Photo by Lowell W. Livezey.

themselves, it is to the wider Jewish community, not to the non-Jewish people of Rogers Parks or to the rest of the city. While their individual members may be quite worldly in other contexts, this was not evident in organizational practice. These Jewish organizations foster an enclave within West Rogers Park and smaller enclaves within that one, but they are defined by the concentration of the Jewish population and institutions, not by exclusion of or hostility toward others. The three organizations do not explicitly espouse "common dreams" (beyond the Jewish community), but neither do they "disunite America." Moreover, we witnessed three solid and solvent institutions, with well-maintained buildings, that actively encouraged residence in the neighborhood and offered tangible support for those who choose to live there. The two synagogues made deliberate decisions not to move out of the neighborhood, not only because of the benefits they received from being in this unique concentration of Jews but also because they would contribute to a stronger Jewish neighborhood, thus helping the city remain attractive to Jewish residents and, in turn, countering the suburban migration that is often part of white flight.

A Catholic Parish and Its Ethnoracial Enclaves

Saint Jerome is a large, hundred-year old Catholic church in the northeast portion of Rogers Parks. The church has six hundred registered families, mostly older and middle-aged white people who have lived in the parish for most of their lives. In addition, by the pastor's estimate, at least four hundred Spanish-speaking families attend mass regularly and participate in various parish activities but are not formally registered as members. Given the larger size of these families, Hispanics comprise a majority of the parish population. In addition, there are about one hundred Haitian families and a few African Americans, Filipinos, and Indians. The six Sunday masses draw more than two thousand worshipers, of whom two-thirds are Hispanic. The church operated a parish school until 1994, when it became a participant in the newly created North Side Catholic Academy, with campuses at other parishes.

Saint Jerome thus exemplifies the traditional territorial parish, which ministers to all baptized Catholics—and informally, to many others—living within its boundaries.[20] Like Saint Nicholas of Tolentine, discussed in chapter 5, its territorial constitution determines that it cannot be a single ethnoracial enclave, since multiple ethnic groups live within its boundaries. It continues to be a social center, as it was for Euro-American ethnic groups in the past, but it is a center that different ethnic groups "use" for their distinct social as well as spiritual purposes. In practice, in the late 1990s, Saint Jerome has formed three differentiated social groups, distinguished by both language and race, each constructing its distinctive culture. The fact that the pastor is trilingual enhances his efforts to provide pastoral leadership to the whole parish, but both the Spanish- and French-speaking groups have their own ordained staff (a priest and a deacon).

Saint Jerome addresses a few programs to the entire church and to the entire neighborhood. A special Easter Mass is conducted in English and Spanish, and the Centennial Mass was celebrated in 1994 in English, French, and Spanish. Each year, the parish attempts other bilingual and trilingual rituals. The annual Via Crucis, a ritual strongly associated with Mexican Catholicism, which Saint Jerome celebrates in response to advocacy by Mexicans, is conducted in English and French as well as Spanish in an effort to symbolize the unity of the diverse parish. This ritually realistic reenactment of Jesus carrying the cross to his own crucifixion helps build community solidarity. By their participation, neighbors of many ethnicities and races acknowledge the status of Saint Jerome Church in the community. As they collectively move through their neighborhood, ceremonially visiting local sites where serious crimes were committed, they call attention to the problem of community violence and their common stake in ending it.

The three Sunday masses in Spanish account for the majority of the attendance, and it is in these that the preponderance of worshipful energy is evident. The Spanish-language choir, singing to the accompaniment of stringed instruments, both expresses cultural themes familiar to the worshipers and enlists their participation in the mass and in the church. Some Hispanics have been parishioners as long as twenty years, and they help organize liturgies and celebrations in Mexican traditions—including the *posadas* during the season of Advent and the *mañanitas* for the Virgin of Guadalupe. The latter, a service of love songs to the Virgin, is devoid of the Mexican nationalism we observed at *mañanitas* in other Chicago communities (perhaps because the population here includes Cubans, Central Americans, and Puerto Ricans), but it is a spirited, energetic affair, and the church is packed with families having a wonderful time.

The Hispanic youth group, Esperanza Latina, attracts fifty or more young people (twelve to thirty years of age) to its weekly meetings, which offer a combination of education in Catholic teaching (the meaning of prayer, of sexuality, of obedience); planning of youth-initiated activities (a Palm Sunday drama to be performed during Mass); and socializing among themselves (a Valentine's Day party). Throughout the many activities youth are asked to think about alternatives, and to deliberate about differences among themselves. Their differences often represent degrees of assimilation to U.S. culture and varying levels of acceptance of Catholic teaching. Saint Jerome fosters the exploration of alternatives, to the extent, for example, of inviting a Mexican American couple who had lived together before their marriage to speak to the group about sexuality, marriage, and family. All discussions are in Spanish (even though most youth speak English well), thus both selecting and encouraging those who are inclined to preserve the cultural heritage of Mexico or of the other Spanish-speaking countries from which they or their parents have come. But young people unable or unwilling to speak Spanish simply do not have a youth program to participate in.

Hispanic Pentecostals

Spanish-speaking youth, and people of all ages, will also find warm welcome and a rich array of programs at the nearby Iglesia de Cristo–Misión Cristiana Elim, a growing Pentecostal church that acquired its large auditorium and educational plant from a Korean congregation in about 1990. Elim, as the church is locally known, is part of a network of Pentecostal churches that was founded in Guatemala and expanded through Central America and Mexico. Some of the six hundred members of Elim were part of the church in Guatemala or Mexico, but most have joined the church since their arrival in Chicago. By 1995 this congregation had started four mission churches, two in Illinois and two in Mexico, forming something of a transnational circuit.

Elim shares many characteristics of "Anglo" and black Pentecostal churches and of Catholic charismatics, including expressive worship styles, rock-style music, physical and emotional healing, speaking in tongues, and many "gifts of the Spirit." Like many such churches, it devotes a great deal of preaching, teaching, and counseling to the promotion and support of nuclear families. While the church has a conservative model of the "good" family, it helps its members find an approach to family life that will work for them in a new and strange environment—urban, North American, and culturally diverse. For example, a marriage retreat promotes negotiation and accommodation between spouses, qualifying the strict patriarchal principle of deference to the husband's authority characteristic of conservative Christian teachings. Similarly, while the Youth Discipleship program includes rather strict moral teaching about chastity until marriage, it also lovingly accepts the unmarried member who becomes pregnant, and it celebrates the birth with a baby shower.

Like Saint Jerome's Hispanic parishioners, Elim's members are living on a number of cultural boundaries—between Mexico and the United States, between traditional and modern, between Christian and secular. These churches offer their members some of the tools for dealing with life on these boundaries. By using the Spanish language only, each church creates a cultural enclave within which its members have a limited protection from the pressures of the new, the urban, the secular. But while each church offers its traditional teaching as moral armor to withstand these pressures, it also offers space within which people can selectively negotiate these boundaries for themselves.

Thus the enclaves are exclusive (of non-Spanish-speakers), but within them people prepare for resilient participation in the multicultural urban world. In contrast to residents of all-Hispanic neighborhoods (for example, Pilsen, discussed in chapter 2), the participants in these churches in Rogers Parks may have no other Hispanic cultural space—unless they join a Latino gang. Both churches know that, as far as youth are concerned, the gangs are their main competitors.

South Asian Muslims

The Al-Madina Islamic Center occupies the entire basement of a large apartment building on Wallen Avenue, not far from the corner of Devon and Clark. The entrance is visible only from the alley, but at the appointed hour for *jum'ah* prayers on Friday afternoons, as many as 250 men and boys can be found there, praying, listening to a short *khutbah* (sermon) in Arabic and to other speeches in Urdu, and then socializing among themselves. Many live or work nearby, but others have chosen this mosque as the place to fulfill their obligation to pray simply because they were in this vicinity at the time. Most of the men are Indo-Pakistanis, some dressed as American laborers and professionals, others in the tunics and hats worn in India and Pakistan. Others appear to be Arabs, Africans, African Americans, Caucasians.[21]

While the *jum'ah* prayer is the central liturgical event of the week— comparable to the Sunday mass or the Shabbat service—it provides only a glimpse of the mosque and its role in Rogers Parks. All the prescribed prayers are conducted—five times every day, according to the officially established lunar timetable. At 4 P.M. Monday through Thursday, neighborhood Muslim boys and girls, often rushing back by public transportation from selective magnet schools around the city, with an Urdu-speaking instructor for lessons in Arabic, the *Qur'an,* and the moral principles of Islam. During the summer, the children spend their days studying the same subjects under the direction of professional teachers whose first language is Arabic. The children's mothers and fathers come in and out, interacting with the teachers and with one another, helping to build a community devoted to making the Islamic way of life meaningful for the next generation of Indo-Pakistani immigrants. Teachers and parents alike encourage students to seize certain opportunities the city presents—to go to the best schools, get the best jobs, advance as far as possible. But a moral discipline must also be preserved: a conservative practice with respect to sexuality and family structure and a recognition of the mosque and the Islamic community as the appropriate source of moral authority.

Participation by parents, teachers, and the mosque's leadership in educational activities, as well as family gatherings for fast-breaking and other community meals, help constitute the mosque as a neighborhood social center for Indo-Pakistani Muslims. Thus, when the men gather to make the decisions about hiring part-time teachers and *imams* or about repairing the drains, they are shaping communal life in a small corner of Rogers Parks, not only the religious practices of those who come to study and pray.

Asian Indian Hindus

The Hare Krishna Temple on Lunt Avenue is the Chicago congregation of the International Society for Krishna Consciousness (ISKCON), which came to the United States from India in 1965.[22] ISKCON was a proselytizing Hindu movement that Westerners saw as a "new religious movement." However, during the 1980s, according to Raymond Williams,[23] and by our own observation in the mid-1990s, while the religious leaders were still primarily Western converts, the regular participants and reliable supporters were mainly Indian immigrants living in Rogers Parks or nearby suburbs.

The temple conducts the prescribed traditional Hindu worship services, offering food and saying prayers to the gods five times each day. The daily practice includes the 4:30 A.M. service, which is omitted by many of the other Hindu temples in the Chicago area, including some whose priests, unlike Hare Krishna's, are Indians. On weekends the temple adds services for the convenience of persons whose work week prevents their daily attendance. The largest of these is the Sunday evening service, which is followed by a meal that not only is strictly vegetarian but is technically what is left over from what the priests have prepared for the gods. Thus the meal has been made with meticulous attention to both cleanliness and taste. Several hundred people, mostly Indians, attend this service and the meal each week.

The temple's education program inculcates Krishna consciousness in the younger members and recent converts, with an emphasis on vegetarianism, nonviolence, avoidance of intoxication and illicit sex, and the regular chanting of the Hare Krishna mantra. The "Straight Talk" program addresses issues of concern to adolescents, including dating and sexual relations. Thus the temple assists Indian parents by conveying moral norms of Hindu and Indian culture. These norms are quite conservative, but since Hare Krishna is a proselytizing sect and interested Westerners often attend the meetings, the presenters attempt to be realistic about the opportunities and pressures of adolescent life in America.

This temple serves as both a cultural and a physical space in which Indian immigrants collectively invent their ethnoracial identities as Indian Americans. The Hindu rituals and the Vedic epics they dramatize identify the participants with India and with the moral values and communal customs of their origins. The predominance of the northern Indian Gujarati and Punjabi languages and customs tends to foster ethnic differentiation from other Indian Americans. For major festivals, these Indians may travel to a larger temple, perhaps a more ecumenical one such as the Hindu Temple of Greater Chicago (see chapter 10); but Hare Krishna on Lunt Avenue is a place they can conveniently gather weekly or even more often. These Indians are dispersed throughout much of Rogers Parks and the adjacent suburbs of Skokie and Evanston but are sufficiently concentrated to make use of a local house of worship. As a result, the temple reinforces the solidarity of Indians as neighbors, as north Indians, and as Hindus.

A Protestant "Parish"

United Church of Rogers Parks is a United Methodist congregation of about 250 members, occupying a large, aging building not far from Saint Jerome, Elim, and Hare Krishna. The regular attenders (no one seems to care much about membership) include English-speaking members of many of the ethnoracial groups of the area—white, African American, and Caribbean. While most of the attenders are middle-income professionals, many are poor, and some suffer from mental problems, alcoholism, and other dysfunctions. In addition, the Indians of the First Telugu Methodist Church, which uses separate space at United Church for its weekly services, participate occasionally in Sunday worship and other programs.

Fig. 6-2. The InSight Arts program for youth provides physically and culturally safe space at United Church of Rogers Park, Chicago. Photo courtesy of United Church of Rogers Park.

United Church is an exception to the pattern developed so far, because rather than building social solidarity on the basis of shared ethnic or racial identity, it attempts, with some success, to make inclusiveness itself a constitutive principle. The church identifies itself as a "safe space" for all, and this metaphor has several meanings. First, the Sunday morning worship service is multicultural, with a rather formal order of service holding together diverse rituals and with music drawn from various (Anglo) American, African American, African, and Caribbean traditions. Prayers and announcements invite concern for fellow human beings throughout the city, suburbs, and the world, often referring explicitly to the many ways in which they are different from the people of United Church and from one another. Worshipers who have trouble relating to the service or to other worshipers—those with mental disorders, for example—are assisted by others who have been trained and authorized to do so.

The InSight Arts program teaches performing and visual arts, but its "ministerial" purpose is to provide community youth a space that is safe from the streets (gang violence), from their homes (domestic violence),

Fig. 6-3. The Good News Church/Iglesia Buenas Nuevas is one church with two congregations—English- and Spanish-speaking—in the North of Howard community, Rogers Park, Chicago. Photo by Paul D. Numrich.

and from social control (artistic censorship). The Children's Learning Center (preschool and aft r school), the Community House (drop-in center), the Community F weekly soup k en), and the Mountain Moving Coffee House (; n organization) all provide security not only from physical harm but from social degradation and personal disrespect. Access to some of these groups is restricted—one must be obey the rules of respect to stay in InSight Arts, and one must be a lesbian or a lesbian's daughter to go to the Coffee House–but they are deliberately inclusive with respect to race and ethnicity.

United Church is widely known to teach a distinct sense of moral responsibility—to respect, include, and care for others—and also to teach that this respect means permitting others to make their own moral choices. In contrast to most of the immigrant congregations we have discussed, the moral culture of United Church fosters conscientious individual choice more than the moral discipline of the community. It is a decidedly liberal congregation that even in its internal life affirms only enough rules to ensure that individuals are safe and that groups can run their own affairs without interference. Thus, while the church prides itself on being inclusive and on sharing and caring among different groups, it is successful in these objectives in part by ensuring the inviolability of separate cultural, and usually physical, spaces. Except for the Telugu congregation, these spaces are not ethnoracial enclaves, but they are groups in which persons, both individually and socially, define their identities for themselves.

A Church in Mission

The Good News Church/Iglesia Buenas Nuevas began as a "house church" and then a storefront church in North of Howard, a very poor section of Rogers Parks. It was a creation of socially and spiritually committed individuals from educational institutions in the adjacent suburb of Evanston. In 1991 it merged with a Hispanic storefront church, and the joint congregation began worshiping together monthly while maintaining separate weekly worship services and prayer and Bible-study meetings. The joint congregation also sponsors a soup kitchen that serves more than one hundred people from the immediate neighborhood every day, with the assistance of suburban congregations that supply food, funds, and volunteers.

Like United Church, Good News is a "mainline Protestant" church (a congregation of the United Church of Christ), and it shares the commitment of service to the people of the neighborhood. Although it has both Spanish-speaking and English-speaking ministers, it works to hold worshipers together in a single congregation through joint activities, a single governing board, and, most important, a common commitment to community service. In some ways this approach may be compared with the distinct services of the three language groups at Saint Jerome; but Good News Church is much smaller than the Catholic parish, and the two language groups have less to do apart from the whole, so that it seems to function much more as a single spiritual community. And while the comparison with United Church is evident in its service orientation and its inclusiveness, Good News has no single, inclusive worship service to project a symbolic unity.

But there is a unity that is both symbolic and practical, and it is to be found in the service to the North of Howard section of Rogers Parks—a section that is almost entirely black and Hispanic and that is the most economically impoverished in the Rogers Parks area. Although a few members come from outside North of Howard, and although suburban churches provide volunteers and financial support, North of Howard defines the congregation as a community.

Religion and Rogers Parks' Ethnoracial Enclaves

Our walk along Devon Avenue showed the ethnoracial diversity of Rogers Parks, but as soon as we left Devon and focused on religious congregations, we found most of them to be much more homogeneous than the neighborhood as a whole, and those that were not homogeneous created distinctive subgroups that were. This looked like a multifaith variant on the aphorism that "eleven o'clock Sunday morning is the most segregated hour of the week," as the new immigrant religions repeated the ethnoracial clustering long characteristic of Protestants, Catholics, and Jews. Moreover, with the exception of United Church, the rituals and activities of each congregation gave symbolic expression to a "we" that was defined not only religiously but ethnoracially. And even United Church, like two of the other four mainline Protestant churches in Rogers Parks, hosted a congregation (Telugu Methodist) that is constituted on an ethnoracial basis.

At a time when the cultural melting pot is being replaced by a mosaic, and when Nathan Glazer confirms that "we are all multiculturalists now,"[24] the simple fact that an apparent majority of congregations actively contribute to the construction of ethnoracial identities is unremarkable. But the content of those identities, the cultural and moral values they embody, may affect how they interface with the neighborhood, the city, and the wider society. As the research on diverse neighborhoods cited earlier makes clear, the sustainability of such neighborhoods depends in part on the ways in which their diversity is interpreted by the residents and on the investment of residents' organizations and local institutions.

With the nonwhite population of Rogers Parks increasing to more than one-third in 1990, and with some census tracts as high as 40 percent Hispanic, 35 percent black, and 27 percent Asian, the area qualifies as a candidate for racial tipping and white flight.[25] Moreover, we found no congregations publicly promoting or defending the racial integration of the area, although United Church, Good News, and Saint Jerome are inclusive organizations. For these congregations of Rogers Parks, diversity is simply a fact of life.

Yet all the congregations have made commitments that add incentives for their members to remain as residents in Rogers Parks. The synagogues and The Ark help maintain a religious and ethnic infrastructure that would be hard to duplicate elsewhere (because it presupposes a geographic concentration of Jews) and thus provide a compelling reason for twenty-six thousand Jews to remain in the neighborhood. Saint Jerome, United Church, and Good News, which represent predominantly white Christian denominations, not only maintain facilities in the neighborhood and offer services to all but also involve their white members in providing those services. The youth programs, which were offered by all the organizations we studied, stabilize the community in two ways. First, parents who might otherwise move to the suburbs to find the support they need for the religious education of their youth have a Jewish, Catholic, Pentecostal, liberal Protestant, Hindu, or Muslim youth group where they now live. Second, the religious groups provide alternatives to illegal youth activities, especially gangs, possibly reducing the danger of tipping by reducing the fear of crime.

These modest positives may be either magnified or eclipsed, however, by the cultural construction of the "we" of these religious groups, the "they" who are not included, and the boundaries between the two. Far from having negative attitudes toward outsiders, these groups are primarily concerned with themselves, apparently feeling it unnecessary to actively distinguish themselves from other ethnoracial groups. Sephardic Jews might take note of their differences from Ashkenazim; German and Austrian Jews might be concerned about Russian immigrants' lack of religious literacy; and Muslims from India might define themselves as Indo-Pakistanis, thus distinguishing themselves from "Indians" and their presumably Hindu culture. Both Pentecostal and Catholic Hispanic youth defined terms of solidarity that excluded the violence, drugs, illicit sex, and *machismo* of the (Latino) gangs. But these are all boundaries within ethnoracial groups, not between them.

But do these organizations do anything positive to promote what they have in common, to build one neighborhood, one community, one American society? They clearly express a kind of American multiculturalism, each ensuring through rituals and education that its particular group will know and value what it means, *within* American society, to be, for example, Jewish, Sephardic Jewish, and Moroccan Sephardic Jewish; to be Muslim and Indo-Pakistani Muslim; to be Catholic, Hispanic, and Mexican Catholic; and so on. But do these congregations dream "common dreams," that is, American dreams? Or, by failing to do so, do they "disunite" America? David Hollinger's distinction between a pluralist and a cosmopolitan multiculturalism[26] is helpful at this point. Whereas both forms share the idea that America should be hospitable to a diversity of ethnoracially specific cultures, pluralist multiculturalism tends to "depict society as an expanse of internally homogeneous and analogically structured units, each possessed of a comparable myth of diaspora." In contrast, the cosmopolitan form shows greater consciousness of the voluntariness of individuals' affiliation with the group and of each group's dynamic interrelationships with more embracing communities, including the neighborhood, city, and America as a whole.

In Hollinger's terms, the organizations described in this chapter are more pluralist than cosmopolitan. Their programs and discourse include relatively little about "America as a whole," about American public life and culture, or about Chicago and the neighborhoods of Rogers Parks. Even the fact that these neighborhoods, because of their diversity and tolerance, include all these groups, without any of them appearing conspicuous, is taken for granted. Our research revealed no programs of education about the other religions and ethnoracial groups in the neighborhood, no intergroup visits or exchanges of musicians or instructors. An interfaith Thanksgiving service—a holdover from a period of much less diversity—was the only joint project during the time of our research. (Since then, an interfaith antihunger project has been developed, and an interfaith agency, the Council for a Parliament of the World's Religions, has organized interfaith dialogues.) United Church, and to a lesser extent, Good News and Saint Jerome, embody a cosmopolitan vision by including multiple ethnoracial groups in the same congregation and by symbolically expressing the unity of different groups through worship, education, and, in the case of Saint Jerome, through the doctrine of the inclusive territorial parish. But as we have seen, even the most cosmopolitan groups achieve their unity by creating separate enclaves in which groups differentiate themselves by race, ethnicity, language, ideology, and sexual orientation.

Yet within the religiously based ethnoracial enclaves we have seen cultural formation that, however differentiated from the wider society, is what much of the wider society claims to want. These groups are building their capacities of moral discourse, forming themselves as morally self-conscious and mutually accountable communities. More ethnically differentiated groups may be, or are trying to be, "communities of memory," constructing shared narratives based on common experiences and using inherited cultural material that they select and adapt according to the criteria of their religious traditions. The United Church, Good News, and Saint Jerome (when it acts as a whole) are ethnically diverse and thus depend more on theological and ideological principles than on shared narrative as a basis for moral formation. Nevertheless, we found all the congregations calling their members to accountability for their relationships and participation in community. If these groups did not, for the most part, define or "socially construct" the wider communities, neither did they allow the individual members to think they were sufficient unto themselves.

Rogers Parks has a variety of enclaves for the variety of people who live there. It appeals to people looking for cosmopolitan urbanity, a dense street life, but not the sort that is conceded to toughs. The area is accessible to families as well as singles. It is attractive to people who want more independence and personal freedom than a family neighborhood in the suburbs or some other parts of the city offer. Its enclaves are real, but they are not ghettos. And while the religious organizations help create and perpetuate the enclaves, they also help ensure that they are defined by the concentration and cultural self-identification of similar people, not by the exclusion or subordination of others.

NOTES

1. Park and Burgess, *The City*.

2. Taub, Taylor, and Dunham, *Paths of Neighborhood Change*, especially chap. 7.

3. Pacyga and Skerritt, *Chicago*.

4. "Racially and Ethnically Diverse Urban Neighborhoods," 23–24 and 131–160.

5. Gronbjerg et al., *Rogers Park*.

6. Chicago Fact Book Consortium, *Local Community Fact Book*, 1980 and 1990, which report U.S. Census data.

7. Young, *Justice and the Politics of Difference*.

8. Hollinger, *Postethnic America*.

9. Fuchs, *American Kaleidoscope*, 77–79.

10. Schlesinger, *Disuniting of America*; Gitlin, *Twilight of Common Dreams*.

11. For discussion of the cultural production of religion, see Wuthnow, *Producing the Sacred*; on cultural production of race and ethnicity, see Omi and Winant, *Racial Formation*.

12. Pacyga and Skerrett, *Chicago*, 146–47.

13. Jewish Federation of Metropolitan Chicago, "Fact Sheet" based on the federation's 1990 study, Chicago, 1992.

14. For the historical context and description, see Cutler, *Jews of Chicago*, esp. 249–254.

15. Sklare, "Conservative Movement," points out that the Conservative movement pioneered the "synagogue center," which offered social and recreational activities.

16. Bellah et al., *Habits of the Heart*, 152–153.

17. Glazer, *American Judaism*, 172; see also 183–186.

18. Danzger, *Returning to Tradition*; Glazer, *American Judaism*, introduction, offers a more qualified view.

19. Cohen and Peck, *Sephardim in the Americas*, especially part 3. On the Sephardim in Chicago, see Cutler, *Jews of Chicago*, 90, 196; and Zenner, "Chicago's Sephardim."

20. On the traditional parish in racially changing contexts, see McGreevy, *Parish Boundaries*.

21. For an enumeration of mosques and their ethnic concentrations in the

Chicago area, see Numrich, "Facing Northeast"; on Muslim immigrants generally, see Haddad, ed., *Muslims of America*.

22. Williams, *Religions of Immigrants*, 129–137 and 234.

23. Ibid., 234.

24. Glazer, *We Are All Multiculturalists Now*.

25. Taub, Taylor, and Durham, *Paths of Neighborhood Change*, 142.

26. Hollinger, *Postethnic America*, introduction and chap. 4. Following quote from p. 12.

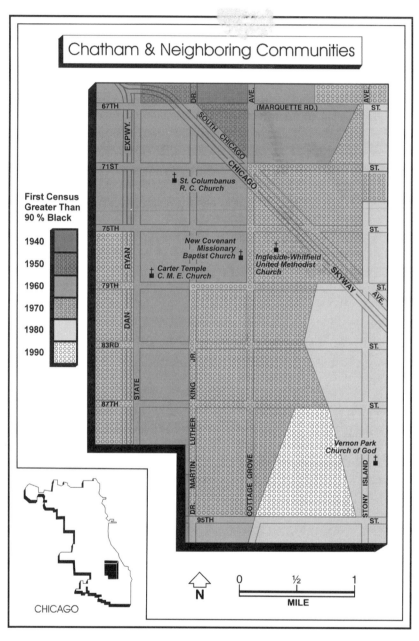

Map 7. Chatham, a comfortable middle-class neighborhood, has been formed by a fifty-year process of racial integration and resegregation. Map by Brian Twardosz, BMT Printing and Cartographic Specialists.

Chapter 7

"Ain't Gonna Let Nobody Turn Me 'Round"
The Politics of Race and the New Black Middle-Class Religion

David D. Daniels III

The brilliance of the new black middle-class religion is exemplified in its combination of various elements that have created a new religious moment in the Black Church. Annual concerts of Handel's *Messiah* and the choral performances of Bach anthems and Negro spirituals join an extensive repertoire in contemporary gospel music. The artful compositions of Edwin Hawkins and Richard Smallwood intermingle with the hard-hitting sounds of composers John P. Kee and Mattie Moss Clark. New black middle-class congregations delight in the diversity of music, applauding the talents and virtuosity of the musicians and vocalists. Although a Methodist, Roman Catholic, or Pentecostal liturgy orders the Sunday morning worship, the congregation seizes liturgical space to offer spontaneous refrains such as "Amen" and "Thank you, Jesus." With black depictions of biblical characters gracing the Sunday worship bulletin and with rites-of-passage programs in the youth ministry, these congregations embrace an Afrocentric Christian orientation. They also strive to connect their Sunday morning worship of God to their weekday service to the community. The diversity of cultural styles that these congregations intertwine each week—from European classical anthems to African American gospel music, Protestant and Catholic liturgies to Afrocentric events, and Sunday worship to community service—reflects the distinctive manner of the new black middle-class religion.[1]

A prime example of the new black middle-class religion is Carter Temple Christian Methodist Episcopal (CME) Church, which is in Chicago's black middle-class neighborhood of Chatham. Carter Temple locates African Americans in the lineage of kings and queens of Africa, not of slaves of white plantation owners. It offers the model of the church as an African village, where people share responsibility for rearing children, regardless of whether the child's father is around, and where men take up their rightful obligations—even if the world around them, including most of the churches, is caught up in "Eurocentric individualism." Carter Temple provides a new, positive symbolic context for elements of African American culture (the extended family, intergenerational respect, even the village life of the American South) and of the structure and traditions of the CME Church (the ministry of stewards to members). Rituals (rites of passage, black male role celebrations, African festivals), symbols (kente cloth, black liberation colors), and new Afrocentric scholarship all are woven into a new collective self-image.

Carter Temple's ministry affirms the humanity of African Americans and recognizes their peoplehood. The congregation joins the battle against the denigration of African Americans in the media, literature, and films by promoting positive images of African American people and life. At Carter Temple, African Americans are taught to respect and love themselves as a people through learning about the contributions of Africans and African Americans in history, the arts, and sciences. The cultural heritage emphasis at Carter Temple serves various functions: it counters the claims that Christianity is a "white man's religion," offers a corrective to the biased Eurocentric interpretation and representation of Christianity and world history, and provides African Americans with information that increases knowledge of their heritage.

Afrocentricity redefines the African American cultural heritage and perspective that Carter Temple expresses. As a worldview, Afrocentricity construes reality from the perspective of the peoples of Africa, both in Africa and in the diaspora. Ethicist Robert Franklin contends that Afrocentricity as a cultural approach "seeks to celebrate the halcyon days of the African past and to affirm black identity in the present through cultural displays." Within the framework of Afrocentricity, black social pathologies are sometimes defined as the products of the African American embrace of Eurocentric values and individualistic culture. To cure the social pathologies in the black community, adherents to the Afrocentric worldview maintain that African Americans need to embrace historical black and African communal values. Thus Afrocentricity offers healing and restoration to the black community, and a Christian Afrocentricity offers salvation.[2] At Carter Temple, sermons juxtapose the individualistic character of American materialism against the communal character of African culture, a communalism in line with Christian virtues.

Afrocentricity frames Carter Temple's engagement of racial politics as the struggle for a liberating construction of African American identity within the sociopolitical context defined by white racism. It inverts the hierarchy of cultural values in the production of racial identity from the best of western culture to the best of African and African American culture. According to philosopher Molefi Asante, "The music and dance of the church may be the essence of our Africanity."[3] Now Africa, not Europe, is the measuring rod of civilization, of the cultural best. Carter Temple, for instance, intentionally valorizes Africa and constructively reappropriates African American folk culture embodied in the mores and customs of the black poor and working class. This leads to a positive reevaluation of the black stereotype that is based in the culture of the black poor. Previously, the black middle class had constructed its identity in contradistinction to the poor and its folk culture; now Carter Temple participates in the construction of black identity utilizing the culture of the poor, especially the folk culture of the poor. The new racial identity encourages cultural and moral identification with the poor, in a rejection of the white American cultural norm. The embrace of features of the stereotype of blacks has facilitated the construction of a common identity stemming from a common history of oppression and achievement, common heritage, and common destiny.[4]

Carter Temple challenges Eurocentric individualism through a number of its various ministries. Especially connected to nurturing an Afrocentric communalism are its Save Our Sons, Project Essence, One-Church-One-School, and Boys to Men conferences. The One-Church-One-School ministry, for instance, links Carter Temple to nearby Ruggles Elementary School, which serves many at-risk children and youth. In each of these ministries, one of the goals is to build the self-esteem of the youth so that they can develop into mature, responsible adults and reject destructive behavior such as gang involvement. These ministries play a double role of strengthening the congregational and neighborhood life.

A distinctive element of Carter Temple's Afrocentricity is its identification with and commitment to the African American community as a whole, including explicitly its more disadvantaged members. Carter Temple strives to define community across class lines; they have formed a partnership with the Olive Branch, a South Side homeless shelter, and

Fig. 7-1. The Lord's Supper is part of the Afrocentric art at Carter Temple CME Church, Chatham area, Chicago. Paintings and stained glass depicting white biblical characters have been removed. Photo by Lowell W. Livezey.

hold a "Come as You Are" Saturday worship service, designed to make the homeless feel comfortable. The congregation aggressively promotes a black male emphasis. In their attempt to "reclaim" the black male, they have stressed patriarchical roles for men and supporting roles for black women. They have also reached out to the prison population, which is predominantly male, in order to include these individuals in the reclaiming endeavor.

The symbolic and stylistic innovations, most obvious in worship, cohere with attempts to broaden the constituency of the church and bridge barriers of class, for example, through inclusion of at-risk children and youth in the Carter Temple family and through the new Saturday "Come as You Are" worship service. This cohesion is effected in part by the incorporation of particular styles of preaching (including escalating, rhythmic intonations known as "hooping") and music (gospel, percussion, rhythm) and "expressiveness" into a setting where inspirational preaching, note-perfect singing, and "sweet hour of prayer" quietness might have been expected—and are still preserved as part of the new mix. The church also sponsors extensive programs in Christian education and mutual support that strengthen the communal life of Carter Temple.

Carter Temple's challenge to Eurocentric individualism spurs its project to redefine community, especially black community. The Afrocentric symbolization at Carter Temple represents only part of a deeper shift in the style of worship and collective identity in what has been a thoroughly middle-class congregation in a denomination identified with the black middle class. The Afrocentricity loosens the grip of the older black middle-class culture, especially the religious dimension of that culture, that critics such as E. Franklin Frazier challenged for its social stratification and paternalistic attitude toward the poor. Carter Temple thus moves away from what might be called the "old black middle-class religion" of its past and, with its particular racial politics, contributes to the construction of a new black middle-class religion.

Diversity within Black Middle-Class Religion

This chapter examines Carter Temple and four other congregations located in the central part of Chicago's South Side, an area we shall call Chatham, although it includes the official community areas not only of Chatham but of Greater Grand Crossing and Avalon Park as well. "Chatham" begins about nine miles south of Chicago's central business district and extends from Sixty-seventh to Ninety-fifth Streets and from the Dan Ryan Expressway to Stony Island Avenue. Politically, this area includes most of the Sixth Ward—long a stronghold of the black component of Chicago's "Regular Democratic Organization"—as well as the western half of the Eighth Ward and a corner of the Fifth. During the midtwentieth century, this area switched from a white to an "integrated" to, finally, an African American community. We call this entire area Chatham, because, as a symbol of the black middle class, the image of Chatham dominates the area. The five congregations discussed in this chapter either moved to Chatham during the 1950s or 1960s or, already located there, became majority African American congregations during the 1960s.

In the 1950s the racial politics of the old black middle-class religion inspired many middle-class African Americans to participate in the integration of Chatham. They were pursuing the American dream of home ownership and the African American dream of integration. The dream of integration, however, faded in the wake of white flight. Chatham, which had virtually no blacks in 1950, saw an increase to 64 percent by 1960 and 98 percent by 1970, along with a significant increase in the total population as black people purchased vacant land and built new homes. Thus, by 1960, Chatham had become established as the preferred area among very limited options for Chicago's relatively affluent black people. William Braden, a respected columnist for the *Chicago Sun-Times*, wrote in 1986 that "Chatham is a bastion of Chicago's black middle class . . . represent[ing] perhaps the largest concentration of middle class blacks in America outside of Harlem and Atlanta."[5]

Chatham is part of Chicago's larger black community and a product of African American integrationists' goals, which spurred the African American relocation into white neighborhoods. Blacks moved into the area in large numbers during the 1950s. The earlier black community, from which African Americans relocated, had been mainly a narrow north-south strip from the Loop to Forty-seventh Street. The area eventually extended to Sixty-seventh Street, due in part to the housing shortages that resulted from the "urban renewal" and "slum clearance" of portions of the pre–World War II area. Urban renewal replaced black people's apartment buildings with Michael Reese Hospital, Illinois Institute of Technology, and the upscale housing of Lake Meadows and Prairie Shores. Restrictive covenants, "white only" home-owner agreements, confined African Americans to particular neighborhoods. The residential boundaries, edging south of Sixty-seventh Street during 1949, expanded through a process of competition for space that was motivated in part by white violence as well as white commercial and political interests. In effect, Chatham became a community where African Americans who possessed the financial resources to purchase or rent housing could integrate, however briefly.[6]

Although the flight of white residents and congregations undermined the integration of Chatham and produced the resegregation of African Americans, a number of factors permitted Chatham to become a vital black middle-class community. The new black residents had the financial resources, the leadership skills, the cultural resources, and the social networks to build and maintain a solid community. Moreover, Chicago's industrial sector was still strong and provided a high concentration of well-paying jobs on the South Side—within an easy commute of Chatham.

African American congregations were at the center of the integration and, later, of the new black middle-class community of Chatham. This chapter contends that the new black middle-class religion, which is represented by three of the five congregations discussed here, signals a shift in the religious culture constructed by African Americans as a response to the reordering of African American society during the 1960s. Sociologist C. Eric Lincoln helps set the stage for our discussion of the new black middle-class religion. In *The Black Church since Frazier,*[7] he contends that during the 1960s a transformation of the Black Church occurred. The pre-1967 Black Church, which has been examined and critiqued in classics such as E. Franklin Frazier's *The Negro Church in America,* collapsed, and a new Black Church emerged. Frazier had been concerned with what I now call the old black middle-class religion. According to Frazier, racial discrimination and segregation defined the social context of the pre-1967 Black Church, which, under segregation, had become a place for African Americans to accommodate to their second-class citizenship. For Frazier, urbanization, social disintegration, social stratification, secularization, and desegregation, especially in the North, marked the twentieth-century Black Church of the pre–Civil Rights era. His project was to distinguish the new social context of the mid-twentieth-century Black Church from the rural location, traditional social organization, predominantly uniform class identification, religious worldview, disfranchisement, and segregation of the post-Reconstruction Negro Church.[8]

Central to Frazier's analysis was the process of achieving status among the black middle class. Two routes to status were occupational and cultural performance. Cultural performance was a vital means to achieving status. The theorists of the old black middle-class religion participated in the designing of a new African American identity. Their cultural production was defined in terms of elite western culture, rejecting African American folk culture and identifying with European and Euro-American elite cultural expressions. The racial politics of old black middle-class church confronted the ideology of African American inferiority through the creative mastery of elite western culture, debunking this debilitating ideology by successfully competing with white Americans on their cultural terrain.[9]

Frazier died before he had the opportunity to witness the change occurring in many black middle-class churches during the 1960s. The theorists of the new black middle-class religion, both reflecting and promoting these changes, rejected the ideology of African American inferiority outright and refused to privilege elite western culture. They preached liberation from white cultural, theological, and intellectual categories and called for the celebration of all things African and African American. This is not to say that they invented black political activism, which began in Chicago, for instance, at the advent of the twentieth century with the pastorates of African Methodist Episcopal Archibald J. Carey Sr. and Baptist Elijah J. Fisher. But the theorists of the 1960s disagreed with the old black middle-class religion about the role of black folk culture in their religion. The contest produced a shift in African American religious culture. Some scholars described the cultural shift as the "birth of a new 'black being.'" Others characterized the shift as a psychological revolution, the overthrow of "the rule of white men in our [African American] minds." The old black middle-class religion, then, operated in a social world dominated by western or Eurocentric cultural values that the theorists of new black middle-class religion supplanted with their own creation.[10]

The five congregations presented in this chapter all existed during the heyday of the old black middle-class religion. They now represent different constituencies within the Black Church. Two congregations are members of historically black denominations, the Christian Methodist Episcopal Church and the National Baptist Convention of America, respectively. The other three congregations are members of predominantly white denominations: the Roman Catholic Church, the Church of God (Anderson, Indiana), and the United Methodist Church (UMC). Three of the congregations were founded by African Americans; one congregation is a merger of a white and an African American congregation; and one congregation began as a white congregation, whose membership became interracial prior to becoming predominantly African American. The congregations vary in membership and attendance at Sunday worship, with more than a thousand people attending Sunday worship at each of two of the churches, while six hundred, five hundred, and one hundred persons, respectively, attend the other three. These congregations bear the marks of their respective histories.

Carter Temple, a congregation with more than twenty-two hundred members and a major community institution by virtue of its membership and neighborhood presence, is located in the west-central part of Chatham on Seventy-ninth Street, a relatively affluent and stable portion of the neighborhood. Founded in 1921, Carter Temple moved to this location and built the present edifice in 1965. Since the Reverend Henry M. Williamson Sr. was appointed pastor in 1986, the church has grown by one thousand members and has added a second Sunday service and a Saturday service. Carter Temple actively supports its denomination, the Christian Methodist Episcopal Church.

Located on Stony Island Avenue at Ninetieth Street on the eastern edge of Chatham, abutting a pleasant residential and commercial area, Vernon Park Church of God was founded in 1955 by its current pastor, the Reverend Claude Wyatt, and his wife, who was later ordained, the Reverend Addie Wyatt. It grew steadily while worshiping in several locations before building its present complex in 1985. At present, it has more than one thousand members and nearly that many in its Sunday morning worship service. It has a wide range of ministries, with an emphasis on pastoral care for both members and nonmembers. Vernon Park is a congregation of the Church of God (Anderson, Indiana) and a member of its National Association, an organization of the denomination's African American clergy.

New Covenant Missionary Baptist Church is located one block west of Cottage Grove Avenue on Seventy-seventh Street (now Reverend Stephen John Thurston Place, in honor of the current pastor). A growing church of fifteen hundred members with a weekly Sunday-worship attendance of more than one thousand, New Covenant was established in 1934 on Forty-fourth Street by the Reverend Elijah Thurston, the grandfather of the current pastor. New Covenant moved to its present location in Greater Grand Crossing during 1956, when only a few of its families lived in its new neighborhood. Its pastor and prominent laypeople are leaders in the National Baptist Convention of America, Inc.

The racial politics of Carter Temple, Vernon Park, and New Covenant represent different trajectories in the new black middle-class religion. For each congregation, racial authenticity became the standard in its liturgy and congregational life. Whether or not an element was authentically black served as a criterion for appropriation. Thus new black middle-class religion adopted gospel music, "hooping," religious dance, expressive and celebrative gestures, and Pentecostal-like spirituality. By the 1980s, the term *Afrocentricity* was employed to provide specificity to racial authenticity. Rites of passage, kente cloth, and African attire were introduced as elements of a specifically African cultural identification. Coupled with the liturgical and cultural elements were emphases on educational ministries related to blacks in the Bible, black religious and social history, and black theology. Instead of attempting to debunk myths of black inferiority through greater adherence to elite western cultural norms, these congregations sought to advance knowledge about Africans as a biblical people and makers of a great ancient civilization as well as a great culture, in order to construct a vibrant religious community buoyed by this knowledge.[11]

Compared with Carter Temple, Vernon Park Church retains more of the characteristics of the "middlebrow," middle-class Black Church, with its note-perfect music, Pastor Claude Wyatt's inspirational preaching, and the pastoral function in all aspects of church life and work. This church exhibits no stereotypical Pentecostal qualities, though its holiness identity is evidenced by the expectation that the gifts of the Holy Spirit should shape the Christian lifestyle more than emotional or expressive forms of praise and worship. Yet, Vernon Park promotes the new Afro-centric perspective that defines the new black middle-class religion. The black liberation flag of red, black, and green hangs in the sanctuary. Kente cloth occasionally adorns the liturgical garments of the clergy. African American art graces the walls of the corridors and the fellowship hall. Black history shapes the educational programs of the church. The ministry supports the PUSH/Rainbow Coalition's goal to create a "just" America, a new America. Afrocentricity at Vernon Park celebrates the achievements and agenda of African Americans. It differs, however, from perspectives that define knowledge by race, are basically separatist in racial orientation, or reinterpret Scripture and the Christian tradition through racial concerns. Vernon Park embraces Afrocentricity along with its progressive political agenda and justice emphasis as a means of empowerment and liberation.

While at Vernon Park there is little systematic differentiation from or critique of "the predominant culture" in terms of race, there is an explicit public concern with the *urban* situation, defined not mainly in terms of race but in terms of conditions and issues that affect everyone. Vernon Park defines itself as engaged in urban ministry rather than in Afrocentric ministry. The church sponsors a food pantry for the poor and a Saturday Academy for youth, an enrichment program funded through the Urban League. At Vernon Park, Pastors Claude and Addie Wyatt model the relevance of political engagement along with other leaders in their congregation, such as the former mayor Eugene Sawyer and the Reverend Willie Barrow of Operation PUSH. Afrocentricity infuses the life of Vernon Park, although it is not central.

New Covenant reflects less of the new black middle-class religion than do Carter Temple and Vernon Park. But it also rejects the old black middle-class religion by appropriating aspects of the black folk church into the new cultural context of the black middle class. New Covenant is also engaged in the redefinition of black religious culture, but the central frame of reference for its innovation is the Black Church in America, not Africa—although the congregation occasionally invokes African symbols. The central lineage of New Covenant members is not the kings and queens of Africa but the Christian slaves who found salvation by trusting in Jesus and—this is crucial—who organized the Black Church. Thus, if African Americans are to find assurance that the Bible is true for blacks today as a minority group in a white, secular culture that dominates them, they must remember that it was also true for the slaves who trusted Jesus.

One might reasonably ask: Where lies the innovation? Nothing being presented about the Black Church is new here, at least not in terms of its history. The innovation is that New Covenant, a historically elite, "upper-class church" (to quote Pastor Stephen Thurston) catering to the very black bourgeoisie studied by Frazier, now seeks to locate itself among the contemporary descendants of slaves who remain oppressed by the dominant culture during the postsegregation era. Rev. Thurston's preaching constantly reminds the congregation that they have arrived not in the promised land but in an alien land. The pastor invites congregants to model an alternative to the dominant culture, not to trust it and certainly not to join it. Those who have not crossed the church's threshold—which is social and cultural as well as physical—may hear its message on its weekly telecast or from a mission group member doing her time of service witnessing on the street or door to door. The congregation welcomes the newcomer into a cultural enclave shaped by the black folk church, one that defines itself over against the dominant culture and embraces all who trust Jesus. Music, preaching, education, and mission combine to define New Covenant as an enclave.

New Covenant's pastor, the Reverend Stephen John Thurston, has expressed his commitment to civil rights through his active involvement in Operation PUSH. To assist the poor, the congregation sponsors a secondhand-clothing store. Although Afrocentricity is not a major focus at New Covenant, in 1993 the church assisted 150 of its youth to visit Africa as a mission-to-Africa trip as well as an activity of religious formation of the youth. Africa represents an important symbol and place in the congregation.

In contrast to the three churches thus far examined, congregations such as Saint Columbanus Roman Catholic Church and Ingleside-Whitfield United Methodist Church have resisted any adoption of the new black middle-class religion in Chatham. Saint Columbanus was built in 1925 on Seventy-first Street in the northwest corner of Chatham, having been created in 1909 for upwardly mobile Irish American residents. The church easily seats one thousand. Since the mid-1960s, Saint Columbanus has been a predominantly African American parish. From the 350 families now registered, perhaps five hundred people attend mass weekly. While the majority of the active members and leadership are age fifty or older, a significant number of younger families with children are active in the parish. Father Phillip Cyscon, a diocesan priest of Polish descent, has been pastor since 1993. With two priests and two deacons, the parish offers daily and three weekend masses. It also operates a highly respected and growing school, whose students come from across the South Side of Chicago.

Saint Columbanus, particularly its older leaders, drew a sharper line between African American culture and Catholic faith than did the African American Catholics who created and promoted the Gospel Mass movement. Saint Columbanus's leadership resisted the developments that endowed African American cultural expressions with religious valence and declined to support campaigns for black cultural liberation within the Chicago Archdiocese, withholding strong attachment to either African religious rituals and holidays or African American religious-based cultural forms. Whereas other black parishes, such as Holy Angels, Saint Sabina, and Saint Benedict the African, celebrated their African and African American heritage liturgically, Saint Columbanus opted to bring the older black middle-class religion into the new religious context.[12]

The parish continues the older black middle-class commitment to racial uplift, defined in terms of social change. It daily opens its gymnasium to the neighborhood youth to provide a "safe place" for recreation. Its parochial school sponsors a before- and after-school program, offering working parents a supervised and structured environment for their youth. To serve the poor, the church stocks a food pantry.

Similar in some respects to Saint Columbanus is Ingleside-Whitfield's adjustment to the new cultural context of the Black Church. A new congregation resulting from the merger of a white and an African American Methodist congregation in 1960, Ingleside-Whitfield is located on Seventh-sixth Street in the central part of Chatham (near New Covenant). Its first African American pastor, the Reverend Edsel Ammons, later a United Methodist bishop, was appointed at the time of the merger. At the time of our study the church had a single worship service, with an average attendance slightly over one hundred. The pastor, the Reverend Danita R. Anderson, was appointed in 1991.

Until the 1990s, Ingleside-Whitfield held to the old black middle-class religion, resisting the appropriation of elements from the black folk church. The introduction of Afrocentric elements and folk worship styles in the last decade of the twentieth century has been divisive. Yet, as with Saint Columbanus, the ties to the old black middle-class religion have included commitment to racial uplift. Ingleside-Whitfield offers a program for younger children sponsored by the Edsel Ammons Nursery School and Kindergarten. A layperson from the church has been the mainstay of the Greater Grand Crossing Organizing Committee, a church-based community organization of modest impact. Saint Columbanus and Ingleside-Whitfield both remain closely aligned to the old black middle-class religion, albeit adapted to the new cultural and social context.

The diversity within black middle-class religion reflects the differing forms of racial politics selected to construct racial identity as well as to advance the full incorporation of African Americans in American society. The post-1967 cultural and social context, while defined by desegregation and later resegregation, reflects the cultural production currently identified with Afrocentricity. Although relative agreement exists on the overall civil rights agenda, widespread disagreement engulfs the cultural agenda of the black middle-class church.[13]

Black Middle-Class Religion in the Age of Segregation and Desegregation

The new black middle-class religion is an heir of the Civil Rights movement, black ecumenism, and black nationalism, and is a product of the black theology movement. It emerged in the 1970s, well after the collapse of the integration of Chatham. Black middle-class congregations supported the integration of communities like Chatham in the 1950s, often relocating their congregations to predominantly white neighborhoods before their memberships did the same (as was the case with New Covenant), thus competing with the "open" white congregations for black middle-class members relocating into these neighborhoods. The racial politics of the old black middle-class religion shaped the aspirations of African Americans moving into Chatham.

By the time African Americans began residing in Chatham, the civil rights activists vigorously promoted integration. They espoused the philosophy of an activist federal government taking "responsibility of making a better life for all its citizens, regardless of race, creed, or color." Encouraged by Franklin Delano Roosevelt's initiatives, they applauded the Supreme Court's efforts to supplant legalized segregation with "an Integrated Equality that included political equality, equality of economic opportunity, and integrated public facilities." They adopted proportionality as a measure of equality and a means to achieve it, advocating open public facilities and even proportional percentages of African Americans and whites in public institutions such as federal housing, public schools, hospitals, and occupations. Since all human beings were the same, they contended that "extensive assimilation and integration of the races was both necessary and desirable."[14]

Housing loomed as a cardinal goal of integration. But housing, like schools, became contested in northern cities such as Chicago. As historian Thomas J. Sugrue demonstrates, in northern cities "the politics of race, home ownership, and neighborhood" spawned the white resistance to integration in the post–World War II era that preceded white flight. Neighborhood civic associations engaged in "defensive localism" and asserted the right to racially homogeneous neighborhoods, a right initially defended even by the HOLC (Home Owners' Loan Corporation) and FHA (Federal Housing Administration) as democratic. During 1946 and 1947, the focal points for this struggle in Chicago were the Airport Homes and the Fernwood Apartments, two temporary veteran housing projects sponsored by the Federal Public Housing Authority and administered by the Chicago Housing Authority.[15]

The people and congregations moving into Chatham in the 1950s were also part of the larger middle-class world of black sororities, fraternities, lodges, and social clubs, with their elaborate rituals and social networks. They had created an alternative world of African American society within the space African Americans cleared in the midst of the racially segregated nation. This achievement demonstrated that African Americans could appropriate and excel at what was considered the best of western bourgeois culture. In the racial politics of the older black middle class, class was defined as culture and status. To traverse the divide between the African American working class and the middle class, African Americans needed to acquire middle-class values and culture. The cultural project of the old black middle-class religion was not mimicry; it involved something new: the creation of African American modern art, dance, music, and literature, by geniuses such as Horace Pippin, Katherine Dunham, William Grant Still, and Zora Neale Hurston.

The old black middle-class church often yoked the social incorporation of African Americans into American society with their cultural productions. The development of an African American middle-class culture served the political purpose of debunking myths about African American racial inferiority through its ability to assimilate culturally. Black pathologies would be exorcised from the black community as a consequence of full assimilation bolstered by a black middle-class culture, proving that these pathologies were the products of social malformation due to racial isolation and racism and were not inherent in black people.[16] Central to the racial project of the old black middle-class church was cultural contact: African Americans had to learn and contextualize the best of white American and European culture.

The hallmark of black cultural production was music. Black middle-class congregations had distinguished themselves in Chicago for their musical productions, ranging from classical concerts to operas, in post–World War I Chicago. Choral study clubs became the primary vehicles for cultural advancement. Historian Michael Wesley Harris notes that these clubs advertised that they were "organized to create a desire for better music among Chicago Negroes and to render musical numbers of the higher type." These clubs excelled in the performances of "Handel's *Messiah*, Gall's *Holy City*, and the choral music of Samuel Coleridge-Taylor." Bethel African Methodist Episcopal Church mounted the first opera sung by African Americans in Chicago with the choir's performance of Friedrich von Flotow's *Martha*. By 1930, the choral study clubs had become the choirs for local congregations. These choirs would sing, in Latin and in English, compositions ranging from Rossini's *Stabat Mater* to Mendelssohn's *Elijah*, from Bach's cantatas to Haydn's *Creation* to Theodore Dubois's *The Seven Last Words*. The complete performance of these works occurred at concerts advertised as "monthly musicales." In addition to European classical music, the choir sang Negro spirituals in choral arrangements by Nathaniel Dett, Hall Johnson, Harry T. Burleigh. The choir members often donned a "black robe with white collar and black cap with tassel."[17]

Yet, in worship, the old black middle-class church did not take the same artistic license. To distance themselves from the stereotype of black religion as sheer emotionalism and ignorance, they de-emphasized rhythmic music, religious dancing, and hooping and stressed note-perfect singing, quietness, and inspirational and intellectual preaching. Music structured the worship service, with hymns representative of mainline Protestant hymnody and choral selections drawn from anthems and spirituals. Even their singing of spirituals was anglicized. The congregational singing reflected little of the urban gospel sound or the rural harmonies associated with long-meter hymns. Black middle-class congregations prided themselves on their ability to worship in a manner deemed as dignified as that of white middle-class Protestants.

The preaching style in these congregations was informational and inspirational, with biblical or theological applications on practical, everyday issues presented in an "intelligent" manner. Vattel Daniel, in his 1940s study of Black Church worship in Chicago, found that black middle-class congregations reflected the social stratification within the black community, and in contrast to lower-class black congregations, their worship tended to be more "ritualistic and deliberative" than "emotional and demonstrative." Willis Laurence Jones described these deliberative black middle-class churches as Europeanized in decorum.[18]

Carter Temple and New Covenant were proud bearers of older black middle-class religion in the pre-1967 era. By the time New Covenant relocated to Chatham in 1956 the congregation had already replaced its southern black religious ethos with the black middle-class religious style. The congregations' identification with the middle class affected their desire to attract middle-class blacks, especially professionals, and to serve as a pillar of the social world of the black middle class; they often restricted leadership positions in the church to the middle-class membership. The Whitfield congregation, prior to the merger with Ingleside during the 1960s, embraced the religious style of the black middle-class church, with its focus on respectability and racial uplift, while Saint Columbanus during the 1960s embraced the ethos of black middle-class Roman Catholicism, with its selective continuation of the traditions, values, and norms of the pre–Vatican II era. These norms related to the status of the parish's parochial school, the activities of the fraternal and social organizations in the parish, and the relationship to the neighborhood, in which Saint Columbanus strove to be a service institution.[19]

The racial politics of the old black middle-class religion found allies in the social and political context in which Americanization or cultural conformity defined the dominant cultural policy for all racial and ethnic

Fig. 7-2. A 1960s black-tie dinner at New Covenant Missionary Baptist Church, Chatham area, Chicago. Formal events remain important to this and many black churches. Photo courtesy of New Covenant Missionary Baptist Church.

groups and in which racial integration framed liberal social policy, especially in the post–World War II era. The racial advancement of the African Americans in this period seemingly illustrated the effectiveness of the racial politics of the old black middle-class religion.

The ideological, political, and cultural changes in the black community of the 1960s undermined the racial politics of the old black middle-class religion. As noted earlier, the late 1960s was the dividing line between the Black Church under and after segregation. Assimilationism, the liberal cultural policy during segregation, lost its appeal to African Americans through the white American Church's explicit and implicit support of the state-sponsored terrorism waged against the Civil Rights movement. This depletion of the moral and cultural standing of white Christians occurred for a significant segment of African Americans. "The Negro Church is dead," noted Lincoln, "because the norms and presuppositions which structured and conditioned it are not the relevant norms and presuppositions to which contemporary Blacks . . . can give their asserevation and support."[20]

The coalition of the black middle-class church and the black folk church in the Civil Rights movement anticipated this shift by the prominence the movement gave to black folk songs and culture, legitimating the "unangli-cized" versions of spirituals and other songs and fashioning individuals into movement people. Black folk Christianity supplied cultural forms, dis-course, and music that formed the core of the mass meetings sponsored by civil rights activists, thus further legitimating black folk culture. These meetings, attended by various pastors of Chicago's black middle-class con-gregations, including Rev. Claude Wyatt and Rev. Addie Wyatt, pastors of Vernon Park Church, employed the spontaneous testimony of the devo-tional service to narrate the experiences of injustices and activism. They adopted old-fashioned preaching, with its accent on realism, application, and inspiration, and the church-rocking singing of congregational and free-dom songs. And they also utilized social analyses, "creating an experience which transformed powerless individuals" into powerful agents of God's new world.[21]

The racial politics of the old black middle class in Chicago was chal-lenged as much by factions within the Black Church as by outside crit-ics. Central to the struggle were the divisions within the old black mid-dle class over the strategies of civil rights campaigns in Chicago. The civil rights struggle over de facto school desegregation and open hous-ing in Chicago led to divisions in Chicago's black middle class in general and in its churches in particular, which were widest in February 1964, after the successful one-day school boycott held on October 22, 1963. The black leadership and congregations were divided over whether to organize a second school boycott. Abstaining from supporting the boy-cott were the Chicago branches of the NAACP (National Association for the Advancement of Colored People) and the Urban League, Chicago's black Democratic leadership, and many prominent African American congregations, including Olivet Baptist Church, pastored by the Rev-erend Joseph H. Jackson. Support for the boycott included other repre-sentatives of the black middle class and their churches, including Ver-non Park Church, Quinn Chapel AME, and First Baptist Congregational Church. Although black leaders and institutions, including churches, were divided over the strategies to promote civil rights in Chicago, part of the black middle and working classes began to support more aggres-sive measures during 1964. During the second school boycott, a number of black congregations housed the "Freedom Schools." A July 1964 rally drew more than thirty thousand protesters to march. The black middle-class religion found itself divided on the role of social activism to achieve racial advancement.[22]

It was within the emergent Black Church of the late 1960s that the nationalist sentiment encountered its most vigorous reception. African American nationalists had led an active campaign to discredit assimilation and integration as means of racial advancement. This led to the repudiation of the "traditional leadership of the black community, which had typically arisen from the well-educated, hard working, successful women and men of the black middle class," because, according to the nationalists, "the black masses had never wanted integration; that always had been a middle-class dream." Nationalists labeled Christianity a "white man's religion." According to theologian Mark Chapman, a key issue addressed by the National Committee of Negro Churchmen during the late 1960s was "the charge that black clergy were representatives of white Christianity." The clergy who leveled the charge, mostly men, belonged to predominantly white denominations and supported black power as a "precondition for any meaningful reconciliation between blacks and whites." The espousal of black power by black clergy fostered a militance that nurtured the political independence of black clergy from white clergy. The former expressed this independence in organizing black caucuses during 1967–1968 in predominantly white denominations such as the United Methodist Church, the denomination of Ingleside-Whitfield.[23]

Related to the call for the political independence of the Black Church was the question of its cultural integrity. In 1968 theologian Henry H. Mitchell argued that African American Christianity needed cultural integrity as well as political independence to refute the nationalist critique. He defined cultural integrity in terms of the "distinctive quality of black religious culture—its music, preaching, worship style and theology."[24] Mitchell's focus on cultural integrity reflected the cultural shift within black middle-class religion, in which black folk culture supplanted the dominant culture as the ideal.

Ready to embrace the new cultural awareness were the recent arrivals to the black middle class. According to Andrew Billingsley, "The proportion of middle-class families doubled during the decade of the 1960s from 12 percent to 25 percent." These tended to be people who came from the black poor to the middle class during the 1960s. The doubling of the black middle class overwhelmed the old black middle class as a group and undermined their cultural hegemony, challenging middle-class leadership and discrediting their organizations. The contest cleared space for the new black middle class to define itself.[25]

The social and political context in which the racial politics of the old black middle-class religion had thrived was changing. The new context inverted the hierarchy of social and cultural values and created an ethos in which the new black middle-class religion would invent itself within the emerging Black Church identified by C. Eric Lincoln. The racial politics that the new black middle class would craft allied itself to the new racial identity and black cultural awareness advanced during the Black Power era.

Conclusion

The black middle-class religion redefines itself in the age of resegregation. The racial politics of these five Chatham congregations play not only a crucial economic, social, and political role in their resegregated community but also a cultural role. The structural changes affecting the neighborhood since the white flight from and the resegregation of Chatham have created a different community by the 1990s than the community some of these black congregations integrated in the 1950s and 1960s. Chatham has been significantly underinstitutionalized due to local and global economics. It is a throwback to the bedroom communities of the 1950s, without many social amenities. There are relatively few community-based organizations and social service agencies. It lacks strong public schools and is without a trauma center or major hospital. The area no longer includes a major shopping center, nor are there nearby employers capable of replacing the steel mills and stockyards.

The role of the new black middle-class churches in this economic context is complicated with regard to their mission, resources, and organizing skills, as well as the larger restructuring occurring in the U.S. economy and society. On one level, these churches provide a major countertrend to the underinstitutionalization of this neighborhood: that is, there are churches here (including those we have studied) that attract people from outside of the neighborhood. While few people come into this neighborhood to work, shop, or go to public school, many come to worship at neighborhood churches and attend parochial schools. These churches are anchor institutions of the community.

Regarding the role of the new black middle-class religion in the racial construction of neighborhoods, there has been a shift away from the devaluing of racial separation and the valuing of integration. While resegregation of neighborhoods by whites is abhorred, the relocations of African Americans to black neighborhoods are interpreted as a positive expression of self-determination and black solidarity. Although whites are welcomed to the neighborhood, they are not needed to give the neighborhood value. Ideals of interracial cooperation and harmony are avowed, but a quest for interracial residential communities is not a focus. The focus is the quest for racial justice and a racially just city and society.

Race is an issue that all five churches confront. None of them takes the racial subordination and abasement of African American people as a given. They all seek, in different ways, to engage in the racial advancement of African Americans. They affirm African Americans and valorize the African American community, and they do so by invoking specific dimensions of their religious life. In some of the congregations, this valorization of African American culture is part of the redefinition and evolution of black religious culture. Its importance extends not only to the vitality of the Black Church (one of the strongest sectors in American Christianity) but also to its prospects for sustaining community when other neighborhood institutions are under siege or fail to undergird it.

Innovations in Christian worship and ministry also contribute to the construction of racial identity and the redefinition of black religious culture. These innovations undermine differentiation in worship styles associated with social stratification and class. The poor and working class can join the middle class in worship and in social-justice endeavors without adopting middle-class religious culture as a prerequisite. The new black middle-class religion actively appropriates elements of black folk religion to fashion its racial and religious identity. This process strengthens black solidarity across class lines. While it also widens the divide between African Americans and whites, it defines the cultural difference in terms of black versus white culture rather than in terms of education and intelligence. By intentionally adopting elements of black folk culture, the new black middle-class church dispels the branding of this culture as inferior and therefore as a sign of African American social inferiority. Thus previously untapped religious and cultural resources are now available for utilization by the new black middle-class religion.

The racial politics of the new black middle-class religion involves more than the differences in cultural strategies between itself and old black middle-class religion. It emerges from the competition between various moral discourses informed by Christianity and by assimilationism, black nationalism, and Afrocentricity. Each moral discourse describes a different role for race to play in the realization of racial justice, as well as a different conception of humanity and culture. The racial politics of the new black middle-class religion coincides with the wider struggle of the identity politics movement that engulfs American society. Although the battle over multiculturalism fails to exhaust the challenge of identity politics in movements for bilingual education, racial and ethnic designations in the federal census, and culturally diverse textbooks for public schools, it nevertheless functions as a focal point for the culture wars raging across the country. The racial politics of the new black middle-class religion stands in the vanguard of the identity politics movement to reshape American society in the late twentieth century.

The new black middle-class religion intersects with myriad social currents such as identity politics, urban revitalization, and social activism. Through its racial politics it participates in reconceiving the dynamic interplay of race, class, and culture within the Black Church. The creation of a new religious and cultural moment in the African American community and American society stands as a result.

NOTES

1. On new black middle-class congregations, see Mamiya, "Social History"; Lawrence, *Reviving the Spirit*. On the new black middle class, see Landry, *New Black Middle Class*.

2. Franklin, *Another Day's Journey*, 42, 59–62.

3. Asante, *Afrocentricity*, 74.

4. Dyson, *Reflecting Black*, 78–87; Asante, *Afrocentricity*, 74; McClain, "What Is Authentic Black Worship?"

5. Chicago Fact Book Consortium, *Local Community Fact Book 1990*, 121, 174, 177; Braden, "Chatham." The 1990 U.S. Census indicates that of Chatham's 36,779 residents, 97 percent are African Americans, with the rest made up of 363 Euro-Americans, 312 Hispanic Americans, 29 Asian Americans, and 23 Native Americans; Greater Grand Crossing population totals 38,644, of whom 99.2 percent are African Americans.

6. Braden, "Chatham," 341; Chicago Fact Book Consortium, *Local Community Fact Book 1990*, 119–121 and 175–177.

7. Lincoln, *Black Church since Frazier*.

8. Frazier, *Negro Church in America*, 89; also, e.g., Mays and Nicholson, *Negro's Church*.

9. Banner-Haley, *Fruits of Integration*, 3–26.

10. Ibid., 37.

11. For example, Carter Temple displayed and sold publications by healing evangelist Kenneth Hagen; Lawrence Mamiya on Bethel AME, Baltimore; Walter McCary's *Black Presence in the Bible;* Charles Copher's *Black Biblical Studies,* among others.

12. See Rivers, *Soulful Worship;* Hovda, ed., *This Far by Faith.*

13. The black neoconservative platform is the major challenge to the civil rights agenda. See West, *Race Matters.*

14. Condit and Lucaites, *Crafting Equality,* 167, 171, 169, 192, 170.

15. Sugrue, *Origins of the Urban Crisis,* 557.

16. Frazier, *Negro Family in Chicago* and *Negro Family in the United States;* Scott, *Contempt and Pity.*

17. Harris, *Rise of Gospel Blues,* 106–108; Ferguson, *History,* 66.

18. Frazier, *Black Bourgeoisie,* 65–71; Lincoln, *Black Church since Frazier,* 73; Daniel, "Ritual Stratification."

19. Lincoln, "Black Methodists"; Irvin, *Unsung Heart,* 32–49; Davis, *History of Black Catholics.*

20. Lincoln, *Black Church since Frazier,* 106–107.

21. The black folk church and the black middle-class church are two segments within the Black Church. The black folk church is recognized for its use of long-meter hymns and congregational songs, as well as for its jubilant preaching. Often associated with the black working class, the black folk church differs from its black middle-class counterpart more by its religious culture than by mere economic and educational factors. See Washington, *Black Sects and Cults;* Boyer, *How Sweet the Sound.*

22. Anderson and Pickering, *Confronting the Color Line,* 125, 118, 133; Travis, *Autobiography of Black Politics,* vol. 1, 319, 327–336, 338, 335; Jackson, *Story of Christian Activism;* and "Joseph H. Jackson," in Paris, *Black Religious Leaders,* 65–98.

23. Condit and Lucaites, *Crafting Equality,* 195; Chapman, *Christianity on Trial,* 38, 77, 82. Black caucuses were formed in the Presbyterian Church (U.S.A.), Presbyterian Church U.S., United Methodist Church, United Church of Christ, Disciples of Christ, Protestant Episcopal Church, American Baptist Churches in the U.S.A., American Lutheran Church, Lutheran Church–Missouri Synod, Reformed Church of America. Also see Lincoln and Mamiya, "The New Black Revolution: The Black Consciousness Movement and the Black Church," in *Black Church,* Chap. 7, 164–95.

24. Mitchell, "Black Power and the Christian Church," 105.

25. Billingsley, *Climbing Jacob's Ladder,* 51.

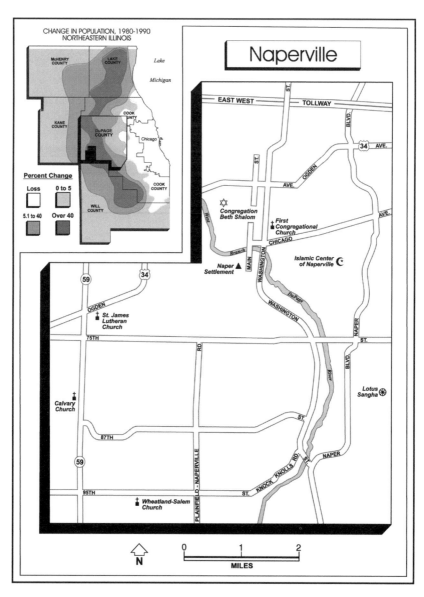

Map 8. Naperville, Illinois, is one of metropolitan Chicago's fastest-growing edge cities. Map by Brian Twardosz, BMT Printing and Cartographic Specialists.

Chapter 8

Change, Stress, and Congregations in an Edge-City Technoburb

Paul D. Numrich

Naperville has become a popular place. During its first summer of operation in 1996, the city's Internet web page received more than twenty-two thousand hits. Three hundred people move into Naperville every month, making it the tenth-fastest-growing municipality in the country. "Naperville has a good reputation," a real estate agent remarks in one of countless local newspaper stories about Naperville's recent growth. "People just want to live here."[1]

Naperville has even established a place for itself in the literature on contemporary American society, with feature articles in the *Atlantic Monthly* and *Inland Architect* and a book-length study of women forging life on the postindustrial frontier. The portrait of Naperville drawn in these pieces, however, tends to be more ambivalent than real estate agents would wish. Nicholas Lemann titled his 1989 *Atlantic* article "Stressed Out in Suburbia," while Sally Helgesen's recent book *Everyday Revolutionaries,* acknowledging its analytical debt to Lemann, describes the overextended lives of Naperville's women, who nevertheless remain optimistic and energized about the opportunities afforded by life here. Michael Ebner's article in *Inland Architect* points out the structural stress on Naperville during its transformation from small town to "technoburb" over the past forty-five years.[2]

This chapter also examines life in contemporary Naperville, but unlike previous studies, it grants institutional religion a central position.[3] Naperville's congregations have participated in the change and stress of the city's recent transformation and, like some edge-city observers, often harbor ambivalent feelings about life in such a popular place.

Their spiritual perspectives on edge-city life certainly help members to alleviate the strains; but do they strike to the underlying causes?

Naperville, Yesterday and Today

The city's namesake, Great Lakes steamship captain Joseph Naper, founded Naperville in 1831.[4] Befriended by local Potawatomis—and protected by Fort Payne on the highest point in the area—Naper's settlement survived the Black Hawk Indian War the following year. Naperville received rail service when the Chicago Burlington and Quincy (today's Burlington Northern) came through in 1864, establishing an economic lifeline for the town. A public library was dedicated in 1898, and in 1913 the Naperville Lounge Company changed its name to Kroehler Manufacturing Company, which would later become the nation's largest furniture manufacturer.

It took three decades for Naperville's turn-of-the-century population of twenty-six hundred to double. The city's centennial fell early in the Great Depression, during which a county guidebook described Naperville as reminiscent of a New England village.[5] But area development accelerated immediately after World War II. Historian Michael Ebner identifies Argonne National Laboratory, built in 1947, as the "high-technology seed" from which sprouted Naperville's present status as the hub of Chicago's technoburb (Robert Fishman's term). "Technoburb" and Joel Garreau's notion of "edge city" insightfully describe places like Naperville—self-contained socioeconomic territories on the urban periphery, dense with high-technology industries, corporate headquarters, retail space, and residents. As Garreau notes, such a place "has it all" today, yet it is nothing like it was only a few years earlier.[6]

According to Ebner, Argonne's arrival in 1947 corresponded with Naperville's new commitment to providing quality public education comparable to prestige school systems around the country. Commuter ridership on the Burlington line increased in the 1950s; parking near the downtown depot became a problem; and the East-West Tollway brought interstate access to Chicago in 1958. From this point it took only about one decade for Naperville's population to double.

Packer Engineering (1962) and Northern Illinois Gas (1963, now Nicor Gas) initiated an influx of technology-based companies. In 1966, AT&T opened a major research facility, Bell Labs (now Lucent Technologies), that would supplant Kroehler Manufacturing as the area's largest employer, employing in the 1990s more than ten thousand people on six campuses in Naperville and adjoining Lisle. Fermi National Accelerator Laboratory, Amoco Research Center, and Nalco Research followed. By the mid-1980s, when Governor James Thompson designated a stretch along the East-West Tollway as the Illinois Research and Development Corridor, Naperville had become what Ebner describes as "the geographic center of Chicago's version of California's Silicon Valley."[7]

Naperville's municipal territory expanded from twelve square miles in 1970 to fifty square miles by the early 1990s, while its population exploded during the same period from just under twenty-three thousand to more than one hundred thousand. Projections call for 135,000 Napervillians by the year 2005 and 160,000 by 2020, an anticipated percentage increase more than three times that of the metropolitan region as a whole. The city's senior planner predicted that up to 75 percent of all future population growth would occur in South Naperville's so-called Sector G.

Indian Prairie School District 204, bridging Aurora and Naperville (including Sector G), is the fastest-growing school district in Illinois and trails only Chicago's public school system in student diversity in the state. Its English as a Second Language program accommodates students from nearly one hundred countries. Enrollment is not expected to peak until the year 2008. With a price tag in excess of $60 million, Neuqua Valley High School, named after one of the friendly Potawatomis who ensured Naperville's early survival, opened in 1997 as the most expensive public school in Illinois history, funded by the state's largest referendum.

Naperville remains a predominantly White community, although Blacks (2 percent) and Asians (over 5 percent) comprise a significant new presence. Naperville's Blacks rank sixth in per-capita income among Blacks in all local communities, while only two suburbs have more Asian residents than Naperville. Asians make up more than 10 percent of Lucent Technologies' work force.

Median family income for Naperville in 1995 was nearly $67,000, $12,000 higher than the DuPage County median, which itself ranks twenty-fourth among all U.S. counties. Less than 2 percent of Naperville residents lived below the poverty line, and the average home value stood at $191,000. A marketing analysis conducted by Virginia-based Claritas Inc. categorized Naperville as an "elite suburb" with predominant "lifestyle clusters" of kids and cul-de-sacs on the one hand and executive suites on the other. Respectively, according to Claritas, people with such lifestyles "buy trivia games, own a piano, read parenting magazines" and "play racquetball, own a video camera, listen to jazz radio."[8] The traditional American nuclear family of two parents with children still characterizes DuPage County demographics more than the national profile. Contrary to a thirty-year trend of decreasing mobility among the American public overall, during the period 1985–1990 over one-fourth of Naperville's new residents relocated from outside of the Chicago metropolitan region.

By most measures, Naperville offers its residents a high—and highly touted—quality of life. Commenting on plans to revive a Black community on Chicago's South Side, Chicago's mayor Richard M. Daley promised that children will feel "like they are in Naperville." Indeed, Zero Population Growth, a Washington, D.C., organization that examines the relation between population growth and quality of life, named Naperville the nation's most child-friendly city. Dining, entertainment, and the arts, once the exclusive purview of downtown Chicago, now lie close at hand for Napervillians.

Thus the Naperville area epitomizes Joel Garreau's edge city, a recent growth area on the urban periphery that offers all the essentials of modern life—job, home, market, education, culture.[9] Naperville strikes many observers as a postindustrial metropolitan success story, having made the transition from quaint small town to thriving technoburb. The old Kroehler factory near the heart of town speaks volumes in this regard: once it cranked out couches for Sears; today it houses upscale restaurants, shops, and condominiums.

But the other side of Naperville's success is visible as well. Vocational anxieties, social problems, congestion from rapid development—to some these signify growing pains soon to be overcome, to others red flags that qualify claims about the satisfaction offered by such edge-city technoburbs.

As Lemann wrote in 1989, "In Naperville the word 'stress' came up constantly in conversations. . . . They complain that between working long hours, traveling on business, and trying to stay in shape they have no free time."[10] A decade later Sally Helgesen filed the same report, noting that life for Naperville's women had become characterized by "the disappearance of time."[11] Lurking behind all of this stands the specter of corporate downsizing, threatening to end Naperville's technoburban heyday. When AT&T announced a nationwide layoff of forty thousand employees in the mid-1990s, the *Chicago Tribune* commented that some workers in

Naperville saw it as "yet another thunderclap in a place often shaken by such storms." Moreover, some of Naperville's high-tech luster certainly dimmed with the recent discovery of twenty cases of brain tumors among former and current Amoco Research Center employees.

In the four-year period 1993–1996, when Naperville's population grew by 12 percent, reported incidents of domestic abuse in Naperville increased over three times that rate. Likewise, although a comprehensive health assessment found the county to be "very healthy," with "good medical and support services," nevertheless negative behavioral choices (e.g., alcohol consumption and cigarette smoking) and pockets of poverty among the overall affluence of the county remained areas of concerns. A 1996 survey of Naperville teens revealed dramatic increases in substance abuse, with marijuana usage significantly higher than the national average. One estimate suggested as many as 150 homeless people in Naperville. With high monthly rental rates and a housing market geared to white-collar residents, one report concluded, affordable housing and home ownership are problematic for a significant portion of Naperville's population.

Contention over Naperville's rapid change and new diversity surfaces periodically, for example, in home-owner resistance to an apartment complex that could tarnish the city's image, in protests of School District 203's minority hiring practices, and in Asian Indian voters' claims of discrimination over a nominating petition for a city council candidate. DuPage County's board chairperson identified growing diversity as the county's "biggest problem."

As in edge cities across the country, the phenomenal development that created today's Naperville carries inherent threats to the overall quality of life of its residents. One county study identified traffic congestion and an imbalanced jobs/housing ratio as key concerns, characterizing Naperville's jobs/housing ratio as "extremely out of balance." Each day nearly 180,000 DuPage residents leave the county for work, while even more— another 220,000—enter the county to work. Add to this the more than 245,000 DuPage residents who commute to work within the county, and the burden on the area's transportation infrastructure becomes obvious, as does the stress on commuting workers.

As a solution, the county planning commission suggested slowing the growth of jobs in the area. The ambivalence of other area planners, however, surfaced in Naperville's decision to allow construction of a four hundred–unit "upscale" apartment complex that would provide affordable housing for interim corporate workers along the Research and Development Corridor. The Naperville City Council approved the complex over the objections of its own planning commission, which saw the parcel of land as a prime location for even more office, research, and industrial development.

Religion in Naperville

Noted church consultant Lyle Schaller, a local resident, identifies some trends about religion in Naperville. At the end of World War I, Naperville had only nine churches, all northern European Christian in heritage. Today Naperville has about sixty congregations, many still northern European Christian but many more of the homegrown American variety, such as Mormons, Jehovah's Witnesses, and Pentecostal groups. Today's congregations place less emphasis on denominational identity and hierarchical polity than the churches of previous generations, and laypeople play a much greater role now, exercising their prerogative of joining the congregation of their choice. Today, Naperville's congregations tend to be bigger and much more competitive than their predecessors in attracting members—like the stores in nearby shopping centers.[12]

Korean and Chinese Christians, along with Jews, Muslims, Baha'is, and Buddhists, have increased Naperville's religious diversity in recent years. New religious facilities sprout up as fast as new subdivisions, and solicitation of new members through mass marketing techniques is commonplace. Pollsters have reported either steady or declining worship attendance nationwide in recent years, but that is the exception rather than the rule among Naperville congregations of all religious identities.

The following congregational profiles illuminate key dynamics of edge-city life in Naperville. How have these congregations participated in the change and stress that characterize life in such places today?

First Congregational Church

On the highest point in town, not far from the site of old Fort Payne, sits Piety Hill, local lingo for the cluster of Naperville's oldest churches. One bears the name First Congregational Church (United Church of Christ), tracing its origins to a weekend gathering of mostly New England Puritans in July 1833. In the early years worship services rotated, with worshipers meeting in a variety of venues—homes, barns, schools, the

Fig. 8-1. First Congregational Church on "Piety Hill" is one of the oldest churches in Naperville, Illinois. Photo by Paul D. Numrich.

courthouse, a Baptist church. Disagreement over a permanent location led to the congregation's first split. A faction withdrew to build their own church south of town, whereas in 1846 First Congregational erected a wooden-frame structure on donated land at its current Piety Hill location, the donor stipulating that the church must always have a cupola and bell. A limestone structure replaced the original church in 1906.

First Congressional's membership declined in the 1960s, but by the early 1970s it began a sustained upturn that would last two decades— precisely the period of Naperville's coming-of-age as an edge-city technoburb. The church's latest schism is directly related to this growth and change.

In 1993 the congregation's Long Range Planning Board (LRPB) concluded that maintaining the church's status quo at the Piety Hill location should not be a long-term option. The next year the LRPB broached the idea of a split-site operation, and in January 1995 it brought a formal recommendation asking that the congregation "aggressively and prayerfully pursue a step-by-step plan to relocate the entire membership to a new facility and establish the [downtown] facility as a Church-led Community Center." The LRPB targeted the high-growth area of South Naperville as the site for the new facility, and the denomination appeared ready to lend financial support to the venture. By a simple majority vote, the congregation approved further study of the LRPB's recommendation.

But ensuing congregational debate about the future of the church proved emotional and, ultimately, schismatic. Other options were discussed, including razing the historic facility and erecting a new one on the site, a notion many could not abide. Rejecting the recommendation of a split-site operation, a previous chair of the LRPB wrote in an open letter to the congregation, "We must support the preservation of our heritage through the delivery of our entire ministry in the downtown location." "We must value organic growth over numerical growth," the letter continued, countering a key rationale for relocation to South Naperville—attraction of young families in the residential boom areas. "Bigger is not necessarily better," wrote one church member, while still another argued that "the church should remain at its present site . . . [since] God doesn't need another big church in a cornfield; He has enough of them already." This last member even raised possible legal ramifications of relocation, given the implicit wish of the nineteenth-century donor of the downtown property that there always be a church, with cupola and bell, on that site. Members who cherished First Congregational's social mission orientation feared that aspect of the church's liberal heritage would be lost through relocation away from downtown Naperville.

After months of debate, it became clear that the faction favoring relocation could not garner the required two-thirds majority congregational vote for the necessary allocation of funds. Forty families subsequently left First Congregational to found Hope Church, which in September 1998 dedicated its new multi-acre site in South Naperville's booming Sector G. Both churches thrive today, having succeeded in attracting different segments of the edge-city baby-boomer population. First Congregational focuses on rechurching the disaffected, many of whom, according to the current pastor, appreciate the historic sanctuary on Piety Hill. It feels like "home," they say, reminding them of the churches of their childhood.

Wheatland Salem Church

"That's it over there," the construction supervisor told me in the summer of 1996, pointing to a slight knoll amid the stakes outlining phase two of Mission Oaks subdivision in Sector G. The knoll betrayed no indication that it had once been a church cemetery, nor even that it had once been surrounded by farmland. The supervisor mentioned that during phase one of development a few Mission Oaks home owners had asked permission to take some of the headstones, presumably for use as yard ornaments. With advice from the local genealogical society, church leaders eventually decided to cover over the graves and remaining markers and to erect a single monument honoring the pioneers of their congregation.

Like its old cemetery, Wheatland Salem Church (United Methodist) nearly passed into oblivion around 1980. The church's remarkable rescue from the brink of institutional demise can be traced to the fortuitous appointment of the right pastor at exactly the right time of residential growth in South Naperville.

Wheatland Salem's roots lay in two congregations of Pennsylvania German farmers affiliated with the Evangelical Association in North America. Copenhagen Church (also known as Salem Church), established in 1852 at the crossroads of Copenhagen Road and today's Illinois Route 59, and Emmanuel Church, established in 1860 several miles to the southwest in Wheatland Township, merged in 1907 to build a new church halfway between the two, at Ninety-fifth Street and Route 59. One old-timer reminisces about going to the church as a child by horse and buggy down Route 59, then a gravel road.

The congregation declined after World War II, and by 1979 membership had dropped to eighty-seven. In 1980 the United Methodist bishop appointed the Reverend Scott Field to preside over Wheatland Salem's imminent closure.

Pastor Scott, as he is often called, did not listen to the bishop. And no one—certainly not the farmers who founded the church—could have predicted what was about to happen in Naperville's Sector G, where the church was located. In 1987, when the area was still considered Naperville's "boondocks," the prestigious White Eagle subdivision opened just to the north, with its signature Arnold Palmer golf course. Less than a decade later, more than thirteen thousand residents lived in the sector. Route 59, the one-time gravel road, expanded to six lanes of fast-moving traffic.

Wheatland Salem's resuscitation paralleled the growth around it. In 1986 the church expanded its facility by three times the original size. The next year the administrative council committed the congregation to a development strategy that shifted the laity into ministry roles and the pastor into the role of manager of ministry. By 1989 the church broke the two hundred mark in worship attendance, and in the 1990s church programming began bursting the seams of the expanded facility. During a personal prayer retreat in 1993, Pastor Scott concluded that further improvement of the current site was much too timid a plan for the future. Besides, he says today, the old farm church would have been a "retrograde fit" in the new development slated around it. When Pastor Scott challenged the congregation to think big and relocate, he was pleasantly surprised at the overwhelmingly positive response.

In the fall of 1997 those big thoughts culminated in the opening of a $6 million "church for the twenty-first century," located on fourteen acres of former farmland east of the old site, in the middle of what Pastor Scott, playing on downtown's Piety Hill, calls Naperville's new Piety Row. The church battled two municipalities and a major land developer over annexation and utilities problems at the new location, and congregational leaders make no bones about using the large mortgage as a "poison pill" tactic against the loss of Pastor Scott through appointment elsewhere.

The new Wheatland Salem Church fits comfortably into its edge-city milieu. Pastor Scott is savvy to the ways of his members' information-age world and adept at strategizing for a twenty-first-century church. "We are using this time of societal and technological change to build a place to serve Christ's Gospel now and in the future," states a professional-quality prospectus on the new church facility. The only "retrograde" features are the stained-glass windows brought over from the old church and the new address, 1852 Ninety-fifth Street, commemorating the year the church was founded.

Pastor Scott is also adept at applying evangelical theology to a congregation often clinging to the edge of their technoburban lives. During the children's sermon one Sunday, he held up a McDonald's cup that bore the likeness of flamboyant Chicago Bulls basketball player Dennis Rodman, noting that some members of the congregation had contributed to the cup's marketing. (Rodman's hair changed color with the temperature of the beverage in the cup.)

"Do you ever worry?" Pastor Scott asked the children.

"Yes," a few answered, sheepishly.

"Do your parents ever worry?" "Yes!" the children all shouted, uncoaxed. Pastor Scott then broached his evangelical topic for the day: "Give all your worries over to Jesus." The sermon for the adults bore the title, "When Maalox Moments Become a Way of Life," and Pastor Scott declared the communion table a "worry-free zone," where the dreaded concept of "Monday" could be left at Jesus' feet.

Pastor Scott holds no naive sentiments about some universal edge-city thirst for intimate relationships that can be quenched by church programming. As he writes:

> Our discovery has been that while friendliness is important to everyone, many newer members are not particularly concerned about "the closeness of the church" in the first place. The primary organizing principle which holds them to this congregation is not the constellation of close relationships built up over years spent together but an attraction to particular programs for themselves or their children, engaging worship experiences, and/or the opportunity to participate in meaningful Christian volunteer opportunities. These members certainly expect to be treated warmly and cordially in their relationships with other church folks, but they also seem to value a degree of distance and privacy.[13]

Such are the needs of many edge-city congregations.

Calvary Church

The person from First Congregational who spoke of big churches in cornfields certainly had this one in mind. Calvary Church (Assemblies of God)[14] is big by any standard, with a massive facility that dominates 116 acres of former farmland and accommodates nearly three thousand worshipers each Sunday.

The church's history parallels Naperville's edge-city growth. Sandwiched between the openings of Bell Labs and Amoco Research, Calvary began its corporate life in 1967 by purchasing a wooden-frame church near the center of town (which now houses Calvary's ministry to the poor); then, in the late 1970s, it erected an eighty thousand–square-foot facility in an early boom area of South Naperville (which now houses Calvary Christian School). The church's current $20 million complex is a stone's throw from the prestigious White Eagle subdivision in Naperville's Sector G.

Calvary Church qualifies as a "megachurch" in its large attendance figures; its full-service programming for a consumer-oriented clientele, including numerous fellowship groups that mete out the big-church experience in manageably small doses; its architectural overtones, reminiscent of a shopping mall or convention hotel. Yet Calvary's unapologetic Pentecostalism cuts against the grain of the most influential megachurch model: Willow Creek Community Church, with its "seeker-targeted" or

Fig. 8-2. Calvary Church and campus in Naperville, Illinois. Calvary is a growing Pentecostal "megachurch," which participates in Naperville's rapid expansion. Photo courtesy of Calvary Church.

"seeker-oriented" sensitivity to today's unchurched, skeptical, disaffected, yet spiritually searching baby boomers. Calvary retains many "cringe factors" that might drive seekers away. A free-standing, forty-foot-high cross outside the main entrance stakes Calvary's Pentecostal claim in full view of busy Route 59. Sunday services feature long sermons replete with extensive biblical expositions. Members prefer songs with unambiguous Christian lyrics, ranging in genre from traditional hymns such as "Blessed Assurance" and "Trust and Obey" to catchy contemporary Christian music. Offering plates are passed with unflinching admonitions to Christian commitment. People speak in tongues occasionally, and many raise their hands in typical Pentecostal fashion during the prayers. Services climax with an old-fashioned altar call for the unsaved to come forward and give their lives to the Lord.

When I asked the assistant pastor if all this might frighten off unsuspecting visitors, he admitted that Calvary's Pentecostalism is "seeker hostile," and that the message of the cross runs counter to the secular humanism and self-centered values of the typical baby boomer. But he also pointed out that even non-Pentecostal Christians have initial misgivings about attending a Pentecostal service. The key is whether a person's pain is great enough to risk anything to find healing, even walking into a Pentecostal church.

Naperville is a "scary" place for many people, the founder of Calvary's counseling ministry told me—an assessment at odds with the usual portrayal of the town. Calvary's youth ministry, which draws hundreds to midweek services that feature rock music with Pentecostal lyrics, exhorts teenagers to take a stand for righteous behavior in their schools, to reject drug-and-sex lifestyles fueled by the ethics of tolerance that dominates modern society, and to encourage nominal Christians in their schools to join them in righteous living. Calvary also offers a ministry to single adults, some of whom are parents struggling to raise the youth just mentioned. Many singles throw themselves into their work, the singles pastor told me, seeking life's entire meaning there. Others add friends and regular workouts at the health club to their work, but this still leaves a spiritual void that Calvary seeks to fill.

I attended one of the church's fellowship group meetings. Seven couples ranging in age from their twenties to their fifties gathered on a Friday night at a home in one of South Naperville's new subdivisions. The group sat in a large circle in the living room, first sharing a time of "praise reports and prayer requests," the latter being the more numerous. One couple had just learned they were expecting a baby, a cause for praise. But another woman shared her dismay at how greatly her extended family was enmeshed in sexual sin without even realizing it (specific details were supplied). Two men spoke of work-related stresses. In one case, high level managers were being terminated without explanation. The man prayed for peace of mind for the most recent casualty. Several people asked prayers for good health and impending surgeries. After this impromptu individual sharing, the group entered into a time of more formal prayer, punctuated by frequent exclamations of "Yes, Lord," "Thank you, Jesus," "Praise God," and the like. The group then sang several contemporary Christian songs and shared more individual prayer requests.

A Bible study would have ensued had there not been a Chicago Bulls playoff game that evening. The group ate popcorn and pizza and analyzed the game like any number of Naperville fans gathered that evening. The difference had been in this group's Pentecostal pregame warm-ups.

Saint James Lutheran Church

Saint James serves as a counterpoint to the visible and exponentially growing congregations of Naperville, such as Calvary and Wheatland

Salem. The church struggles with problems of location and membership loss, in addition to addressing the stresses of edge-city life.

Saint James (Evangelical Lutheran Church in America) began in 1979 as a denominational mission enterprise in the home of its founding pastor. The congregation met in a public elementary school at the intersection of Routes 59 and 34 (Ogden Avenue) before moving to its present site, about one block east, in September 1989. At that time the church and an adjacent landscaper had the only structures in the area, but eventually they were joined on the west and north by commercial developments piggybacking on nearby Fox Valley Center mall. Moreover, Routes 59 and 34 have become major traffic arteries, and a residential subdivision will likely be developed soon on open land immediately to the south.

This site has become a source of concern for the congregation. Although the location would appear choice for attracting new members, the church building itself, a small, A-shaped sanctuary with an attached multipurpose wing, is engulfed by surrounding development to the point of near obscurity. Particularly galling for some is the view approaching from the west on Route 34, which is dominated by a flooring store that the current pastor, the Reverend Roger Timm, calls "a two-story monstrosity."

The congregation has mounted efforts to overcome this visibility problem, for instance, through flyer distributions in nearby subdivisions. An Advent caroling party in 1995 doubled as a time to decorate the front of the church in order to catch the eyes of passersby. Newly dedicated stained-glass windows led the pastor to reflect in 1996, "It really has added to [our] morale. We have always feared that our church looks like part of a strip mall, but these windows are a sign that we are a church."

Much of the recent low congregational morale derives from the forced resignation of the founding pastor in February 1992, which caused a great upheaval in the church and a precipitous decline in membership. Early in his tenure at Saint James, the present pastor held cottage discussions and other activities in order to determine the mood of the congregation. The church's current motto—"A welcoming place for sharing the love of God"—developed out of those discussions, and the pastor feels that the congregation has now appropriated this view of itself. By 1996, membership loss appeared to have bottomed out.

Most of the congregation are middle-class professionals who suffer from vocational stress, overextension, and anxiety about corporate downsizing. Saint James has responded by trying to create a comfortable,

Fig. 8-3. Saint James Lutheran Church, eclipsed by commercial developments in Naperville, Illinois, attempts to be a respite from the stress of edge-city life. Photo by Paul D. Numrich.

face-to-face community where harried, unappreciated, and anxious people can take heart that God loves them and calls them to a life of love in an often unloving society. People know each other here and share a friendly Christian fellowship together. The pastor's sermons emphasize God's loving care and its transformative power in people's daily lives. Posing the question in one sermon "Would it make any difference if Saint James didn't exist?" the pastor answered that the result would be one less place "to gather to worship and to listen to the message of God's love for us and God's will for our lives, . . . one less place in our fast-paced, impersonal world where we can experience personal caring."

The pastor's approach to job loss and transition within the congregation illustrates this emphasis. He addresses such issues about once a month in his sermons. He feels the church's role is to maintain people's sense of self-esteem by showing them that they are loved throughout their ordeals. People can get help with their résumés elsewhere—the church is where they feel worthwhile in spite of a situation where they are made to feel otherwise. Christian commiseration is key. What does one do, the pastor asked in a sermon, if one's position requires letting other people go at their place of employment? The answer:

No easy answer. Quitting in protest wouldn't do much good except to add one more person to the unemployment rolls. Can you lay someone off lovingly? Words of sympathy and appreciation may seem hollow, and your authority to act may be limited. But concern for justice, fairness, and compassion can shape how you act and what support is offered to the people affected.

One lay leader spoke about the role Saint James plays in many members' lives. This person sees the local church as providing an alternative to the corporate and residential contexts in which people work and live. The church allows people to express their faith and to enrich their lives in ways not found on the job or in the neighborhood. One simply does not discuss certain things with one's neighbors, who typically are more passing acquaintances than close friends. Also, since many members have no extended family in the area, the one continuity in their transient lives becomes church membership. In this lay leader's own case, the family had lived in five different states, but in each new area they found a church to join.

Congregations Reflecting Naperville's New Diversity

The *Naperville Sun*'s sesquicentennial edition in 1981 captured some of the town's growing religious diversity, featuring Unitarian (established 1955), Jehovah's Witness (1956), and Mormon (1966) congregations in addition to many of the earlier and mainline churches. Much more diversity would come to town in the 1980s and 1990s. For instance, DuPage Korean United Methodist Church, the largest of eight Korean Christian congregations in the area, has shared space in one of Naperville's original Piety Hill churches since 1986. The congregation's membership of nearly one hundred is predominantly professional and well educated, including several engineers from Argonne National Laboratory. In 1996 a Chinese Lutheran congregation bought Naperville's historic Nichols Library. As one member put it, "I really do feel this is the place God wanted us to be in."

Three relatively new congregations—Jewish, Muslim, and Buddhist—have particularly poignant tales to tell about their place in edge-city Naperville.

Congregation Beth Shalom, affiliated with the Jewish Reconstructionist Federation and one of two DuPage County synagogues, began in 1972 through the efforts of local Jewish residents, virtually all of whom have since moved away. In 1985, Beth Shalom purchased a former Evangelical Free Church facility north of downtown Naperville, which it eventually outgrew. The congregation constructed a new building in 1998, DuPage County's first synagogue to be built from the ground up, on a donated site not far from Naperville's Piety Hill.

Rabbi Michael Remson characterizes his congregation as mostly young, relatively economically secure, corporate employees. Several work at Amoco, Argonne, and Lucent. Were it not for the mobility of the membership, the rabbi says, Congregation Beth Shalom would not exist. The membership is a conglomeration of religious backgrounds—Reform and Conservative Jews, even many Christians through marriage—for whom the synagogue's Reconstructionist affiliation may be the most workable institutional compromise. Beth Shalom does not represent the "home synagogue" for most members, a fact evident when many return to their childhood synagogues to celebrate Jewish holy days.

One constant for most members is their choice to live in Naperville. "We west-suburban Jews are a self-selected community," the rabbi pointed out at a forum held in Chicago's heavily Jewish North Side. "We like it in Naperville," he explained. Jews remain a small minority, and they must endure occasional ignorance about Judaism as well as the "seasonal pain" of Christmastime, but Jewish life in Naperville is unpretentious and less intense than in other settings, and other minority religious groups are around to deflect attention. As one member of Beth Shalom explained, the town is rather homogeneous on most levels: "Jew or not Jew, look who's living in Naperville. We're not all that different from the rest of the folks who live in Naperville."

Still, to be a Jewish community in Naperville has a unique social geography. I noticed the unconscious language used by virtually every person interviewed at Congregation Beth Shalom: they talked about being Jews "out here" in the western exurbs, implying a qualitative difference from Jewish life "in there," that is, in the thickly settled Jewish northern suburbs and the North Side of Chicago. After moving to Naperville from Wilmette in the early 1980s, Beth Shalom's lay president would quip to friends and family that he had joined the Diaspora.

Since Congregation Beth Shalom is "the only show in town," to quote one member, it devolves upon the synagogue to bring Judaism to bear on Naperville's edge-city lifestyle. Some in the congregation fear that the influence runs too much in the opposite direction. A synagogue board member with nearly thirty years of teaching experience at an area public school lamented the priorities of many members' lives, in this order: house, car, vacations, work, and Judaism. When I asked about potential conflicts between school athletic events and Sabbath services on Friday nights, he replied that there is no conflict, since the kids are at the game.

"Throughout this year, I have had quite a hectic schedule," wrote one tenth grader in her culminating essay for confirmation class. "High pressure and academic demands have been my life!" We might speculate about what her adult life will be like, given her hectic life already as a sixteen-year-old, yet she contends: "I know how [difficult] it is to hold a busy schedule and [still] attend Sunday School, but it is possible."

For several years Beth Shalom has run a Havurah (fellowship) program of adult small groups. According to the program's founder, these groups fill a void in many members' lives. Naperville is more like California than the Jewish North Side of Chicago, he explained. Life here is so spread out, and there is no strong sense of "community," but it can be created within congregations like Beth Shalom. Another member gave unexpected confirmation of this opinion during an interview. A committed Jewish feminist who remembers Beth Shalom's beginnings, she bemoaned the small number of like-minded feminist members today. Yet, when asked why she stays, she pointed to the symbolic significance of the synagogue and also to a certain "richness" in the relationships she has developed here.

Workplace anxiety—and not a little anger—struck several of Beth Shalom's members when both Amoco and AT&T downsized. The congregation's adult members also suffer the added anxiety of being the "sandwich generation," that is, concerned about the quality of life of both aging parents and maturing children. In his 1995 newsletter message to the congregation during Sukkoth, the Jewish festival in which temporary shelters (*sukkahs*) were traditionally constructed, the rabbi advised: "The sukkah reminds us that life is not secure; that worrying is part of the human condition. . . . So, at least we aren't crazy for being afraid. Come; eat in the sukkah. If life is insecure at least it can be fun."

On the other side of town from Congregation Beth Shalom, the Islamic Center of Naperville occupies the former Jehovah's Witnesses Kingdom Hall. Like other American mosques, the Islamic Center of Naperville features a communal prayer room oriented toward the holy city of Mecca. Because of the Chicago area's historical pattern of building on a north-south-east-west grid, such an orientation means that the focal point (*mihrab*) of the prayer room is the northeast corner, the direction to Mecca following the curvature of the globe. Thus, symbolically, American Muslims in prayer place themselves slightly askew of the dominant culture. To be a Muslim congregation in a place like Naperville thus carries a unique sense of spiritual distinction.[15]

The Islamic Center of Naperville emerged from discussions among mostly Indo-Pakistani professionals in the late 1970s. Around 1980, leaders from several western suburbs formed an organization for the purpose of building a mosque, but a proposed site in Woodridge never materialized. Instead the community established a short-lived Islamic school while continuing to raise funds for a mosque. When Muslims in nearby Villa Park opened their mosque and school in 1983, Naperville Muslims joined that venture.

The distance to the Villa Park mosque proved inconvenient to many, however. A small group began meeting in Naperville homes for evening prayer, and employees of Bell Labs reserved a conference room for Friday's midday communal prayer, signing in non-employees as visitors. The present mosque facility was purchased in 1992 and offers all five daily prayers, as well as an Islamic school in the afternoons. The congregation now comprises Arabs and other ethnic groups in addition to the Indo-Pakistani majority.

Perhaps, a founding member told me, the Islamic Center of Naperville would not have experienced problems with its neighbors had the congregation not sought to renovate their facility. But the subsequent contention between the center and its non-Muslim neighborhood has brought the marginal status of immigrant Muslims into focus. "Every Friday in a quiet Naperville neighborhood," opens one of many newspaper accounts, "a weekly clash of communities begins just before 1 p.m." The issue has to do with traffic congestion at prayer time, which the neighbors fear will be exacerbated by the proposed renovations. Still, when a neighbor purportedly exclaimed to members, "Why don't you go back where you came from?" the intent likely was not to send them back to their own suburban neighborhoods.

The notion of "neighborliness" has been invoked many times. The center's president, an Arab engineer, has consistently maintained that his members try to be "good neighbors" to the area. Parking attendants protect access to residential driveways and curbside mailboxes, for instance, banning mosque attenders who disobey their rules of parking etiquette three times. Still, the center may not be long in this neighborhood, since it hopes eventually to build a new facility in another location.

Come what may, we can expect the mosque's president to be consistent with his *khutbah* (sermon) theme during a recent Eid Ul-Adha holy day service. There is no better prayer than to pray to be a good Muslim, he said—better than to pray for a new house, a new car, or even children. Being better Muslims will make us better people, he stressed, and the community around us will be a better community.

Lotus Sangha (established 1995) gathers regularly in a private residence in one of Naperville's newer subdivisions.[16] Followers of well-known Vietnamese monk Venerable Thich Nhat Hanh, the immigrant Vietnamese members of Lotus Sangha are simply too busy to establish a full-fledged Buddhist temple, according to the group's coordinator. Lotus Sangha arranges periodic visits by out-of-town Buddhist monastics who apply Hanh's Zen Buddhist insights to members' lives and concerns during extended meditation/teaching sessions. People attend from throughout the metropolitan area, attracted by Lotus Sangha's particular combination of ethnic identity and Buddhist practice.

I observed three sessions that typify Lotus Sangha's approach. The first, a day-long mindfulness retreat, featured different forms of meditation in the morning and afternoon. In the evening, sixteen adults attended a two-hour *dharma* (teaching) talk by a Buddhist monk from San Diego, though the style was much more dialogical than a traditional Buddhist *dharma* talk. The session began with everyone introducing themselves and identifying where they live. After a brief ritual honoring the Buddha, the group heard the monk's message about clearing their minds and meditatively cultivating a peacefulness that is "empty" of either excessive happiness or depression. The key here, the monk explained, is to do everything with complete concentration.

A man who identified himself as an architect pressed the monk on how to accomplish this. It is easy to talk about concentration, he proposed, but difficult to put into practice. The man found it particularly difficult in his occupation, where he faces tense situations and even anger, where fellow workers argue with him and challenge his work. He feels he must not back down, otherwise he will be labeled a "loser," anathema in today's work world. The monk suggested ways to discuss issues without becoming angry, since anger will consume a person and create negative results in family and other relationships. Others in the room eagerly joined the discussion, though not in English. A time of singing followed. One woman offered a solo in French; another woman sang several emotional solos "about our homeland and how we miss it," as she announced in English. The title of the final group song translated as "Get Together" or "Come Closer," an expression of Lotus Sangha's cohesiveness around the compassion and mutual understanding they find in the Buddha's *dharma*.

At the second session, the same monk from San Diego gave an hour-long *dharma* talk to the children. True understanding and true happiness come from being a Buddha, he said. The lotus flower grows in ponds in Vietnam, the country of your parents, and it is like your mind: the true mind or Buddha mind rises above the mud of the ordinary world and is pure. Practice mindfulness meditation in everyday life—if you are mindful, you will discover something beautiful already within your body and mind. We should get in touch with the energy of a clear mind in order to become intelligent, happy, and loving people. Be good children so your parents will be happy, and you will be happy too. The essence of Buddhism is to live with true understanding, to live mindfully, to help others, to refrain from doing bad things or making people angry.

The third session marked Ullambana or Vulan, the Vietnamese Mother's Day. Two Vietnamese nuns from Michigan led the dialogue about how to maintain a peaceful mind in everyday life. The question arose as to how to have a peaceful family, especially if you are the only one in your family who meditates. One fiftyish man, an accounting manager, described his daily practice in detail. His stressful week involves long commutes and very demanding work. He listens to peaceful music (from Thich Nhat Hanh), pauses for focused breathing exercises before getting out of the car to go into work, meditates during his breaks, and stops at a park on the way home for fifteen to thirty minutes of practice. He and his wife both practice, and because of this they have no marital problems, he testified.

The nuns gave advice throughout the evening. It is not easy to practice daily, but we should use our time wisely. Don't eat or fight in the car, rather use that time to practice. When you feel a physical pressure in your chest, it indicates some kind of worry in your life. But the mind controls everything in this world—a good mind makes everything around you good, but a "devil mind" (my translator's term) makes everything around you bad.

Conclusion: Ambivalence over Edge-City Life

Like other corporate entities, congregations participate in the social and structural dynamics that create edge-city technoburbs like Naperville. Some congregations contribute directly to the physical reconfiguration of such places, riding the crests of residential growth patterns and building new religious facilities consistent with the new landscape. Wheatland Salem Church (which owes its continued existence to the building boom in Sector G), Calvary Church (whose history parallels Naperville's coming-of-age as an edge city), and Congregation Beth Shalom (with a membership turnover of virtually 100 percent since its establishment) stand out in this regard. All three recently opened new facilities architecturally appropriate to their edge-city niches—even Calvary's "big church in a cornfield" would not strike typical edge-city commuters as out of place as they whiz past it on Route 59. Other edge-city congregations try to buck the reconfiguration trends swirling around them, but they evolve vis-à-vis those trends nonetheless. First Congregational Church (which split over the issue of relocation from its historic downtown site) and Saint James Lutheran Church (which has suffered from poor visibility and a downward trend in membership) provide cases of relative ill ease or ill fit with edge-city transformations.

Edge-city congregations also contribute to the increasing social and cultural diversity of these "places apart" within the restructuring metropolis of contemporary America. Most residents of outer-ring or exurban enclaves may still be Christian, but some of their Christian neighbors now hail originally from Asia instead of Europe. And other neighbors now profess non-Christian faiths such as Islam and Buddhism, in addition to the more familiar Judaism. The cultural landscapes of places like Naperville now include synagogues, mosques, and temples alongside churches. To a great extent, the congregations served by these religious institutions were formed by the dynamics of edge-city technoburban development and are affected by those same dynamics, no matter whether they call themselves Christians, Muslims, Buddhists, or Jews.

Edge-city congregations confront the stresses of edge-city life, offering religion's transcendent perspective and spiritual comfort to people in need in the midst of general material abundance. Naperville is a popular place, yet its congregations are not always happy about what Naperville has become. The hectic pace of life, anxieties in the workplace, social problems, congestion from rapid development—these represent the downsides of prosperity, the costs of successful transition to technobur-ban status. But religion has always measured "success" by more than one yardstick. At heart, the search is the same no matter the denominational label—the search for spiritual meaning in "the most materialistic com-munity in America," in the words of one local Baptist pastor. The ambiva-lence of edge-city religion is that it nearly bites the hand that feeds it, so to speak; for in the midst of obvious material success, edge-city congrega-tions ask: Is this worth the costs? Is this all there is to life?

Intriguingly, religion's ambivalence over edge-city life is shared by many edge-city analysts, despite their relative lack of interest in edge-city religious life. From a mall owner's perspective, religious facilities may represent simple "noncompeting low-density [land] use," but Joel Gar-reau suggests that religion is an important purveyor of "community" and "connectedness" amid the centrifugal forces of edge-city life, and thus re-ligion helps make an edge city a livable place. Provocatively, Garreau points to religion's rather uncomfortable fit in the edge-city environ-ment—after all, what need is there for religion's vision of a life more abundant in the midst of such material abundance?[17]

As Garreau sees it, these exurban enclaves are the wave of the future, though it remains to be seen what kind of future this wave will bring in its wake. "Are we satisfying our deepest yearnings for the good life with Edge City?" Garreau asks. "Or are we poisoning everything across which we sprawl?"[18] Whereas Garreau's concern for the good life may be moti-vated largely by civic and aesthetic considerations, edge-city congrega-tions pose the same questions for spiritual reasons, seeking satisfying an-swers in sermons, fellowship, and programs of various types. The case studies presented in this chapter suggest that congregations in edge-city technoburban milieus may tend to offer spiritual palliatives for individu-als rather than structural alternatives for edge-city technoburban life. Fellowship, prayer, and meditation mitigate the stresses of this lifestyle. They do not advocate substituting a less stressful, alternative lifestyle.

NOTES

My thanks to Nancy L. Eiesland for her helpful comments on an earlier version of this chapter. Research for this chapter began in October 1995.

1. In the interests of space and readability, newspaper reports, primary docu-ments, and personal interviews are cited sparingly. These sources include numer-

ous articles published between 1995 and 1998 in the *Beacon News* (Aurora, Illinois), the *Naperville Sun,* the *Daily Herald,* the *Chicago Sun-Times,* and the *Chicago Tribune.* Primary documents were provided by the city of Naperville, the Fox Valley Genealogical Society, the DuPage County Regional Planning Commission, the DuPage County Development Department, and Indian Prairie School District 204.

2. Ebner, "Technoburb"; Helgesen, *Everyday Revolutionaries;* Lemann, "Stressed Out in Suburbia."

3. Ebner does not consider religion, while Lemann devotes one paragraph to Naperville's congregations. Helgesen considers religion throughout her book, but her analysis takes a predominantly individualistic perspective.

4. Historical information from Towsley, "View of Historic Naperville"; Keating and Lebeau, *North Central College and Naperville.*

5. Ebner, "Technoburb," 56.

6. Fishman, *Bourgeois Utopias;* Garreau, *Edge City,* 7. Eiesland, *Particular Place,* surveys the literature on such places.

7. Ebner, "Technoburb," 59.

8. Claritas divided the United States into sixty-two lifestyle clusters based on census data, opinion polls, and product purchases, assigning each cluster a clever nickname. Reardon, "New Geography," reports the view of the National Opinion Research Center director that these nicknames both are "too cute" and tend to imply that the difference between these types are greater than they are. Even so, the labels do capture aspects of Naperville's lifestyle.

9. See Garreau, *Edge City,* 428.

10. Lemann, "Stressed Out in Suburbia," 42.

11. Helgesen, *Everyday Revolutionaries,* 51–53.

12. Lyle E. Schaller, phone interview with Paul D. Numrich, February 7, 1996.

13. Field, "'Let My People Go,'" 84–85.

14. For a fuller treatment of this congregation, see Numrich, "Pentecostal Megachurch on the Edge."

15. See Numrich, "Facing Northeast."

16. Though not in Sector G as Helgesen, *Everyday Revolutionaries,* 226, reports.

17. Garreau, *Edge City,* 63–65, 288, 291–94, 454.

18. Ibid., 11–12.

Part III

Religion and the New Metropolitan Context

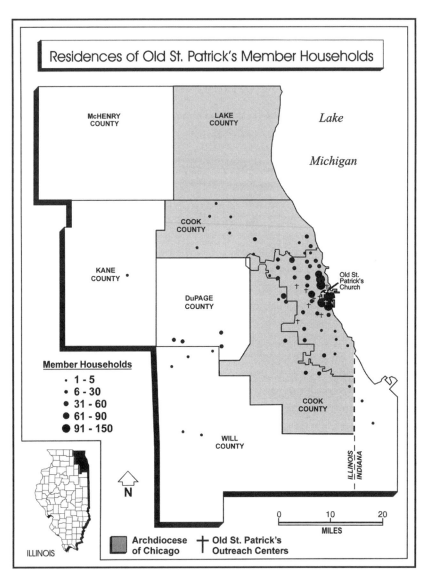

Map 9. Old Saint Patrick's Roman Catholic Church draws members from throughout—and beyond—the Archdiocese of Chicago, while also serving as a local parish. Map by Brian Twardosz, BMT Printing and Cartographic Specialists.

Chapter 9

Catholic Spirituality in a
New Urban Church

Elfriede Wedam

"They welcomed a stranger . . . that's how Abraham and Sarah got started. . . . I think the church ought to model for the world that virtue of hospitality." So responds Father Jack Wall, the pastor of Old Saint Patrick's Church, to the question of how to meet the challenges of pairing old understandings with new times. Hospitality is only the first step, but it suggests an older virtue that may affect the uneasy balance between the changes many urban Americans have made and those to which they have been subject. The religious practices of American Catholics have always stood at the junction of faith and world, and this chapter assesses what has happened in one urban Catholic church in an attempt to learn where current change might lead.

In the mid-1960s, the west side of Chicago's business district was home to skid row. There were no residences, and the area had retained few of the commercial activities that were generated by overland rail and Great Lakes ship traffic during industrial growth of the city. But Old Saint Patrick's Catholic Church, the oldest public building in Chicago, founded in 1846 by Irish railroad workers, remained. The church's yellow bricks, joined in a Romanesque revival style, contain museum-quality stained-glass windows that use motifs from the *Book of Kells*.[1] Each of its mismatched towers, representing eastern and western Christendom, is topped by a Celtic cross.

Succeeding waves of Italians, Mexicans, and other immigrants were served by Old Saint Patrick's Church as they passed through this tenement district, which was also the home of Jane Addams. In 1931, the local archdiocesan newspaper wrote that Old Saint Pat's served "the Loop workers and transients because of its convenience to the hotels in the central part of the city."[2] The printers from the South Loop Printers Row came for the 3:30 A.M. Sunday mass, created for them after their shift. Today the church has made a place for a new transient population—middle-class urbanites, both returnees from the suburbs who now prefer to live in the city again and young adults who work in the Loop.

The current story began in the mid-1980s, when Old Saint Patrick's was redefined as a regional or magnet church. Because the church had been designated a historic landmark in 1964 it had remained open, although used more as meeting space than as a functioning parish, since only one residential building was located inside the parish boundaries. But Old Saint Patrick's captured the interest of Fr. John J. Wall, a diocesan priest whose own Irish bloodlines were connected to both the Catholic and the political history of the city. A church at a major expressway interchange that was also within walking distance of the Loop suggested to him centrality and access—a way to create a second-generation, postimmigrant urban church.

Since few people live within the parish territorial boundaries, fluid membership categories were deliberately created. One could simultaneously belong to Old Saint Patrick's and to one's neighborhood parish, or just belong to Old Saint Pat's, or simply participate in one of the church's many opportunities for volunteering or socializing. By the mid-1990s the church had fifteen hundred registered members, the majority from various city neighborhoods and about 25 percent from the suburbs. The 1998 rolls reveal twenty-eight hundred members and a mailing list of over twelve thousand. New building construction and conversions of lofts and warehouses added residences where there were none before. The members are predominantly white, with a handful of African Americans and an occasional Asian or Hispanic, and are overwhelmingly white-collar professional and business people, and young adult and middle-aged. Church programs on work and faith, spirituality, and young adult issues, as well as social events and community outreach, attract from hundreds to thousands of participants. Successful fund-raising, anchored by the popular but increasingly secular "World's Largest Block Party" each July, has produced an annual budget over $1 million. The church has turned more to stewardship as the staff strives to reduce the financial dependence on vagaries such as the weather and the popularity of the rock bands at the block party. Old Saint Pat's recently undertook a multimillion-dollar restoration of the architectural and artistic features of the

Fig. 9-1. Saint Patrick and reredos behind the altar in Old Saint Patrick's Roman Catholic Church, Chicago. The Celtic cross symbolizes the church's understanding of the relationship to the city: the circle represents the city boundary and the cross, the meeting point of the people. Photo by Erin Jaeb. Used by permission.

church, entirely financed through the parish's own efforts. Their elementary school, the first to open under Catholic auspices in twenty-five years in Chicago, has a substantial waiting list. While not the only post–Vatican II model of "being church," the successful revival of Old Saint Patrick's has been much noticed in an archdiocese that has struggled mightily to keep open the doors of its urban parishes.

A New Organizational Form

A Catholic parish is a manifestation of universal Catholicism at the most local level, and Old Saint Patrick's has been innovating and experimenting with alternative forms of that manifestation. When the social and cultural structures that support a particular model of parish relationships change, members of parishes begin to seek new models. Scholars have noted that the story of this local expression—the "origins, size, activities, inner dynamics and how they responded to the religious needs of their members—has not yet been told."[3] This chapter is about a parish that is responding to the changed urban realities by evolving a new ecclesiology that will continue to support communal relationships not tied to the territorial parish.

The innovation inevitably raises important questions: What is essential to the idea of a parish? Which elements of a parish can be changed before it is no longer a parish? The question was put positively by theologian Langdon Gilkey:

> How can this center, that is, the parish remain vital in a "revised" ecclesia that recognizes historical change and hence change in all the church's structures and expressions, including its forms of ultimate authority, its liturgy and liturgical sacramental rites, its exclusive rules of participation, and its surrounding ecclesiastical dogmas?[4]

When vitality of parish life becomes the goal, as at Old Saint Pat's, there is much room for creating and changing structures to support it.

One of the changes in ecclesiastical dogma that has given Old Saint Pat's the opportunity for innovation and growth is the status of parish territorial boundaries. The 1983 Revised Code of Canon Law states that "as a general rule a parish is to be territorial . . . whenever it is judged useful, however, personal parishes are to be established."[5] Yet this increased flexibility in practice suggests a change in religious identity. If a baptized

Catholic chooses what parish to belong to, does that mean she is in some sense choosing Catholicism and therefore creating a Catholic identity, rather than accepting historical circumstances as a given? Furthermore, can she reject that identity just as easily? While the answer may seem obvious to Protestant and modern secular observers, it is a question about a Catholic self-concept—this ascriptive or inherited status—that has been tied to the assumption of membership in the geographic parish. So now, with parish boundaries less decisive for where and how Catholics belong to their church, the theological and ecclesiological question arises of whether the meaning of being Catholic has changed as a result.

Another question is whether and how culturally constructed (as opposed to geographic) boundaries that demarcate the rules of participation can foster the communal relationships historically associated with the Catholic parish. When a parish like Old Saint Pat's shifts the emphasis from geographic to cultural and social boundaries, what happens to the cohesion of the group? When identity becomes less ascribed and increasingly a matter of choice about whom members associate with, what kinds of relationships will result?

Our ethnographic observation of Old Saint Patrick's Catholic Church mainly provides evidence on the sociological questions about communal relationships, although there are interesting clues for the ecclesiological and theological questions as well. This is in part because Old Saint Patrick's connects the meaning of the cultural and social boundaries to personal identity as a Catholic.

The "loss" of community and the excesses of American individualism are historical themes that crystallized in the imaginations of the present generation through the 1985 publication of Robert Bellah and colleagues' *Habits of the Heart*. Applying these themes to the Catholic Church in *Religion and Personal Autonomy,* Phillip Hammond argues that when choice of parish is available, Catholics lose the primary-group ties that anticipate the obligations parishioners have for one another. The group ties give way to a drive for personal expression, to preoccupation with the question "What am I getting out of this?"[6]

In this study of Old Saint Patrick's Church, I argue not only that this fundamental shift accords with Vatican II but, more important, that it need not result in the loss of the communal character of Catholic parish life. The kind of participation Old Saint Pat's asks of its members respects the broad pluralism of everyday urban life; at the same time, it refuses to build a church simply around their needs. Nevertheless, this new integration is a work in progress, with gaps in concept and execution. This new form reveals losses as well as gains in modifying tradition—serious considerations as the American Catholic Church undergoes the "most significant changes in parish life since the U.S. church mobilized to meet the needs of immigrants."[7]

Old Saint Patrick's is in some respects what R. Stephen Warner calls a "*de facto* congregation," an informal polity of a "gathered assembly," members who are drawn together rather than required to be there—a practice Warner says is becoming increasingly common in America, even among Catholics and others whose religion has historically been ascribed and whose institutions express strong central authority.[8] Yet, Old Saint Patrick's demonstrates that a *de facto* congregation may be quite collective in its actions and communal in its social networks, depending on the propensities of the members and which traditions they draw on. Old Saint Patrick's respects the voluntary commitment that makes a congregation but at the same time consciously seeks to rebuild a corporate foundation to support all aspects of parish life. This rebuilding attempts to respond to urban realities with a new model of parish that will work in a metropolitan—not just a neighborhood—context.

Church Practice in an Urban Setting: Theology and Social Theory

Styles of parish life are determined in part by the theological mission of a particular diocese, the quality of lay and clerical leadership, and the desires of the Catholics in the pews. Intersecting with these factors is the process of "inculturation," which requires innovation to achieve "the proper relationship between faith and culture" in each local setting.[9] Thus the local context helps determine the particular shape and voice of the local churches, so there are different legitimate cultural modes of expressing the "ancient faith" in the contemporary understanding of faith and cultures. Since the Revised Code of Canon Law cited above, several types of nonterritorial parish models have been developed (or redeveloped) around ethnic identification and language, young adult ministries, and urban outreach. One type is like Old Saint Patrick's, located in the downtowns of aging industrial cities without large residential populations. These nonterritorial parishes have open boundaries but still focus on the theological mission of the communion of the church.[10]

The social character of Catholic identity is expressed in many ways that do not depend on territory. For example, gathering around the table, the communion feast, is a collective expression.[11] Yet Catholic churches vary in their communal expression. Phillip Hammond describes a three-stage move of church affiliation from that of a primary-group model to a secondary- and voluntary-group model. Old Saint Pat's is, in many respects, an example of "individual-expressive" relationships, in which secondary- and voluntary-group ties form the basis of its associational life. This contrasts with the "collective-expressive" model, which represents inherited relationships with several overlapping primary-group ties.[12] The collective-expressive model of human agency emphasizes the obligations of the human condition—being a member of something, such as the parish, that is greater than the individual ego and makes claims upon it.

However, Hammond argues, when people *choose* their religious affiliation, including whether to affiliate at all, the nature of religious expression and hence its role and impact on individuals changes. This is the basis of his critique of the increasingly voluntary nature of American religion. While Protestants have long celebrated the "voluntary principle"[13] in American religious affiliation, it is mainly since the 1960s that choosing whether and where to affiliate has increased as a form of personal autonomy for Catholics. Hammond argues empirically that personal autonomy correlates with an erosion of local, primary ties and an acceptance of a new morality based heavily on individual conscience and choice. Personal autonomy among Catholics is revealed in how they choose personal parishes over territorial ones and evidence lower rates of parish involvement. The decline of involvement in parish life is accompanied by a change in the meaning of that involvement; that is, increasingly, parish involvement is a vehicle for self-expression only.[14]

Although Hammond notes how personal autonomy resulted from structural and cultural changes, his formulation is nevertheless nonreflexive. His collective-expressive model assumes that people are Catholic because they have always been Catholic and go to church out of habit. He argues that this mode permits the church to mediate for its members against the autonomy of the state and the market. The church's authority rests on its claim that its members constitute a perduring group and do not just come together to pursue temporary interests. In contrast, observers like José Casanova note that although the Catholic Church has not, for example, been able to shape public policy on abortion, it has been extremely effective in stimulating, informing, and focusing a public debate.[15] Universal education enhanced the ability of ordinary Catholics to decide whether or not their parish fosters the development of their inner spiritual life. Their reform efforts echo the Council of Trent, which determined that parish territorial reform was needed "for the spiritual good of souls."[16]

Phillip Hammond's collective-expressive view of the church is consistent with a theological interpretation of parish that "the church is not an object that they, as individuals, may freely accept or reject."[17] Some Catholic writers have argued that the church is not "merely a private reality, solely at the service of its members. It is the divinely constituted Body of Christ in history, an essentially public entity."[18] In this view, assent is more a matter of fulfilling a destiny of faith than of engaging a positive preference.[19] But choosing to attend a particular Catholic church is different from choosing to live as a practicing Catholic. Does being a practicing Catholic imply attendance at one's territorial parish? Not necessarily. Unlike Protestants, who may change denominations in the process of choosing a congregation, for Catholics, institutional identity does not change with a change in parish affiliation.

Catholics are retaining a fundamentally institutional identity, regardless of what parish they choose to join or attend. For example, national (that is, ethnically defined) parishes are not territorial either, despite the convenient clustering of European immigrants in ethnic enclaves, often encouraged by pastors to foster commitment to "their" parish (but not necessarily for theological reasons).[20] The primary-group ties created by shared language, national culture, and immigrant status are dependent on a particular historical circumstance. In the typically large ethnic parishes of two thousand or more families, the intimacy implied in primary group ties would have been difficult to find. I hesitate, therefore, to link members' "choosing" of Old Saint Patrick's with "wanting" rather than "having" to go to church. These Catholics *have* to go to church, but they find Old Saint Patrick's contemporary style is intellectually, aesthetically, and spiritually more satisfying than that in their neighborhood parishes. The same can be said of ethnic immigrants' desires to worship in national parishes where a common language and cultural style were and continue to be valued. This is also an expression of choice, but I question that such voluntariness reduces the ability to fulfill one's destiny as a baptized Catholic.

Nevertheless, Hammond's analysis points to important concerns. What is the consequence for community when removed from territory?

What is the further consequence, then, for identity? While American Protestant congregational life is strong and extensive, its social character is different from that of Catholicism. One reflection of this is the difference in commitment to locale, especially to the neighborhood and one's neighbors. I agree with John McGreevy that Catholics' theological and social commitments to neighborhoods had negative consequences for race relations in the United States, but he and other scholars still point to certain positive consequences for security, safety, and the building of civic infrastructure.[21] Sharon Zukin is right that "men and women still want to live in specific places,"[22] that is, a geography they can point to and identify with. Place continues to have meaning, and the construction of meaning cannot rest solely on issues and relationships about which people can freely choose. Personal identity is partially derived from where one lives and the kinds of ties one makes there.

Old Saint Patrick's can be usefully compared to the medieval cathedral churches which were built in the major towns and served the entire region, particularly on liturgical holidays. Similarly, Old Saint Patrick's members are revising—regionalizing—the geographic basis of (social) ascription. They may reject their inherited relationships (with neighbors they, in fact, do not know), but Old Saint Patrick's is nevertheless a necessary expression of their theological inheritance: they *must* go to church, and they must go to a Catholic church with other Catholics.

Old Saint Patrick's: A Model for the World

At Old Saint Pat's, the whole city of Chicago is construed as a metaphor for the territorial parish, and the church is the "meeting at the crossroads" symbolized by the bars on the Celtic cross. The cross is surrounded by a circle, a symbol used on ancient city maps to represent the walls protecting the city residents. Old Saint Pat's has reinterpreted and used this symbolism to connect the church with the city as a whole, reaching beyond traditional parish boundaries. The church draws on Vatican II, which redefined a universal conception of the church so as to make porous the boundaries of the parish center, making the parish "open to the world."[23] Consequently, the focus of the parish is continually outward-looking rather than parochial.

The church is organized around the mobility of young adults for whom "the whole country is their backyard," as associate pastor Father

John Cusick put it. By creating programs around their transitory circumstances rather than lamenting their unpredictability, the church has opened new patterns of attendance and involvement. Outreach efforts then call for the development of new—or rediscovered—virtues, beginning with hospitality.

Hospitality is not only highlighted in the church's mission statement but articulated in every liturgy, particularly by the clergy when they welcome the congregants. The liturgy begins with a greeting to "neighbors" surrounding the worshiper in the pew. This "encounter" with the stranger is vested with spiritual meaning. "Everything is meeting a stranger, is opening yourself up to that gift of the stranger," continued the pastor.

Hospitality has more valence in the church than does the discussion of building a community—the relationship among intimates commonly attributed to the traditional parish. At the same time, the tension between welcoming the seeker, the traveler, or simply the curious and addressing the continuing assembly, who have put down their roots, enrolled their children, and volunteered on a steady basis, is self-consciously balanced. For example, support for family programs has been increased by the addition of staff and a family mass. At the same time, a renewed emphasis on young adults in their twenties has resulted in new programming because of a leveling off of membership.

In part, this tension exists because of the continual movement and impermanence, or at least very conditional stability, of urban life. Old Saint Pat's shares this sense of movement rather than the more fixed sense of neighborhood or traditional "community." The Near West Side surroundings lack an identity, including a "turf." In exchange, the church has centrality and accessibility, which make its programs available for a metropolitan constituency.

Because this is a downtown church with a mission to reach the Loop workers, the church has organized its programs and activities around the schedules and rhythms of the business world. This includes the timing of activities but also the mode of addressing members, who may be transferred to another city or country next month. Many programs are organized with built-in end points—"so people know how to get out of something before they commit to it," Fr. Cusick explained.

Old Saint Pat's has diverse programs for many kinds of Catholics. Through the many community volunteering programs and social programs, its members have reinterpreted their roles as lay Catholics for their own generation. Volunteering is a direct expression of the outward-looking mission of the church, explicitly designed to get away from a clublike model of "meeting members' needs." One volunteer described the involvement of himself and his wife as a calling to "share their gifts." The entirely lay-run Community Outreach Group is the church's cornerstone mission project, with more than five hundred members. It has reduced bureaucratic demands on participants—there are no bylaws or regular meetings—so they can focus on relationship building with those they serve, and on efficiently achieving their goals. One can volunteer for any level of commitment, and exiting is built into the system. The group offers a variety of venues to work in—elementary school tutoring in a black Catholic parish, adult literacy and employment training at both Catholic and non-Catholic locations, pediatric visits at a non-Catholic hospital, working at two Franciscan homeless shelters, an athletic program for Hispanic youth in a Latino parish, holiday sustenance drives, and even a wine auction to raise funds for a home for the mentally handicapped.

A built-in transience is also evident in the content of parish programs, which have none of the traditional membership requirements such as running for office and having monthly meetings; nor is a continuous commitment expected. Instead, this programming resembles an active conference center wherein a variety of lectures, forums, and discussion groups are held—often over an affordable breakfast, lunch, or dinner—and speakers address issues interesting to professional workers. These programs focus on spiritual, ethical, and civic concerns and, together with the archdiocesan young adult ministry led by Fr. Cusick, programs for young adults addressing relationship issues.

The rich mix of activities at Old Saint Pat's means that the parish is a vital social center, continuing the intensive and extensive group life that American Catholics have created as a legacy of the "immigrant church."[24] To be sure, contemporary practices are less devotional and more social than those of the nineteenth century.[25] Nevertheless, they continue to be expressions of faith and are certainly no less collective in character. Indeed, those nineteenth-century devotional activities were also a pursuit of personal spiritual growth, albeit less critical of church ecclesiology or doctrine.

The metaphor of the parish as a community is used sparingly at Old Saint Pat's. The ideal moral construction of community as a relationship among intimates may not adapt well to the kinds of relationships these urban people actually have. Joseph Fichter suggested this in the mid-1950s: "I say an urban parish cannot be a community—it can't be; it's too

Fig. 9-2. Old Saint Patrick's Roman Catholic Church and "the World's Largest Block Party," which raises over half a million dollars each year for parish activities. Photo by Gail Pollard, courtesy of Old Saint Patrick's Roman Catholic Church.

big. The typical urban parish is a secondary association within which there are maybe a dozen to twenty or twenty-five primary groupings; and this is all to the good."[26]

Old Saint Patrick's Church contains different combinations of primary and segmental relationships of the sort Fichter and others since have observed.[27] Its activities foster overlapping friendship groups. The welcoming atmosphere at meetings, for example, is deliberately organized but appears to emanate spontaneously from the attendees. Rather than a solemn atmosphere before the beginning of each mass, the pews buzz with friendly conversation, and a priest can often be spotted socializing in the aisles. The peace greeting during the liturgy is an occasion for warm and enthusiastic exchanges among the priest celebrant and members spilling into the aisles.

The mass celebrations exhibit immediacy, a sense of participation, and informality. One Sunday the celebrant suggested that because two choir members got married the day before, the choir was a little hung over. Congregants talk about the church as an attraction—something they look forward to, something "you didn't want to miss." But their vibrancy may derive less from intimacy than from the rich variety of intellectually stimulating opportunities that the church offers, including preaching that responds to events in congregants' lives in an intellectually engaging way.

In only a matter of weeks I easily identified familiar faces in a half dozen different church venues, suggesting that many of the members know one another in multiple contexts, partially offsetting the segmental character of urban social life. Such multifaceted arrangements have always characterized urban life; whereas urban relationships are less spatially proximal than in rural areas, Claude Fischer argues that they are not less solid or intimate. The urban environment is one of higher density and more massive scale and separates our relationships into specialized roles. Our neighborhood friends and our work friends, for example, are not likely to know each other. But the relationships around occupation or ethnicity or religious membership are often intimate, face to face, and deep.[28] Old Saint Pat's provides a site for these relationships to form and thrive.

Pluralism, Experimentation, and the Laity

Old Saint Pat's members are thoroughly invested in an incarnational theology that values spirituality over dogma, experience-centeredness rather than rule-centeredness, and presence in this world more than preparation for the next. The theology is inclusive and pluralistic, best seen in the establishment of the Jewish-Catholic Dialogue Group, a dual worshiping group of mixed-marriage couples. Clergy from Old Saint Pat's and a Reform rabbi from a downtown synagogue share ministry to this group. Innovative activities include dual-faith liturgies, such as a naming ceremony and baptism. The family that originated the ceremony described it as "the most meaningful thing we have ever done. It was a real turning point in our religious lives." The dual-faith religious education program for primary-grade children, entirely written and taught by the members, received an award from the Archdiocese of Chicago for its innovative content and quality of lay leadership. Some families in the group emphasize one faith over the other, but others respect both equally, and the content of the religious education school and curriculum reflects the latter approach.

Typically, couples seek out the dialogue group when looking for help in holding a dual-liturgy marriage ceremony. One point of pride is the number of nonpracticing Jews and Catholics who returned to observance after joining. But the deeper response has been the unalloyed relief among couples who have discovered they do not have to yield to marriage the faith of their birth or abandon faith altogether in the desire for familial harmony. They have found a "third way." They can connect their concrete, personal, and pluralistic life situation with what their bylaws call "a meaningful way to find God."

Through their leadership with the dialogue group, Old Saint Patrick's clergy express a theological—not just an ecumenical—pluralism. The group works effectively because clergy help them explicate the role of Christ as a Jew in Jewish history and seek out the symbolic, universal meaning of Christ. For the annual talk on the relationship between Passover and the Lenten-Easter season, the group invited a priest-theologian, who challenged the wall of hostility between the faiths erected over the historical events. He said Jesus "was born a Jew, lived and died as a believing Jew" and then explained how integrating such an idea into the ritual practices of both Christians and Jews directly reflects the content of Jesus' personal ministry.

When asked how this approach stands the test of evangelization, Old Saint Patrick's clergy say they prefer that people be brought into spiritual awareness and practice rather than into doctrinal adherence or conversion. They also point out that a small number of Jews and Protestants have become regular members.

The search for new models of an urban church depends heavily on lay initiative, enabled by Vatican II's reversal of the four hundred years of lay passivity the Tridentine reforms had effected.[29] Many of Old Saint Pat's programs are developed because a layperson suggests a need such as discussion groups focusing on inner spirituality, which are the sodalities of the twentieth century. In Progress (young adult issues), Sunday Suppers (speakers for the "seasoned" adult), the Men's Spirituality Group, and Pray Allways (prayer group) are examples of this. Others, especially the volunteering groups, are more outward-looking. The mission statement orients the effort of Old Saint Patrick's to "serve the life and work of the laity in the world." Staff provide opportunities based on members' experience rather than a prescriptive model of what people "should" do. Yet, while the communal experience is enriched by the bazaar of activities available, a certain busyness may obstruct the ability to achieve deeper self-insight.

A lay-initiated group heralding from a previous era but being redefined by the current membership is the Council on Working Life, which was once an activist organization concerned with the problems of blue-collar workers. Currently, the members have shifted their focus from public issues to individual members' struggle to understand the current economic environment. Reported one member: "What the Council is willing to talk about is ways to humanize the workplace, advise and encourage people to shape the small space which they occupy in their work into something they can live with and keep their sanity." Although some on the Catholic Left will criticize this shift, Monsignor Daniel Cantwell, the chaplain to the group, whose credentials include the labor movement and civil rights, redefined activism in other terms. He declared that being "psychologically and spiritually involved" in everyday life is preferable to testing the correctness of people's positions.

Much of the discourse in the church's programs, as in the wider culture, centers on the notion of interests rather than commitments, and this comes at a cost. The pursuit of self-interest weakens a communal model, because interests are based on individual needs that will change as they become fulfilled, forcing churches (and other institutions) continually to adapt.[30] Therefore, the pursuit of individual interests may fracture communal well-being. For example, interests draw like-minded and like-status people together; hence, while pluralism in Old Saint Patrick's is an expressed ideal, homogeneity of race and class still predominates. The rhetoric of inclusion is part of the self-presentation of Old Saint Pat's, but that presentation appears not to connect with the non-English-speaking or the poor or the nonwhite. For example, exchanges of choirs on Martin Luther King Jr.'s Birthday do not bring African Americans into the congregation. Old Saint Pat's high quality liturgical choir with professional-level soloists and orchestral accompaniment, appeals to middle- and upper-middle-class whites but has not attracted middle- and upper-middle-class African Americans and Hispanics.

Despite the 30 percent nonwhite component in the elementary school, the nonwhite parents are not visible in the congregation. Despite the extensive volunteering in the poor areas of the city, it is hard to spot anyone without a middle-class appearance. While the metropolitan locality constitutes the de facto parish boundaries for inclusion in this church, other symbolic boundaries—middle-classness, professional job status, like-mindedness in taste and style—form the exclusive boundaries.

These choices are probably not intentionally exclusive. Singing music that reflects one's ethnic heritage or taste is a meaningful experience. But the consequences for groups or individuals not privileged to be included can be overlooked or ignored. The metropolitan reach created by Old Saint Pat's overcomes the limitations of access that parishes of the "club mentality" tend to foster. But it promotes an ideology of access without creating the necessary structures to implement it. Such criticism is familiar to the leadership at Old Saint Patrick's. "I want concrete strategies, not condemnations," complained Fr. Cusick to me. "Tell me how to do it!"

In spite of these potential and existing areas of exclusivity, some Old Saint Pat's members who grew up in ethnic or national parishes recounted how Old Saint Patrick's provides an inclusivity they had not previously experienced. One member cited how cliquishness and vested interests in her home parish created "us versus them" styles of relationships. Yet the shift from the boundaries of ethnicity to the boundaries of class, while a freeing experience for many, replaces rather than eliminates definitions of "otherness." At the annual, well-attended Seder Supper, Fr. Wall asked members to make their offering for the needy in order "to expand our community." He reflects an awareness of the limits of the congregation's self-identity but does not directly challenge it. Nevertheless, Fr. Wall acknowledges that Catholics in general are "missing out on the multicultural experience."

Old Saint Patrick's has developed an urban church that is universalistic, theologically pluralistic, fluid, and outward-looking. There are some costs—a certain kind of familiarity, shared identity based on ethnicity, language, historic memory, or even long-term membership, does not exist. Transitory and segmented relationships and a consumer orientation to participation mitigate against an integrated continuity of relationships. Through appropriation of Celtic aesthetics, the church celebrates an Irish heritage that has more to do with the Saint Patrick's Day parade and political connections in the city than with the Irish religious heritage. Pluralism in race and class has not been achieved. The fluidity of membership offers choices, but choices also limit the construction of broader visions that might require a more demanding discipline. "Commitment to relationships is one of the most daunting challenges of our culture," writes Philip Murnion. "Parishes need to keep calling people into commitment to family and friendship, to parish and public life."[31]

What is gained, though, is an inventiveness in the creation of programs inspired by the outward-looking orientation of both the leaders and the members. Music, theater, and artistic expressions in the liturgy are well developed and sensually pleasing. The emphasis on the practical, nondogmatic, nonmoralistic, and holistic understanding of spirituality challenges middle-class, well-educated Catholics with an approach that is worldly and pluralistic. This "non-ideological" theology, as Fr. Cusick calls it, also permits the word from the homilist to be more publicly critical of contemporary society and politics, as when he criticized the warmongering of both the United States and Iraq during the 1991 Persian Gulf War, and to be more cognizant of the ironic than if he were preaching a dogmatic theology. In offering their non-ideological theology, the pastors invoke the Vatican II document *Pastoral Constitution on the Church in the Modern World* in support of a critical understanding of the world by Catholic believers, who are expected to become more open to the world, not to retreat from it.[32]

A non-ideological theology can also limit the range of discussion. At Saint Patrick's, for example, tension points within Catholic dogma—a married clergy, ordination of women, and the abortion issue—are rarely discussed. The effort to avoid moralism and rigidity results in avoiding conversations in which the issues contain stark and oppositional views. The so-called culture wars debate shows the limits of our language to interpret and communicate experiences that contain morally different resolutions, so it may not be surprising that at Old Saint Pat's such conversations are avoided. Leaders at Old Saint Pat's have observed that the young people who come to the church are interested in their relationships and in work; by contrast, "the ordination of women is not high on young people's list of importance." But recent ethnographic studies have also shown how groups actively seek to overcome polarization.[33]

Church programs that focus on workplace issues are under the leadership of the Crossroads Center for Faith and Work, the brainchild of former staffer John Fontana, a self-styled "religious entrepreneur."[34] The center provides forums for professionals to discuss topics ranging from the costs of downsizing to the economic necessity of redeveloping Chicago's poorest neighborhoods. These discussions are infused with the language of transformation: "The church is a reflective community engaging in public dialogue to transform the world." "How can we transform religious convictions into public issues?" "The purpose of the church is not to do ministry but to be captured by mission." In practice, however, the appeal is usually to individual rather than social tranformation. As Fontana concludes, "Discussion often comes back to small transformations in each layperson in accordance with roles, responsibilities, and the use of power and authority in their worlds of work, family, community life, and citizenship."

Charles Shaw, the developer of Lake Point Tower and other upscale Chicago high-rises, has spearheaded a development in North Lawndale, a poor African American neighborhood on the West Side. He speaks compellingly on the necessity of a commitment to the urban core. At Civic Forum, a regular series sponsored by the Crossroads Center, Shaw reminded his audience that in great part the infrastructure of the outlying areas was built at the expense of the city. He stated his belief in both the free market and social responsibility and suggested that we "must know how to blend them together." His vision, however, is focused on the "fundamental power of individuals." Similarly, the moral issues surrounding the responsibility of CEO members of the church who order massive labor cuts is avoided. Questions about responsibility for social justice are answered with "These are educated people. We cannot tell them what to do. Instead we show them the Gospel and encourage their understanding of the power to live out the Gospel." The language of transformation usually refers to the influence one has over the small area around oneself, yet members of the elite, whose sphere of influence is considerably larger, are not challenged to extend their responsibility likewise. The church's principal response is a retreat to spiritual personalism.

The program presentations I was able to observe were mute on the suggestion that Catholicism or Christianity or Christ should permeate or direct decisions in members' work lives. The In Progress series is devoted to discussions on issues that "touch the lives of young adults in the

1990s." There was little discussion about how religion could be a resource to solve problems in the work life. To some extent, these members saw the church as a haven from the unethical or amoral work environment.

Other programs on faith and work focused on the psychological costs of work-life problems—identity crises, consumer numbness, lifestyle hollowness, which result from work chosen for the income it may provide, regardless of intrinsic worth or the collective costs. One speaker repeated the now-familiar warning that "a lifestyle is not a life." When audience members probed for alternatives, he suggested only that individuals elevate satisfying work choices—"do what you really like to do"—above financial considerations and "hope for the best." He did not, for example, suggest that a refashioned union movement could be a fruitful approach, even though his answers to other questions reminded his listeners of the taken-for-granted benefits of past labor struggles.

In a similar way, the problems of corporate downsizing were addressed with a reactive and adaptive perspective, focusing entirely on survival strategies and advising members to "adapt to changes in the business environment." Such shunning of prescriptive approaches makes religious values difficult to articulate. Labor perspectives received a couple of slots during other Civic Forum seasons, but only one speaker suggested any serious role for religion. He was a labor lawyer who included churches with unions as types of organizations that can mediate between the individual and the changes occurring in the global economy. An Old Saint Pat's member likened the non-ideological approach of the church to that which "comes up to the doorway, but does not cross the threshold."

The church's relationship to change is complex, eagerly looking forward yet somewhat stymied by the cultural compromises it finds itself making and the limitations of a focus on personal spirituality. The explicit consensus is that Old Saint Pat's is not involved in structural change. One member commented that the priests of Old Saint Pat's want to ameliorate abuses but not change structures. If members want a challenge, they can find it, but it's not a requirement for participation. Invited speakers have addressed the death penalty, consumerism, unionism, and poverty. Homilies have addressed war and racism. But as one member voiced, "We can talk about issues here, but there is no collective experience that can lead to change."

New ways of connecting individual with collective forms must be constructed. Most Americans speak comfortably the language of individualism as their "first language," asserted the authors of *Habits of the*

Heart.[35] The language of collective expression, however, is more difficult to find and is mostly located where most Americans are not, that is, in "communities of memory." Such groups share a tradition and a past that are continually retold to its members through ritual and story but also through interdependent sharing and decision making. Critics of *Habits of the Heart* have pointed out that while in many ways the language of the collective has been held hostage by the limitations of our current therapeutic, individualistic culture, it can be found in the process of telling the story, more so than in the structures of the group per se. These critics argue that transcending individualism can occur, for example, in the narratives that families pass down and in communities of choice in which the rituals and activities of the members help them interpret their lives and pass the stories on to others.[36] Different forms of communities, those that do not depend on history and tradition, can develop a moral discourse about their shared life with deliberate and self-conscious strategies.

Volunteering is a type of practice that offers the possibility of transcending the self. First, volunteering with others is a way to experience, however fleetingly, a different life. This exposure creates possibilities for volunteers to deal with issues in their own personal situations in a totally different way. Second, it is a way to express altruism, even if it is minimal. At an adult literacy and employment training program in a poor area near the church, a small but tenacious and resourceful staff direct the professionals from Old Saint Patrick's who volunteer each evening. Sister Virginia Phillips, the Catholic nun who runs this program, is impressed with the church for a membership that "has gathered for others." She thinks the Catholic yuppies and their parents who come to Old Saint Patrick's are hungry to serve others, and that is why the church is growing and successful. Sister Virginia views the social-service approach vis-à-vis the more activist social-justice model positively. When volunteers witness small victories in the lives of individual poor people, these suggest larger hopes. The interaction between the Old Saint Pat's members and the members of the center leads to communication and sometimes friendship. Sister Virginia pointed with delight to the warmth and sociality among the Christmas party guests at the large annual event, which brings social mingling between the volunteers and the people they serve. One church staff member reminded me that "outreach is a human thing. It's vested in a human person, not just a program." Through their own reflection, Old Saint Pat's volunteers bring what they have learned to their work settings, where there may be a long-term, though likely not an immediate, potential for wider social change.

Old Saint Patrick's is also attempting to transcend the limits of therapeutic culture by suggesting that members reflect on the experience of others as they reflect on their own experience. The creative potential of this approach was demonstrated in a courageous presentation by Father Larry Craig, director of Maximilian Kolbe House, the ministry to prisoners at Cook County Jail. He offered a Catholic view of capital punishment on the eve of the sentencing of John Wayne Gacy, the most notorious serial killer from Chicago since Richard Speck. He asked the group of two hundred Old Saint Patrick's professionals how many favored capital punishment; more than half raised their hands. Through a narrative describing issues faced by the prison inmates to whom he ministers, Fr. Craig raised questions—without taking an explicit position—about the uses of death in the American criminal justice system. The result was to make his listeners uncomfortable as they reflected on their own positions.

Labor and civil rights activist Msgr. Cantwell was in residence at Old Saint Patrick's when he died of cancer in early 1996. He was known to have spoken out for women's ordination during his homilies. Staff members felt privileged by his presence but also noted his singular courage. Nevertheless, Msgr. Cantwell was not disappointed in the absence of a countercultural stance among Old Saint Pat's members. "A certain kind of activism turns me off," he explained, "especially the kind that comes in from the outside telling [people] what to do." The role of leadership, he felt, was to "encourage people to do what they want and help them see how it fits into the larger whole" of what they want to accomplish. He noted that the strong involvement of young adults in Old Saint Pat's was distinctive—"we're making other parishes wonder what happened to their young adults"—as well as hopeful for the church in general. "There is life here," he told me.

Conclusion: "What the Church Is For"

Old St. Patrick's changed its name from "parish" to "church" to reflect its mission to serve all Catholics who choose to come here. While Old Saint Pat's members voluntarily identify with the church, they continue to carry out a corporate identity of obligations. Voluntarily joining the church has not made attending church less obligatory. Moreover, while choice does not automatically translate into commitment, the latter can be developed in parishes like Old Saint Patrick's, in part because of what Nancy Ammerman calls the "consonance" of individual choice with individual identity and purposiveness.[37] Even religious inheritance, which translates into religious identity, does not automatically result in commitment. Andrew Greeley estimates that about 15 percent of cradle Catholics leave the church.[38]

Catholic identity is not just inherited; it is also constructed by a combination of achievement and ascription. How one grew up was mediated by the interpretative abilities of the earlier generation to connect theology with the social context of their time. It is the same for the next generation. Furthermore, one's identity as a Catholic is the result not just of continually reinterpreted history and tradition but also of religiously legitimated parish and archdiocesan planning (see chapters 5 and 11). The inculturation process connects in an ongoing dialogue the institutional with the personal through the action of the local church.

There is no singular unfolding of history in the development of Catholic parishes. As noted above, the earliest church models were urban but not territorial. Lay initiative was responsible for much of the development of the early American church.[39] Yet current ecclesiological structures emerged from systems of relationships that are now either antiquated—the feudal agrarian model of European parishes—or rare—the small-town American congregations.[40]

Many Catholics, not just those from Old Saint Patrick's, have rejected ideologies of the left and the right on public issues in favor of a focus on and commitment to their private work and family lives. Perhaps they are avoiding larger society-wide moral obligations; alternatively, they may truly be looking for new ways—"for new insights," suggests Fr. Cusick. Creating common understandings about societal obligations in a pluralistic society will require changing our understanding of community and its connection to territory. To accomplish this, the individual-expressive and collective-expressive modes of relationship may need a new fusion. While analytically distinct and clarifying for many purposes, both modes have always been present in some combination and to different degrees, the emphasis shifting with different historical and cultural epochs. When the collective mode had primary agency, individuals tended to become passive, as the recent history of American Catholicism demonstrates. To compensate, individuals exercised choice by being only tangentially related to parishes, as in "Christmas and Easter Catholics." Many pastors have noted that the active core of parishioners consists in only about 10 percent of the members.

Old Saint Pat's acknowledges that it sits in the tension between recourse to individual conscience and the teaching power of the church in moral matters. There, too, it draws on a theological tradition revised and reemphasized in the Second Vatican Council's *Declaration on Religious Freedom*. Thus Old Saint Patrick's signifies one type of the individual-expressive mode of being church. As a case study, it gives evidence of a level of activity and commitment considerably above what is found in the "typical" parish. This evidence is contrary to Hammond's finding that high parish activity and commitment correlate with local ties and implicit acceptance of collective authority in matters of moral issues. Also contrary to Hammond, Old Saint Patrick's demonstrates that the individual-expressive model can be a center of social life and community service, and not just a deliverer of services to members. Old Saint Patrick's may well represent the fusion I argued for above, although the form is still emerging.

Yet there are worries among some members that the church may fall victim to its own successes. Despite the positive atmosphere and high rates of participation, some have noticed a two-class system coming to hand. As one member remarked, a "furs and hats" crowd has developed, some of whom receive celebratory treatment because of their financial giving. Some of the social events carry a big price tag and further stratify the congregation. Moreover, the church is "too packed to be pleasant," especially on holy days, she said. And she worried that people who come for the prestige element are not "volunteering and participating in the regular life of the church." This member fears "the loss of intimacy" as the social cost for Old Saint Patrick's institutional success. Another member ruefully admitted regarding the World's Largest Block Party, while "it's great to have so much money that will sponsor such great programs, the block party is not a Catholic event any more." These are important concerns because, as John McGreevy recently pointed out, the danger of a religious consumerism based on individual autonomy is that it offers "little resistance to 'absorption by business culture.'"[41]

The challenge for the members of Old Saint Patrick's, as for every Catholic church, is to answer the question of mission posed by Fr. Wall, "how to stay focused on what the church is for, and not to somehow respond in the narrow way to one's own needs." This requires "searching for new elements of the transcendent . . . by listening with a 'third ear' to the

symbolic and moral content of existing religious traditions which res-
onate with the contemporary scene."[42] Although the case is hopeful, it is
yet unclear whether the emerging identity of Old Saint Patrick's provides
a model of an urban church based on a dialectical relationship between
the current social context and the theological teachings of the church or
is primarily an adaptation to the prevailing ideas of materially prosperous members.

The members of Old Saint Patrick's Church are middle-class, city-cen-
tered people who participate in several forms of community—segmental
yet multidimensional, through primary *and* secondary relationships. As a
parish, the compliance with parish territorial boundaries is subordinate to
more practical, critical questions of effective church mission and effective
connections with individual spiritually hungry Catholics. So, although Old
Saint Patrick's Church may be a *de facto* congregation, it retains and reen-
acts some of the essential qualities and functions of a parish. In short, I believe it is responding to the restructured urban setting by using the inherited Catholic tradition, the innovations of Vatican II, and the resources of
the city itself to construct multivalent connections among its members in
order to develop new metropolitan forms of belonging.

NOTES

For comments on earlier versions of this chapter, I thank my Religion in Urban
America Program colleagues and, Penny Becker, Kevin Corn, Art Farnsley, John
Hickey, Robert Lammers, Rhys Williams and Patricia Wittberg.

1. Barton, "Celtic Revived."
2. Quoted in Koenig, *History of the Parishes,* 757.
3. Coriden, *Parish in Catholic Tradition,* 18.
4. Gilkey, "Christian Congregation," 113.
5. Coriden, Green, and Heintschel, eds., *Code of Canon Law,* canon 518,
418–419. See also Warner, "Place of the Congregation," 79.
6. Bellah et al., *Habits of the Heart;* Hammond, *Religion and Personal Autonomy.*
7. Murnion, review of *The Parish in Catholic Tradition.*
8. Warner, "Work in Progress"; and Warner, "Place of the Congregation," 63,
68, 73.
9. Schreiter, "Faith and Cultures."
10. For additional examples in Chicago, see Marciniak and Droel, "Future of
Catholic Churches."

11. Michael Novak cites Aquinas on the social nature of Catholic thought in *Catholic Ethic,* 301.

12. Hammond, *Religion and Personal Autonomy,* 3–11.

13. Handy, "Voluntary Principle in Religion," 129–140.

14. Hammond, *Religion and Personal Autonomy,* 171.

15. Casanova, *Public Religions.*

16. Coriden, *Parish in Catholic Tradition,* 31.

17. Hammond, *Religion and Personal Autonomy,* 3.

18. Linnan, "Re-thinking the Urban Parish," 5.

19. Gilkey, "Christian Congregation," 105–106.

20. For an elaboration of this complex subject, see McGreevy, *Parish Boundaries,* 19; Conzen, "Forum," 112.

21. McGreevy, *Parish Boundaries;* also McGreevy, "Faith and Morals," 247.

22. Zukin, *Landscapes of Power,* 275.

23. Linnan, "Re-thinking the Urban Parish," 25.

24. Avella, *This Confident Church.*

25. Orsi, *Madonna of 115th Street.*

26. Quoted in Linnan, "Re-thinking the Urban Parish," 7.

27. Fischer, "Subcultural Theory of Urbanism" and *To Dwell among Friends;* Gannon, "Religious Tradition and Urban Community."

28. Fischer, *To Dwell among Friends.* Also see Ammerman *Congregation and Community,* 354.

29. Coriden, *Parish in Catholic Tradition,* 32.

30. Bellah et al., *Habits of the Heart;* also Hammond, *Religion and Personal Autonomy.*

31. Murnion, "Parish," 7.

32. See Linnan, "Re-thinking the Urban Parish," 25; and Coriden, Green, and Heintschel, eds., *Code of Canon Law.*

33. See examples in Becker and Eiesland, *Contemporary American Religion.*

34. Fontana, "Religious Entrepreneur," 1420.

35. Bellah et al., *Habits of the Heart.*

36. Hall and Neitz, *Culture,* 38–43. See also Reynolds and Norman, eds., *Community in America.*

37. Ammerman, *Congregation and Community,* 354.

38. Greeley, *Catholic Myth,* 111.

39. Dolan, *American Catholic Experience.*

40. Green, ed., *Churches, Cities and Human Community.*

41. McGreevy, "Faith and Morals," 248.

42. Gannon, "Religious Tradition and Urban Community," 299.

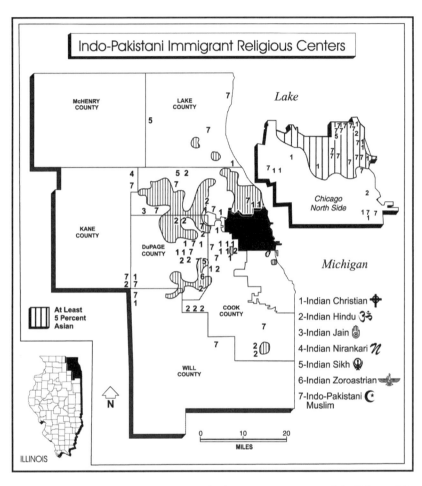

Map 10. Indo-Pakistani immigrants and religious centers are widely disbursed in metropolitan Chicago, with concentrations based more on class than on language or country of origin. Map by Brian Twardosz, BMT Printing and Cartographic Specialists.

Chapter 10

Recent Immigrant Religions and the Restructuring of Metropolitan Chicago

Paul D. Numrich

America's most recent immigrant religions face many of the same dynamics of Americanization encountered by their classical counterparts. Confronted by the cultural travail that necessarily accompanies migration to another country, immigrant groups transplant familiar Old World religious practices and institutions to their New World communities. Of course, exact duplication of the Old World cannot be accomplished; although traditional roots may be put down, transplantation inevitably becomes transformation as growth and change occur in a new sociocultural environment.[1]

Classical and recent (post–World War II) immigrant religious groups differ, however, with regard to the respective urban contexts that they entered and helped shape, and which in turn shaped them. Since World War II, urban restructuring has created a new American metropolis characterized by deindustrialization, regional reconfiguration, socioeconomic polarization, and demographic diversification. This chapter thus has a dual purpose: first, to identify classically "immigrant" aspects of the recent immigrant religious experience; second, to examine the interrelation of recent immigrant religions and the post–World War II restructuring of metropolitan Chicago.[2] We highlight Indo-Pakistanis here, due to their relatively large numbers and current scholarly interest in their experiences.[3]

We begin with case studies of three Indo-Pakistani immigrant congregations in the Chicago region. The first two, a Hindu temple and a Muslim mosque, have self-consciously sought to bridge ethnoreligious differences within the immigrant community; the third, a Sikh *gurdwārā*, maintains its distinctive ethnoreligious identity. The Hindu and Sikh congregations have built commuter religious centers in relatively well-off exurban locations; the Muslim center is located in an area of transition within the city of Chicago and serves both a neighborhood and a commuter clientele. Institutionally, all three congregations are well integrated into the larger American society. These case studies illustrate the classical functions fulfilled by recent immigrant religious centers, wherein Old World traditions and identities are both transplanted and transformed in a New World context. These case studies also provide local texture to the dynamics of post–World War II urban restructuring.

The Hindu Temple of Greater Chicago (Southwest Cook County)

More intentionally than perhaps any other Indian congregation in the Chicago area, The Hindu Temple of Greater Chicago (HTGC) pursues what has been called an "ecumenical adaptive strategy."[4] HTGC accommodates the various sectarian and regional/linguistic groups within the Indian immigrant community by facilitating multiple expressions of Hinduism. The inclusive name chosen for the temple bespeaks this, as other local temples specify their particularist emphases—for example, Sri Venkateswara (Balaji) Temple of Greater Chicago (a South Indian temple) and Chinmaya Mission of Chicago (a sectarian temple).

HTGC's membership draws on immigrants from all regions of India, and the temple offers various region-specific programs as well as classes in several Indian vernacular languages. Two other Hindu congregations meet in HTGC's facility. When asked about the distinct groups associated with HTGC, leaders stressed the larger, shared identity as Hindu Indians. As one said, "It depends on how you look at it. I have come, and we have come, [from] far away, so we can see India from above, from the point of view of the whole." HTGC also cultivates broader interreligious dialogue—it served as a cosponsor of the 1993 Parliament of the World's Religions and has representation in the DuPage (County) Interfaith Resource Network.

HTGC's priests provide daily *pūjās* (worship services) and *āratīs* (light ceremonies) for individuals, families, and groups visiting the temple, usually several hundred people per week. Special *pūjās* are held on a regular basis throughout the year, and the temple offers various *samskāras*, or religious ceremonies marking life-cycle passages such as birth and marriage. Hinduism's major religious celebrations, such as Shivaratri (a vigil to the god Shiva) and Diwali (a festival of lights), all of which follow a traditional lunar calendar, can draw as many as four thousand people.

HTGC's Cultural Committee, often working with other area organizations, coordinates many events featuring Indian arts and customs. Well-known Indian artists perform at the temple periodically. Also, a popular summerfest called Greeshma Mela, offering regional Indian cuisines, clothing and jewelry sales, entertainment, and free health screenings, has been organized since 1991. The Humanitarian Committee tends to the social and personal needs of the temple's elderly, most of whom have joined children and grandchildren through family reunification provisions of the immigration laws and who often feel lonely and unproductive in their new surroundings. It also coordinates relief efforts for the economically needy in both India and the United States.

"As the children in these new families grew older," HTGC's own written history observes, "it became important to preserve traditional religious and cultural values." One observer elaborates on the broader phenomenon of local temple-building: "So the temples of Chicago have become the focal point of culture propagation among second-generation Indians, something that the first generation sees as a very critical issue, if not *the* single most important issue, at this stage in their development as an ethnic group."[5]

Through its Education Committee and some twenty-five volunteers, HTGC offers Sunday school classes twice monthly. The Sunday school began in 1984 with only four children but today serves well over one hundred. The children learn various subjects, such as scriptures, *bhājan* (a sacred devotional song), and vernacular Indian languages. Two Sunday school teachers we interviewed stressed the importance of language instruction. It is much easier, they insisted, to teach traditional Indian values through the native languages of Indian culture than through English. Language instruction allows the children to discover their cultural roots, they continued, and in knowing their roots, children can begin to take pride in their identity. Such pride is imperative for those children who experience anti-Asian or anti-Indian prejudice in the public schools.

In 1991 high school and college-age youth formed a group called In the Wings, which by 1995 had some three hundred members. As a flyer puts it, "'Waiting In the Wings' means waiting to take over; these youths are the future of our temple." In the Wings organizes twenty to twenty-five programs annually, including social events, sports activities, and a summer camp. The group also schedules a discussion series called Youth Speaks to address topics such as prejudice, drugs and alcohol, and AIDS.

Marriage appears to be a very touchy subject between the youth and their parents. Ironically, during our interviews at the temple we heard an adult leader predict that marriages with non-Indian Americans would soon become common, whereas a youth leader stated that most of the temple's young people would prefer to marry a fellow Indian.

Every committee has youth representation, though some youth complain that their elders often do not take their opinions seriously. An adult liaison brokers disputes with the board of trustees. One youth leader reported to us that "most of the time [the liaison] successfully resolves the conflict and almost always there is a compromise." As the children become more Americanized through the influences of peers and popular culture, the temple serves as the venue for both challenge and compromise vis-à-vis their Indian heritage. Confrontation most often occurs when individualistic values of the youth clash with Indian values regarding family and respect for elders. Adults may show dismay over the situation, but at the same time they have taken steps to address it positively. For instance, one temple committee has organized open forums to help parents answer their children's questions about Hinduism's relevance in modern America. Moreover, adults have shown a willingness to concede to changes in traditional practices. In commenting on why doughnuts are served during Sunday school as part of *prasāda* (the food consumed at the conclusion of a *pūjā*), one person generalized that such accommodations to the tastes of the younger generation must be made if the temple is to retain these children as its future leaders. "It is impossible," this person pointed out, "to impose strict, conservative, Indian values on American-born kids."

Another group of note in HTGC is Akshaya ("Perennial"), made up of adults in their twenties and thirties "who are seeking to explore, learn, and expand upon their knowledge of the Hindu religion," as the group's flyer puts it. "We are affiliated with The Hindu Temple of Greater Chicago (HTGC)," the flyer continues, "and our goals are to begin the transition to future leadership of the temple and increase public awareness of the HTGC and its goals."

The Hindu Temple of Greater Chicago traces its origin to discussions among South Indian community leaders beginning in 1977. Two important decisions were made in the organization's early years. First, Sri Rama was chosen as the principal deity for the temple. One of the popular *avatāras* (literally, "descents," savior figures) of the god Vishnu and the title character of the *Ramayana* epic, Rama was seen by temple leaders as a pan-Indian deity that all Hindu immigrants could recognize and honor.

The second important decision concerned a suitable location for the proposed temple. The organization considered more than thirty sites around the metropolitan region and eventually purchased an eighteen-acre parcel of undeveloped bluff property near southwest suburban Lemont. Three considerations sealed the choice, according to the temple's written history: "[a] its proximity to I-55 and other major highways, [b] its quiet spot secluded from thickly populated residential and commercial areas, as well as [c] budgetary constraints." Considerations [a] and [b] clearly presupposed a commuter clientele.

For several years the organization gathered building funds from a variety of sources, including local fund-raising activities and loans from both an Indian-owned Chicago bank and the Tirumala Tirupati Devasthanam, a popular and wealthy Sri Venkateswara temple in South India.[6] In 1982–1983 temporary facilities for ritual practices and community gatherings were set up in west and southwest suburban locations, first in a Lombard residence, then in rented halls in Downers Grove and Romeoville.

By 1983–1984, however, the strain of the project began to show. Several years had passed, the temple's history reports, "and yet there was nothing concrete on the Lemont site, [thus] the patience of the devotees was getting exhausted." A group headed by Telugu professionals pulled out of the Lemont project to build a South Indian temple in west suburban Aurora, with Venkateswara (Balaji) as its principal deity. Groundbreaking for that temple took place in May 1985 and dedication the following June.[7] This split off of the Aurora temple poignantly testifies to the challenges inherent in HTGC's ecumenical agenda. As Padma Rangaswamy summarizes in rather dramatic terms, "The history of temple building in Chicago is also the story of bitter infighting among rival groups."[8] And as Raymond B. Williams notes specifically with regard to HTGC, "The difficulties encountered in developing the plans and in raising the funds for the temple indicate how hard it is to unite people from the various regions and sects in support of one project."[9]

The Lemont group carried through with its plans nonetheless. June 1984 saw the chief minister of the Indian state of Andhra Pradesh lay the foundation stone for the Rama temple. The *kumbhābhishēkam* (dedication ceremony) was held on the Fourth of July 1986.

The temple compound today rises impressively above Lemont Road, two miles south of Interstate 55. The white exterior of the Rama temple exhibits key architectural features of traditional South Indian temples—a

Fig. 10-1. Gopuram of Rama Temple, The Hindu Temple of Greater Chicago in Lemont, Illinois. Photo by Paul D. Numrich.

large, pyramid-shaped entryway (*gopuram*) as well as smaller towers surmounting the cubicles of three of the temple's deities. The main hall on the upper level features shrines to several deities, including Ganesha and Hanuman. A room to one side contains images of Krishna and Radha; an opposite room contains Venkateswara and two goddess consorts. The focal point of the hall itself is the sanctum, with its images of Rama and his brother Lakshmana and wife Sita. The ceiling in this part of the hall drops dramatically so that the worshiper approaching the sanctum will experience a sense of entering the *garbhagriha* (womb chamber), the sacred center of the spiritual mountain symbolized by a Hindu temple.[10]

The Hindu Temple of Greater Chicago recently completed a project transforming the original building on the site into a temple honoring the deities Ganesha, Shiva, and Durga. The *kumbhābhishēkam* for this temple was performed in the summer of 1994. The tower surmounting the Shiva sanctum here follows the North Indian architectural style, so the two temples together express HTGC's pan-Indian ecumenism. HTGC plans next to build the Kalyana Mandapam and Community Center, a large, three-level facility housing an auditorium, dining hall, and multipurpose classrooms.

With its traditional Old World architectural symbolism and its inclusive ecumenical approach, The Hindu Temple of Greater Chicago functions like a regional "cathedral" for the widespread immigrant Hindu community of metropolitan Chicago. Its impressive physical plant bespeaks a significant resource base within that community, particularly among exurban Indian professionals. At the same time, many less-well-off Hindus living around Devon Avenue on the North Side of the city of Chicago cannot easily travel to the southwest suburban Lemont temple to perform their ritual practices. For these Hindus, the ISKCON (International Society for Krishna Consciousness) temple in the Rogers Parks area of Chicago has taken on increasing importance in recent years. The ISKCON temple conducts all the prescribed daily Hindu services, including the 4:30 A.M. service that the Lemont temple does not provide. The ISKCON temple also adds special weekend services for the convenience of those who work during the week. Gujarati Indians predominate at this temple, most of them small-business owners and working-class people.

Fig. 10-2. International Society for Krishna Consciousness (Hare Krishna Temple), formerly a Masonic lodge, is clustered with Catholic and Protestant churches in Rogers Park, Chicago. Photo by Paul D. Numrich.

Muslim Community Center (Albany Park, Chicago)

Muslim Community Center (MCC) is the oldest of the Chicago region's Indo-Pakistani mosques. From its inception, MCC has articulated its mission in light of both recent immigration trends and the Islamic theological ideal of *ummah*, that is, the greater Muslim community that transcends differences of nationality or ethnicity. Looking back on MCC's history, the program booklet for its twenty-fifth anniversary celebration explained: "Its birth was part of the global vision in which Muslims from diverse cultural backgrounds welded into one with one common goal: the establishment of a dynamic and vibrant Islamic Community in North America." A banner hangs today at the front of MCC's prayer hall proclaiming, in both Arabic and English, the Qur'anic injunction "Thus We [Allah] have made you a model community that you may be witnesses to the nations." Commenting on the typically negative perception of Islam held by the American public, MCC's president challenged the Muslim audience at the anniversary celebration to present a balanced picture of Muslims in America. If other Americans saw Muslims as people who do more than just sit around all day reading the Qur'an, he suggested, then knee-jerk negative reactions such as those in the aftermath of the Oklahoma City bombing would be less likely to occur.[11] MCC served as a cosponsor of the 1993 Parliament of the World's Religions and is a member of the Council of Islamic Organizations of Greater Chicago.

MCC has a substantially mixed ethnic congregation. At Friday *jum'ah* prayers, which draw two thousand people during the sacred month of Ramadan, MCC's worshiping body is approximately 70 percent Indo-Pakistanis, 25 percent Arabs, and 5 percent Blacks, Whites, and others. Attendance at daily prayers runs half-and-half Indo-Pakistanis and Arabs. MCC's highest leadership has always been predominantly Indo-Pakistani, but a special committee organizes all programs for Arab members. The center has no appointed *imām* ("exemplar," the Muslim equivalent of clergy), an unusual situation partly explained by a concern that an *imām* might favor one Islamic school of thought (*fiqh*) over others. Each week a different person gives the Friday sermon (*khutbah*) at the center in both Arabic and English, the latter the common language among worshipers. In 1994, MCC elected its first non-immigrant president, a Harvard-educated Black convert, thus expressing the center's awareness of the racial diversity of America's largely urban Muslim community.

MCC facilitates the living of a full Islamic lifestyle by its members. All five daily prayers are observed at the mosque. During Ramadan, many Muslims gather in the evening for the special prayers (*tarāwīh*) and to break the daily fast. The center's Rehab and Welfare Committee organizes the collection and redistribution of the obligatory Islamic alms (*zakāh*). In 1993 these funds totaled about $83,000, more than 90 percent of which came from Indo-Pakistani donors; more than three hundred individuals and families (65 percent of them Black, 20 percent Arab) received the funds. The Darul Qadah Committee offers counseling and handles disputes among the Islamic membership, including divorce cases. The Women's Committee holds health fairs, study groups, and clothing and food sales. Weddings, social events, and funerals take place regularly at the center; members who cannot afford funeral expenses may receive financial assistance.

MCC pays special attention to programming for children and youth. In its guidelines for classroom behavior, MCC's School of Islamic Studies reminds each student, "As a Muslim you are expected to behave in a dignified, respectful manner at all times." Students and parents both sign the guidelines with this vow: "I have read the rules of classroom behavior and will Inshallah [God willing] abide by them to help me learn more about Islam and be a good Muslim." MCC's Arabic Saturday school draws nearly three hundred students, virtually all Arabs, and a Sunday school conducted in Urdu and English serves an equal number of Indo-Pakistani students. The weekend school's curriculum is extensive, as this sampling from a tenth-grade theology class reveals: Qur'an (scripture), Hadith (traditions from the Prophet Muhammad), Fiqh (schools of thought), Sharia (Islamic law), Haram and Halal (prohibited and acceptable actions), and Contemporary Social Problems (e.g., homelessness, drugs, sex, and abortion).

In 1989, MCC opened its full-time day school, the Muslim Education Center (MEC), in a former public elementary school in near north suburban Morton Grove. The school offers both a preschool and an elementary school program through the fifth grade and has an enrollment of 150 students from city and suburbs, the majority Indo-Pakistani. (MEC also runs a weekend school for 250 students.) Much of the impetus for establishing MEC came from parents concerned about "losing" their children to the surrounding non-Islamic culture, as this wording from MEC's statement of philosophy reveals: "The school's foremost objective is to provide an Islamic environment for the education of young Muslims . . . [that] affirms in our children their identity and pride in the Islamic legacy. . . . As is widely accepted, the education of our children in an

Islamic environment is the only genuine alternative to public school education to avoid their exposure to un-Islamic mannerism[s] and practices
such as sexual permissiveness and undue emphasis on materialism."

The precise parameters of an "Islamic environment" are often negotiated at MEC, given its various constituencies and their variant interpretations of and degrees of adherence to Islamic requirements. For instance,
on the matter of separation of the genders in the school, three views may
be found among MEC parents: no separation at all, total separation, or
separation only after the fourth grade. At the time of our field study,
MEC did not separate the students at all. An issue facing Muslim girls in
American society is whether or not to wear the traditional head covering
(*hijāb*). Confronted with peer ridicule in the public schools, some girls
leave home covered but uncover themselves at school. Such daily dilemmas compel some Muslim parents to enroll their daughters in MEC.

Muslim Community Center runs an annual summer youth camp in
rural Illinois for as many as one hundred youth, ages twelve and older. As its
flyer explains, "Muslim Youth Camp is one week during the entire year
where a young person can live with other young Muslims in an Islamic atmosphere of learning and fun." MCC's organizational structure includes a
Youth Council, and its board of directors is required to include two youth
representatives. In his keynote address at the twenty-fifth anniversary celebration, MCC's president outlined his aspirations for expanding youth programming. For instance, a $1 million athletic facility is being planned that
will provide Muslim youth a controlled Islamic environment for recreation.
Also, the president challenged MCC to develop Islamic high schools to
combat negative social influences on Muslim youth, as well as to consider
establishing an Islamic university. Instead of sending our Muslim children
to a Catholic school like Notre Dame, he asked, why not send them to a
Muhammad University or something of the kind?

Muslim Community Center was established in 1969 primarily by
Indo-Pakistani immigrants and students, who initially gathered wherever
they found space, such as at the University of Chicago and the Illinois Institute of Technology. In the early years MCC developed a close relationship with other Muslim centers already in the Chicago region, but according to an MCC source, these groups eventually parted company over
the issue of multiethnic membership.

MCC purchased its first facility in 1972, a former Danish community
center on Kedzie Avenue in the Humboldt Park area on Chicago's West Side.
The site was available and affordable, and the area had some Muslim pres-

ence, but MCC experienced vandalism and harassment there. By 1975, MCC had appointed a planning committee to study the possibility of relocation. In January 1977 the committee recommended constructing an Islamic complex in a "Proposed Muslim Neighborhood" within specific boundaries on Chicago's North Side, in order "to answer the challenge faced by the Muslim community in its efforts to lead a truly Islamic life in a non-Muslim environment." The neighborhood in question—roughly within the areas of West Rogers Park, North Park, and Forest Glen (the upper part of the break-out portion of Map 10)—fulfilled several of the committee's criteria, including attractive urban conditions, availability of housing, proximity of jobs, and adequate transportation. MCC's eventual choice in 1982, a former movie theater in Albany Park, about a mile south of the designated area, fulfilled two other criteria in particular: (1) a relatively dense and potentially expanding Muslim population and (2) a suitable facility. In 1993, MCC purchased fifteen hundred burial lots for Muslims in Rosehill Cemetery, which may be seen as part of its intention to establish a Muslim neighborhood on Chicago's North Side. Previously, North Side Muslims buried their dead inconveniently in the western and southern suburbs.

Clearly, serving a neighborhood community was an important factor in the decision to relocate to Albany Park, and today the majority of MCC's primary ethnic constituencies (Indo-Pakistanis and Arabs) live near the mosque. Nevertheless, during the annual Eid religious holidays these two groups part company, as Arabs travel to Mosque Foundation in southwest suburban Cook County to celebrate with fellow Arabs, while Indo-Pakistanis gather at McCormick Place, Chicago's largest convention center. Independent Arab mosques have operated on the North Side of the city twice in recent years, apparent indication that North Side Arabs wish to have a nearby mosque "of their own."

Most of MCC's leaders have been immigrant professionals—its past presidents include several engineers and two college professors—and suburbanites. The center thus serves an affluent and influential suburban commuter clientele in addition to its majority of typically less affluent city dwellers. A controversy stemming at least partly from this dichotomy arose over the location of the Muslim Education Center. Eventually, those favoring a suburban site over a city site prevailed, as MCC purchased the Morton Grove facility despite significant opposition in that municipality. Also regarding the issue of suburban influence in MCC, we note that MCC claims to have established several "daughter" mosques to serve residential concentrations of Indo-Pakistanis in the northern and western suburbs.

Fig. 10-3. Muslim Community Center in the Albany Park neighborhood is one of the largest of Chicago's mosques. Once a dinner club and theater, it accommodates 1,500 for weekly prayers and 600 children for weekend school. Photo by Paul D. Numrich.

Muslim Community Center and its suburban daughter institutions have mustered the resources necessary to renovate existing facilities for use in worship, education, and other programming. The purchase of the Morton Grove school marked a clear step in the direction of moving MCC itself away from the city, yet speeches at MCC's twenty-fifth anniversary celebration betrayed continuing ambivalence over the issue of city/suburb siting. The current president spoke of hopes to open a retreat center someday in Wisconsin, away from the "cesspool" of the city's un-Islamic influences. Yet a former MCC president pressed for the erection of a "grand *masjid*" (namely, a mosque with Old World Islamic architecture) in MCC's North Side vicinity as a "permanent landmark of the community." If such a mosque materializes, it will become the first Old World–style "cathedral" erected within the city limits of Chicago by any Indo-Pakistani congregation.

Sikh Religious Society of Chicago (Northwest Cook County)

The United States has lately become the preferred destination for emigrants from the worldwide Sikh diaspora.[12] Even so, "the Sikhs remain a largely unknown ethnic group to most Americans."[13] Unfortunately, when Sikhism emerges into American public consciousness, misconceptions and prejudices often ensue. Ethnic Sikhs in America have sometimes suffered from stereotyping as "terrorists," especially around the time of the Golden Temple incident and its aftermath in 1984.[14] Oddly, Chicago Sikhs experienced difficulties a few years earlier, during the Iranian Revolution in 1979—mistaken for Iranians, some Sikhs were accosted with shouts of "Ayatollah go home," and vandals broke many of the plateglass windows in the Sikhs' newly constructed suburban religious center. In December 1994 the local Sikh community was thrust into headline news after the tragic murder of a Sikh child at that center by a mentally disturbed Sikh visitor to the area. Sikhs once again faced the task of clarifying the nature of Sikhism to a generally uninformed American public— a Chicago TV news anchor initially identified the site of the slaying as a Hindu temple—despite years of cultivating local civic and interreligious connections, including through the Asian American Coalition, the Parliament of the World's Religions, and municipal events. In fact, the civic activism of one area Sikh youth had resulted in national legislation exempting turbaned Sikhs from military uniform requirements.

As one member summarized, the Sikh Religious Society offers a "psychological niche" of solidarity and solace for the immigrant generation within the community, as well as a "strong cultural anchor" of Punjabi-Sikh identity for the American-born and -raised generations. The society's goals include a stress on worship, education of the second generation, and "unity among our community." The matter of communal unity among ethnic Sikhs in America has taken on added significance since the Golden Temple incident, and the Sikh Religious Society of Chicago prides itself on having one of the more harmonious *gurdwārās* in the country.[15]

"The *gurdwārā* ['gateway or doorway of the guru'] has always been a crucial institution for knitting together the Sikh community, . . . it has been a multipurpose institution: a place of worship, a political center, an educational institution, and a center for hospitality and service."[16] On average, approximately 250 congregants gather in the *darbar sahib* (worship hall) of the Sikh Religious Society's *gurdwārā* for each of two Sunday morning religious services. For the most part, men sit on one side of the hall, women and children on the other. The women typically dress in traditional Indian fashion. Perhaps one-third of the men are *sahajdhārīs,* their clean-shaven faces and trimmed hair marking them as either uninitiated into the Khalsa or (more likely) assimilated into Western society through abandonment of the five Ks.[17] Religious services usually include *kīrtan,* devotional singing of praise and love to God under the leadership of trained musicians and singers (*rāgis*); *gurbāni,* reading of passages from the Guru Granth Sahib (the Sikh scripture), followed by a homily interpreting and applying the meaning of the passages; and *ardās,* congregational prayers. A *granthī* ("Granth-keeper," the Sikh equivalent of clergy) presides over the service, though lay Sikhs are allowed to read from and expound upon the Granth. Toward the conclusion of the service, all participants receive *parshād,* a small piece of warm, sweet dough. After the service, the congregation gathers downstairs for the *langar,* a communal meal open to all.

Four key events from Sikh history call forth major celebrations at the *gurdwārā,* each drawing as many as fifteen hundred people. The birth of founder Guru Nanak (b. 1469) is honored around the full moon of October/November. In December/January the tenth Guru's birth is honored. Baisakhi, in April, both commemorates the establishment of the Khalsa and marks the beginning of the Indian lunar New Year. This celebration demands several months of preparation each year and involves some two hundred performers. Last, the martyrdom of the fifth Guru is commemorated in June. Life-cycle religious ceremonies such as marriages and funerals also take place regularly at the *gurdwārā.*

Sikhism considers service to others, or *sevā,* a religious obligation. *Sevā* takes many forms at the *gurdwārā,* from checking coats and shoes at the entrance to preparing and serving the Sunday *langar* meals, the latter a formidable task considering the numbers attending on a typical weekend. In an effort to reclaim the original meaning of the *langar* as a *sevā* to all persons, regardless of caste or other distinctions, and also as an expression of concern for the poor, *gurdwārā* volunteers organize a monthly food distribution through the Salvation Army in the Uptown area of Chicago. The Sikh Religious Society also conducts an annual on-site blood drive, contributes to local and national disaster relief efforts, and supports various charitable organizations.

A sign announcing rehearsal for the singers who lead congregational worship every third Sunday of the month reads: "Bring a friend, make friends, meet old friends, and JAM with Kirtan!!!!" Their elders may feel that the sign's tone lacks a proper respectfulness for the religious tradition, but in this and other ways the second generation at the *gurdwārā* hopes to make that tradition both attractive and meaningful to young Sikhs. For an hour each Sunday morning, some sixty children receive Sunday school instruction in scripture, Sikh history, and the Punjabi language. A week-long summer Gurbani Camp—analogous to a Christian "Bible Camp"—has been organized locally for over a decade. Also, the *gurdwārā* facilitates discussions among older Sikh youth concerning issues of peer relationships.

During our interviews, adult members openly shared their concerns about the next generations of Sikhs, as well as their hopes that the *gurdwārā* will expand its programming for them. It appears that high school and college youth tend to drift away from the *gurdwārā*. For some, Punjabi culture has lost its appeal. Others complain that the immigrant generation is unwilling to relinquish control of the institution. Among the younger children, however, there seems to be a revival of interest in Sikh traditions and values. In years past, one interviewee noted, summer camp participants tended to be skeptical of Sikhism's relevance to an American context. Now they show a keen desire to be "good Sikhs," which has at times evoked prejudice in their schools, especially toward Sikh boys wearing turbans. Moreover, Sikh youth sometimes express dissatisfaction with their parents' emphasis on occupational success and material values and long for something more spiritual.

Most of the first Sikhs to settle in the Chicago region were students in the 1950s who met together socially in each other's homes and apartments, often with non-Sikh Indians in attendance. One University of Chicago couple set aside a room for the Guru Granth Sahib, the only such facility in the area at the time. According to one local source, the Sikh Study Circle was formed in 1956 and evolved into the Sikh Religious Society of Chicago in 1972.

Professionals, particularly physicians and engineers, dominated the first local wave of post-1965 Sikh immigrants, many of whom eventually settled in the western and northwestern suburbs. As the community grew in numbers in the early 1970s, social/religious gatherings moved from homes to rented facilities such as the Park District center in west suburban Lombard. Once the decision was made to secure a permanent location, debate emerged over whether to renovate an existing structure in Chicago or to locate in one of the suburbs in anticipation of further suburban Sikh settlement. The latter opinion won out, and in 1972 the community purchased an affordable parcel of land in the northwestern suburb of Palatine and

Fig. 10-4. The *gurdwārā* of the Sikh Religious Society of Chicago, Palatine, Illinois, is home to metropolitan Chicago's largest Sikh congregation. Photo by Paul D. Numrich.

began planning construction of a *gurdwārā*. According to one source, ten Sikh individuals (nine medical doctors and a taxi driver) put up $30,000 each to guarantee the mortgage. Groundbreaking took place in 1976; the first services were held in 1979.

The Palatine *gurdwārā*, tucked away unobtrusively in a modest residential area, does not have obviously "religious" architectural features. Reportedly, its Sikh architect sought to express the openness and simplicity of Sikhism through an uncomplicated design.[18] The upstairs *darbar sahib* feels spacious and airy, with glass on all sides. One's attention is drawn toward the front of the room to the *manji sahib,* the canopied place of honor for the Guru Granth Sahib. Around the perimeter of the lower-level *langar* hall one notices striking expressions of Sikh identity and concerns: a display of key events in Sikh history, including graphic photos of the Golden Temple incident and its aftermath; a sign proclaiming Khalistan as the "Sikh Homeland" (Khalistan is a name given to the Punjab region by those seeking an independent Sikh territory); and a list of "Our Gurus," from Guru Nanak to the Guru Granth Sahib.

Recently the Sikh Religious Society began a major fund-raising campaign to expand the Palatine *gurdwārā*. Phase one will see construction of larger facilities to accommodate the *langar* meal. Plans for later phases focus on a new center for the educational program and the library, both currently housed next door to the *gurdwārā* in the chief *granthī*'s residence. The local Sikh community typifies many of the dynamics of the metropolitan region's Indian immigrant community. A second wave of Sikh immigrants came beginning in the mid- to late 1970s. Today, according to one community source, only spouses, students, asylum seekers, and illegals continue to enter the United States. Clustering especially near Devon Avenue on Chicago's North Side, most of these newest Sikh arrivals differ from the earlier immigrants in socioeconomic status. Thus a bimodal Sikh community has developed, with the more established and better-off professionals living mostly in the western and northwestern suburbs and the less well-off newcomers living mostly in the city. It would not be unusual to hear members of the former group disparage the status of the latter, and members of the latter group begrudge the fortunate circumstances of the former. Due to the dispersed Sikh settlement around the greater metropolitan Chicago region, many in both groups find it either difficult or inconvenient to travel to the Palatine *gurdwārā*. This partially explains the opening of several new *gurdwārā*s in the late 1990s: in the West Rogers Park area of Chicago,

Fig. 10-5. Gurdwara Sahib of Chicago is a Sikh religious center in the space above this carpet store in West Rogers Park, Chicago. Photo by Paul D. Numrich.

serving less affluent North Side Sikhs living around Devon Avenue; in Oak Brook, serving more affluent western suburban Sikhs, for whom the drive to Palatine may take an hour; and in Milwaukee, Wisconsin, and Merrillville, Indiana. In addition, a Sikh *dera* (spiritual mission center) has been established in Island Lake, Lake County, Illinois.

Recent Immigration and Unprecedented Urban Diversity

The three case studies just presented illustrate certain patterns in recent U.S. immigration history and the resulting unprecedented ethnic and religious diversity now found in our largest cities. Prior to World War II, America's immigration "door" stood nearly shut for Asian groups.[19] Relatively small numbers of Asians entered the United States as measures such as the Chinese Exclusion Act (1882), the Gentlemen's Agreement with Japan (1908), the Asiatic Barred Zone (1917), and the Oriental Exclusion Act (1924), as well as Supreme Court decisions denying U.S. citizenship to Asians in the 1920s, effectively served notice that this country did not welcome such groups. The reversal of Chinese exclusion (1943), passage of the War Brides (1945) and McCarran-Walter Acts (1952), and growing civil rights sentiments in the post–World War II period brought a steady, though still relatively small, influx of Asians into the United States. The 1965 Immigration Act (implemented in 1968) opened wide America's immigration door to previously excluded or restricted groups. The number of Indo-Pakistani immigrants, for instance, increased approximately 4,000 percent between 1965 and 1984.[20] The 1990 census counted just over 815,000 Indians and eighty-one thousand Pakistanis in America. Thus, since World War II, and particularly since the 1960s, immigration patterns have been sculpting a "new face" for the American people, significantly less European in its contours than in the classical period of American immigration.

A remarkable socioeconomic diversity characterizes post-1965 immigrant groups. Professionals, technicians, and skilled workers predominated in the early years, as the 1965 act gave preference to such occupations and thus precipitated a "brain drain" of valuable human capital from certain Third World countries. Since the mid-1970s a more occupationally and educationally varied mixture has characterized the immigration flow, especially through "chain migration" of relatives of the earlier immigrants and the influx of large numbers of Southeast Asian refugees after the end of the Vietnam conflict in 1975. The post-1965 wave of

American newcomers, Alejandro Portes and Ruben Rumbaut observe, is far more diverse in origins, motivations for migration, and adaptation strategies than any wave of immigrants in U.S. history.[21] Whereas most immigrants during the classical period entered American society at the lower socioeconomic strata,[22] recent immigrants "cluster bimodally in both blue- and white-collar occupations": "Today's immigrants include first generation millionaires and topflight engineers and scientists; at the other extreme, they also include destitute refugees and undocumented workers."[23] Relatively speaking, Indo-Pakistanis have been a successful group, with many professionals and small-business owners among them, though the latest immigrants include less elite subgroups.

Post-1965 immigrants have tended to settle in America's largest metropolitan regions.[24] Chicago, which typified America's classical immigration, now ranks fourth behind New York City, Los Angeles, and Miami in the total number of recent immigrants received.[25] According to the 1990 census, the top nine Asian groups in the six-county Chicago metropolitan region are Filipinos, Indians, Chinese, Koreans, Japanese, Pakistanis, Vietnamese, Thais, and Cambodians. Chicago ranks second to New York as the preferred urban destination for Indians;[26] it also has a slightly higher ratio of Pakistanis to Indians (about 1:6) than the national ratio (about 1:10).

This new diversity of immigrant groups has created an unprecedented diversity of religions in America's urban areas. Estimates of the numbers of adherents of selected recent immigrant religions are controversial and vary widely depending on the source. Though arguable, the following figures capture the new diversity of religions in metropolitan Chicago:[27] more than three hundred thousand Muslims (making Islam the second-largest religion, slightly ahead of Judaism though still far behind Christianity); 131,000 Buddhists (over half the number of Orthodox Christians in the area); eighty thousand Hindus (more than the number of Anglicans in the Episcopal Diocese of Chicago); five thousand Jains; five thousand Sikhs; and five hundred Zoroastrians. Non-European Christian groups add to the variety. For instance, the majority of the thirty-six thousand Koreans in metropolitan Chicago are Protestants, and the patriarch of the Assyrian Church of the East has established that church's headquarters in Chicago, where a reputed sixty-five thousand adherents now live.[28]

As the foregoing paragraphs imply, the diversity of the recent immigrants creates a complex, interrelated web of social identity according to ethnicity, race, and religion. Taking the Indo-Pakistani case, we note that Pakistani immigrants are predominantly Muslim, though they represent Sunni, Shi`i, and heterodox (e.g., Ahmadiyya) traditions within Islam, while some Pakistanis are Christian. "Hinduism" is the religious tradition of the majority of Indians, though that term only loosely ties together a variety of practices and emphases sharing a religious family resemblance; additionally, India is home to millions of Muslims, Sikhs, Jains, Zoroastrians, and Christians. Indian immigrants in America distinguish themselves according to homeland regional/linguistic provenance and religious tradition. A regional/linguistic group can include several religious traditions (e.g., Gujaratis can be Hindu, Muslim, Jain, or Christian); by the same token, a religious tradition can include several regional/linguistic groups (e.g., Gujarati, Tamil, and Telugu Hindus). Sometimes several regional/linguistic Hindu groups are subsumed under the broader designations "North Indian" and "South Indian" because of shared cultural characteristics.

"Ethnicity" has to do with a "sense of peoplehood [that] rests mainly on such things as language, custom, and the perception of shared ancestry."[29] It is socially constructed and therefore changes as groups migrate from one society to another. The terms *South Asian* and *Indo-Pakistani*, for instance, take on new meaning for immigrants to the United States. Certainly, for Indo-Pakistanis to be subsumed under the label "Asians" and thus lumped together with Southeast and East Asians stems from their newfound American context.

Whether by ethnicity, race, or religion, most recent immigrant groups occupy a minority position in America and thus face the prejudice and discrimination, both actual and potential, that continue to characterize U.S. society. The largest and most visible of the non-Christian religions practiced by the recent immigrants—Buddhism, Hinduism, Islam, Sikhism—suffer from generally poor public images.[30] A recent national survey, for instance, ranked Buddhism and Islam just after atheism and Scientology as the most negative influences on American society.[31] Despite their collective socioeconomic success as a recent immigrant group, South Asians still face personal harassment and vocational "glass ceilings,"[32] which may stem largely from public ambiguity over the racial identity of South Asians. A U.S. Supreme Court decision in the 1920s ruled that although Indians may technically be Caucasians, they were not "White" under U.S. law and thus not eligible for either citizenship or land ownership. A 1978 national survey showed that 11 percent of respondents saw Indians as White, 15 percent as Black, 23 percent as Brown, 38 percent as Other, and 13 percent did not know what race Indians were.[33] In 1993 the Illinois Chapter of the Association of Indians in America established a Council on Education and Legal Defense to deal with incidents of prejudice and discrimination.

Minority status and other dynamics of post–World War II urban restructuring help explain the prolific differentiation of recent immigrant religious centers according to ethnic, subethnic, and sectarian religious identities. A notable fact about metropolitan Chicago's recent immigrant religious centers is that most serve single-ethnic constituencies, that is, one ethnic group comprises more than 80 percent of the congregation. Yen Le Espiritu and Ivan Light summarize the situation on a general level:

> Partially as a result of urban restructuring, . . . America's immigrants confront a more complex political, economic, and social landscape than did earlier generations of immigrants. These complex and often threatening conditions encourage them to band together around common linguistic and cultural identities in order to influence their life chances and living conditions.[34]

Even more than during the classical period of predominantly European immigration, immigrant institutions today perform vital functions vis-à-vis the larger society. They serve as safe havens from antagonisms of minority daily life and often stand "over against" the majority society, offering social criticism of American values and behaviors—Hindus criticize the individualism, Muslims the moral breakdown of American society, for instance. But at the same time these institutions help broker an advantageous relationship between their constituents and the larger society. As Williams explains:

> The formation of religious groups by immigrants, even those with the most narrowly conceived ethnic or hierarchical boundaries, do [*sic*] not function primarily to separate persons from the rest of the population, but rather to provide the necessary basis on which the individual and group can negotiate effective relations with the majority population as variously defined.[35]

Coalitions for a variety of purposes have arisen among the recent immigrant groups, though success has been uneven. For instance, several religious groups have sponsored the local Asian American Coalition and the Parliament of the World's Religions (the latter held in Chicago in 1993). Intrafaith coalitions include the Buddhist Council of the Midwest and

the Council of Islamic Organizations of Greater Chicago. Many population groups remain isolated, however, either unwilling or unable to forge
relationships with other groups. As we attempted to compile comprehensive lists of religious centers, it appeared that even within a single ethnic
population, one religious segment was unaware of (or unwilling to identify) other religious segments.

Siting of Recent Immigrant Religious Centers

Map 10 plots the sites of religious centers serving eighty-nine predominantly Indian and Indo-Pakistani congregations in the six-county
Chicago metropolitan region, broken out by religious identity (Muslim,
Christian, Hindu, etc.).[36] The map reveals much about the dynamics involved in the siting of recent immigrant religious centers.

One-third (thirty of eighty-nine) of the religious centers are located
within the city limits of Chicago (break-out portion of Map 10). Distribution across the city is highly circumscribed, with centers found in only
twelve of Chicago's seventy-seven "community areas" and significant
clustering of centers found only on the city's North Side. Their placement
typically shadows Asian settlement patterns—ten of the twelve community areas contain more than fifteen hundred Asian residents each—and
typically avoids the predominantly Black areas on Chicago's South and
West Sides, continuing immigration trends from the 1960s and 1970s.[37]
Nevertheless, five of the twelve community areas now have a Black population of 20 percent or more, mostly as a result of simultaneous Black in-
migration to immigrant port-of-entry areas. Moreover, nine of the twelve
areas have a combined Black and Hispanic population of 20 percent or
more. A striking example is Rogers Park, discussed in chapter 6. These
facts point to an important shift in settlement patterns among recent immigrant groups, namely, their growing inability to avoid the traditional
American minority areas of the city. Also, markedly larger percentages of
the Muslim (about half) and Christian (more than one-third) centers are
found within the city limits of Chicago than is the case with other Indian
(Hindu, Sikh, etc.) religious centers (about 10 percent).

Turning to the suburban centers (Map 10), comprising two-thirds of
the metropolitan total, we find that the great majority cluster in two of
the region's six counties (Cook and DuPage). Siting generally shadows recent immigrant settlement preferences for predominantly White north-

TABLE 1
Congregations per Religious Group Meeting in Areas
above/below Regional Median Family-Income Level
*Community Areas of Chicago and Suburbs**

Group	City: #Above	City: #Below	Suburbs: #Above	Suburbs: #Below
Indian Christian	0	10	16	3
Indian Hindu, Sikh, etc.	1	2	19	3
Indo-Pakistani Muslim	2	15	12	6
Other Muslim	2	5	1	2
Buddhist	5	12	9	3
Totals	10	44	57	17

* Income figures reported in Chicago Fact Book Consortium, *Local Community Fact Book,*
1990; the regional median family-income level for 1990 was $42,292.

ern and western suburban areas over predominantly Black suburbs, again continuing trends from the 1960s and 1970s.[38] Nevertheless, as with the situation in the city of Chicago, we also see an increasing inability of recent immigrant groups to avoid settling in traditionally American minority areas, indicated by the fact that four suburbs with a Black population of 20 percent or more and eleven suburbs with a combined Black and Hispanic population of 20 percent or more have Indo-Pakistani religious centers. At the same time, unlike the situation in the city of Chicago, where the religious centers largely perpetuate the classical model of "neighborhood" or "parish" institutions that normally serve surrounding residential communities, the diffuse settlement and increased mobility of suburban immigrant populations have given rise to several "commuter" religious centers that draw much (sometimes virtually all) of their congregations from outside the municipalities in which they are located. Less than half (thirteen of thirty-one) of the suburban municipalities with large Asian populations (more than 1,500) have Indo-Pakistani religious centers; conversely, fifteen suburban municipalities with very small Asian populations (less than 250) do have Indo-Pakistani centers—obviously, such centers draw "commuter" congregations. We note again here that Indo-Pakistani Christians and Muslims lag behind fellow ethnics (Hindus, Sikhs, etc.) in establishing religious centers in the suburbs.

Indications of the socioeconomic status of the various religious groups may be seen in Tables 1 and 2. Two additional religious groups—"other" immigrant Muslims (namely, non-Indo-Pakistanis) and immigrant Buddhists—have been added to the analysis for comparative purposes.

Table 1 shows the number of congregations in each religious group that meet in locations either above or below the regional median family-income

TABLE 2
Suburban Congregations per Religious Group
Meeting in Desirable Municipalities*

Group	Total Congregations	#Desirable	%Desirable
Indian Christian	19	9	47%
Indian Hindu, Sikh, etc.	22	12	55%
Indo-Pakistani Muslim	18	7	39%
Other Muslim	3	1	33%
Buddhist	12	7	58%
Totals	74	36	49%

* A "desirable" municipality has both an income above the regional median level (see Table 1) and a crime rate lower than the median rate for all regional municipalities. Crime-rate data from *Chicago Regional Report*, which does not disaggregate the rates for Chicago's seventy-seven community areas.

level, broken out by community areas of the city of Chicago and suburban municipalities. For virtually all groups, regardless of religious identity, the tendency for suburban centers to be located in higher-income areas and city centers to be located in lower-income areas is dramatically evident. Religious identity appears to be salient in the Muslim case, where the percentage of centers in higher-income areas, particularly in the suburbs, lags markedly behind other groups, including fellow ethnics in the case of Indo-Pakistani Muslims vis-à-vis Indians of other religions.

Table 2 focuses exclusively on the suburbs and provides a caveat against a simplistic dichotomization of city versus suburban conditions. Overall, less than half of the suburban groups meet in municipalities that qualify as "desirable" in terms of both income and safety from crime. Religious identity appears to have salience here again: Muslims lag significantly behind the other groups, Indo-Pakistani Muslims behind their fellow ethnics.

The foregoing discussion illuminates the interrelation of recent immigrant religions and the post–World War II restructuring of the Chicago metropolitan region. Ethnic residential enclavism, characteristic of the classical period of American immigration,[39] has given way to a socioeconomically determined, bimodal geography, as poorer, less assimilated, and less successful immigrants cluster in depressed and transitional metropolitan areas, while better-off, more assimilated, and more successful immigrants gravitate to attractive city locations or disperse throughout exurbia.[40] This typifies "the widening 'social divide' [that] is a striking feature of the post-industrial metropolis."[41] Significantly, this "social divide" includes ethnoreligious features. Bluntly stated, in the Indo-Pakistani case, one's chances of worshiping in a desirable area of the city or suburbs increase in roughly the following sequence: from Muslim to Christian to Hindu, Sikh, and so forth.

Some observations about facilities elaborate this analysis. Most recent immigrant congregations rent or rehabilitate existing facilities to serve as religious centers, a practice also followed by some classical immigrant groups.[42] The variety of converted places—for example, homes, apartments, businesses, schools, churches—reveals both the dynamics of urban restructuring and the practical constraints on these religious groups when securing suitable facilities. Recent Christian immigrants offer an interesting variation on the theme of facility adaptation. Like their non-Christian counterparts, these groups typically cannot yet afford to erect new buildings. As Christians, however, they share the religious identity of the majority in American society, which provides an option typically unavailable to non-Christian congregations: renting a facility from an Anglo-Christian congregation. Fox Valley Muslim Community Center in far west suburban Kane County provides an exception; it rented space from a Christian church. After several years it constructed its own mosque.

In post–World War II metropolitan regions like Chicago, where land is at a premium and construction costs are considerable, erecting a new religious facility, particularly in an Old World architectural style, has become the prerogative of the successful and thus a less realistic dream for many groups than it was during the classical period of American immigration. Very few "cathedrals," new structures whose architectures carry Old World religio-symbolic power, serve the recent immigrants of metropolitan Chicago or attract regional pilgrims. For instance, local immigrant Buddhists have erected only one such structure and immigrant Muslims, four (two of them Indo-Pakistani), whereas non-Christian Indian religious groups (Hindus, Sikhs, etc.) have been proportionally more productive, with as many as six already completed and two more under construction. Of all these "cathedrals," only one is located within the city limits of Chicago, a Japanese Buddhist temple built in 1971 in fashionable, affluent Lincoln Park. Assuming that the urban "social divide" continues to widen, many recent immigrant religious centers will remain in impoverished metropolitan areas. Upward social mobility and geographic relocation to attractive neighborhoods, whether city or exurban, are not inevitable for all recent immigrant groups or subgroups.

Conclusion

As this chapter demonstrates, Chicago's recent immigrant religions follow many patterns from the classical period of American immigration. Through cultural celebrations, religious activities, and educational and other programming, the newest religious centers preside over the transplantation and transformation of Old World traditions. In so doing, these centers perpetuate ethnically, racially, or religiously distinct identities even more prolifically than did their classical European counterparts. Today's Indo-Pakistani mosque is analogous to the classical Italian Roman Catholic parish, that is, a particular ethnonational expression of a major religion. Likewise, today's Indian regional/linguistic Hindu temples are analogous to German provincial Protestant churches (i.e., Old World parochial variations of a single national religion), while today's Jain temples and Sikh *gurdwārās* are analogous to Polish Roman Catholic churches and Jewish synagogues, respectively (i.e., distinct major religions within a single ethnonational group). A significant departure from such differentiation is found in ecumenically minded congregations such as The Hindu Temple of Greater Chicago and Muslim Community Center, though as we have seen, the ecumenical ideal is not easily realized.

A crucial difference between the experience of the recent immigrant religions and that of the classical period stems from post–World War II urban restructuring. The arrival of the recent immigrants both coincided with and contributed to the new urban context in the latter half of the twentieth century. These immigrants constitute the primary source of the new ethnic, racial, and religious diversity of America's metropolitan regions, and their social bimodalism, patterns of residential settlement, and siting of religious centers have participated in the latest transformation of Chicago and other large American cities. In this sense the recent immigrants share more with their contemporaries in the majority society than did previous immigrant groups.

The evolution of immigrant enclavism is most striking. Classically, Swedes, Italians, Jews, and others formed relatively distinct ethnoreligious neighborhoods within the city of Chicago or in certain suburbs, and when one group moved to a different area, another group occupied its territory and converted its religious centers. It took decades for most classical groups to disperse throughout the metropolitan region; in the Italian case, this did not occur until after World War II.[43] It appears that ethnicity per se no longer constitutes the most salient factor in immigrant enclavism. Rather, socioeconomic status now seems most salient, even though socioeconomic status includes variables of ethnoreligious identity (as seen, for instance, in the geographic distribution of religious centers within the Indo-Pakistani group). Today, well-off groups or sub-groups occupy desirable areas while the less well-off cluster in poorer areas of the city of Chicago and in certain suburbs. Classical, neighbor-hood-type immigrant religious centers can still be found, mostly in the city, but now many exurban commuter-type religious centers serve widely scattered and mobile immigrant congregations. Centers of both types have followed the classical pattern of occupying the facilities of pre-vious religious groups, but only in rare instances, mostly in well-off exur-ban locations and among certain religious groups, have recent immigrant congregations been able to construct new religious facilities according to Old World architectural models.

An ever-widening gap between America's rich and poor cuts across the entire society, including recent immigrant groups.[44] As Robert Manning and Anita Butera observe, "The old urban centers . . . are becoming in-creasingly populated by disadvantaged native minorities and recent im-migrants who lack the necessary social and human capital for negotiating the more favorable terrain of the suburban economy."[45] Prosperous areas remain few, while many other areas see prosperity receding from sight. America's newest religious immigrants are like their classical predeces-sors in important ways, yet their experience also differs due to the great "social divide" of the new metropolis where they now live.

NOTES

Some ideas and wording in this chapter previously appeared in Numrich, "Recent Immigrant Religions in a Restructuring Metropolis: New Religious Landscapes in Chicago," *Journal of Cultural Geography* 17, 1.

1. See Park and Miller, *Old World Traits Transplanted;* Handlin, *The Uprooted;* Herberg, *Protestant-Catholic-Jew;* Bodnar, *The Transplanted;* Fenton, *Transplant-ing Religious Traditions;* Numrich, *Old Wisdom.* Portes and Rumbaut, *Immigrant Americans,* 144, point out the shared etymology of *travel* and *travail.* The term *recent* refers to post–World War II waves of immigrants, particularly those com-ing since the 1965 Immigration Act. "Classical" immigrants include both the "old" immigrant waves (predominantly northern European and Protestant, up to 1880) and the "new" immigrant waves (largely southern and eastern European, and Roman Catholic, Orthodox Christian, and Jewish, from 1880 to 1924).

2. On the interrelation of recent immigration and urban restructuring, but without consideration of religion, see, e.g., Soja, Morales, and Wolff, "Urban Restructuring"; Waldinger, "Immigration"; Manning and Butera, "From City to Suburbia."

3. The U.S. Immigration and Naturalization Service has counted Indians and Pakistanis separately since 1973, but ethnic studies often conflate them into a single category of "Indo-Pakistanis."

4. Williams, *Religions of Immigrants* and *Sacred Thread*.

5. Rangaswamy, "Asian Indians," 449.

6. Williams, *Religions of Immigrants*, 229.

7. Ibid., 231–33.

8. Rangaswamy, "Asian Indians," 450. Also, on 448, she reports: "Many Indians feel that groupism is far more pronounced in Chicago [than in other U.S. cities] but are at a loss to explain why this is so."

9. Williams, *Religions of Immigrants*, 229.

10. Eck, *Darsan*, 62–63.

11. Some media commentators assumed immediately that the April 1995 bombing of a federal facility in Oklahoma City represented the work of Muslim extremists.

12. Dusenbery, "Introduction."

13. La Brack, *Sikhs of Northern California*, 421.

14. Indian government troops and militant Sikh partisans engaged in a violent confrontation at the Golden Temple in Amritsar. A few months later, Prime Minister Indira Gandhi was assassinated by her Sikh bodyguards.

15. Cf. Williams, *Religions of Immigrants*, 81, 240.

16. Helweg, "Sikh Diaspora," 80.

17. Sikhism's tenth and last historical Guru (Teacher) established the Khalsa (the "Pure"), a status conferred by initiation and characterized by adoption of the surnames Singh (males) or Kaur (females) as well as distinguishing personal marks known as the five Ks: *kesh* (uncut hair, which males cover with a turban), *kanghā* (comb), *karā* (bracelet), *kachhā* (a certain kind of undershorts), and *kirpān* (ceremonial sword).

18. Williams, *Religions of Immigrants*, 240. Our own source pointed out that the congregation gave the architect a free hand in designing the facility because he did so without charge.

19. Reimers offers this useful metaphor in *Still the Golden Door*.

20. Minocha, "South Asian Immigrants," 348–350.

21. Portes and Rumbaut, *Immigrant Americans*, 6–8.

22. Bodnar, *The Transplanted*, 170.

23. Espiritu and Light, "Changing Ethnic Shape," 36, 42; see Rumbaut, "Passages to America," 225, 228.

24. Waldinger, "Immigration and Urban Change," 211.

25. Fuchs, *American Kaleidoscope,* 296–304; Portes and Rumbaut, *Immigrant America,* 36.

26. Portes and Rumbaut, *Immigrant America,* 37.

27. These are 1997 self-estimates reported by the Chicago and Northern Illinois Region of the National Conference for Community and Justice, formerly the National Conference of Christians and Jews.

28. Galloway, "Place to Call Home."

29. Becker, "Ethnicity and Religion," 1477; Conzen et al., "Invention of Ethnicity."

30. E.g., Williams, *Religions of Immigrants,* 290; Haddad, ed., *Muslims of America,* 3.

31. Dart, "Most View Christians."

32. Minocha, "South Asian Immigrants," 363.

33. Takaki, *Strangers;* Xenos, Barringer, and Levin, *Asian Indians.*

34. Espiritu and Light, "Changing Ethnic Shape," 49–50.

35. Williams, *Sacred Thread,* 255.

36. We adopt the generic term *religious center,* i.e., a particular place where a congregation gathers regularly for religious activities, in order to avoid imperialistic use of one group's term (e.g., church) to refer to other groups' sacred places (e.g., temple, mosque, *gurdwārā*). The term *congregation,* defined as "a local, religious association of people" (cf. Wind, *Places of Worship,* xvii), has gained acceptance beyond its initial Judeo-Christian context, though to be sure, temples, mosques, etc., in America do not always function like classical American churches or synagogues. We have not considered size—whether of membership or programming—when including particular religious centers in our tally, but we have excluded special-purpose groups and centers with one-dimensional programming, such as Muslim Student Associations and Friday Islamic prayer places. Note that the eighty-nine total represents the number of *congregations* in our study; the number of *religious centers* is slightly less, due to some congregational sharing of centers.

37. Carlson, "Settling of Asian Immigrant Groups."

38. Ibid.

39. E.g., Pacyga and Skerrett, *Chicago;* Holli and Jones, eds., *Ethnic Chicago,* 3rd and 4th eds.

40. Waldinger, "Immigration and Urban Change"; Espiritu and Light, "Changing Ethnic Shape."

41. Manning and Butera, "From City to Suburbia."

42. Pacyga and Skerrett, *Chicago;* Cutler, *Jews of Chicago.*

43. Candeloro, "Chicago's Italians."

44. Cf. Hirt, "Shifts in Labor Market."

45. Manning and Butera, "From City to Suburbia."

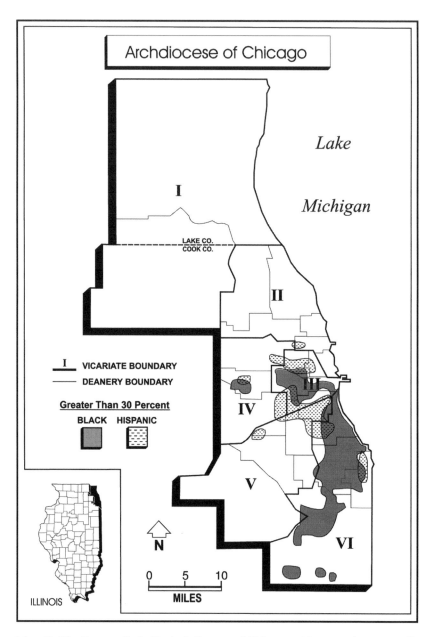

Map 11. The Roman Catholic Archdiocese of Chicago, with more than two million people, is the largest religious body in metropolitan Chicago. Map by Brian Twardosz, BMT Printing and Cartographic Specialists.

Chapter 11

Catholic Planning for a Multicultural Metropolis, 1982–1996

Peter R. D'Agostino

A sadness fell over Chicago with the death of Cardinal-Archbishop Joseph Bernardin (1982–1996). Although a principal architect of the postconciliar Catholic Church on the national level, Bernardin also oversaw a host of local (archdiocesan) reforms. These addressed familiar characteristics of late-twentieth-century America such as deindustrialization, multiculturalism, and the shift of power from city neighborhoods to suburbs. The planning processes and institutional changes enacted during Bernardin's episcopacy, although sometimes the source of conflict, became a model for other dioceses. This chapter describes and interprets the normative vision of the local church that drove the reforms enacted during Bernardin's tenure. I construct this vision through a narrative of institutional changes and an analysis of explanations offered to legitimate change. I describe this vision as a process ecclesiology.

This chapter's archdiocesan analysis complements the ethnographic studies of congregations and parishes presented in the rest of this book, at a time when Catholic authorities beyond the reach of congregations are closing parishes and schools. These closings have profound implications for education, politics, and ethnoracial developments in urban America. Church authorities beyond the parish have baptized multiculturalism as the normative ideology of American and Catholic identity, transforming the design of parish programs and shaping interparish dynamics in new ways.

Although not readily apparent to the ethnographer immersed in a rich congregational universe, Catholic parishes increasingly reconstitute archdiocesan organizations and reforms, and they are increasingly forced to work across parish boundaries on terms established by the archdiocese. In other words, the archdiocese both limits and facilitates parochial initiatives. It is what sociologist Anthony Giddens and historian William Sewell call a deep structure.[1] To describe contemporary urban parishes without reference to it is to analyze words without a grammar. We have, of course, learned a great deal about the Archdiocese of Chicago from our ethnographic analysis within parishes. However, the Religion and Urban America Program realized, and this chapter demonstrates, that an understanding of public religion and urban transformation, particularly in Chicago, is greatly illuminated by an analysis of the Archdiocese's process ecclesiology.

By a process ecclesiology I mean the permanent integration of a dynamism of adaptation into the church at all levels of organization. Bernardin's reforms promoted awareness of interdependence among Catholic institutions and people. This consciousness, cultivated through cooperative planning, culminated in institutional reforms made in a dialectic with the larger environment, which itself was always in flux. Bernardin and his coworkers in relevant archdiocesan agencies—planners or "experts"—hoped the church would institutionalize adaptation to the changing realities of modern life, as it simultaneously mobilized its material, social, and spiritual resources to transform society.

Bernardin's reforms diverged from many local traditions. Both the reorganization of the Archdiocese's administration, governance, and ecclesial geography and the theology of structural reforms challenged Chicago's Catholics. To demonstrate the innovative character and limits of Bernardin's fourteen-year episcopacy, I give a brief analysis of the Archdiocese's planning processes, elementary school reforms, and rethinking of the normative relationship between faith and culture.

The Archdiocese of Chicago and the
Myth of Chicago Catholicism

The size and history of the Archdiocese of Chicago are daunting. At the end of 1995, the Archdiocese was a geographic space of 1,411 square miles; a political space identical to Lake and Cook Counties in the state of Illinois; an ecclesial space comprising 6 vicariates, 25 deaneries, and 377 parishes; and a complex organization including the Pastoral Center at the hub, 46 cemeteries, 200 operational units of Catholic Charities, 19

Catholic hospitals, 6 Catholic colleges and universities, 377 parishes, 281 elementary schools, 48 high schools, 3 archdiocesan seminaries, and the nation's largest theologate—the Catholic Theological Union. In terms of personnel, the Archdiocese was composed of Bernardin, 7 auxiliary bishops, 988 diocesan priests, 861 religious priests in residence, 457 religious brothers in residence, 3,574 women religious in residence, 587 deacons, 148 pastoral associates (which included some deacons and religious), a total of 6,664 teachers and administrators in the school system, and 4,719 employees of Catholic Charities. There were 18,876 employees of the Catholic archbishop of Chicago, not including those employed at Catholic hospitals and universities. The total population of the Archdiocese was 5,712,000, which included a Catholic population of 2,342,000 of which 62 percent was White (non-Hispanic), 31 percent Hispanic, 4 percent African American, and 3 percent Asian.[2]

These numbers only hint at the pluralism embedded in its many regional, ethnic, clerical, and class subcultures. Thus the Archdiocese has a strong, "thick," multifaceted personality. The shared stories, personalities, movements, and buildings that Chicagoans, American Catholics, and scholars associate with the Archdiocese of Chicago suggest it readily becomes a multivalent symbol. Communities of memory transform the Archdiocese of Chicago into a corporate personality, which I shall call Chicago Catholicism.[3]

The Archdiocese of Chicago transformed by memory and values into Chicago Catholicism functions as a myth. The myth tells the story of tight-knit neighborhoods and struggles of proud ethnic groups for local democracy, land ownership, and political clout. Within the myth, the parish-school plant symbolizes the neighborhood community. It embodies, protects, and dramatizes the values of the neighborhood as it bridges generations of neighborhood residents. The parish-school plant marks urban boundaries, brings order out of chaotic urban space, and gives each neighborhood a distinctive history and name recognizable throughout the metropolitan area. The myth has a normative dimension that preserves the history of the Archdiocese of Chicago in selective ways. Deviations from the myth generate resistance. Thus some Chicagoans assert that every parish once had a school, that every Catholic child attended that school, and therefore, that every parish ought to maintain a school today. Bernardin tried to portray aspects of his reform in continuity with the myth. But pan-parochial planning and alternatives to powerful parochial loyalties met resistance from many

Catholics who were mourning the loss of urban parishes and schools intimately associated with memories of family and community.[4]

Bernardin arrived as an outsider to Chicago Catholicism. Born and raised in Columbia, South Carolina, by immigrants from northeastern Italy, his experiences had been administrative, as auxiliary bishop in Atlanta and as a formative figure in the National Conference of Catholic Bishops. Although he had been the bishop of Cincinnati from 1972 to 1982, a large, deindustrialized, heterogeneous city such as Chicago was new to him. In contrast to his twentieth-century predecessors, Bernardin was not Roman-trained and did not have an authoritarian or autocratic style of leadership. He came to Chicago as a healer to reinvigorate an archdiocese and city that had become disenchanted, with charges of corruption and insensitivity aimed at his predecessor.

Administration, Governance, and Geography

Upon his installation on August 25, 1982, Bernardin oversaw reforms in the administration, governance, and ecclesial geography of the Archdiocese. In December 1982, Bernardin appointed an Administrative Reorganization Advisory Committee to review the organizational structure of the archdiocesan Chancery Office (renamed the Pastoral Center). To delegate authority and promote greater coordination and fiscal efficiency, he consolidated sixty-nine agencies and offices into six departments: Evangelization and Christian Life, Financial Services, Human Services, Ministry Formation, Personnel Services, and Communications and Development.

In March 1985 the Archdiocesan Pastoral Council (APC) held its first regular meeting. Established to receive input from parishes and regions throughout the Archdiocese, the APC had four standing committees with forty-six voting members, 67 percent of whom were laypeople. The APC served as a consultative body to the archbishop. In this way the APC legitimized consolidations and closings of parishes and schools. In 1986, the Presbyteral Senate also formed a task force on consolidations, which the cardinal consulted, as required by canon law. Bernardin oversaw the creation of parish councils, made mandatory by 1990, which were necessary to integrate parishes into archdiocesan long-range planning processes. In January 1988 only 65 percent of the Archdiocese's parishes had a parish council, and only 30 percent of the councils operated according to archdiocesan guidelines. An Office for Parish Councils provided workshops to train parishioners on the theology of parish councils.

By January 1984 the Archdiocese was divided into six territorial vicariates (see map 11), each under an auxiliary bishop acting as an episcopal vicar. Each vicariate included deaneries—whose number rose from twelve to twenty-five by 1995—with a representative pastor serving as dean. Within each deanery, clusters were formed from groups of geographic parishes whose priests or lay representatives met to discuss common concerns. This new ecclesial map encouraged parishes operating in similar urban environments to identify common problems, compare solutions, and form common local strategies. This permitted urban problems to be addressed regionally rather than either parochially—where resources were scarce and knowledge was limited—or on the archdiocesan level, which seemed distant or insensitive to local residents. In this sense, geographic reorganization was both a delegation of authority and decision making from the center to the periphery and a loss of parish autonomy. Furthermore, to the extent that local entities were compelled to meet and plan, one could argue these reforms represented a type of episcopal authority imposed in an indirect bureaucratic manner, rather than through a traditional monarchical personal-command structure.

These ecclesial units—vicariates, deaneries, clusters—were by no means symmetrical in terms of size, resources, or character. They exhibited a variety of levels of cooperation, planning, cohesion, and trust. Ethnicity, race, neighborhood traditions, and leadership qualities conditioned their operation. Many pastors knew little of or actively resisted cooperation and planning within these units. In fact, some pastors generated and maintained parish identity and solidarity by defining themselves against the Pastoral Center as a beleaguered congregation protecting itself against an uncaring "bureaucracy." In contrast, one West Side cluster had a long tradition of lay involvement and activism. Lay representatives from cluster parishes had been meeting for twenty years to discuss common public concerns, and the parishes in that cluster had joint Lenten services. Reforms built on local traditions were more likely to succeed.

These reforms required episcopal reinforcements to man each vicariate. On December 13, 1983, four new bishops were consecrated to Chicago to join the two existing auxiliaries. These appointments reflected sensitivity to the cultural geography of the Archdiocese. The importance of bonds forged between bishops and Catholics of the same race or

ethnicity could either weaken or strengthen the territorial identities of
the vicariate system. Thus, from 1983 until his reassignment to the Diocese of Belleville, Bishop Wilton Gregory, an African American, was the
vicar of the South Side of Chicago (vicariate 6), which included a high
proportion of African American residents (69 percent in 1995). Those
residents often articulated the idea of a Black Catholic Church on the
South Side of Chicago that had its own bishop, in spite of Bishop Gregory's self-proclaimed commitment to be a bishop for all Chicagoans.
From 1983 until his reassignment to the Diocese of Lubeck, Bishop
Placido Rodriguez was the episcopal vicar of the Near West Side (vicariate 3, 46 percent Hispanic in 1995), which included the overwhelmingly
Mexican Pilsen and Little Village neighborhoods. Like the African Amer-
ican Catholics in regard to Bishop Gregory, Hispanics throughout
Chicago thought of Bishop Rodriguez as their bishop.

Planning: Modernization and Legitimation

The reforms described above facilitated strategic planning at every level
of church organization. Strategic planning, in Bernardin's vision, was
the means whereby the corporate reflection of "the people of God"
would emerge. While planning embodied the Catholic principle of sub-
sidiarity, it also legitimated change. The reforms of the administration,
governance, and geography of the Archdiocese coincided with highly
publicized controversial closings and consolidations of schools and
parishes. In this conflictual context, the cardinal promoted planning as
a type of religious activity, a devotion of the new people of God to discern God's will.

John A. Grindel's work helps us understand how planning linked to
institutional change was a religious activity. Grindel describes a pastoral
circle with four parts: insertion, social analysis, theological reflection, and
pastoral planning, which leads back to insertion to complete the circle.
The first moment of the circle, insertion into the individual and corporate Catholic experience, begins with the thoughts and feelings of Catholics, who go on to share and analyze their experiences. Through theological reflection, Catholics understand those experiences in the light of
their "faith, Scripture, church teaching and the resources of tradition." Finally, pastoral planning involves designing an effective short- and long-
term plan. In a similar way, Bernardin hoped the Archdiocese would in-

ternalize this pastoral circle, creating a dynamic organization in a constant process of renewal. Grindel describes the process as a circle because it "must be gone through again and again. Every time a pastoral plan is implemented it gives rise to another set of experiences which once again must be analyzed and reflected on in order to do further pastoral planning." Grindel warns that social analysis enters "into the realm of controversy," and "any analysis is implicitly linked to some ideological tradition." Thus part of the process requires "conversion," the explication of values one brings to social analysis.[5]

In the Archdiocese planning was conceived as a corporate devotion implemented to discover the mission of the church and to transform Catholics. In 1986, archdiocesan Personnel Services director Father J. Cletus Kiley asked:

> What is the mission of this Church? What does it mean to be a Roman Catholic in Cook and Lake County? . . . One of the fears that a lot of us have is we are using management language and we are a Church, not a business. The challenge is to take the best that management has learned and remember to keep our identity as a people of God with a spiritual mission. . . .
>
> We don't know the future. We see trends, we use sociology or whatever. . . . But at the same time there is always room for the Spirit. It's the blending the two, spirituality and science. In management they talk about "organizational transformation." We're using the word "conversion." Business uses the word "good management." We talk about "stewardship."[6]

In 1988, Bernardin published a four-part series in *Chicago Catholic,* the archdiocesan weekly, titled "Why Do We Need to Plan?" in which he linked planning to the core of the church's mission. When "wave upon wave of immigrants" constituted the church, national parishes were "a good and effective approach to pastoral needs," Bernardin noted. He went on to say, however, that they also "tended to go their separate ways, fragmenting the archdiocese. People thought of themselves more as parishioners of a particular parish than as members of the larger church. A certain degree of parochialism or congregationalism set in, and it is still present." Bernardin reasoned that since "we are no longer primarily an immigrant church, . . . the church's mission has changed." In light of demographic changes, "the archdiocese has no choice but to be a careful manager of all its resources—facilities, finances and, especially, personnel. . . . Planning . . . is increasingly becoming a fact of life in the archdiocese."[7] Bernardin believed the situation had reached crisis proportions: "To be candid, the number of parishes in need of arch-diocesan assistance, as well as the number of parishes merely breaking even, is somewhat alarming." The financial crisis "make[s] . . . planning essential. Otherwise, there will continue to be an unwise and inequitable allocation and distribution of archdiocesan resources."[8]

Bernardin connected planning with the idea of just, responsible stewardship. "Within the archdiocese in the past, planning has often been somewhat informal, sporadic or local. However, we can no longer afford to proceed with business as usual." Finally, he addressed the larger issue of Catholic identity and its relationship to planning:

> Perhaps the greatest challenge of all is to expand our personal concept of what it means to be a Catholic, to belong to a church that extends beyond our own parish. . . . An authentic theology of the church underlies this concept, however, and it must be reflected in all our pastoral efforts.[9]

His theological reflections on a postconciliar Catholic identity challenged the operative myth of Chicago Catholicism and troubled many Chicago Catholics. Some associated the requirements to participate in planning with a subterfuge to legitimate parish closings. Planning generated suspicion and, in some cases, instigated resistance.

Bernardin had planted the seeds for a permanent process of self-evaluation in his 1985 pastoral letter "In Service of One Another." In November 1986 the cardinal's cabinet distributed *Criteria for Parish Planning and Evaluation,* endorsed by the Presbyteral Senate, which established guidelines for parish self-evaluation. The guidelines included references to distances between parishes (no more than two miles, not less than one-half mile), population (registered families should not exceed three thousand nor dip beneath three hundred in number), ministerial personnel, religious formation and education, and parish finances. Parish planning in the Archdiocese culminated in a program called Tomorrow's Parish, first implemented in 1992 and henceforth required of all parishes. Bernardin's archdiocesan planning process, completed in 1994, culminated in the publication of *Decisions for the Future of our Church.*

Tomorrow's Parish, in theory a nine-month planning process, was implemented in 1992 by twenty-nine parishes and was required of all parishes by 1998. It was designed to create a three- to five-year plan. The materials the Office of Research and Planning provided to implement Tomorrow's Parish offered detailed but flexible criteria that a planning team used to reflect on its parish. These criteria related to ministerial life—spirituality, human concerns, education, parish life—and planning—ministerial personnel, demographics, religious education, finances. Once this assessment was complete, the parish council and pastor implemented changes to realize their vision for the parish. The process allowed for input from parishioners, neighboring parishes, and deanery, vicariate, and archdiocesan representatives. It was meant to be a prayerful as well as a sociological experience, one that promoted greater awareness among active participants of all dimensions of parish life. Archdiocesan planners hoped to see each parish go through this planning process every five years, thus entering a permanent cycle of reflection on identity and mission that would strengthen the parish and perpetually reintegrate it into its ecclesial and social environments.[10]

Before the cardinal's death, the Archdiocese completed the initial stages of an archdiocesan strategic-planning process. In the spring of 1993, Bernardin identified two priorities: (1) evangelization and education and (2) ministerial leadership. With input from two writing teams that consulted with more than eight thousand Catholics, the cardinal put forth *Decisions for the Future of Our Church* in the spring of 1994 and appointed a committee that published a five-year *Decisions Implementation Plan*, with concrete goals based on a financial assessment.[11]

Decisions for the Future of Our Church acknowledged a break with Chicago Catholicism. In *Decisions,* Bernardin emphasized the need to overcome strictly parochial commitments in order to develop cooperation and collaboration across territorial and ethnic and racial boundaries:

> We belong to a universal Church whose teaching and experience we must respect. We are not a "congregational" church. . . . Each of our parishes and institutions is part of the local Church we call the Archdiocese. They do not exist in isolation. Planning for the future requires a greater degree of collaboration and sharing than has been our custom in the past.

The document anticipated further restructuring of deaneries to define them by "natural groupings [which] will make it easier to plan collaboratively for the promotion of the Church's primary mission of evangelization, of which its educational mission is an integral part." While Bernardin promoted collaboration across territorial and ethnic and racial boundaries, he also insisted on the maintenance of traditional structures, particularly schools for all Catholics and the urban poor. Thus, Bernardin asserted the value of regional or consolidated schools—a school for more than one parish—but he agreed that the "*parochial* nature of our elementary schools must be maintained." Thus he broke from Chicago Catholicism's traditional parish-school unit but hoped to harness its spiritual, social, and material capital for his innovation.[12]

Tomorrow's Parish and *Decisions* followed the financial crisis that had culminated in extensive parish and parish school closings. According to Thomas J. Gannon, S.J., and David F. Schwartz, the financial crisis grew out of "a large and continuing increase in grants to parishes; higher costs of labor and employee benefits, specifically medical benefits; and rising operational costs for parish and archdiocesan buildings." In 1989 parish operating revenues fell $26.3 million short of expenses, and the Pastoral Center incurred a $20.8 million deficit. Nearly two-thirds of the Archdiocese's parishes were unable to meet expenses from income. The parochial schools' average collective deficit from 1987 to 1992 was $68 million, a sum historically paid from excess parish income.[13] Bernardin took steps to raise funds and cut budgets, including administrative cutbacks for the Pastoral Center. Since 1986, twenty-seven parishes had already been closed or consolidated. By June 1990 an additional twenty-eight parishes, eighteen elementary schools, two missions, and a minor seminary were closed. Five more parishes and two more elementary schools were closed by June 1991. Many Chicagoans who felt closings were implemented without consultation cried foul. After 1990, they often associated planning with a purely financial response to a financial problem and evinced little interest in the theological framework for planning and for a new postconciliar Catholic identity. This limited the success of planning in the 1990s.

Catholic Elementary Schools

The Archdiocese of Chicago boasts the largest Catholic school system in the United States. Powerful affective bonds to schools constitute a central feature of Chicago Catholicism. But Bernardin inherited a school system in decline. According to the *Official Catholic Directory,* enrollment dropped from 286,670 students in 429 elementary schools in 1965, to 160,129 in 394 schools in 1975, to 125,786 in 361 schools in 1985, to 105,030 in 281 schools in 1995. Of these remaining 281 elementary schools, only 207 (74 percent) were strictly parochial—under the authority of one parish and its pastor—conforming to the parish-school unit that has constituted a principal component of Chicago Catholicism. Seventy-four (26 percent) were not traditional parish-school plants and fell under the authority of two or more parishes or the Archdiocese. These trends represented a break with Chicago Catholicism.[14]

At the Third Plenary Council of Baltimore (1884), the American Catholic bishops had commanded the construction of a school for each parish and required Catholic children to attend. Although these ideals were never realized, the importance of the school in the parish community was considerable. Consequently, many parishioners today have difficulty conceiving of a parish without a school. Furthermore, although some ethnic groups, such as Italians, Puerto Ricans, and Mexicans, never sent a high proportion of their children to Catholic schools, those Chicagoans with stronger familial ties to parochial schools "remember" a time when all Catholic children went to them and learned the Baltimore catechism. Thus, Cardinal Bernardin's efforts to close or consolidate parochial schools, due to a shortage of religious who had formerly administered and taught at Catholic schools for little compensation, came as a challenge to Chicago Catholicism.[15]

In the 1980s, Bernardin reorganized the archdiocesan Offices for Catholic Education and Religious Education to cultivate better communication between the schools, principals, pastors, and archdiocesan offices and to integrate them into the broader planning processes. School planning had become institutionalized in 1976 with the establishment of a Planning Department under the Superintendent of Schools. Between 1977 and 1985, forty-five elementary schools completed a planning process, but in each case it was implemented in isolation from the sponsoring parish or neighboring schools.[16]

From 1985 to 1996, school planning was linked to mandatory parish planning. Each school was required to undergo an evaluation process, developed in response to the 1990 letter from the Catholic Bishops titled "In Support of Catholic Elementary and Secondary Schools." The process entailed a self-evaluation by the principal and teachers, with input from parish staff and board members, followed by a three-day visitation from a team composed of representatives from the Office of Catholic Education, principals, and teachers. The school then became responsible for implementing the recommendations given by the visiting team. In addition, the Office of Catholic Education implemented a "Catholic Identity Process" to help each school reflect on its identity and mission. The Identity Process engaged principal, parents, and faculty in discussion. Although voluntary, by the spring of 1994 more than two hundred Catholic elementary schools had participated. The process cultivated self-awareness of the distinctive identity of each school, which often depended on the character of the neighborhood and its traditions. This process revealed that some schools understood their identity as Catholic because they nurtured students into the life of the church, while others considered themselves Catholic because they had a mission to transform society in line with Catholic social teaching.

The financial strains on the Archdiocese led to a reorganization of the school system. This generated controversy because it usually culminated in closing some parochial schools and consolidating others into regional schools, breaking with the traditions of Chicago Catholicism. Each consolidation required the new regional school to cultivate a new identity not grounded in strictly parochial traditions and conceptions of urban space. Bernardin hoped this new identity would be more inclusive, evincing a greater awareness of cultural and economic diversity.[17]

A Multicultural Church

Ethnic and racial diversity has shaped the Archdiocese. Numerous national parishes were constructed in industrial cities for continental European immigrants. Frequently, religious congregations took the lead in pastoral care over ethnic groups. The Resurrectionists for the Poles, the Scalabrinians for the Italians, the Claretians for the Mexicans, and the Divine Word Fathers for African Americans, served as pastors and representatives to diocesan or Vatican authorities. Italian, Puerto Rican, Mexican, and African American men were rarely found in, or were segregated from, Saint Mary of the Lake, the archdiocesan seminary, and almost never worked in archdiocesan offices before World War II. Chicago's Polonia, in contrast, became a significant Catholic power bloc and still commands considerable leverage.[18]

Before 1965 the metaphor of the "melting pot" symbolized the dominant ideology of the Catholic Church, which sought to facilitate the assimilation of immigrants and their children into a common American Catholic nationality. The segregation of African American Catholics within the church stood out as a contradiction of this ideal, and the pre–World War II separatism of some Poles or Italians, prolonged by their own clergy, lingered, but it did not undermine faith in the process of assimilation. Although divided by language and history, Catholic parishes increasingly resembled one another in most aspects of their liturgical and congregational life.

After 1965 some activists and intellectuals in the Catholic Church advocated cultural pluralism.[19] Within a Catholic context, they sought to recapture or preserve distinctive religious rituals, symbols, and affective experiences associated with European homelands or immigrant neighborhoods. The public affirmation of cultural pluralism, often coupled to a condemnation of the melting pot metaphor, helped legitimate the persistence and even expansion of distinctive archdiocesan offices and cultural centers for ethnic groups whose immigrant populations had dwindled. The investments of some religious congregations, who themselves had become symbols of ethnicity within Catholic culture, also assured an institutional presence. On his arrival in 1982, Bernardin inherited an ethnic apostolate composed of thirteen full-time employees, with eleven offices dedicated to separate ethnic, racial, or language groups. Each office spoke for "its" people, set up programs or events for "its" people, petitioned for resources for "its" people, and worked in relative isolation from other ethnic offices.

With the financial crisis of 1989, Bernardin reorganized these offices into a new Office for Ethnic Ministries, which opened in 1991. I will analyze the significance of this reorganization in regard to theology and multiculturalism after a historical overview of some of the ethnic apostolates that were reorganized. This overview cannot do justice to the tensions among religious congregations, factions of diocesan clergy, archdiocesan institutions, and lay interest groups that spanned the postwar period. Symbolic boundaries based on ethnicity, race, visions of the political and economic order, and conceptions of religious authority make any brief narrative unsatisfactory. My goal is only to provide the background to archdiocesan planning processes that baptized contemporary multiculturalism as an ideology embodied in the Office for Ethnic Ministries in the 1990s.

Hispanic Ministry

Pastoral care for Spanish-speaking immigrants in the 1950s diverged from a pattern in which European immigrant clergy had worked with "their" own, with little archdiocesan oversight. A cohort of progressive

White Chicago diocesan clergy emerged, with an interest in Hispanic urban ministry. No organization of diocesan clergy had ever sought out a specialized ministry among Czech, Italian, African American, or Mexican Catholics before.

In 1956, Cardinal-Archbishop Samuel A. Stritch (1940–1958) formed the Cardinal's Committee for the Spanish Speaking (CCSS) under the direction of diocesan clergy—Fathers Leo Mahon (1956–1963) and Donald Headley (1963–1968).[20] The CCSS grew out of Mahon's initiatives with Puerto Ricans at Holy Cross Church and supplemented the Claretians' work at Mexican parishes. The CCSS, however, integrated Hispanics into parishes where they lived and organized lay Puerto Ricans for leadership roles. In the late 1950s and 1960s, the Hermanos en la Familia de Dios, an organization of lay men founded to organize Puerto Ricans, and El Cursillo de Cristiandad fostered political activism among Hispanics. Eventually the CCSS developed into the Archdiocesan Latin American Committee (ALAC).

In 1963, with the support of Cardinal-Archbishop Albert Meyer (1958–1965), Mahon established a mission at San Miguelito in the Archdiocese of Panama, where he remained until 1975 as vicar of eastern Panama. With Headley after 1968, Mahon cultivated lay leaders through base communities and hoped to expose Chicago seminarians and priests to a lay-led church. Under the tenure of Cardinal-Archbishop John Patrick Cody (1965–1982), however, the Panama mission did not play the role Mahon had envisioned. Although it became an active center for Latin Americans, Cody neither publicized the mission's activities nor tapped its potential to train Chicago clergy.

The change from national parishes of European ethnics under religious clergy into Mexican parishes under diocesan clergy in the Pilsen and Little Village neighborhoods was also significant for Hispanics' pastoral care. In 1968 the ALAC tried a team ministry approach in Pilsen with eleven diocesan priests, eleven sisters, and one layman. This "18th Street Team" coordinated pastoral care of seven area parishes, integrating community organizations and parish resources on behalf of Mexican interests. Not all the parishes in the area participated, however, and by 1971, eight of the sisters and six of the clergy had left the active ministry. The dissolution of the 18th Street Team left priests reluctant to attempt a coordinated approach again.[21]

In 1974 the first Encuentro Hispano held in Chicago recommended the formation of a Center for Hispanic Ministry. Although Cody appointed Bishop Nevin Hayes, O. Carm., as a vicar for Spanish-speaking Catholics in 1978, many clergy believed Cody had ignored their initiatives and was not prepared for the growing Hispanic population. Consequently, in 1978 a committee of thirty-three priests formed the Hispanic Caucus, which soon included a number of women religious. The caucus encouraged better preparation for seminarians, called for improvements to public schools attended by Hispanics, tried to place Hispanic students at Catholic colleges, demanded more priests in Hispanic parishes, and protested against the Immigration Reform and Control Act of 1986.

Soon after his arrival in Chicago, Bernardin created the Office of the Hispanic Apostolate under Claretian priest Father Pedro Rodriguez. The purpose of the office was to promote Hispanic ministry and integrate the concerns of the caucus into archdiocesan organizations. Through the initiatives of the caucus and the Office of the Hispanic Apostolate, programs for Hispanic evangelization, liturgists, and catechists developed. Since 1982, an annual festival to celebrate Hispanic faith and culture has marked the massive Hispanic presence in the Archdiocese. In 1983, Chicago received its first Hispanic bishop, and by 1986 an archdiocesan Spanish-language paper was established. In 1987 the Hispanic Caucus presented a plan to Bernardin for a new mission in Latin America, which opened in July 1989 in Chilapa, Mexico. In 1988, Bernardin established as his advisory body a Hispanic Pastoral Council of fourteen laypeople, with at least two from each vicariate, and the next year the Office of the Hispanic Apostolate was replaced by a Hispanic Pastoral Commission under the direction of Angelina Marquez.

African American Ministry

During the decades before Bernardin's arrival, an active cohort of diocesan clergy worked with African Americans in the struggle for civil rights and to facilitate the difficult racial transition in Chicago parishes. This often pitted progressive clergy advocating interracialism against confreres who maintained segregation. In the years after the civil rights movement, many of the charismatic clergy and sisters who had worked in the Black community left the active ministry. Perhaps this explains in part why no equivalent of the Hispanic Caucus developed among priests and sisters working with African American Catholics in Chicago.

On Bernardin's arrival in Chicago, he conferred with African American Catholics and their priests and affirmed their desire for an African

American auxiliary bishop and an office for Black Catholics. Bishop Gregory was consecrated to Chicago in December 1983. Before the establishment of the Office for Black Catholic Ministries in 1985, the Office for Chicago Catholic Evangelization handled African American affairs. African American Catholics began meeting annually at the "Comfort My People" festival in 1982, which provided a forum to discuss pastoral issues and to plan for evangelization. In 1984 the ten African American bishops in the United States issued their first pastoral letter, "What We Have Seen and Heard." In October 1985, African Americans gathered for the first annual archdiocesan revival, held in Holy Name Cathedral.

In March 1987 the first archdiocesan Black Catholic Congress was held, promoted by the Office for Black Catholic Ministries. The congress developed plans to strengthen lay leadership and to build connections among African American parishes and agencies, and it prepared for Chicago's participation in the National Black Catholic Congress in Washington, D.C., that May. At this first National Black Catholic Congress of the century, fifteen hundred African American delegates from 110 dioceses developed a national pastoral plan. The implementation of the national plan for evangelization revealed the Archdiocese's strengths and weaknesses. While it had both an auxiliary bishop and an Office for Black Catholic Ministries, as of 1990 only one of two hundred pastoral associates and ten of 466 directors of religious education were African Americans. After the national congress, the Archdiocese promoted the training of Ministers of Care, whose parish apostolate stresses African American cultural values, theology, spirituality, and catechetics.

Polonia

The institutional history of Polish pastoral care dates back to the nineteenth century. Chicago quickly became the largest Polish area of settlement outside Europe and has played an important role in the evolution of Polish ethnicity and in Poland–United States relations. The massive network of Polish national parishes and schools, the presence of the Resurrectionists and several Polish orders of women religious, the strife between the Polish Roman Catholic Union and the Polish National Alliance, and the cold war struggle contributed to Polish ethnic consciousness in the Archdiocese.

In May 1984, Bernardin met with four of his bishops and seventy-four priests to begin a study of the Polish apostolate in the Archdiocese, where there were 752,000 Americans of Polish descent. At this heated meeting the cardinal emphasized that he did not want to set up parallel programs for each ethnic group, but he acknowledged the need for better coordination among Polish ministries. Considerable divisions existed between various generations of Polish Americans, Polish immigrants, and Polish and Polish American clergy. Although 282 of 1,232 students in the archdiocesan seminary system were of Polish descent, only ten spoke Polish. In 1988 the Holy Trinity Mission was established to serve post–World War II arrivals, and the archdiocesan Polish Apostolate was reorganized into the Office of Ministry to Polonia. The office worked to integrate Polish immigrants in existing parishes and to promote the teaching of Polish language and liturgy at Saint Mary of the Lake Seminary.

Chicago auxiliary bishop Alfred Abramowicz served as the national executive director of the Catholic League for Religious Assistance to Poland, established in 1943. Its annual collection instigated division between those who believed Polish American resources ought to support Polish American concerns and those who wanted the resources to support Poles in Poland. Nevertheless, in 1991, Bishop Abramowicz provided the Polish church with $270,000 for the training of priests; $143,000 for churches, convents, monasteries, and soup kitchens; and $25,000 for radio broadcasting and Vatican communications. The collection also supported the Polish Pontifical College in Rome and the Polish Seminary in Paris.

Centers and Missions

Other groups in the Archdiocese established ethnic ministry centers and missions that hosted social and sacramental services to Latin- and non-Latin-rite Catholics. Furthermore, cultural centers with a Catholic affiliation, such as the Lithuanian Cultural Center in Lemont and the Italian Cultural Center in Stone Park, institutionalized ethnic identity in the Archdiocese. Centers and missions are of particular importance to Asian Catholics. By 1990, Chicago hosted the Holy Trinity Polish Mission, the Blessed George Matulaitis Lithuanian Mission, the Angel Guardian Croatian Catholic Mission, the Saint Therese Chinese Catholic Mission, the Syro-Malabar Catholic Mission, the Knanite Syro-Malabar Catholic Mission, the Kananaya Catholic Mission, the Syro-Malankara Catholic Mission, the Haitian Catholic Center, the Indo-Chinese Catholic

Center, the Korean North Suburban Catholic Center, and the Korean Catholic Center at Queen of Angels Parish.

Office for Ethnic Ministries

From Bernardin's arrival until the financial crisis of 1989, the ethnic apostolates were reorganized to express solidarity between the archbishop and his people. The new archdiocesan offices were meant to be receptive to input from ethnic and racial groups, input many felt had not been welcomed by Bernardin's predecessor. Still, the institutional organization of ethnic and racial apostolates reflected a cultural pluralist model in which each group with enough "clout" had an autonomous office. The distinctive history of African Americans in comparison with European ethnic groups and the enormous Hispanic presence had not been institutionally affirmed in any clear manner. Furthermore, the diverse groups of Asian Catholics, who lacked the institutional history that provided patrons and power, required greater attention. The new Office for Ethnic Ministries, created in 1991, emerged both from downsizing the Pastoral Center during the financial crisis of 1989 and from reconceptualizing pastoral care. Its organizational structure embodied a Catholic baptism of the ideology of multiculturalism, and its mission of evangelization was linked to a Catholic theology of inculturation.

In the new office, four consultants were hired to direct four "desks"— for European Americans, Hispanic Americans, Asian Americans, and African Americans. A full-time director assisted by two secretaries coordinated the office. There was also a part-time Polish liaison, a Resurrectionist appointed to coordinate the transfer of clergy and seminarians from Poland to the Archdiocese.

Each consultant oversaw an advisory board that represented either ethnic groups within each desk or regions of the Archdiocese. For example, the European consultant had an advisory board that met bimonthly and included eleven representatives (Slovak, German, Latvian, Italian, Croatian, Polish, Lithuanian, Hungarian, Czech, Irish, and Slovenian). This advisory board kept the office aware of festivals, conflicts, and other concerns in its respective ethnic communities. Similarly, the Asian American and Hispanic American consultants had advisory boards that represented the variety of ethnic groups within their desks. Because the African American desk housed less ethnic diversity (although it included Haitians), its representatives where chosen from geographical regions of the Archdiocese. The Hispanic American desk, unlike the others, had vicariate Hispanic coordinators in each of the six vicariates, who served as regional representatives of the office. The office was reorganized along the lines of the National Conference of Catholic Bishops and the United States Catholic Conference, which in 1990 had four similar desks, thus anticipating coordinated national and international networks and initiatives.

The Office for Ethnic Ministries served as a consultant to parishes and archdiocesan agencies with regard to intercultural relations. Sharing a common space with the other desks in the Pastoral Center, each consultant had responsibilities beyond advocacy for one group. Put another way, the organization of the office acknowledged a need not only to represent distinct constituencies but also to cultivate sensitivity to minority issues among all groups and to promote the recognition and celebration of diverse Catholic identities. This task included educating Catholics about the theological significance of diversity, and encouraging residents to welcome newcomers in their parishes. The office institutionalized a commitment to interaction and understanding among groups, in contrast to isolated ethnic factions bickering for resources.

Organized in a manner sensitive to changes in immigration patterns, American cultural self-understanding, and Catholic theology, the office institutionalized the ideology of multiculturalism. Multiculturalism divides the American population into what David Hollinger has called an "ethno-racial pentagon" of European Americans, African Americans, Hispanic Americans, Asian Americans, and Native Americans.[22] The office's alignment with national and international Catholic institutional networks signaled how a multiculturalism conceptualized within a global framework had become normative for the church in Chicago. The ethic of mutual recognition among all Catholics across racial or ethnic boundaries, along with the emphasis on intercultural interaction and celebration, was a break from the separatist ethnic boosterism of the past. This ethic, described by Charles Taylor in his commentary on multiculturalism as the "politics of recognition," shapes the activities of the consultants.[23]

"Inculturation," a concept used to understand the proper relationship between faith and culture in the process of evangelization, provided the theological underpinnings for the Office for Ethnic Ministries. Conciliar and postconciliar documents have emphasized the need for local churches to embrace the plurality of cultures the church meets. The church has endorsed the idea that it must evangelize cultures, not merely individuals within cultures. A. A. Roest Crollius states:

> Inculturation of the Church is the integration of the Christian experience of a local Church into the culture of its people, in such a way that this experience not only expresses itself in elements of this culture, but becomes a force that animates, orients and innovates this culture so as to create a new unity and communion, not only within the culture in question but also as an enrichment of the Church universal.[24]

The dialogical relationship between church and culture implied in the concept of inculturation has served to legitimate multiculturalism among Catholics engaged in evangelization.

Conclusion

Planning and institutional reorganization marked Bernardin's fourteen years as the archbishop of Chicago. He envisioned what I have called a process ecclesiology: an integrated institutional structure, in a dialectical relationship with a changing environment, animated by an ethic of responsibility and stewardship among members. He tried to harness the resources of Chicago Catholicism, although he acknowledged that many changes were a break from that tradition.

Bernardin's tenure spanned a period of economic scarcity for significant sectors of the city of Chicago, while the Archdiocese's edge cities and suburbs grew in numbers and power. Most urban neighborhoods did not have resources to build new institutions. Before 1960, the Archdiocese had been built upon a century of remarkable industrial growth. What has been called "the immigrant church" might also be called "the industrial church." Many Chicago Catholics were industrial workers, civil servants, and small-scale entrepreneurs who lived in urban industrial neighborhoods. The relatively unregulated economy, notwithstanding unpredictable booms and depressions, allowed European immigrants and their children to attain high levels of property ownership and to build parish-school plants.

Postconciliar Catholicism is largely a "post-industrial church." Deindustrialization, out-migration of middle-class Catholics, weakened labor unions, and diminished urban social services and neighborhood political power have drastically restricted the possibilities for the Catholic Church in

urban America. Sadly, many Catholic discussions about the closing of institutions do not fully take into account this transformation. These discussions tend to evaluate the moral intentions of fellow Catholics and can become highly accusational. Bernardin did not initiate a massive reallocation
of resources from suburbs to the city. Through voluntarism, such as the Big
Shoulders program or parish sharing efforts, some suburban resources were
directed toward city parishes and schools. But like all American bishops
reigning over midwestern and eastern urban dioceses in the 1980s,
Bernardin presided over the dismantling of the industrial church in urban
neighborhoods. In that context, Bernardin tried to give institutional reorganization theological meaning linked to a new Catholic identity.

Bernardin claimed that this identity was more genuinely Catholic than
an exclusively parish-centered consciousness of Chicago Catholicism.
Nothing Bernardin said, however, indicated a hostility toward the territorial or national parish, the parish school, or the preconciliar devotional
ethos that had passed away among middle-class Catholics. He tried to
mobilize the symbolic and social capital of Chicago Catholicism to support his reforms. But the parish, according to Bernardin, while fundamental to Catholic formation and identity, could no longer be the only
commitment, particularly because parishes were competing with one another for scarce resources.

One generous interpretation of the reorganization of institutions would
be that postconciliar Catholicism is analogous to the immigrant church. Between 1880 and 1940 the church promoted assimilation through "Americanization," generating confusion and conflict as a new American Catholic
identity was forged from the children of European immigrants. Today, new
forms of Catholic consciousness that require higher levels of activity, planning, and sharing across parish and racial boundaries will also take a generation to become normative in the imagination of a new generation of
Catholics.

Two factors limit the realization of Bernardin's vision. First, in some
cases collaborative planning and decision making do not work smoothly
because lay Catholics harbor ambivalence about taking responsibilities,
setting agendas, and forming visions. Many Catholics do not participate
in their parishes with enough regularity or at a level of sufficient intensity
to experience the corporate reality of the church. Unlike those whom
James Castelli and Joseph Gremillion have defined as "core" Catholics,
they prefer to have clerical authorities lead, and they remain unaware of
or indifferent to planning processes or church governance.[25]

The ambiguity of authority in postconciliar Catholicism also hampers the realization of Bernardin's vision. Tension exists between democratic and hierarchical church structures. The laity, or in some cases the clergy, are not certain that their decisions will be followed even after they participate in an intensive planning process.

This ambiguity of authority is systemic. Since Vatican Council II, Catholic bureaucracies, agencies, councils, and conferences have proliferated. Many are canonically required consultative and advisory bodies that give Catholics a voice, but not power, in the church. The collaborative participatory model of the church, which some contend is normative for postconciliar Catholicism and which Bernardin's career symbolized, exists in tension with the juridical-canonical definition of the church. On the one hand, local organizations sensitive to local needs suggest a church with empowered laity, in which the Pastoral Center functions as a resource to help Catholics develop innovative approaches to solve their own problems. This is a church not explicitly hierarchical. It uses social-scientific research to implement decisions in a pragmatic, responsive manner. On the other hand, a hierarchical structure remains. Canonically, bishops remain the monarchs of dioceses and pastors remain the princes of their parishes and schools. In sum, consultative and advisory bodies have no formal authority.

Observers have noted the ambiguity of authority in the postconciliar church. John Grindel states, "Gradually, the bishops have been opting for a participative style of life in the Church. This participative style has its roots in the American principle of 'self-governing association' that is at the basis of all other aspects of life in the United States." But he adds a caveat. The church's "ecclesial structure has remained quite Roman and hierarchical, a structure that is creating tensions with a membership much more attuned to equality, due process, and participation in decision making."[26]

NOTES

The data for this essay are derived from the archdiocesan weekly *Chicago Catholic* (renamed the *New World*), 1982–1996; more than fifty structured interviews with Catholic administrators, priests, and laypeople; many more informal conversations with Catholics throughout Chicago; and numerous observations of liturgical services and religious group activities. Thanks to Religion in Urban America Program colleagues and to John McGreevy for comments on earlier drafts.

1. Giddens, *Constitution of Society;* and Sewell, "Theory of Structure."
2. *Data on the Organization, Resources and Activities of the Archdiocese of Chicago* (1996).
3. On the history of Catholicism in Chicago, see Shanabruch, *Chicago's Catholics;* Kantowicz, *Corporation Sole;* Avella, *This Confident Church;* Dahm, *Power and Authority;* Sanders, *Education of an Urban Minority.*
4. For works that question the notion that the parish-school unit was the central marker of the neighborhood, see Zorbaugh, *Gold Coast and Slum;* Suttles, *Social Order of the Slum;* Hunter, *Symbolic Communities.*
5. Grindel, *Whither the U.S. Church?* 10, 11, 12.
6. *Chicago Catholic,* September 12, 1986, 1, 14.
7. Ibid. June 3, 1988, 2.
8. Ibid. June 10, 1988, 2.
9. Ibid. June 24 and July 1, 1988, 2.
10. *Tomorrow's Parish: Guide for Planning; Tomorrow's Parish: Criteria for Planning.*
11. Bernardin, *Decisions for the Future of Our Church* (Spring 1994); *Decisions for the Future of Our Church: Implementation Plan* (Fall 1994).
12. Bernardin, *Decisions* (Spring 1994), 2 n. 1, 6, 10.
13. Gannon and Schwartz, "Church Finances in Crisis," 112.
14. *Data,* 81, 99. For similar trends in high schools, see Fornero, "Expansion and Decline."
15. Buetow, *Of Singular Benefit;* Hunt and Kunkel, "Catholic Schools."
16. Schuster, "Study of the Local School Long-Range Planning Process."
17. On schools and controversies, see Beaudoin, "Elementary Schools"; Harris, "Is the American Catholic Church Getting Out?"; O'Brien, *Mixed Messages;* Kealey, "Collision Course"; McCready, "Catholic Schools and Catholic Identity."
18. Parot, *Polish Catholics in Chicago;* Davis, *History of Black Catholics;* D'Agostino, "Missionaries in Babylon."
19. Gleason, *Keeping the Faith.*
20. The next several paragraphs draw on an unpublished working paper by Charles Dahm, O.P., "A Brief Analysis of Some Historical Developments in Hispanic Ministry in the Archdiocese of Chicago."
21. Kelliher, "Mexican Catholics and Chicago's Parishes."
22. Hollinger, *Postethnic America.*
23. Taylor, *Multiculturalism.*
24. Schreiter, "Faith and Cultures," quotes Crollius, "What Is So New about Inculturation? A Concept and Its Implications"; quote on p. 735.
25. Castelli and Gremillion, *Emerging Parish.*
26. Grindel, *Whither the U.S. Church?* 92, 96, 97.

Part IV

Epilogue

Epilogue
Building Religious Communities at the
Turn of the Century

R. Stephen Warner

When I met Lowell Livezey late in 1991, he had received a planning grant for this project from the Lilly Endowment, and as I recall Lilly wanted him to investigate what "urban ministry"—an ideal that had flourished in Chicago from the 1920s through the 1950s—could mean in the context of radically changed American cities at the end of the twentieth century. In the years surrounding World War II, urban ministry had come to center on the responsibility that privileged white Protestant denominations assumed for cities that were increasingly alien to their own once rural, now increasingly suburban, constituencies, as the cities of the nation's industrial heartland became more Catholic, more colored, and more poor. At the end of the century, it was time for another look at the place of religion in such cities. Their industrial base had eroded into a "Rust Belt" that their white inhabitants, Protestant and Catholic alike, continued to flee in the face of newer and yet more alien people—new immigrants from the third world—even as white Protestant religious institutions had lost much of the vigor that had sustained urban ministry ideals. Such, as I understood it, was the agenda with which Livezey was presented.

During the planning process, Livezey made three fateful decisions that decisively shaped the research that he and his associates report in this book—locating the project at the University of Illinois at Chicago (UIC), defining the city as a place of ongoing religious activity, and conducting the field research from the neighborhood up.

First, Livezey knew that the project would have to engage non-Christian religious communities, and, as he told me, he thought that entrée to such communities would be facilitated if the project were to be housed at a secular university. For many reasons, McCormick Theological Seminary, the distinguished Presbyterian institution where his wife, Lois Gehr Livezey, teaches theology and ethics, would have been a suitable home, not least for its having housed Carl Dudley's Church and Community Ministry Project in the late 1980s.[1] But Livezey wanted to allay any suspicion on the part of Muslims and Jews, among others, that the project had a particularly Christian agenda, and so he shopped around for a more neutral venue. John Gardiner, of UIC's Office of Social Science Research, whose significant contributions to the project are acknowledged in the Preface, opened doors for the project at UIC, promising office space and administrative savvy and introducing Livezey to me and other potential collaborators. Settling in at UIC, not previously known as a home for research in contemporary American religion and oblivious to urban ministry, Livezey's Religion in Urban America Program (RUAP) was enmeshed in a matrix of urban-oriented social science departments, including a sociology department that enshrined the tradition of Chicago school field research. Elfriede Wedam, who had been trained in that tradition and was soon to finish her Ph.D., became central to the RUAP team. UIC was also home to a large and diverse student body of undergraduate and graduate students, for many of whom Chicago was home, from whose number RUAP was able to recruit many capable research assistants.

The second decision, bound up with the first, was a far-ranging conceptual one: to define the city for religious purposes not in terms of its needs or deficits but in terms of the religious communities already on the ground. Instead of assuming that the city was the religious responsibility of the white Protestant elite who had dominated its early years,[2] RUAP would approach the city expecting to find a diverse array of religious institutions—fledgling, struggling, and flourishing—who understood one or another part of the city's territory or population to be their special bailiwick.[3] It makes a huge difference whether one's approach toward urban populations is foremost concerned with what they lack (good jobs, decent housing, effective schools, anchor institutions, and so forth) or one instead assumes that the point of departure must be their religious activities and self-understandings. Foreign missionaries face an analogous conceptual choice, but for them the challenge is to respect the indigenous, usually non-Christian, religious tradition. In the case of contemporary American cities, the indigenous population is very likely to be Christian but followers of Christian traditions that practitioners of urban ministry often find alien and suspect, such as fundamentalism, evangelicalism, and Pentecostalism. Defining "religion in urban America" from the ground up and having at hand potential research assistants stemming from some of these indigenous urban religious communities, Christian and otherwise, RUAP avoided the deficit perspective.

Finally, as Livezey organized his RUAP research team, they decided to follow the Chicago school tradition of urban research (including the *Local Community Fact Book,* which since 1985 has been produced at UIC)[4] and to conduct the research primarily from the perspective of neighborhoods. Thus, for the most part the field sites of the research were local religious communities—congregations, parishes, Islamic centers, temples, and *gurdwārās*—that were found, prominently or obscurely, by surveying the neighborhoods. The exceptions are mostly represented in part 3, where we read about one Roman Catholic congregation (or "magnet parish") that serves a population drawn from the entire metropolitan area (chapter 9), congregations of new immigrants, many of which draw their members from similarly dispersed residential communities (chapter 10), and the most important supracongregational judicatory in Chicago, the Roman Catholic archdiocese (chapter 11).

The neighborhood-based method is a decisive alternative to focusing the study on those religious institutions identified with Chicago's ecumenical and interfaith movement, as represented for example in the local chapter of the National Conference for Community and Justice (NCCJ) and the Council for a Parliament of the World's Religions (CPWR). Had RUAP sampled religious institutions for the study through the NCCJ or the CPWR, it no doubt would have encountered a higher proportion of religious energies directed toward social activism and external ministry, but it would have missed the smaller, less ecumenically inclined but arguably no less effective churches, synagogues, mosques, and other nascent institutions that turned up in RUAP's exhaustive, on-the-ground inventory of local congregations.[5] The neighborhood-based method may thus underrepresent what metropolitanwide activism exists. Yet the particular neighborhoods chosen for the study also underrepresent other religious communities that are similar to those sampled, including those of Korean Protestants, Chinese Evangelicals, and Puerto Rican Pentecostals, as well as the nation's most prominent megachurch, Willow Creek

Community Church, located in one of the edge cities of the metropolitan region. Inclusion of such communities would, as I shall argue below, only have strengthened the findings of the study.

On the basis of these three practical, conceptual, and methodological commitments, RUAP was poised to discover the actual ways that religious institutions in Chicago engage their urban (and metropolitan) context. RUAP's findings will likely disappoint those who expect urban churches to be activist cadres dedicated to social change.[6] Indeed, the picture of American religion that emerges in these pages is, although far more varied in confessional terms, not unlike one that could be drawn about other American times and places characterized by rapid population movement and economic change, whether in the early republican period, on the frontier in the 1830s, in the cities between the wars, suburbia in the 1950s, or exurbia in the 1970s: Americans are inclined to use their religious institutions to build community in the face of social change.[7]

Throughout this book, we read of religious institutions made up of people of every color and creed that invite their members to get acquainted with one another, provide safe havens for members' (and neighbors') children, promote family values, facilitate homeownership, attempt to channel behavior in constructive directions and discourage indulgence in temptations, promote concern for others who themselves are expected to hew to the standards of the group, nurture positive identifications when negative ones are so near at hand, offer moral support and a psychological shield against a perceivedly hostile society, and promote spiritual growth where pressures of the job are experienced as soul-deadening.

Adapting for our purposes Penny Becker's typology of congregations,[8] we can say that religious institutions tend to specialize in one of four callings, being primarily (1) places of worship, where the religious ideals of the group are inculcated and expressed, (2) networks of relationships, where quasi-kinship bonds and interpersonal networks of caring are nurtured, (3) communities of discourse, where members' values are expressed and implications debated, or (4) activist organizations, where members' values and leaders' initiatives are devoted to changing the surrounding society. In terms conventional around Protestant seminaries, activities of the first two types tend to be classified as focusing on "private" religion while the fourth type, and lately the third, are lifted up as "public" involvements.[9] From this point of view, it is remarkable how much religion of the second type, where members work at building internal solidarity, shows up in RUAP's Chicago. Shall we follow the conventional wisdom and call this a pattern of "privatization"?

It was perhaps easier to do that in the 1950s, when the nascent communities tended to be suburban and their constituents so heavily white and middle class and disproportionately Protestant.[10] Under such circumstances, for white middle-class Protestant social critics to call their own people to moral account, demanding that they subordinate their "private" interests to their "public" obligations, was seen as prophecy, not prejudice. The new suburbanites were affluent, they appeared to have good jobs and stable families, and public policies like federally guaranteed mortgages and federally subsidized highways were stacked in their favor. They seemed to have no moral right to be collectively involuted, and to the extent that they were so, they were perceived as socially conformist, politically quiescent, and religiously effeminate.[11]

But when the inhabitants of urban America themselves, the people that self-centered suburbanites were cajoled to care about, show up in research like that reported in this book as dedicated to the social construction and moral self-improvement of their own communities (alongside the development of their material infrastructure), what are the erstwhile critics to say? Stepping out of the mode of conventional thought, Livezey boldly asserts (chapter 1), that their efforts at cultural production (which one might classify under Becker's first type) are one form of public religious action.

The fact is that community, which was to be the necessary infrastructure for religious social action and urban ministry, cannot be taken for granted at the end of the twentieth century, whether we are speaking of the formation of noninstrumental social bonds in a suburban development, an urban ethnic neighborhood, a church congregation, or even a family. It is not that community has been eclipsed or that it is only a relic of the past. In America, communities have been and must still be regularly created anew, particularly in times, like our own, of rapid social change. Robert Putnam has recently raised the specter of "bowling alone," leisure activity without social bonds, in his concern for the erosion of social capital.[12] Although his portrait has been criticized for its exaggeration (and although his concentration on the decline of service clubs and sports leagues ignores the greater vitality of local religious congregations), it is not absurd to worry with him about individualistic fragmentation in American society, where each person can feel so free to go his or her own way and so lonely in the going.[13] Much of modern art and drama is built around such themes, where even the joining of one person to one other has to count as a triumph.

But the precariousness of social capital is not only a problem for our time, nor—and this is a major theme in this book—are the worries about fragmentation only those of white Americans feeling displaced by multiculturalism. Those new to America recognize what many of the natives ignore, that American culture is thoroughly steeped in individualism.[14] Long before the supposedly unprecedented 1960s, Americans had been urged to follow Jesus regardless of mother and father, to go west and leave family behind, to sample the charms of Kansas City and not to be fenced in. Individualism was, and likely still is, a functional ethic for a society so devoted to economic growth and mastery of the natural environment, where the lessons a father learned about making a living were likely to be obsolete by the time his son was old enough to have to earn his own keep. Surely the value of individualism—practical as well as moral—was accentuated by the 1960s, when with postwar prosperity and the baby boom more and more Americans became heir to the culture's promises. Adapting older aspirations, some of them replaced Jesus with Buddha, others went north instead of west, and the lure of Kansas City was eclipsed by that of San Francisco's Castro district for gay men.[15] The economic devaluation of parents' learning, which young men had long been led to expect, became something many young women experienced; to the father-son disjunction was added one between mothers and daughters.[16] These individualizing currents were new but distinctly American; our culture has always been one that values mobility and individual opportunity.

The American middle class—the old WASP establishment now firmly upper middle class—has long lived with the tension between individualistic ideals and sociological realities. In the middle third of the century the nuclear family ideal—where the unit of mobility was the "two-person career"—was an apparent temporary resolution to the tension between individual and community, and parents had the expectation, backed by their resources, that prodigal children would return to the fold after their experiment with youth culture.[17] Not only did this ideal eventually reveal its bias against the aspirations of women,[18] but it also was vulnerable at the less privileged end of the white social scale to employers who had no interest in supporting more than the one person who could be induced to work for wages offered. For the lower middle class and the working class who in the 1960s finally became heirs to its promises, the nuclear-family ideal was undermined by the economic system to which it had seemed so exquisitely adapted.[19] One response of the white middle class was to lay even more stress on small-scale interpersonal responsibilities, women to men, men to women, parents to children and children to parents, an appeal to family values.

For white Appalachians, African Americans and other people of color, and Hispanics, as well as new immigrants, the American system offered both promise and threat, as barriers to mobility were lowered along with guarantees against disaster and where ethics of mutual help and deference that had helped sustain these communities in older times and other places seemed to be in jeopardy. In the post-1960s world, a family could hope for fame and fortune for a child but had good reason also to fear disgrace and poverty. Hear how often the religious communities portrayed in this book express their distrust of "the culture": the Hispanic families of Emmanuel Presbyterian and *Iglesia de Cristo,* who worry about gang recruitment of their children; the struggling African American families of the Revival Center Church of God in Christ on the West Side, who call by the name of Satan the many threats to their members; the Muslim families repulsed by the "cesspool" of un-Islamic influences to be found in American culture; the black middle-class families of New Covenant Missionary Baptist Church who are told not to trust the culture of the surrounding society; even the affluent edge-city families who think "Naperville is scary."

Largely missing, except among the volunteer tutors at Fourth Presbyterian, is the confident conviction that young people of all backgrounds need to learn the tools that would allow them full participation in the society, both its economy and its culture. Also heard little in these chapters is the idea that the wider culture should be changed. (This lacuna may be an artifact of the concentration of chapters 2 and 11 on organizational aspects of the tall-steeple Protestant churches and the archdiocesan office to the relative neglect of the sermons preached in their respective cathedrals, and of the absence altogether of megachurches in the conservative Calvinist mold.) Instead one reads that each community in question typically finds the culture lacking in religiocultural and moral guidelines for them and their children to live by; providing these guidelines for their own people they take to be their responsibility.[20]

"The culture" that is so distrusted seems for the most part nameless, except for the label "American." It seems clear enough implicitly that what one group disdains (e.g., sexual permissiveness for Muslims) may not be the same as another's anathema (e.g., violence, drugs, or even stress). It is doubtful than any single package of reforms would mend the culture to the satisfaction of all the groups; they have different complaints. Yet it also seems that the threat perceived from the culture is to a large extent an internal one, where the culture is seen as posing moral temptations to members of the group itself, particularly its young people, rather than physical threats to their possessions. What threatens most of the groups here is not other groups or other persons but less tangible cultural and ideological currents that are thought to undermine the group's intergenerational and interpersonal solidarity. Thus, moral boundaries are often drawn within the group (as they are by the Revival Center) rather than between groups. Backsliders and the nonobservant are harshly or lovingly corrected and admonished, but few of the groups portrayed here enjoy the kind of unambiguous group solidarity that would be capable of identifying the threat as coming solely from outside.[21]

Within-group moral boundaries are what we might expect to find, at least on the surface, in a culture so heavily influenced by evangelical Protestantism and its ideology of individual responsibility, including the ideal of the self-made man. In such a culture, it is incumbent on the individual to maintain his or her respectability, and dereliction weighs more heavily on the miscreant and reflects less on the reputation of the family or community than is the case in more communal cultures. Protestant churches can surely foster interreligious prejudice, especially anti-Semitism, and, in their guise as social clubs, they offer breeding grounds for narrow intergroup sympathies. Yet evangelical Protestantism is universalistic—salvation is open to all—and gives no ideological support for ethnic particularism between groups of evangelicals (a communion that includes most African Americans and increasingly Asian Americans). Evangelical churches are *supposed to* welcome everyone regardless of race or nationality; that is their value system. With spiritualized conceptions of virtue (where lust in the heart is seen as equivalent to adultery), there is no way other than vigilant self-control to keep the enemy at bay.

Similarly, perhaps because American Jews have come to recognize intermarriage and assimilationism as a greater threat to their future than pogroms,[22] the Jewish enclave of West Rogers Park that Livezey writes about is "defined by the concentration of the Jewish population and institutions, not by exclusion of or hostility toward others." For Rogers Parks in general "Far from having negative attitudes toward outsiders, these groups are primarily concerned with themselves. . . . [The] boundaries [are] within ethnoracial groups, not between them" (chapter 6).

Many religious communities whose stories are missing from these pages because of RUAP's sampling method manifest similar within-group boundaries, as Korean American churches are increasingly differentiated by generation, the first generation oriented to Korean culture and the Korean language and the second to American-style evangelicalism and the English language.[23] Korean immigrant parents have learned not to scorn "Americans," for that category now includes their own children. Community building in the form of intergenerational solidarity is a problem and a priority for most new immigrant communities; they cannot easily build fences to protect themselves because who they are is precisely what is at issue.[24]

Similarly, it is not only conservatives who seek to build community in the face of socially destructive forces, to bolster internal solidarity as much as to keep enemies at bay. Gays and lesbians, who owe to a culture of individualism their greater freedom to "come out" and express their sexual identities, nonetheless have to exert themselves to reconstruct relationships that were strained by their disclosures and to build new ones in place of the old.[25] The social centrifuge of the 1960s and 1970s both freed them from roles and expectations to which they were not suited and sorted them into new enclaves where they could begin to build their own cities on a hill.[26] Had RUAP sampled religious institutions in other Chicago neighborhoods—particularly Lakeview—this book would have featured more, and more diverse, instances of internally directed community building.

In sum, the religious institutions portrayed in this book devote considerable energies to community construction; they attempt to counteract the demoralizing effects of American culture on their members' lives by strengthening the group's subculture and promoting awareness of mutual accountability. Yet their enhancement of subcultural particularity is not tantamount to the promotion of divisiveness in American society. Religious communities in our country do not simply mirror preexisting social divisions.

The organizational repertoires of American religion offer two contrasting modes of building local communities, the congregational model prevalent in the reformed branch of American Protestantism (especially the Baptist churches) and among American Jews, and the parish model most thoroughly institutionalized until recently in the U.S. Roman Catholic Church.[27] As the word etymologically implies, the congregational model defines the local community socially as a gathering of like-minded people, people brought together by virtue of their ideals. By contrast, the parish model (from a Greek word indicating propinquity) defines the community geographically, as the territory under the authority of the local representative of the broader church. Within Janise Hurtig's Pilsen we see both models, in Emmanuel Presbyterian and Saint Pius, respectively. More broadly, we see the congregational model across the entire religious spectrum of Livezey's Rogers Park and Paul Numrich's Naperville, whereas the parish model still seems to dominate the public culture of Wedam's Southwest Side.

Both parishes and congregations can be moral communities and networks of concern, and those who are struggling to rebuild communities can operate on either set of paradigms, building a new neighborhood community within the frame of the Catholic parish (as in the Southwest Side) or a series of congregational enclaves (as in Rogers Park). We see in the case of Pilsen's Saint Pius and the churches of the Southwest Side that the parish is oriented to taking care of people, feeling responsible for them whether or not they participate. They do not really have to participate in religious activities to fall under the care of the parish, because the parish is responsible for the territory. But precisely that expectation makes for conflict with newcomer "others," because they are not "us," they are not "my neighbor." The congregation, by contrast, looks after itself and demands a lot of its members in terms of both participation and behavior. In order for care to be given, congregations tend to demand that the recipient be morally accountable to the group, not merely a resident of the neighborhood, and they therefore tend to discriminate, in terms discussed by Matthew Price, between the deserving and undeserving poor. Congregations tend to promote moral crusades, whereas parishes lend themselves to turf wars.

But that demand for moral accountability means that the congregation has a stronger impact on changing people; it gets under their skin. Livezey proposes that under conditions of a restructured metropolis, the social network of the congregation can conceivably provide social bridges to the outside, thus alleviating the social isolation that is the most serious problem of the urban underclass. But Wedam gives us reason to think that the parish model is better than the congregation at providing a potential forum for intergroup contact and dialog.

Because of its comprehensiveness as a local community, the parish model requires explicit negotiation among groups and invites the question, "Whose place is this?" and the demand, "You have to speak my language to come in." Congregations, however, are built on cultural, especially religiomoral, consensus, instead of place. Coexistence among different congregations may require only mutual toleration and civil inattention. The Jews of West Rogers Park, who are congregational, seem to understand how to deal with religious diversity at both the community and the enclave levels. As we have seen, Protestants may not always welcome cultural diversity, but unlike Catholics, they are not used to owning urban turf.

The racial history of Chicago offers mixed lessons about these two models and no clear verdict on the superiority of one over the other. As Chicago neighborhoods have undergone racial change, it is relatively easy for congregationally based institutions to move with their constituents to new city neighborhoods or the suburbs, depriving the old neighborhood of some of its social capital, whereas parish-based institutions are far more likely to stay as anchors in old neighborhoods and to be ready to minister to their new residents. On the other hand, the physical capital of fleeing congregations, their often substantial buildings, can be made available by sale to the congregations that actually represent the newcomer population. Moreover, the carefully inculcated loyalty to parish territory has tragically fueled fierce resistance to neighborhood racial change.[28] It is not clear that one model is superior to another in building community relations.

As much as they cannot be dismissed as "privatized," the efforts at community construction and restructuring portrayed in these pages still leave much to be desired. Too few of them seem to address issues of concern across the entire metropolitan area, let alone the nation as a whole, an important matter given the decreasing capacity of the city, even of its elites, to govern its own destiny. Those who might have the resources to do so—the churches of affluent, growing Naperville—seem not to address tractable issues that their members appear to be aware of, their hard-driven, materialistic lifestyles. Another church of the affluent, Old Saint Pat's, seems to offer little challenge to its parishioners to employ humanely what power they enjoy in their workplaces. The downtown churches seem on the verge of losing much of the raison d'être of their urban ministry, as the Cabrini Green housing project, whose children they tutor, seems doomed before the rising tide of real estate values. None

of these congregations seems to have much to say about extreme and rising economic inequality in the United States. In these chapters, only the
Catholic archdiocese seems even remotely capable of a policy of modest
redistribution, in which affluent suburban churches might subsidize the
efforts of poor urban ones. Perhaps more along such lines is going on in
these churches than appears in this book, as well as in the many religious
institutions RUAP could not cover.

Yet the achievement of the book—and the efforts of the religious institutions we read of in it—should not be slighted. These churches, synagogues, mosques, temples, and *gurdwārās* devote themselves to building
cultural coherence and social bonds in the face of powerful individualizing currents. Those who attempt to improve the material lot of their constituents do so using methods that are both material and spiritual, both
structural and cultural. State-centered attempts to further economic
equality should take seriously the methods found in at least some of these
churches, where effective material aid in the form of the Earned Income
Tax Credit (to cite one example of an effective tool of social policy)
would be insufficient without a continuing rhetorical attack on drug and
alcohol abuse. Although none of these religious communities may have
the right answer for improving the condition of the truly disadvantaged,
thoughtful outsiders who would like to call themselves progressives
should respectfully consider as models of policy the religious schooling
some provide and the moral strings others attach to charitable aid. The
stalemate of left/right politics and the dichotomy of "structural" versus
"moral" approaches to policy should end, and this book makes an important contribution to that goal.

NOTES

1. Dudley, *Basic Steps toward Community Ministry*.
2. Stockwell, "A Better Class of People."
3. A similar shift in perspective can be seen in comparing the chapter on context in Carroll, Dudley, and McKinney, eds., *Handbook*, with the chapter on ecology in Ammerman et al., eds., *Studying Congregations*.
4. Chicago Fact Book Consortium, *Local Community Fact Book*, 1980 and
1990.
5. There is a paradox to interfaith efforts, which, sampling on the dependent
variable of willingness to engage in cross-boundary dialog, misrepresent the
range of American religious diversity, typically excluding those who do not wish

to be included among the ecumenically inclined—Pentecostal Christians, Orthodox Jews, and conservative Muslims, among others.

6. See Ducey, *Sunday Morning.*

7. See Mathews, "Second Great Awakening as an Organizing Process"; Miyakawa, *Protestants and Pioneers;* McGreevy, *Parish Boundaries;* Winter, *Suburban Captivity of the Churches;* and Warner, *New Wine in Old Wineskins.*

8. Becker, *Congregations in Conflict.*

9. Marty, "Public and Private."

10. W. H. Whyte, in *The Organization Man,* and Bennett M. Berger, in *Working-Class Suburb,* wrote of Jewish and working-class suburbs, respectively.

11. Warner, "Changes in the Civic Role of Religion," 238.

12. Putnam, "Bowling Alone."

13. Wuthnow, *Restructuring of American Religion.*

14. Bellah et al., *Habits of the Heart.*

15. See Tipton, *Getting Saved from the Sixties;* Lemann, *Promised Land;* and FitzGerald, *Cities on a Hill.*

16. Stacey, *Brave New Families.*

17. Parsons, "Age and Sex in Social Structure."

18. Friedan, *Feminine Mystique.*

19. Stacey, *Brave New Families.*

20. Warner, "Changes in the Civic Role of Religion."

21. See also Pattillo, "Sweet Mothers and Gangbangers."

22. Notwithstanding the racism and anti-Semitism that Benjamin Smith and the World Wide Church of the Creator brutally visited upon this community on July 2, 1999.

23. Kwon, Kim, and Warner, eds., *Korean Americans and Their Religions.*

24. Warner and Wittner, eds., *Gatherings in Diaspora.*

25. Wilson, *Our Tribe.*

26. FitzGerald, *Cities on a Hill;* Warner, "Metropolitan Community Churches and the Gay Agenda."

27. Warner, "The Place of the Congregation."

28. McGreevy, *Parish Boundaries.*

Appendix
Religious Organizations Studied and Names of Principal Contact Persons

Chapter 2. Pilsen

Iglesia Presbiteriana Emanuel
1850 S. Racine Avenue
Chicago, IL 60608
Rev. Rolando Cuellar, pastor

Pilsen Resurrection Project
1818 S. Paulina Street
Chicago, IL 60608
Raoul Raymundo, executive director

St. Paul Roman Catholic Church
2127 W. 22nd Place
Chicago, IL 60608
Rev. George Ruffolo, pastor

St. Pius V Roman Catholic Church
1919 S. Ashland Avenue
Chicago, IL 60608
Rev. Charles W. Dahm, O.P., pastor

Temple Bethel Church of God
1924 S. Leavitt Street
Chicago, IL 60608
Rev. Jose Vasquez, pastor

Chapter 3. Loop and Near North Side

First United Methodist Church, Chicago Temple
77 W. Washington Street
Chicago, IL 60602
Rev. Eugene Winkler, pastor

Fourth Presbyterian Church
126 E. Chestnut Street
Chicago, IL 60611
Rev. John M. Buchanan, pastor

LaSalle Street Church
1136 N. LaSalle Street
Chicago, IL 60610
Rev. Bruce Otto, associate pastor

The Moody Church
1609 North LaSalle
Chicago, IL 60614
Rev. Erwin Lutzer, pastor
Rev. Daryl Worley, associate pastor

Old St. Patrick's Roman Catholic Church
122 S. Des Plaines Street
Chicago, IL 60661
Rev. John J. Wall, pastor

Park Community Church
108 W. Germania Place
Chicago, IL 60610
Jim Sharkey

Episcopal Cathedral of St. James
65 E. Huron Street
Chicago, IL 60611
Rev. Todd Smelser, dean

St. Joseph's Roman Catholic Church and School
1065 N. Orleans Street
Chicago, IL 60610
Sr. Stephanie Schmidt

Temple Sholom
3480 N. Lake Shore Drive
Chicago, IL 60657
Rabbi Frederick Schwartz

Chapter 4. Near West Side

First Baptist Congregational Church
1613 W. Washington Boulevard
Chicago, IL 60612
Rev. Arthur D. Griffin, pastor

Greater Pleasant Valley Missionary Baptist Church
1709 W. Washington Boulevard
Chicago, IL 60612
Rev. Robert Skinner, pastor

People's Church of God in Christ
4244 W. Madison Street
Chicago, IL 60624
Rev. William M. Elder, pastor

Presentation Roman Catholic Church
734 S. Springfield Avenue
Chicago, IL 60624
Rev. Thomas P. Walsh, pastor

Revival Center Church of God in Christ
1956 W. Washington Boulevard
Chicago, IL 60612
Rev. Benjamin Bowman, pastor

St. Malachy Roman Catholic Church
2248 W. Washington Boulevard
Chicago, IL 60612
Rev. Ralph E. Starus, pastor

St. Stephen AME Church
2000 W. Washington Boulevard
Chicago, IL 60612
Rev. Albert D. Tyson III, pastor

Spirit of Joy Lutheran Church
1345 N. Karlov Avenue
Chicago, IL 60651
Rev. Maxine Washington, pastor

Chapter 5. Southwest Side

Almuhajireen Mosque and School
Pulaski Avenue at 63rd Street
Chicago, IL 60629
Khawla Razeq, lay member

Congregation Lawn Manor Beth Jacob
6601 S. Kedzie Avenue
Chicago, IL 60629
Janice Kay, lay member

Covenant Group of Churches
6012 S. Laflin Street
Chicago, IL 60636
Mary Foley, coordinator

Greater Southwest Development Corporation
2601 W. 63rd Street
Chicago, IL 60629
Jim Capraro, director

St. Adrian Roman Catholic Church
7000 S. Fairfield Avenue
Chicago, IL 60629
Rev. Theodore Ostrowski, pastor

St. Bruno Roman Catholic Church
4751 S. Harding Avenue
Chicago, IL 60632
Rev. Joseph P. Grembla, pastor

St. Clare de Montefalco Roman Catholic Church
5443 S. Washtenaw Avenue
Chicago, IL 60632
Rev. Anthony Pizzo, pastor

St. Gall Roman Catholic Church
5511 S. Sawyer Avenue
Chicago, IL 60629
Rev. David Dowdle, pastor

Nativity BVM Roman Catholic Church
6812 S. Washtenaw Avenue
Chicago, IL 60629

St. Nicholas of Tolentine Roman Catholic Church
3721 W. 62nd Street
Chicago, IL 60629
Rev. Stanley G. Rataj, pastor

St. Rita of Cascia Roman Catholic Church
6243 S. Fairfield Avenue
Chicago, IL 60629
Rev. William E. Lego, O.S.A., pastor

Southwest Organizing Project
(formerly Southwest Catholic Cluster Project)
2601 W. 63rd Street
Chicago, IL 60629
Jay Caponigro, executive director

Southwest Youth Collaborative
3154 W. 63rd Street
Chicago, IL 60629
Camille Odeh, director

New Life Community Church
1700 W. 44th Street
Chicago, IL 60609
Rev. Mark Jobe, pastor

First Christian Church
3600 W. 79th Street
Chicago, IL 60652
Rev. Alan White, pastor

Ashburn Lutheran Church
3345 W. 83rd Street
Chicago, IL 60652

Chapter 6. Rogers Park and West Rogers Park

Al-Madina Islamic Center
(also Wallen Community Center)
1701 W. Wallen Avenue
Chicago, IL 60626

The Ark
6450 N. California Avenue
Chicago, IL 60645
Renee Lepp, executive director

Congregation Ezra Habonim
2620 W. Touhy Avenue
(now 2800 W. Sherwin)
Chicago, IL 60645
Rabbi Robert Rhodes
Fred Sinay, president
Ralph Reubner, chair, Pulpit Committee

First Telugu Methodist Church
1545 W. Morse Avenue
Chicago, IL 60626
Rev. Jacob Agepog, pastor

Good News Church/Iglesia Buenas Nuevas
7649 N. Paulina Street
Chicago, IL 60626
Rev. Karen Mosby-Avery, pastor
Rev. Haracio Sedio-Peralta, pastor

Iglesia de Cristo–Misión Cristiana Elim
1615 W. Morse Avenue
Chicago, IL 60626
Rev. Hector Nufio, pastor

International Society for Krishna Consciousness (ISKCON)
(Hare Krishna Temple)
1716 W. Lunt Avenue
Chicago, IL 60626
Prithusrava Dasa, president
Shankara Pandit, vice president

St. Jerome Roman Catholic Church
1709 W. Lunt Avenue
Chicago, IL 60626
Rev. Harold A. Bonin, pastor

Sephardic Congregation
1819 W. Howard Street
Evanston, IL 60202
Rabbi Michael Azose
Yehoshua Ben Avraham, president

United Church of Rogers Park
1545 W. Morse Avenue
Chicago, IL 60626
Rev. Kermit Krueger, pastor
Anita Alcantara, minister of community life

Unity Church
1925 W. Thome Avenue
Chicago, IL 60660

Chapter 7. Chatham and Greater Grand Crossing

Carter Temple CME Church
7841 S. Wabash Avenue
Chicago, IL 60619
Rev. Henry M. Williamson Sr., pastor

Ingleside-Whitfield United Methodist Church
929 E. 76th Street
Chicago, IL 60619
Rev. Danita Anderson, pastor

Israel Methodist Community Church
7620 S. Cottage Grove Avenue
Chicago, IL 60619
Rev. Hiram Crawford, pastor

New Covenant Missionary Baptist Church
740 E. 77th Street
Chicago, IL 60619
Rev. Stephen J. Thurston, pastor

St. Columbanus Roman Catholic Church
331 E. 71st Street
Chicago, IL 60619
Rev. Phillip Cyscon, pastor

Vernon Park Church of God
9011 S. Stony Island Avenue
Chicago, IL 60617
Rev. Claude Wyatt and Rev. Addie Wyatt, pastors

Chapter 8. Naperville, Illinois

Calvary Church
9S200 Route 59
Naperville, IL 60564
Rev. Robert Schmidgall, pastor (deceased)
Rev. Keith Boucher, assistant pastor
Mark Strohm, principal, Calvary Christian School

Congregation Beth Shalom
1433 N. Main Street
Naperville, IL 60563
Rabbi Michael M. Remson

First Congregational Church
25 E. Benton Avenue
Naperville, IL 60540
Harold Gosselink, lay member and historian

Islamic Center of Naperville
450 S. Olsen Drive
Naperville, IL 60540
Faisel Hamoudeh, president

Lotus Sangha
1520 Canyon Run Road
Naperville, IL 60565
Amelia Nguyen, lay member

St. James Lutheran Church
2844 W. Ogden Avenue (Route 34)
Naperville, IL 60567
Rev. Roger Timm, pastor

Wheatland Salem Church
Route 59 and 95th Street
Naperville, IL 60564
Rev. Scott Field, pastor

Chapter 9. Old Saint Patrick's Roman Catholic Church

Old St. Patrick's Roman Catholic Church
122 S. Des Plaines Street
Chicago, IL 60661
Rev. John J. Wall, pastor
Rev. John C. Cusick, associate pastor
Eileen Smith, lay member

Chapter 10. Recent Immigrant Congregations

Chinmaya Mission
11 S. 80, Route 83
Hinsdale, IL 60521
Brother Sharan Chaitanya

The Hindu Temple of Greater Chicago
10915 Lemont Road
Lemont, IL 60439
Marella L. Hanumadass, president

International Society of Krishna Consciousness (ISKCON)
1716 W. Lunt Avenue
Chicago, IL 60626
Prithusrava Dasa

Jain Society of Metropolitan Chicago
435 N. Route 59
Bartlett, IL 60103

Mosque Foundation
Harlem Avenue and 93rd Street
Bridgeview, IL   60455
Rafeeq A. Jaber, president

Muslim Community Center
4380 N. Elston Avenue
Chicago, IL   60641
NeQuiniso Abdulla, president

Sikh Religious Society of Chicago
P.O. Box 864
Palatine, IL   60067
Granthi Mohinder Singh

Sri Venkateswara (Balaji) Temple of Greater Chicago
1145 Sullivan Road
P.O. Box 1536
Aurora, IL   60507-1536

The Thai Buddhist Temple (Wat Dhammaram)
7059 W. 75th Street
Chicago, IL   60638-5934
Ven. Chuen Phangcham

Wat Phrasriratanamahadhatu
4735 N. Magnolia
Chicago, IL   60640
Phra Ratana Thongkrajai

Chapter 11. Archdiocese of Chicago

The Pastoral Center
155 E. Superior Street
Chicago, IL   60611
Joseph Cardinal Bernardin, archbishop of Chicago (deceased)
Rev. David E. Baldwin, director of the research and planning
Elaine Schuster, superintendent of Catholic schools

Bibliography

Adelman, William J. *Pilsen and the West Side*. Chicago: Illinois Labor History Society, 1977.

Ammerman, Nancy T. *Congregation and Community*. New Brunswick, NJ: Rutgers University Press, 1997.

Ammerman, Nancy T., Jackson W. Carroll, Carol S. Dudley, and William McKinney, eds. *Studying Congregations: A New Handbook*. Nashville, TN: Abingdon, 1998.

Anderson, Alan B., and George W. Pickering. *Confronting the Color Line: The Broken Promise of the Civil Rights Movement in Chicago*. Athens: University of Georgia Press, 1986.

Anderson, Elijah. "The Code of the Streets." *Atlantic Monthly*, May 1994, 81–94.

———. *Streetwise: Race, Class, and Change in an Urban Community*. Chicago: University of Chicago Press, 1990.

Anderson, Nels. *The Hobo*. Chicago: University of Chicago Press, 1923.

Anzaldúa, Gloria. *Borderlands/La Frontera: The New Mestiza*. San Francisco: Spinsters/Aunt Lute, 1987.

The Archdiocese of Chicago: Antecedents and Developments. Des Plaines, IL: St. Mary's Training School, 1920.

Asante, Molefi Kete. *Afrocentricity*. Trenton, NJ: Africa World, 1988.

Asian American Handbook. Chicago: National Conference of Christians and Jews, Asian American Journalists Association, and Association of Asian Pacific American Artists, 1991.

Avella, Steven. *This Confident Church: Catholic Leadership and Life in Chicago, 1940–1965*. Notre Dame, IN: University of Notre Dame Press, 1992.

Badillo, David. "The Catholic Church and the Making of Mexican-American Parish Communities in the Midwest." In *Mexican Americans and the Catholic Church, 1900–1965*, edited by Jay P. Dolan and Gilberto M. Hinojosa, 254–256. Notre Dame, IN: University of Notre Dame Press, 1994.

Bakke, Raymond J. *The Expanded Mission of "Old First" Churches*. Valley Forge, PA: Judson, 1986.

———. *A Theology as Big as the City*. Downers Grove, IL: InterVarsity, 1997.

Banner-Haley, Charles. *The Fruits of Integration: Black Middle Class Ideology 1960–1990*. Jackson: University Press of Mississippi, 1994.

Barton, Timothy. "Celtic Revived: The Artistry of Thomas O'Shaughnessy." In *At the Crossroads: Old Saint Patrick's and the Chicago Irish,* edited by Ellen Skerrett, 85–101. Chicago: Wild Onion, 1997.

Bass, Dorothy C. "Congregations and the Bearing of Traditions." In *American Congregations,* vol. 2: *New Perspectives in the Study of Congregations,* edited by James P. Wind and James W. Lewis. Chicago: University of Chicago Press, 1994.

———, ed. *Practicing Our Faith: A Way of Life for a Searching People.* San Francisco: Jossey-Bass, 1996.

Beaudoin, David M. "Elementary Schools in the United States: Catholic and American." *Chicago Studies* 28 (November 1989): 303–319.

———. "Evangelization, Christian Initiation and Catholic Schools." *Catechumenate* 14 (July 1992): 12–20.

Becker, Laura L. "Ethnicity and Religion." In *Encyclopedia of the American Religious Experience: Studies of Traditions and Movements,* edited by Charles H. Lippy and Peter W. Williams, 1477–1491. New York: Scribner's, 1988.

Becker, Penny E. *Congregations in Conflict: Cultural Models of Local Religious Life.* Cambridge: Cambridge University Press, 1999.

Becker, Penny E., and Nancy L. Eiesland, eds. *Contemporary American Religion: An Ethnographic Reader.* Walnut Creek, CA: AltaMira, 1997.

Bellah, Robert N., Richard Madsen, William M. Sullivan, Ann Swidler, and Steven M. Tipton. *Habits of the Heart: Individualism and Commitment in American Life.* Berkeley: University of California Press, 1985.

Berger, Bennett M. *Working-Class Suburb.* Berkeley: University of California Press, 1960.

Bernardin, Joseph Cardinal. *Decisions for the Future of Our Church.* Archdiocese of Chicago, Chicago, Spring 1994.

———. *Decisions for the Future of Our Church: Implementation Plan, Evangelization and Education, Ministerial Leadership.* Archdiocese of Chicago, Chicago, Fall 1994.

———. *The Gift of Peace: Personal Reflections.* Chicago: Loyola University Press, 1997.

Billingsley, Andrew. *Climbing Jacob's Ladder: The Enduring Legacy of African-American Families.* New York: Simon & Schuster, 1992.

Blank, Rebecca M. *It Takes a Nation: A New Agenda for Fighting Poverty.* Princeton, NJ: Princeton University Press, 1997.

Bluestone, Daniel. *Constructing Chicago.* New Haven, CT: Yale University Press, 1991.

Bodnar, John. *The Transplanted: A History of Immigrants in Urban America.* Bloomington: Indiana University Press, 1985.

Bole, William. "Closing the Doors." *Catholic World Report* 4, no. 5 (May 1994): 30–33.

Boyer, Horace Clarence. *How Sweet the Sound: The Golden Age of Gospel.* Washington, DC: Elliott & Clark, 1995.

Braden, William. "Chatham: An African-American Success Story." In *Ethnic Chicago: A Multicultural Portrait,* edited by Melvin G. Holli and Peter d'A. Jones, 4th ed., 341–345. Grand Rapids, MI: William B. Eerdmans, 1995.

Branch, Taylor. *Parting the Waters: America in the King Years, 1954–1963.* New York: Simon & Schuster, 1988.

Browning, Don S. *A Fundamental Practical Theology: Descriptive and Strategic Proposals.* Minneapolis: Fortress, 1991.

Buchanan, John M. *Being Church, Becoming Community.* 1st ed. Louisville, KY: Westminster John Knox, 1996.

Buetow, Harold A. *Of Singular Benefit: The Story of U.S. Catholic Education.* New York: Macmillan, 1970.

Burgess, Ernest W. "The Growth of the City: An Introduction to a Research Project." In *The City,* by Robert E. Park and Ernest W. Burgess. Chicago: University of Chicago Press, 1925.

Butler, Francis J., ed. *American Catholic Identity: Essays in an Age of Change.* Kansas City, MO: Sheed & Ward, 1994.

"Cabrini Youths Take Shot at Film Making." *Chicago Defender,* 28 September 1994.

Candeloro, Dominic. "Chicago's Italians: A Survey of the Ethnic Factor, 1850–1990." In *Ethnic Chicago: A Multicultural Portrait,* edited by Melvin G. Holli and Peter d'A. Jones, 4th ed., 229–259. Grand Rapids, MI: William B. Eerdmans, 1995.

Carlson, Alvar W. "The Settling of Asian Immigrant Groups in the Chicago Metropolitan Area, 1965–76." *Philippine Geographical Journal* 28 (1984): 22–40.

Carroll, Jackson W., Carl S. Dudley, and William McKinney, eds. *Handbook for Congregational Studies.* Nashville, TN: Abingdon, 1986.

Caruso, Jorge, and Eduardo Camacho. "Latino Chicago." In *Ethnic Chicago,* edited by Melvin G. Holli and Peter d'A. Jones, 4th ed. Grand Rapids, MI: William B. Eerdmans, 1995.

Casanova, José. *Public Religions in the Modern World.* Chicago: University of Chicago Press, 1994.

Castelli, James, and Joseph Gremillion. *The Emerging Parish: The Notre Dame Study of Catholic Life since Vatican II.* San Francisco: Harper & Row, 1987.

Cateura, Linda Brandi, ed. *Growing Up Italian: How Being Brought Up as an Italian-American Helped Shape the Characters, Lives, and Fortunes of Twenty-four Celebrated Americans.* New York: William Morrow, 1987.

Cenkner, William. *The Multicultural Church: A New Landscape in U.S. Theologies.* New York: Paulist, 1995.

Chapman, Mark L. *Christianity on Trial: African American Religious Thought before and after Black Power.* Maryknoll, NY: Orbis Books, 1996.

Chaves, Mark. "Secularization as Declining Religious Authority." *Social Forces* 72, no. 3 (March 1994): 749–774.

Chicago Fact Book Consortium. *Local Community Fact Book, Chicago Metropolitan Area: Based on the 1980 Census.* Chicago: The Chicago Review, 1985.

———. *Local Community Fact Book Chicago Metropolitan Area 1990.* Chicago: Academy Chicago, 1995.

Chicago Housing Authority. *Statistical Profile: The Chicago Housing Authority, 1991–1992.* Chicago: Chicago Housing Authority, 1992.

Chicago Regional Report. National Growth Management Leadership Project, October 1996.

Cohen, Anthony. *The Symbolic Construction of Community.* London: Routledge, 1985.

Cohen, Martin A., and Abraham J. Peck, eds. *Sephardim in the Americas: Studies in Culture and History.* Tuscaloosa: University of Alabama Press, 1993.

Coleman, James. "Families and Schools." *Educational Researcher* 32 (August 1987): 32–38.

———. *Foundations of Social Theory.* Cambridge, MA: Belknap Press of Harvard University Press, 1990.

———. "Social Capital in the Creation of Human Capital." *American Journal of Sociology* 94 (1988): S95–121.

Coleman, John, S.J. "True and False Multi-Culturalism." Address to National Catholic Charities Convention, Washington, DC, 1 October 1994.

Condit, Celeste Michelle, and John Louis Lucaites. *Crafting Equality: America's Anglo-African Word.* Chicago: University of Chicago Press, 1993.

Conzen, Kathleen Neils. "Forum: The Place of Religion in Urban and Community Studies." *Religion and American Culture* 6, no. 2 (1996): 112.

Conzen, Kathleen Neils, David A. Gerber, Ewa Morawska, George E. Pozetta, and Rudolph Vecoli. "The Invention of Ethnicity: A Perspective from the U.S.A." *Journal of American Ethnic History* 12, no. 1 (1992): 3–41.

Copeland, Warren R. *And the Poor Get Welfare: The Ethics of Poverty in the United States.* Nashville, TN: Abingdon, 1994.

Coriden, James A. *The Parish in Catholic Tradition: History, Theology and Canon Law.* New York: Paulist, 1997.

Coriden, James A., Thomas J. Green, and Donald E. Heintschel, eds. *The Code of Canon Law: A Text and Commentary.* New York: Paulist, 1985.

Cose, Ellis. *The Rage of a Privileged Class: Why Are Middle-Class Blacks Angry? Why Should America Care?* New York: HarperCollins, 1993.

"Criteria for a Good Parish." *Origins* 24, no. 3 (2 June 1994): 1, 35.

Cruse, Harold. *Plural but Equal: A Critical Study of Blacks and Minorities and America's Plural Society.* New York: William Morrow, 1987.

Cutler, Irving. *The Jews of Chicago: From Shtetl to Suburb.* Chicago: University of Illinois Press, 1996.

D'Agostino, Peter R. "The Crisis of Authority in American Catholicism: Urban Schools and Cultural Conflict." *Records of the American Catholic Historical Society of Philadelphia* 108 (Fall–Winter 1997–1998): 87–122.

———. "Missionaries in Babylon: The Adaptation of Italian Priests to Chicago's Church, 1870–1940." Ph.D. diss., University of Chicago, 1993.

———. "Recent Research." *American Catholic Studies Newsletter, Cushwa Center for the Study of American Catholicism* 21, no. 2 (September 1994): 16–18.

Dahm, Charles, O.P. "A Brief Analysis of Some Historical Developments in Hispanic Ministry in the Archdiocese of Chicago." Unpublished paper, October 1990.

———. *Power and Authority in the Catholic Church: Cardinal Cody in Chicago.* Notre Dame, IN: University of Notre Dame Press, 1981.

Daniel, Vattel Elbert. "Ritual Stratification in Chicago Negro Churches." *American Sociological Review* 7 (June 1942): 73.

Daniels, David D., III. "The Cultural Renewal of Slave Religion: Charles Price Jones and the Emergence of the Holiness Movement in Mississippi." Ph.D. diss., Union Theological Seminary, 1992.

Danzger, M. Herbert. *Returning to Tradition: The Contemporary Revival of Orthodox Judaism.* New Haven, CT: Yale University Press, 1989.

Dart, John. "Most View Christians, Jews as Good Influences, Survey Finds." *Los Angeles Times,* 17 February 1996, B1.

Data on the Organization, Resources and Activities of the Archdiocese of Chicago: Facts and Figures for Year Ending 1995. Chicago: Archdiocese of Chicago Office of Research and Planning, 1996.

Davis, Cyprian. *The History of Black Catholics in the United States.* New York: Crossroad, 1993.

"Declaration on Religious Freedom." In *The Documents of Vatican II: In a New and Definitive Translation,* edited by Walter M. Abbott, S.J., 675–696. New York: Herder & Herder, 1966.

Demerath, N. J., III, and Rhys H. Williams. *A Bridging of Faiths: Religion and Politics in a New England City.* Princeton, NJ: Princeton University Press, 1992.

———. "Secularization in a Community Context: Tensions of Religion and Politics in a New England City." *Journal for the Scientific Study of Religion* 31, no. 2 (1992): 189–206.

"Developer Building a Dream at Cabrini." *Chicago Tribune,* 20 June 1998.

Díaz-Stevens, Ana María, and Anthony M. Stevens-Arroyo. *Recognizing the Latino Resurgence in U.S. Religion.* Boulder, CO: Westview, 1998.

"Diocesan Offices: Organization and Reorganization." *Center Papers* 6 (1994): 1–12.

"Diocesan Reorganization." *Center Papers* 2 (December 1985): 1–12.

Dolan, Jay P. *The American Catholic Experience: A History from Colonial Times to the Present.* Garden City, NY: Doubleday, 1985.

Dolan, Jay P., and Gilberto M. Hinojosa, eds. *Mexican Americans and the Catholic Church, 1900–1965.* Notre Dame, IN: University of Notre Dame Press, 1994.

Drake, St. Clair, and Horace R. Cayton. *Black Metropolis: A Study of Negro Life in a Northern City.* New York: Harper & Row, 1962.

Drucker, Peter F. "The Age of Social Transformation." *Atlantic Monthly,* November 1994, 53–80.

Ducey, Michael. *Sunday Morning: Aspects of Urban Ritual.* New York: Free Press, 1977.

Dudley, Carl S. *Basic Steps toward Community Ministry: Guidelines and Models in Action.* Washington, DC: Alban Institute, 1991.

Dudley, Carl S., and Sally A. Johnson. "Congregational Self-Images for Social Ministry." In *Carriers of Faith: Lessons from Congregational Studies,* edited by Carl S. Dudley, Jackson W. Carroll, and James P. Wind, 104–124. Louisville, KY: Westminster John Knox, 1991.

Dudley, Carl S., Jackson W. Carroll, and James P. Wind, eds. *Carriers of Faith: Lessons from Congregational Studies.* Louisville, KY: Westminster John Knox, 1991.

DuPage County Development Department, Planning Division. *Profile: DuPage County Statistical Handbook.* 1992.

DuPage County Regional Planning Commission. *DuPage County Jobs/Housing Study.* February 1991.

Dusenbery, Verne A. "Introduction: A Century of Sikhs beyond Punjab." In *The Sikh Diaspora: Migration and the Experience Beyond Punjab,* edited by N. Gerald Barrier and Verne A. Dusenbery, 1–28. Delhi: Chanakya, 1989.

Dyson, Michael E. *Reflecting Black: African-American Cultural Criticism.* Minneapolis: University of Minnesota Press, 1993.

Ebner, Michael H. "Technoburb." *Inland Architect* 37, no. 1 (January 1993): 54–59.

Eck, Diana L. *Darsan: Seeing the Divine Image in India.* 2d ed. Chambersburg, PA: Anima, 1985.

———. *World Religions in Boston: A Guide to Communities and Resources.* Cambridge, MA: Pluralism Project, Harvard University, 1995.

Edington, Howard. *Downtown Church: The Heart of the City.* Nashville, TN: Abingdon, 1996.

Ehrenhalt, Alan. *The Lost City: Discovering the Forgotten Virtues of Community in the Chicago of the 1950s.* New York: Basic Books, 1995.

Eiesland, Nancy L. *A Particular Place: Urban Restructuring and Religious Ecology in a Southern Exurb.* New Brunswick, NJ: Rutgers University Press, 2000.

Elshtain, Jean Bethke. *Democracy on Trial.* New York: Basic Books, 1995.

Engel, Ronald J. *Sacred Sands: The Struggle for Community in the Indiana Dunes.* Middletown, CT: Wesleyan University Press, 1983.

Espiritu, Yen Le, and Ivan Light. "The Changing Ethnic Shape of Contemporary

Urban America." In *Urban Life in Transition,* edited by Mark Gottdiener and Chris G. Pickvance, 35–54. Newbury Park, CA: Sage, 1991.

Etzioni, Amitai. "The Responsive Community: A Communitarian Perspective— 1995 Presidential Address." *American Sociological Review* 61, no. 1 (February 1996): 1–11.

Faith and Culture: A Multicultural Catechetical Resource. Washington, DC: United States Catholic Conference, 1987.

Faramelli, Norman, Edward Rodman, and Anne Scheibner. "Seeking to Hear and Heed in the Cities: Urban Ministry in the Postwar Episcopal Church." In *Churches, Cities, and Human Community: Urban Ministry in the United States 1945–1985,* edited by Clifford J. Green, 97–122. Grand Rapids, MI: William B. Eerdmans, 1996.

Farr, Marcia. "Language, Culture, and Literacy in a Transnational Community: Old Traditions in New Settings." Unpublished manuscript, 1997.

Fenton, John Y. *Transplanting Religious Traditions: Asian Indians in America.* New York: Praeger, 1988.

Ferguson, Margaret Geneva. *The History of St. Paul C.M.E. Church, Chicago, Illinois 1907–1988.* Chicago: Margaret G. Ferguson, 1988.

Ferman, Barbara. *Challenging the Growth Machine: Neighborhood Politics in Chicago and Pittsburgh.* Lawrence: University Press of Kansas, 1996.

Fichter, Joseph H. *Social Relations in the Urban Parish.* Chicago: University of Chicago Press, 1954.

Field, Scott N. "'Let My People Go!' Breaking the Two Hundred Barrier at Wheatland Salem United Methodist Church through Lay Ministries." Ph.D. diss., Asbury Theological Seminary, 1991.

Fischer, Claude S. "The Subcultural Theory of Urbanism: A Twentieth-Year Assessment." *American Journal of Sociology* 101, no. 3 (November 1995): 543–577.

———. *To Dwell among Friends: Personal Networks in Town and City.* Chicago: University of Chicago Press, 1982.

Fish, John, Gordon Nelson, Walter Stuhr, and Lawrence Witmer. *The Edge of the Ghetto: A Study of Church Involvement in Community Organization.* New York: Seabury, 1968.

Fishman, Robert. *Bourgeois Utopias: The Rise and Fall of Suburbia.* New York: Basic Books, 1987.

FitzGerald, Frances. *Cities on a Hill: A Journey through Contemporary American Cultures.* New York: Simon and Schuster, 1986.

Fitzpatrick, Joseph P., S.J. *One Church, Many Cultures: The Challenge of Diversity.* Kansas City, MO: Sheed & Ward, 1987.

Fontana, John. "A Religious Entrepreneur in the World of Work." *Catholic World* 237 (July 1994): 1420.

Fornero, George V. "The Expansion and Decline of Enrollment and Facilities of

Secondary Schools in the Archdiocese of Chicago, 1955–1980: A Historical Study." Ph.D. diss., Loyola University of Chicago, 1990.

Fox Valley Genealogical Society. *Copenhagen Cemetery*. Naperville, IL, 1997.

Franklin, Robert M. *Another Day's Journey: Black Churches Confronting the American Crisis*. Minneapolis: Fortress, 1997.

———. "My Soul Says Yes: The Urban Ministry of the Church of God in Christ." In *Churches, Cities, and Human Community: Urban Ministry in the United States 1945–1985*, edited by Clifford J. Green, 77–96. Grand Rapids, MI: William B. Eerdmans, 1996.

———. "The Safest Place on Earth: The Culture of Black Congregations." In *American Congregations*, vol. 2: *New Perspectives in the Study of Congregations*, edited by James P. Wind and James W. Lewis, 257–284. Chicago: University of Chicago Press, 1994.

Frazier, E. Franklin. *Black Bourgeoisie*. New York: Collier Books, 1962.

———. *The Negro Church in America*. New York: Schocken Books, 1974.

———. *The Negro Family in Chicago*. Chicago: University of Chicago Press, 1932.

———. *The Negro Family in the United States*. Chicago: University of Chicago Press, 1939.

Friedan, Betty. *The Feminine Mystique*. New York: Norton, 1963.

Fuchs, Lawrence H. *The American Kaleidoscope: Race, Ethnicity, and the Civic Culture*. Hanover, NH: Wesleyan University Press, 1990.

Galloway, Paul. "A Place to Call Home: Assyrian Church Brings Headquarters to Chicago." *Chicago Tribune*, 8 September 1995, sec. 2, p. 9.

Gannon, Thomas. "Religious Tradition and Urban Community." *Sociological Analysis* (1979): 283–302.

Gannon, Thomas, and David F. Schwartz. "Church Finances in Crisis." *Social Compass* 39, no. 1 (March 1992): 111–120.

Garraghan, Gilbert J. *The Catholic Church in Chicago, 1673–1871: An Historical Sketch*. Chicago: Loyola University Press, 1921.

Garreau, J. *Edge City: Life on the New Frontier*. New York: Doubleday, 1991.

Geertz, Clifford. *The Interpretation of Cultures*. New York: Basic Books, 1973.

———. *Local Knowledge: Further Essays in Interpretive Anthropology*. New York: Basic Books, 1983.

Giddens, Anthony. *The Constitution of Society: Outline of a Theory of Structuration*. Berkeley: University of California Press, 1984.

Gilkes, Cheryl Townsend. "The Storm and the Light: Church, Family, Work, and Social Crisis in the African-American Experience." In *Work, Family, and Religion in Contemporary Society*, edited by Nancy T. Ammerman and Wade C. Roof, 177–198. New York: Routledge, 1995.

Gilkey, Langdon. "The Christian Congregation as Religious Community." In *American Congregations*, vol. 2: *New Perspectives in the Study of Congregations*, edited by James P. Wind and James W. Lewis, 100–132. Chicago: University of Chicago Press, 1994.

Gilligan, Carol. *In a Different Voice: Psychological Theory and Women's Development.* Cambridge, MA: Harvard University Press, 1982.

Gitlin, Todd. *The Twilight of Common Dreams: Why America Is Wracked by Culture Wars.* New York: Metropolitan Books–Henry Holt, 1995.

Glazer, Nathan. *American Judaism.* 2d rev. ed. The Chicago History of American Civilization, edited by Daniel J. Boorstin. Chicago: University of Chicago Press, 1989.

———. *We Are All Multiculturalists Now.* Cambridge, MA: Harvard University Press, 1997.

Gleason, Philip. *Keeping the Faith: American Catholicism Past and Present.* Notre Dame, IN: University of Notre Dame Press, 1987.

———. "What Made Catholic Identity a Problem?" In *The Challenge and Promise of a Catholic University,* edited by Theodore M. Hesburgh, C.S.C., 91–102. Notre Dame, IN: University of Notre Dame Press, 1994.

Goozner, Merrill. "What Ails Post-Industrial Chicago." In *Chicago's Future in a Time of Change,* edited by Dick Simpson, 77–87. Champaign, IL: Stipes, 1993.

Gottdiener, Mark. *The Social Production of Urban Space.* 2nd ed. Austin: University of Texas Press, 1994.

Gottdiener, Mark, and Joe R. Feagin. "The Paradigm Shift in Urban Sociology." *Urban Affairs Quarterly* 24 (1988): 163–187.

Gottdiener, Mark, and Chris G. Pickvance, eds. *Urban Life in Transition.* Newbury Park, CA: Sage, 1991.

Greeley, Andrew M. *The American Catholic: A Social Portrait.* New York: Basic Books, 1977.

———. *The Catholic Myth: The Behavior and Belief of American Catholics.* New York: Scribner's, 1990.

——. "Catholic Schools: A Golden Twilight?" *America* (11 February 1989): 106–118.

Green, Cathy, and Monique Irvin. "The National Black Catholic Congress." *In a Word* 5 (July–August 1987): 2.

Green, Clifford J. "History in the Service of the Future: Studying Urban Ministry." In *Churches, Cities, and Human Community: Urban Ministry in the United States 1945–1985,* edited by Clifford J. Green, 1–22. Grand Rapids, MI: William B. Eerdmans, 1996.

———, ed. *Churches, Cities, and Human Community: Urban Ministry in the United States 1945–1985.* Grand Rapids, MI: William B. Eerdmans, 1995.

Green, Paul M., and Melvin G. Holli, eds. *Restoration 1989: Chicago Elects a New Daley,* Chicago: Lyceum Books, 1991.

Grimshaw, William J. *Bitter Fruit: Black Politics and the Chicago Machine, 1931–1991.* Chicago: University of Chicago Press, 1992.

Grindel, John A., C.M. *Whither the U.S. Church? Context, Gospel, Planning.* Mary-knoll, NY: Orbis Books, 1991.

Griswold, Wendy. *Cultures and Societies in a Changing World.* Thousand Oaks, CA: Pine Forge, 1994.

Gronbjerg, Kirsten A., Katy Crossley, Lorri Platek, Natalya Zhezmer, and Toni Migliore. *Rogers Park: A Tradition of Diversity—Laying the Foundation for Economic Development.* Loyola University, Chicago, November 1993.

"Growth Is at the Root of Cabrini Youth Garden." *Chicago Tribune,* 30 June 1993.

Guidelines for Development Strategy for Metropolitan Mission. New York: Division of Church Strategy and Development, Board of National Missions, United Presbyterian Church U.S.A., 1967.

Hacker, Andrew. *Two Nations: Black and White, Separate, Hostile, Unequal.* New York: Macmillan, 1992.

Haddad, Yvonne Yazbeck, ed. *The Muslims of America.* New York: Oxford University Press, 1991.

Haider, Donald. "Chicagoland 2005." In *Chicago's Future in a Time of Change,* edited by Dick Simpson, 114–132. Champaign, IL: Stipes, 1993.

Hall, John R., and Mary Jo Neitz. *Culture: Sociological Perspectives.* Englewood Cliffs, NJ: Prentice-Hall, 1993.

Hall, Suzanne E. *A Catholic Response to the Asian Presence.* Washington, DC: National Catholic Educational Association, 1990.

Hammond, Phillip E. *Religion and Personal Autonomy: The Third Disestablishment in America.* Columbia: University of South Carolina Press, 1992.

Handlin, Oscar. *The Uprooted: The Epic Story of the Great Migrations That Made the American People.* Boston: Little, Brown, 1951.

Handy, Robert T. "The Voluntary Principle in Religion and Religious Freedom in America." In *Voluntary Associations,* edited by D. B. Robertson. Richmond, VA: John Knox, 1966.

Harding, Vincent. "Toward a Darkly Radiant Vision of America's Truth: A Letter of Concern, an Invitation to Re-Creation." In *Community in America: The Challenge of Habits of the Heart,* edited by Charles H. Reynolds and Ralph V. Norman, 67–83. Berkeley: University of California Press, 1988.

Harkins, William. *Introducing the Catholic Elementary School Principal: What Principals Say about Themselves, Their Values, Their Schools.* Washington, DC: National Catholic Educational Association, 1993.

Harris, Joseph C. "Is the American Catholic Church Getting Out of the Elementary School Business?" *Chicago Studies* 31, no. 1 (April 1992): 81–92.

Harris, Michael W. *The Rise of Gospel Blues: The Music of Thomas Andrew Dorsey in the Urban Church.* New York: Oxford University Press, 1992.

Hefley, James C. *The Church That Takes on Trouble.* Elgin, IL: D. C. Cook, 1976.

Helgesen, Sally. *Everyday Revolutionaries: Working Women and the Transformation of American Life.* New York: Doubleday, 1998.

Helweg, Arthur W. "The Sikh Diaspora and Sikh Studies." In *Studying the Sikhs: Issues for North America,* edited by John Stratton Hawley and Gurinder Singh Mann, 69–93. Albany: State University of New York Press, 1993.

Herberg, Will. *Protestant-Catholic-Jew: An Essay in American Religious Sociology.* Garden City, NY: Doubleday, 1956.

Higginbotham, Evelyn B. *Righteous Discontent: The Women's Movement in the Black Baptist Church, 1880–1920.* Cambridge, MA: Harvard University Press, 1993.

Hirsch, Arnold. *Making the Second Ghetto: Race and Housing in Chicago, 1940–1960.* New York and Cambridge: Cambridge University Press, 1983.

Hirt, Jane. "Shifts in Labor Market Increase Wage Gap between Rich and Poor." *Chicago Tribune,* 20 June 1996, sec. 1, p. 6.

Hochschild, Jennifer L. *Facing Up to the American Dream: Race, Class, and the Soul of the Nation.* Princeton, NJ: Princeton University Press, 1995.

Holli, Melvin G., and Peter d'A. Jones, eds. *Ethnic Chicago: A Multicultural Portrait.* 3rd ed. Grand Rapids, MI: William B. Eerdmans, 1984.

———. *Ethnic Chicago: A Multicultural Portrait.* 4th ed. Grand Rapids, MI: William B. Eerdmans, 1995.

Hollinger, David A. *Postethnic America: Beyond Multiculturalism.* New York: Basic Books, 1995.

Hopewell, James F. *Congregation: Stories and Structures.* Edited by Barbara G. Wheeler. Philadelphia: Fortress, 1987.

Hovda, Robert W., ed. *This Far by Faith: American Black Worship and Its African Roots.* Washington, DC: National Office for Black Catholics, 1977.

Hunt, Thomas C., and Norlene M. Kunkel. "Catholic Schools: The Nation's Largest Alternative School System." In *Religious Schooling in America,* edited by James C. Carper and Thomas C. Hunt, 1–34. Birmingham, AL: Religious Education, 1984.

Hunter, Albert. "The Gold Coast and the Slum Revisited: Paradoxes in Replication Research and the Study of Social Change." *Urban Life* 11, no. 4 (1983): 461–476.

———. *Symbolic Communities: The Persistence and Change of Chicago's Local Communities.* Chicago: University of Chicago Press, 1974.

Hunter, James Davison. *Culture Wars: The Struggle to Define America.* New York: Basic Books, 1991.

Interfaith Organizing Project. *The New "West Side Story": The Story of the Interfaith Organizing Project.* Chicago: Interfaith Organizing Project, 1992.

Irvin, Dona L. *The Unsung Heart of Black America: A Middle-Class Church at Midcentury.* Columbia: University of Missouri Press, 1992.

Jackson, Joseph H. *A Story of Christian Activism.* Nashville, TN: Townsend, 1980.

Jackson, Kenneth T. *Crabgrass Frontier: The Suburbanization of the United States.* New York: Oxford University Press, 1985.

Janowitz, Morris. *The Community Press in an Urban Setting.* Chicago: University of Chicago Press, 1967.

Jones, Ezra Earl, and Robert L. Wilson. *What's Ahead for Old First Church.* 1st ed. New York: Harper & Row, 1974.

Kantowicz, Edward R. *Corporation Sole: Cardinal Mundelein and Chicago Catholicism.* Notre Dame, IN: University of Notre Dame Press, 1983.

Kasarda, John D. "Urban Industrial Transition and the Underclass." In *The Ghetto Underclass: Social Science Perspectives,* edited by William J. Wilson, 26–47. Newbury Park, CA: Sage, 1993.

Kealey, Robert J. "Collision Course: Clergy and Laity on Catholic Schools." *Chicago Studies* 28 (November 1989): 277–291.

Keating, Ann Durkin, and Pierre Lebeau. *North Central College and Naperville: A Shared History, 1870–1995.* Naperville, IL: North Central College, 1995.

Kelliher, Thomas G. "Mexican Catholics and Chicago's Parishes." *Working Paper Series, Cushwa Center for the Study of American Catholicism* 25, no. 2 (March 1993).

Kennedy, Eugene C. *Cardinal Bernardin: Easing Conflicts and Battling for the Soul of American Catholicism.* Chicago: Bonus Books, 1989.

———. *My Brother Joseph: The Spirit of a Cardinal and the Story of a Friendship.* New York: St. Martin's, 1997.

Kerr, Louise Año Nuevo. "Mexican Chicago." In *Ethnic Chicago: A Multicultural Portrait,* edited by Melvin G. Holli and Peter d'A. Jones, 3rd ed. Grand Rapids, MI: William B. Eerdmans, 1984.

Kincheloe, Samuel C. "The Behavior Sequence of a Dying Church." In *The Church in the City,* edited by Yoshio Fukuyama, 31–50. Chicago: Exploration, 1989.

Kniss, Fred. "Culture Wars: Remapping the Battleground." In *Cultural Wars in American Politics: Critical Reviews of a Popular Myth,* edited by Rhys H. Williams, 259–282. New York: Aldine de Gruyter, 1997.

Koenig, Harry C., ed. *A History of the Parishes of the Archdiocese of Chicago.* 2 vols. Chicago: Archdiocese of Chicago, 1980.

Kostarelos, Frances. *Feeling the Spirit: Faith and Hope in an Evangelical Black Storefront Church.* Columbia: University of South Carolina Press, 1995.

Kotlowitz, Alex. *There Are No Children Here: The Story of Two Boys Growing Up in the Other America.* New York: Anchor Books, 1992.

Kunjufu, Jawanza. *Countering the Conspiracy to Destroy Blacks Boys.* 2 vols. Chicago: African-American Images, 1985–86.

Kwon, Ho-Youn, Kwang Chung Kim, and R. Stephen Warner, eds. *Korean Americans and Their Religions.* University Park: Pennsylvania State University Press, 2000.

La Brack, Bruce. *The Sikhs of Northern California 1904–1975.* New York: AMS, 1988.

Laderman, Gary, ed. *Religions of Atlanta: Religious Diversity in the Centennial Olympic City*. Atlanta: Scholars, 1996.

Lamont, Michele, and Marcel Fournier, eds. *Cultivating Differences: Symbolic Boundaries and the Making of Inequality*. Chicago: University of Chicago Press, 1992.

Landry, Bart. *The New Black Middle Class*. Berkeley: University of California Press, 1987.

Lasch, Christopher. *The Culture of Narcissism*. New York: W. W. Norton, 1978.

Lawrence, Beverly H. *Reviving the Spirit: A Generation of African Americans Goes Home to the Church*. New York: Grove, 1996.

Lemann, Nicholas. "Stressed Out in Suburbia." *Atlantic Monthly*, November 1989, 34–48.

———. *The Promised Land: The Great Black Migration and How It Changed America*. New York: Knopf, 1991.

Lerner, Michael. *The Politics of Meaning: Restoring Hope and Possibility in an Age of Cynicism*. Reading, MA: Addison-Wesley, 1996.

Levitt, Peggy. "Local-Level Global Religion: The Case of U.S. Dominican Migration." *Journal for the Scientific Study of Religion* 37, no. 1 (1988): 74–89.

Lewis, James W. *The Protestant Experience in Gary, Indiana, 1906–1975: At Home in the City*. Knoxville: University of Tennessee Press, 1992.

Lincoln, C. Eric. *The Black Church since Frazier*. New York: Schocken Books, 1974.

———. "Black Methodists and the Middle-Class Mentality." In *Experiences, Struggles, and Hopes of the Black Church*, edited by James S. Gadsen, 58–68. Nashville, TN: Tidings, 1975.

Lincoln, C. Eric, and Lawrence H. Mamiya. *The Black Church in the African American Experience*. Durham, NC: Duke University Press, 1990.

Linnan, John, C.S.V. "Re-thinking the Urban Parish." Unpublished manuscript, 1995.

Liptak, Dolores. *Immigrants and Their Church*. New York: Macmillan, 1989.

Livezey, Lois Gehr. "The Fourth Presbyterian Church of Chicago: One Congregation's Response to the Challenges of Family Life in Urban America." In *Tending the Flock: Congregations and Family Ministry*, edited by K. Brynolf Lyon and Archie Smith Jr., 119–144. Louisville, KY: Westminster John Knox, 1998.

Livezey, Lowell W., ed. *Religious Organizations and Structural Change in Metropolitan Chicago: The Research Report of the Religion in Urban America Program*. Chicago: Office of Social Science Research, University of Illinois at Chicago, 1996.

Lydersen, Kari. "Lawsuits Claim Realtors Pander to Racial Fears." *Streetwise*, 22 December 1998, 5.

Mamiya, Lawrence H. "A Social History of the Bethel African Methodist Episcopal Church in Baltimore: The House of God and the Struggle for Freedom." In

American Congregations, vol. 1: The Portraits of Twelve Religious Communities, edited by James P. Wind and James W. Lewis, 221–293. Chicago: University of Chicago Press, 1994.

Manning, Robert D., and Anita C. Butera. "From City to Suburbia: The 'New' Immigration, Native Minorities, and the Post-Industrial Metropolis." American Sociological Association Meeting, New York, 19 August 1996.

Marciniak, Edward, and William Droel. "The Future of Catholic Churches in the Inner City." *Chicago Studies* 34 (2 August 1995): 172–186.

Marty, Martin E. *The Public Church: Mainline-Evangelical-Catholic.* New York: Crossroad, 1981.

———. "Public and Private: Congregation as Meeting Place." In *American Congregations, vol. 2: New Perspectives in the Study of Congregations,* edited by James P. Wind and James W. Lewis, 133–166. Chicago: University of Chicago Press, 1994.

Massey, Douglas, Rafael Alarcón, Jorge Durand, and Humberto Gonzalez. *Return to Aztlan: The Social Process of International Migration from Western Mexico.* Berkeley: University of California Press, 1987.

Mathews, Donald G. "The Second Great Awakening as an Organizing Process, 1780–1830: An Hypothesis." *American Quarterly* 21 (Spring 1969): 23–43.

Mays, Benjamin E., and Joseph W. Nicholson. *The Negro's Church.* New York: Arno, 1969.

McAlister, Elizabeth. "The Madonna of 115th Street Revisited: Vodou and Haitian Catholicism in the Age of Transnationalism." In *Gatherings in Diaspora: Religious Communities and the New Immigration,* edited by R. Stephen Warner and Judith G. Wittner, 123–160. Philadelphia: Temple University Press, 1998.

McClain, William B. "What Is Authentic Black Worship?" In *Experiences, Struggles, and Hopes of the Black Church,* edited by James S. Gadsen, 69–84. Nashville, TN: Tidings, 1975.

McCready, William C. "Catholic Schools and Catholic Identity: Stretching the Vital Connection." *Chicago Studies* 28 (November 1989): 217–231.

McGreevy, John. "Faith and Morals in the U.S., 1865–Present." *Reviews in American History* 26 (1998): 239–254.

———. *Parish Boundaries: The Catholic Encounter with Race in the Twentieth-Century Urban North.* Chicago: University of Chicago Press, 1996.

McRoberts, Omar M. "Understanding the 'New' Black Pentecostal Activism: Lessons from Ecumenical Urban Ministries in Boston." *Sociology of Religion* 60, no. 1 (March 1999): 47–70.

Meyers, Eleanor Scott, ed. *Envisioning the New City: A Reader on Urban Ministry.* Louisville, KY: Westminster John Knox, 1992.

Minocha, Urmil. "South Asian Immigrants: Trends and Impacts on the Sending and Receiving Societies." In *Pacific Bridges: The New Immigration from Asia and the Pacific Islands,* edited by James T. Fawcett and Benjamin V. Carino, 347–373. New York: Center for Migration Studies, 1987.

Mitchell, Henry H. "Black Power and the Christian Church." *Foundations* 11 (April–June 1968): 99–109.

Miyakawa, T. Scott. *Protestants and Pioneers: Individualism and Conformity on the American Frontier.* Chicago: University of Chicago Press, 1964.

Moore, Joan. "'Hispanic/Latino': Imposed Label or Real Identity?" *Latino Studies Journal* 1, no. 2 (1990): 33–47.

Mukenge, Ida Rousseau. *The Black Church in Urban America: A Case Study in Political Economy.* Lanham, MD: University Press of America, 1983.

Murnion, Philip J. "Parish: Covenant Community." *Church* 12, no. 1 (March 1996): 7.

———. Review of *The Parish in Catholic Tradition: History, Theology, and Canon Law. Church* 14, no. 4 (Winter 1998): 50.

"The National Black Catholic Congress." *In a Word* 10 (August–September 1992): 2.

Nelson, Ellis. *Where Faith Begins.* Richmond, VA: John Knox, 1967.

Niebuhr, H. Richard. *The Social Sources of Denominationalism.* New York: Henry Holt, 1957.

Novak, Michael. *The Catholic Ethic and the Spirit of Capitalism.* New York: Free Press, 1993.

———. *The Rise of the Unmeltable Ethnic: Politics and Culture in the Seventies.* New York: Macmillan, 1972.

Numrich, Paul D. "Facing Northeast in a Midwestern Metropolis: The Growth of Islam and the Challenge of the Ummatic Ideal in Chicago." In book forthcoming from the Auburn Project on the History of Religion and Urban America, 1875–present. Auburn Theological Seminary, NY.

———. *Old Wisdom in the New World: Americanization in Two Immigrant Theravada Buddhist Temples.* Knoxville: University of Tennessee Press, 1996.

———. "A Pentecostal Megachurch on the Edge: Calvary Church, Naperville, Illinois." In *Tending the Flock: Congregations and Family Ministry,* edited by K. Brynolf Lyon and Archie Smith Jr., 78–97. Louisville, KY: Westminster John Knox, 1998.

———. "Recent Immigrant Religions in a Restructuring Metropolis: New Religious Landscapes in Chicago." *Journal of Cultural Geography* 17, no. 1 (Fall/Winter 1997): 55–76.

Oboler, Suzanne. *Ethnic Labels, Latino Lives: Identity and the Politics of (Re)Presentation in the United States.* Minneapolis: University of Minnesota Press, 1995.

O'Brien, J. Stephen. *Mixed Messages: What Bishops and Priests Say about Catholic Schools.* Washington, DC: National Catholic Education Association, 1987.

Omi, Michael, and Howard Winant. *Racial Formation in the United States: From the 1960's to the 1990's.* New York: Routledge, 1994.

Orellana, Marjorie Faulstich, and Barrie Thorne. "Year-Round Schools and the Politics of Time." *Anthropology and Education Quarterly* 29, no. 4 (1998): 446–471.

O'Rourke, Lawrence M. *Geno: The Life and Mission of Geno Baroni.* New York: Paulist, 1991.

Orr, John B., Donald E. Miller, Wade Clark Roof, and J. Gordon Melton. *Politics of the Spirit—Religion and Multiethnicity in Los Angeles.* Los Angeles: University of Southern California Press, 1994.

Orsi, Robert A. *The Madonna of 115th Street: Faith and Community in Italian Harlem, 1880–1950.* New Haven, CT: Yale University Press, 1985.

———. *Thank You, St. Jude: Women's Devotion to the Patron Saint of Hopeless Causes.* New Haven, CT: Yale University Press, 1996.

Orum, Anthony M. *City-Building in America.* Boulder, CO: Westview, 1995.

Pacyga, Dominic A. "Chicago's Ethnic Neighborhoods: The Myth of Stability and the Reality of Change." In *Ethnic Chicago: A Multicultural Portrait,* edited by Melvin G. Holli and Peter d'A. Jones, 4th ed., 604–617. Grand Rapids, MI: William B. Eerdmans, 1995.

Pacyga, Dominic A., and Ellen Skerrett. *Chicago: City of Neighborhoods.* Chicago: Loyola University Press, 1986.

Padilla, Felix M. *Latino Ethnic Consciousness: The Case of Mexican Americans and Puerto Ricans in Chicago.* Notre Dame, IN: University of Notre Dame Press, 1985.

Paris, Arthur E. *Black Pentecostalism: Southern Religion in an Urban World.* Amherst: University of Massachusetts Press, 1982.

Paris, Peter J. *Black Religious Leaders: Conflict in Unity.* Louisville, KY: Westminster John Knox, 1991.

———. *The Social Teaching of the Black Churches.* Philadelphia: Fortress, 1985.

Park, Robert E. "The City as a Social Laboratory." In *Chicago: An Experiment in Social Science Research,* edited by T. V. Smith and Leonard D. White. Chicago: University of Chicago Press, 1968.

Park, Robert E., and Ernest W. Burgess. *The City.* Chicago: University of Chicago Press, 1925.

Park, Robert E., and Herbert A. Miller. *Old World Traits Transplanted.* Salem, NH: Ayer, 1921.

Parot, John Joseph. *Polish Catholics in Chicago, 1850–1920: A Religious History.* De Kalb: Northern Illinois University Press, 1981.

Parsons, Talcott. "Age and Sex in the Social Structure of the United States." *American Sociological Review* 7 (October 1942): 604–616.

"Pastoral Constitution on the Church in the Modern World." In *Catholic Social Thought: The Documentary Heritage,* edited by David J. O'Brien and Thomas A. Shannon, 166–237. Maryknoll, NY: Orbis Books, 1992.

Pattillo, Mary E. "Sweet Mothers and Gangbangers: Managing Crime in a Black Middle-Class Neighborhood." *Social Forces* 76 (March 1998):747–774.

Philpott, Thomas Lee. *The Slum and the Ghetto.* New York: Oxford University Press, 1978.

Policy Research Action Group. *The Black Churches of West Humboldt Park.* Chicago: DePaul University, January 1999.

Portes, Alejandro, and Rubén G. Rumbaut. *Immigrant America: A Portrait.* Berkeley: University of California Press, 1990.

Provost, James, and Knut Walf, eds. *Catholic Identity.* Concilium 5. New York: Orbis Books, 1994.

Putnam, Robert D. "Bowling Alone: America's Declining Social Capital." *Journal of Democracy* 6, no. 1 (January 1995): 65–78.

———. "The Prosperous Community." *American Prospect* (March 1993): 5–19.

Racially and Ethnically Diverse Urban Neighborhoods. Cityscape: A Journal of Policy and Research 4, no. 2 (1998): 1–269. Special issue.

Rangaswamy, Padma. "Asian Indians in Chicago: Growth and Change in a Model Minority." In *Ethnic Chicago: A Multicultural Portrait,* edited by Melvin G. Holli, and Peter d'A. Jones, 4th ed., 438–462. Grand Rapids, MI: William B. Eerdmans, 1995.

Ranney, David C. "Transnational Investment and Job Loss in Chicago." In *Chicago's Future in a Time of Change,* edited by Dick Simpson, 88–98. Champaign, IL: Stipes, 1993.

Reardon, Patrick T. "The New Geography." *Chicago Tribune Magazine* 10, 5 November 1995: 15–28.

Reese, Thomas J. *Archbishop: Inside the Power Structure of the American Catholic Church.* New York: Harper & Row, 1989.

Reimers, David M. *Still the Golden Door: The Third World Comes to America.* New York: Columbia University Press, 1992.

Reynolds, Charles H., and Ralph V. Norman, eds. *Community in America: The Challenge of Habits of the Heart.* Berkeley: University of California Press, 1988.

Richesin, L. Dale. "Eighty Years of Ministry 1907–1987." In *1988–1990 Greater Chicago Religions Directory and Buyers Guide,* edited by L. Dale Richesin, 153–170. Chicago: Church Federation of Greater Chicago, 1988.

Rieder, Jonathan. *Canarsie: The Jews and Italians of Brooklyn against Liberalism.* Cambridge, MA: Harvard University Press, 1985.

Rieff, Philip. *The Triumph of the Therapeutic.* New York: Harper & Row, 1966.

Rivers, Clarence Joseph. *Soulful Worship.* Washington, DC: National Office for Black Catholics, 1974.

Roeser, Thomas R. "A Letter from Chicago: Is America's Greatest Archdiocese Really in Decline?" *Crisis: A Journal of Catholic Lay Opinion* 12 (July 1994): 43–47.

Roozen, David A., William McKinney, and Jackson W. Carroll. *Varieties of Religious Presence: Mission in Public Life*. New York: Pilgrim, 1984.

Rouse, Roger. "Mexican Migration and the Social Space of Postmodernism." *Diaspora* 1, no. 1 (1991): 8–23.

———. "Questions of Identity: Personhood and Collectivity in Transnational Migration to the United States." *Critique of Anthropology* 15, no. 4 (1995): 351–380.

Rumbaut, Rubén G. "Passages to America: Perspectives on the New Immigration." In *America at Century's End*, edited by Alan Wolfe, 208–244. Berkeley: University of California Press, 1991.

Sánchez, George J. *Becoming Mexican American: Ethnicity, Culture, and Identity in Chicano Los Angeles, 1900–1945*. New York: Oxford University Press, 1993.

Sandel, Michael J. *Democracy's Discontent: America in Search of a Public Philosophy*. Cambridge, MA: Belknap Press of Harvard University Press, 1996.

Sanders, Cheryl J. *Saints in Exile: The Holiness-Pentecostal Experience in African American Religion and Culture*. New York: Oxford University Press, 1996.

Sanders, James W. *The Education of an Urban Minority: Catholic in Chicago, 1822–1965*. New York: Oxford University Press, 1977.

Sandoval, Moises. *On the Move: A History of the Hispanic Church in the United States*. Maryknoll, NY: Orbis Books, 1990.

Schaller, Lyle E. "Foreword." In *Downtown Church: The Heart of the City*, by Howard Edington. Nashville, TN: Abingdon, 1996.

Schiller, Nina Glick, Linda Basch, and Cristina Blanc-Szanton. "From Immigrant to Transmigrant: Theorizing Transnational Migration." *Anthropology Quarterly* 68, no. 1 (January 1995): 48–63.

———. "Transnationalism: A New Analytic Framework for Understanding Migration." In *Towards a Transnational Perspective on Migration: Race, Class, Ethnicity, and Nationalism Reconsidered*, edited by Nina Glick Schiller, Linda Basch, and Cristina Blanc-Szantin, 1–24. Annals of the New York Academy of Sciences, vol. 645. New York: New York Academy of Sciences, 1992.

Schlesinger, Arthur M., Jr. *The Disuniting of America: Reflections on a Multicultural Society*. New York: W. W. Norton, 1992.

Schreiter, Robert J. "Faith and Cultures: Challenges to a World Church." *Theological Studies* 50 (1989): 744–760.

Schroeder, W. Widick, and Victor Obenhaus. *Religion in American Culture: Unity and Diversity in a Midwestern County*. New York: Free Press of Glencoe, 1964.

Schuster, Elaine. "A Study of the Local School Long-Range Planning Process in the Archdiocese of Chicago." Ph.D. diss., University of Illinois at Chicago, 1987.

Scott, Daryl Michael. *Contempt and Pity: Social Policy and the Image of the Damaged Black Psyche, 1880–1996*. Chapel Hill: University of North Carolina Press, 1997.

Scroggs, Marilee Munger. "Making a Difference: Fourth Presbyterian Church of Chicago." In *American Congregations*, vol. 1: *Portraits of Twelve Religious Communities*, edited by James P. Wind and James W. Lewis, 464–519. Chicago: University of Chicago Press, 1994.

Sennett, Richard, ed. *Classic Essays on the Culture of Cities*. Englewood Cliffs, NJ: Prentice-Hall, 1969.

Sewell, William H., Jr. "A Theory of Structure: Duality, Agency, and Transformation." *American Journal of Sociology* 98, no. 1 (July 1992): 1–29.

Shanabruch, Charles. *Chicago's Catholics: The Evolution of an American Identity*. Notre Dame Studies in American Catholicism 4. Notre Dame, IN: University of Notre Dame Press, 1981.

Shaw, Stephen J. *The Catholic Parish as a Way-Station of Ethnicity and Americanization: Chicago's Germans and Italians, 1903–1939*. New York: Carlson, 1991.

Simpson, Dick, ed. *Chicago's Future in a Time of Change*, Champaign, IL: Stipes, 1993.

Skerrett, Ellen, ed. *At the Crossroads: Old Saint Patrick's and the Chicago Irish*. Chicago: Wild Onion, 1997.

Skerrett, Ellen, Edward R. Kantowicz, and Steven M. Avella. *Catholicism: Chicago Style*. Chicago: Loyola University Press, 1993.

Sklare, Marshall. "The Conservative Movement: Achievements and Problems." In *The Jewish Community in America*, edited by Marshall Sklare, 175–192. New York: Behrman House, 1974.

Slater, Philip E. *The Pursuit of Loneliness: American Culture at the Breaking Point*. Boston: Beacon, 1970.

Slayton, Robert A. *Back of the Yards: The Making of a Local Democracy*. Chicago: University of Chicago Press, 1986.

Smith, Carl S. *Urban Disorder and the Shape of Belief: The Great Chicago Fire, the Haymarket Bomb, and the Model Town of Pullman*. Chicago: University of Chicago Press, 1995.

Smith, Gary Scott. "When Stead Came to Chicago: The 'Social Gospel Novel' and the Chicago Civic Federation." *American Presbyterian* 68 (1990): 193–205.

Soja, Edward W. *Postmodern Geographies: The Reassertion of Space in Critical Social Theory*. New York: Verso, 1989.

Soja, Edward, Rebecca Morales, and Goetz Wolff. "Urban Restructuring: An Analysis of Social and Spatial Change in Los Angeles." *Economic Geography* 59 (1983): 195–230.

Sollors, Werner, ed. *The Invention of Ethnicity*. New York: Oxford University Press, 1989.

Soot, Siim, Ashish Sen, Kevin Curtin, and Paul Metaxatos. "Analysis of Employment Hubs and Work Trip Patterns in the Chicago Metropolitan Region." Urban Transportation Center, University of Illinois at Chicago, Chicago, 12 October 1994.

Spalding, David. "The Negro Catholic Congresses, 1889–1894." *Catholic Histori-cal Review* 55 (1969): 337–357.

Squires, Gregory D. *Capital and Communities in Black and White: The Intersec-tions of Race, Class, and Uneven Development.* Albany: State University of New York Press, 1994.

Squires, Gregory D., Larry Bennett, Kathleen Mccourt, and Philip Nyden. *Chicago: Race, Class, and the Response to Urban Decline.* Comparative Ameri-can Cities series, edited by Joe T. Darden. Philadelphia: Temple University Press, 1987.

Stacey, Judith. *Brave New Families: Stories of Domestic Upheaval in Late Twentieth Century America.* New York: Basic Books, 1990.

Stark, Robert. "Religious Ritual and Class Formation: The Story of Pilsen, St. Vitus Parish and the 1977 Via Crucis." Ph.D. diss., University of Chicago Di-vinity School, 1981.

Stead, William T. *If Christ Came to Chicago! A Plea for the Union of All Who Love in the Service of All Who Suffer.* Chicago: Laird & Lee, 1894.

Stockwell, Clinton E. "A Better Class of People: Protestants in the Making of Early Chicago." Ph.D. diss., University of Illinois at Chicago, 1992.

———. "Graham Taylor—Urban Pioneer." *Chicago Theological Seminary Regis-ter* 86, no. 1 (December 1996): 1–23.

Stout, Harry S. "The Place of Religion in Urban and Community Studies." *Reli-gion and American Culture: A Journal of Interpretation* 6, no. 2 (June 1996): 110–122.

Sugrue, Thomas J. *The Origins of the Urban Crisis.* Princeton, NJ: Princeton Uni-versity Press, 1996.

Suttles, Gerald D. *The Social Construction of Communities.* Chicago: University of Chicago Press, 1972.

———. *The Social Order of the Slum: Ethnicity and Territory in the Inner City.* Chicago: University of Chicago Press, 1968.

Swidler, Ann. "Culture in Action: Symbols and Strategies." *American Sociological Review* 51 (1986): 273–286.

Takaki, Ronald. *Strangers from a Different Shore: A History of Asian Americans.* Boston: Little, Brown, 1989.

Taub, Richard P., D. Garth Taylor, and Jan D. Dunham. *Paths of Neighborhood Change: Race and Crime in Urban America.* Chicago: University of Chicago Press, 1984.

Taylor, Charles. *Multiculturalism: Examining the Politics of Recognition.* Prince-ton, NJ: Princeton University Press, 1992.

Thompson, Richard H. *Theories of Ethnicity: A Critical Appraisal.* New York: Greenwood, 1989.

Tipton, Steven M. *Getting Saved from the Sixties: Moral Meaning in Conversion and Cultural Change.* Berkeley: University of California Press, 1982.

Todd, George C. "Presbyterian Ministry in Urban America, 1945–1980." In *Churches, Cities, and Human Community: Urban Ministry in the United States 1945–1985,* edited by Clifford J. Green, 151–178. Grand Rapids, MI: William B. Eerdmans, 1996.

Tomasi, Silvano M., C.S. "A Lesson from History: The Integration of Immigrants in the Pastoral Practice of the Church in the United States." *CMS: Occasional Papers: Pastoral Series* 7 (1987).

———. *Piety and Power: The Role of the Italian Parishes in the New York Metropolitan Area, 1880–1930.* New York: Center for Migration Studies, 1975.

———. "The Response of the Catholic Church in the United States to Immigrants and Refugees." *CMS: Occasional Papers: Pastoral Series* 3 (August 1984).

Tomorrow's Parish: Criteria for Planning. Chicago: Office of Research and Planning, Archdiocese of Chicago, 1993.

Tomorrow's Parish: Guide for Planning. Chicago: Office of Research and Planning, Archdiocese of Chicago, 1993.

Towsley, Genevieve. "A View of Historic Naperville from the Sky-Lines: A Collection of Articles of Historic Significance." *Naperville Sun,* 1975.

Travis, Dempsey J. *An Autobiography of Black Politics.* Volume 1. Chicago: Urban Research Press, 1987.

———. *"Harold" the People's Mayor: An Authorized Biography of Mayor Harold Washington.* Chicago: Urban Research Press, 1989.

Troy, Leander, O. Carm. *The Dandelion Bishop: Nevin Hayes of Chicago.* Chicago: Croatian Franciscan Press, 1994.

Tutor/Mentor Connection 2 (September 1994).

U.S. Bureau of the Census. *1990 Census of Population and Housing.* Summary tape file 3. September 1992.

Van Engen, Charles. "Constructing a Theology of Mission for the City." In *God So Loves the City: Seeking a Theology for Urban Mission,* edited by Charles Van Engen and Jude Tiersma, 241–269. Monrovia, CA: Mission Advanced Research and Communication Center, 1994.

Van Engen, Charles, and Jude Tiersma, eds. *God So Loves the City: Seeking a Theology for Urban Mission.* Monrovia, CA: Mission Advanced Research and Communication Center, 1994.

Vecoli, Rudolph J. "Prelates and Peasants: Italian Immigrants and the Catholic Church." *Journal of Social History* 2 (March 1969): 217–268.

Verba, Sidney, Kay Lehman Schlozman, and Henry E. Brady. *Voice and Equality: Civic Voluntarism in American Politics.* Cambridge, MA: Harvard University Press, 1995.

Villafañe, Eldin. *The Liberating Spirit: Toward an Hispanic American Pentecostal Social Ethic.* Lanham, MD: University Press of America, 1992.

———. *Seek the Peace of the City: Reflections on Urban Ministry.* Grand Rapids, MI: William B. Eerdmans, 1995.

Walch, Timothy. *The Diverse Origins of American Catholic Education: Chicago, Milwaukee and the Nation.* New York: Garland, 1988.

Waldinger, Roger. "Immigration and Urban Change." *Annual Review of Sociology* 15 (1989): 211–232.

Wall, A. E. P. *The Spirit of Cardinal Bernardin.* Chicago: Thomas Moore, 1983.

Wallwork, Ernest. "A Constructive Freudian Alternative to Psychotherapeutic Egoism." In *Community in America: The Challenge of Habits of the Heart,* edited by Charles H. Reynolds and Ralph V. Norman, 202–216. Berkeley: University of California Press, 1988.

Warner, R. Stephen. "Changes in the Civic Role of Religion." In *Diversity and Its Discontents: Cultural Conflict and Common Ground in Contemporary American Society,* edited by Neil J. Smelser and Jeffrey C. Alexander, 229–243. Princeton, NJ: Princeton University Press, 1999.

———. "The Metropolitan Community Churches and the Gay Agenda: The Power of Pentecostalism and Essentialism." In *Sex, Lies, and Sanctity: Religion and Deviance in Contemporary North America,* edited by Mary Jo Neitz and Marion S. Goldman, 81–108. Greenwich, CT: JAI Press, 1995.

———. *New Wine in Old Wineskins: Evangelicals and Liberals in a Small-Town Church.* Berkeley: University of California Press, 1988.

———. "The Place of the Congregation in the Contemporary American Religious Configuration." In *American Congregations,* vol. 2: *New Perspectives in the Study of Congregations,* edited by James P. Wind and James W. Lewis, 54–99. Chicago: University of Chicago Press, 1994.

———. "Work in Progress toward a New Paradigm for the Sociological Study of Religion in the United States." *American Journal of Sociology* 98, no. 5 (March 1993): 1044.

Warner, R. Stephen, and Judith G. Wittner, eds. *Gatherings in Diaspora: Religious Communities and the New Immigration.* Philadelphia: Temple University Press, 1998.

Warner, Sam Bass, Jr. *The Urban Wilderness: A History of the American City.* New York: Harper & Row, 1972.

Washington, Joseph R. *Black Sects and Cults.* Garden City, NY: Doubleday Anchor Books, 1973.

Wedam, Elfriede, and Stephen R. Warner. "Sacred Space on Tuesday: A Study of the Institutionalization of Charisma." In *"I Come Away Stronger": How Small Groups Are Shaping American Religion,* edited by Robert Wuthnow, 148–178. Grand Rapids, MI: William B. Eerdmans, 1994.

Wellman, James K. Jr. "Boundaries of Taste: A Gold Coast Church and Cabrini Green." Unpublished manuscript, 19 February 1994.

———. "A Counter-Example of Liberal Protestant Decline: A Case-Study of an Elite Downtown Protestant Church." Paper presented at the Association for the Sociology of Religion, Los Angeles, CA, August, 1994.

West, Cornel. *Race Matters.* Boston: Beacon, 1993.

Whyte, William H. *The Organization Man.* New York: Simon and Schuster, 1956.

Williams, Melvin D. *Community in a Black Pentecostal Church: An Anthropological Study.* Pittsburgh: University of Pittsburgh Press, 1974.

Williams, Raymond Brady. *Religions of Immigrants from India and Pakistan: New Threads in the American Tapestry.* New York and Cambridge: Cambridge University Press, 1988.

———. *A Sacred Thread: Modern Transmissions of Hindu Traditions in India and Abroad.* Chambersburg, PA: Anima, 1992.

Williams, Rhys H. "Religion as Political Resource: Culture or Ideology?" *Journal for the Scientific Study of Religion* 35, no. 4 (1996): 368–378.

Williams, Rhys, and Fred Kniss. "Approaching Religion as Culture." *Newsletter of the Sociology of Culture* 8, no. 1 (December 1994): 1, 5–8.

Wilson, Nancy L. *Our Tribe: Queer Folks, God, Jesus, and the Bible.* San Francisco: Harper Collins, 1995.

Wilson, William Julius. *The Truly Disadvantaged: The Inner City, the Underclass, and Public Policy.* Chicago: University of Chicago Press, 1987.

———. *When Work Disappears: The World of the New Urban Poor.* New York: Alfred A. Knopf, 1996.

———, ed. *The Ghetto Underclass: Social Science Perspectives,* Newbury Park, CA: Sage, 1993.

Wind, James P. *Places of Worship: Exploring Their History.* Nashville, TN: American Association for State and Local History, 1990.

Wind, James P., and James W. Lewis. "Memory, Amnesia, and History." In *Carriers of Faith: Lessons from Congregational Studies,* edited by Carl S. Dudley, Jackson W. Carroll, and James P. Wind, 15–39. Louisville, KY: Westminster John Knox, 1991.

———, eds. *American Congregations.* vol. 1, *Portraits of Twelve Religious Communities.* vol. 2, *New Perspectives in the Study of Congregations.* Chicago: University of Chicago Press, 1994.

Winter, Gibson. *The Suburban Captivity of the Churches: An Analysis of Protestant Responsibility in the Expanding Metropolis.* New York: Macmillan, 1962.

Wirth, Louis. *The Ghetto.* Chicago: University of Chicago Press, 1928.

———. "Urbanism as a Way of Life." In *Classic Essays on the Culture of Cities,* edited by Richard Sennett, 143–164. Englewood Cliffs, NJ: Prentice-Hall, 1969.

"Without Sweeps, CHA Crime Might Be Worse." *Chicago Tribune,* 26 October 1992, sec. 1, p. 9.

Wolfe, Alan, ed. *America at Century's End.* Berkeley: University of California Press, 1991.

Wuthnow, Robert. *Loose Connections: Joining Together in America's Fragmented Communities.* Cambridge, MA: Harvard University Press, 1998.

Wuthnow, Robert. *Meaning and Moral Order: Explorations in Cultural Analysis.* Berkeley: University of California Press, 1987.

———. *Producing the Sacred.* Chicago: University of Illinois Press, 1994.

———. *Restructuring of American Religion,* Princeton, NJ: Princeton University Press, 1988.

———, ed. *"I Come Away Stronger": How Small Groups Are Shaping American Religion.* Grand Rapids, MI: William B. Eerdmans, 1994.

Xenos, Peter, Herbert Barringer, and Michael J. Levin, *Asian Indians in the United States: A 1980 Census Profile.* Honolulu: East-West Population Institute, 1989.

Young, Iris Marion. *Justice and the Politics of Difference.* Princeton, NJ: Princeton University Press, 1990.

Younger, George D. *The Church and Urban Power Structure: Christian Perspectives on Social Problems.* Philadelphia: Westminster, 1952.

Zenner, Walter P. "Chicago's Sephardim: A Historical Exploration." *Chicago Jewish History* 12, no. 3 (March 1989).

Zorbaugh, Harvey Warren. *The Gold Coast and the Slum: A Sociological Study of Chicago's Near North Side.* Chicago: University of Chicago Press, 1929.

Zukin, Sharon. *The Cultures of Cities.* Cambridge, MA: Blackwell, 1995.

———. "The Hollow Center." In *America at Century's End,* edited by Alan Wolfe, 245–261. Berkeley: University of California Press, 1991.

———. *Landscapes of Power: From Detroit to Disney World.* Berkeley: University of California Press, 1991.

Contributors

Peter R. D'Agostino
Assistant Professor of History and Religious Studies, Stonehill College

David D. Daniels III
Associate Professor of Church History, McCormick Theological Seminary

Janise D. Hurtig
Postdoctoral Research Associate, Center for Research on Women and Gender, University of Illinois at Chicago

Isaac B. Laudarji
Pastor, Evangelical Church of West Africa

Lowell W. Livezey
Director, Religion in Urban America Program, University of Illinois at Chicago

Paul D. Numrich
Research Associate, The Park Ridge Center for the Study of Health, Faith, and Ethics

Matthew J. Price
Postdoctoral Fellow, J. M. Ormond Center, Duke University Divinity School

R. Stephen Warner
Professor of Sociology, University of Illinois at Chicago

Elfriede Wedam
Senior Research Associate, The Polis Center, and Adjunct Assistant Professor of Sociology, Indiana University–Purdue University at Indianapolis

Index

Willow Creek Community Church, as model
of "megachurch," 197–198
Wilson, William Julius, *The Truly Disadvantaged,* 72, 76
Wirth, Louis, *The Ghetto,* 15–16
Within-group boundaries, 302–303
Womb chamber, in Hindu Temple of Greater
Chicago, 244
Working families, in downtown churches, 77
Working poor
Mexican immigrants, 7
vs. desperately poor, 78–79
Workplace issues, response to
at Congregation Beth Shalom, 204
at Old Saint Patrick's Church, 230–231
at Saint James Lutheran Church, 200–202
"World's Largest Block Party," 214, 224f
Worship
at First Baptist Congregational Church, 87
at Hindu Temple of Greater Chicago,
240–241
incorporation of African-American culture
into, 22, 183
at Old Saint Patrick's Church, 225
as outreach to homeless persons, by Carter
Temple Christian Methodist Episcopal
Church, 165–166
at Revival Center Church of God in Christ,
83–84
at Saint Jerome Roman Catholic Church,
147–148
at Saint Malachy Roman Catholic
Church, 86

at Saint Pius V Roman Catholic Church,
29, 42
at Saint Stephen African Methodist Episcopal Church, 85–86
at Sephardic Congregation, 143
at Sikh Religious Society of Chicago, 252
Wuthnow, Robert
on culture of community, 109
Producing the Sacred, 21
on religious restructuring, 6

Young, Iris Marion, on "politics of difference,"
137–138
Young adults, ministry to, at Old Saint
Patrick's Church, 221–222
Youth programs
as alternative to gangs, 53
of Calvary Church, 199
of Emmanuel Presbyterian Church, 48f,
52–53
of Hindu Temple of Greater Chicago,
241–242
of Iglesia de Cristo, 149
InSight Arts Program of United Church of
Rogers Parks as, 153, 153f, 155
of Muslim Community Center, 247–248
of Saint Jerome Roman Catholic Church,
147–148
as source of neighborhood stability, 157

Zapatista movement, 42
Zorbaugh, Harvey, *The Gold Coast and the
Slum,* 62

9320